Better Homes and Gardens®

diabetic LIVING™

Our Best
Diabetic Living
Recipes

VOLUME 1

Meredith® Books
Des Moines, Iowa

Berry Pie with
Creamy Filling
recipe, page 326

(letter from the editor)

When you or someone in your family has diabetes, healthful eating has to be a priority. But it's not always easy. I know because I have type 1 diabetes and I want to serve food that is good for me and my family. Fortunately, the recipes in this book make it much easier to eat well—and feel well—while taking care of your diabetes.

We've gathered the best recipes from the pages of *Diabetic Living* magazine. Each recipe is approved by our Test Kitchen as delicious, nutritious, and easy to make. Our registered dietitians have calculated the calories, carbohydrates, fat, and more so you can see the nutritional benefits you'll receive from each serving.

There are hundreds of wonderful dishes to make in these pages, but I'll point out a few that I can't do without. For a dessert that pleases adults and kids alike, I turn to Rocky Road Parfaits, page 319. For a dinner that I can place into the slow cooker and forget about until it's ready, I depend on Beef and Chipotle Burritos, page 206. I turn to Cherry-Almond Snack Mix, page 278, to offer my husband and son a healthful crunchy snack.

In two special chapters, "Cooking with The Diabetic Chef®" and "From Our Kitchen to Yours," visit the homes and kitchens of families who understand that you needn't cut flavor or satisfaction from food to fit it into your meal plan. Every recipe in this book shows that yes, you can eat what you love while controlling your diabetes!

Kelly Rawlings, editor
Diabetic Living® magazine

ON THE COVER: Grilled Beef and Avocado Salad with Cilantro-Lime Vinaigrette (recipe, page 143).

Better Homes and Gardens® Diabetic Living™
 Our Best Diabetic Living Recipes
Editor: Kelly Rawlings
Designer: Ted Rossiter
Copy Chief: Doug Kouma
Copy Editor: Kevin Cox
Contributing Project Editor: Kristi Thomas, R.D.
Contributing Graphic Designer: Jill Budden
Publishing Operations Manager: Karen Schirm
Edit and Design Production Coordinator: Mary Lee Gavin
Editorial Assistant: Sheri Cord
Book Production Managers: Marjorie J. Schenkelberg,
 Mark Weaver
Contributing Proofreaders: Jean Baker, Nicole Clausing, Brenna Eldeen
Contributing Indexer: Elizabeth Parson
Test Kitchen Director: Lynn Blanchard
Test Kitchen Product Supervisor: Laura Marzen, R.D., L.D.
Test Kitchen Culinary Specialists: Marilyn Cornelius,
 Juliana Hale, Maryellyn Krantz, Jill Moberly,
 Colleen Weeden, Lori Wilson
Test Kitchen Nutrition Specialists: Elizabeth Burt, R.D.,L.D.;
 Laura Marzen, R.D., L.D.

Meredith® Books
Editorial Director: John Riha
Managing Editor: Kathleen Armentrout
Creative Director: Bridget Sandquist
Brand Manager: Janell Pittman
Senior Associate Design Director:

Director, Marketing and Publicity: Amy Nichols
Executive Director, Sales: Ken Zagor
Director, Operations: George A. Susral
Director, Production: Douglas M. Johnston
Business Director: Janice Croat
Vice President and General Manager, SIM: Jeff Myers

Better Homes and Gardens® Magazine
Editor in Chief: Gayle Goodson Butler
Deputy Editor, Food and Entertaining: Nancy Hopkins

Meredith Publishing Group
President: Jack Griffin
Executive Vice President: Doug Olson

Meredith Corporation
Chairman of the Board: William T. Kerr
President and Chief Executive Officer: Stephen M. Lacy
In Memoriam: E. T. Meredith III (1933–2003)

Test Kitchen

Our seal assures you that every recipe in *Our Best Diabetic Living Recipes* has been tested in the Better Homes and Gardens® Test Kitchen. This means that each recipe is practical and reliable, and meets our high standards of taste appeal. We guarantee your satisfaction with this book for as long as you own it.

contents

**Summer Vegetable Pilaf
recipe, page 67**

bright-start breakfasts

Tex-Mex Spinach Omelet

Breakfast is a must for both on-the-go weekdays and kick-back weekends. You can stir up some of our recipes the night before and bake in the morning. Others take just a few minutes to prepare. They all give your day a healthful, delicious start.

Tex-Mex Spinach Omelet

A colorful corn relish brightens an otherwise simple dish.

PER SERVING: 142 cal., 5 g total fat (3 g sat. fat), 12 mg chol., 393 mg sodium, 9 g carb., 2 g fiber, 17 g pro. Exchanges: 2 very lean meat, 1.5 vegetable, 1 fat. Carb choices: 0.5.

1 cup refrigerated or frozen egg product, thawed, or 4 eggs
1 tablespoon snipped fresh cilantro
Dash salt
Dash ground cumin
Nonstick cooking spray
¼ cup shredded Monterey Jack cheese with jalapeño chile peppers, reduced-fat cheddar cheese, or reduced-fat Swiss cheese
¾ cup fresh baby spinach leaves
1 recipe Corn-Pepper Relish (see recipe, below)

1. In a medium bowl, combine egg, cilantro, salt, and cumin. Use a wire whisk to beat until frothy.

2. Coat an unheated 10-inch nonstick skillet with flared sides with nonstick cooking spray. Preheat skillet over medium heat.

3. Pour egg mixture into prepared skillet. Cook, without stirring, for 2 to 3 minutes or until it begins to set. Run a spatula around edge, lifting mixture so uncooked portion flows underneath. Continue cooking until egg is set but still glossy and moist.

4. Sprinkle with cheese. Top with three-fourths of the spinach and half of the Corn-Pepper Relish. Using the spatula, lift and fold an edge of omelet over filling. Top with remaining spinach and relish. To serve, cut omelet in half. Makes 2 servings.

Corn-Pepper Relish: In a small bowl, combine ¼ cup chopped red sweet pepper; ¼ cup frozen whole kernel corn, thawed; 2 tablespoons chopped red onion; and 1 tablespoon snipped fresh cilantro. Makes ¾ cup.

Rosemary Potato Frittata

To cut the fat, you cook the potatoes and onions in water instead of sautéeing them in butter.

PER SERVING: 168 cal., 4 g total fat (3 g sat. fat), 13 mg chol., 407 mg sodium, 15 g carb., 2 g fiber, 17 g pro. Exchanges: 1 starch, 2 very lean meat, 0.5 fat. Carb choices: 1.

- 4 ounces tiny new potatoes, cut into ¼-inch slices (1 cup)
- ¼ cup chopped red or yellow onion
- ¼ cup chopped red, green, and/or yellow sweet pepper
- 1 cup refrigerated or frozen egg product, thawed, or 4 eggs
- ½ teaspoon snipped fresh rosemary or ¼ teaspoon dried rosemary, crushed
- ⅛ teaspoon salt
- ⅛ teaspoon ground black pepper
  Nonstick cooking spray
- ¼ cup shredded Swiss cheese (1 ounce)
  Fresh rosemary (optional)

1. In a covered 6- to 7-inch nonstick skillet with flared sides, cook potatoes and onion in a small amount of boiling water for 7 minutes. Add sweet pepper. Cook, covered, for 3 to 5 minutes more or until vegetables are tender. Drain in a colander.

2. Meanwhile, in a small bowl, whisk together egg, ½ teaspoon rosemary, salt, and pepper. Set aside.

3. Wipe out skillet; lightly coat with cooking spray.

Rosemary Potato Frittata

Return vegetables to skillet. Pour egg mixture over vegetables. Cook over medium heat, without stirring, about 1 minute or until egg mixture begins to set. Run a spatula around the edge, lifting mixture so uncooked portion flows underneath. Continue cooking and lifting edges until egg is almost set but still glossy and moist.

4. Remove skillet from heat. Sprinkle with cheese. Let stand, covered, for 3 to 4 minutes or until top is set and cheese is melted.

5. To serve, cut frittata into wedges. If desired, top each serving with fresh rosemary. Makes 2 servings.

Bacon 'n' Egg Pockets

Creamy scrambled eggs and Canadian bacon pack these pita breads with protein.
It's the perfect breakfast to eat at home or on the go.

PER SERVING: 162 cal., 4 g total fat (1 g sat. fat), 118 mg chol., 616 mg sodium, 18 g carb., 2 g fiber, 13 g pro. Exchanges: 1 starch, 1.5 very lean meat, 0.5 fat. Carb choices: 1.

- 2 eggs
- 4 egg whites
- 3 ounces Canadian-style bacon, chopped
- 3 tablespoons water
- 2 tablespoons sliced green onion (optional)
- ⅛ teaspoon salt
  Nonstick cooking spray
- 2 large whole wheat pita bread rounds, halved crosswise

1. In a medium bowl, combine eggs, egg whites, Canadian bacon, the water, green onion (if using), and salt. Beat with a wire whisk until mixed.

2. Coat an unheated large nonstick skillet with cooking spray. Preheat over medium heat.

3. Add egg mixture to skillet. Cook, without stirring, until mixture begins to set on the bottom and around the edge. Using a large spatula, lift and fold the partially cooked egg mixture so the uncooked portion flows underneath. Continue cooking about 2 minutes or until the egg mixture is set but still glossy and moist. Remove from heat.

4. To serve, fill pita halves with egg mixture. Makes 4 servings.

Breakfast Tortilla Wrap

Turkey bacon, refrigerated or frozen egg product,
and a tortilla add up to an extra lean,
extra delicious breakfast in a bundle.

PER SERVING: 209 cal., 5 g total fat (1 g sat. fat), 10 mg chol., 687 mg
sodium, 29 g carb., 3 g fiber, 12 g pro. Exchanges: 2 starch, 1 very lean
meat. Carb choices: 2.

1   slice turkey bacon
    Nonstick cooking spray
2   tablespoons chopped green sweet pepper
⅛   teaspoon ground cumin
⅛   teaspoon crushed red pepper (optional)
¼   cup refrigerated or frozen egg product, thawed, or
    2 egg whites, slightly beaten
2   tablespoons chopped tomato
3   dashes bottled hot pepper sauce (optional)
1   8-inch flour or whole wheat tortilla, warmed*

1. Prepare turkey bacon according to package
directions; crumble and set aside.

2. Coat a medium nonstick skillet with nonstick cooking
spray. Heat skillet over medium heat; add sweet pepper,
cumin, and, if desired, crushed red pepper. Cook and
stir until sweet pepper is tender, about 3 minutes. Add
egg; cook, without stirring, until mixture begins to set
on the bottom and around edge. With a spatula or large
spoon, lift and fold the partially cooked egg mixture so
that the uncooked portion flows underneath. Continue
cooking for 2 to 3 minutes or until egg mixture is cooked
through but is still glossy and moist.

3. Stir in bacon, tomato, and, if desired, hot pepper
sauce. Spoon onto tortilla; roll up. Makes 1 serving.

*Test Kitchen Tip: Wrap tortilla in white microwave-safe
paper towels; microwave on high for 15 to 30 seconds or
until softened. (Or preheat oven to 350°F. Wrap tortilla in
foil. Heat in oven for 10 to 15 minutes or until warm.)

Breakfast Pizza

A purchased Italian bread shell makes
a perfect base for an Italian-style topper.

PER SERVING: 233 cal., 7 g total fat (2 g sat. fat), 11 mg chol., 579 mg sodium, 29 g carb., 2 g fiber, 15 g pro. Exchanges: 2 starch, 1.5 lean meat. Carb choices: 2.

Nonstick cooking spray
1½ cups loose-pack frozen diced hash brown potatoes with onions and peppers
 1 clove garlic, minced
1½ cups refrigerated or frozen egg product, thawed
 ⅓ cup fat-free milk
 1 tablespoon snipped fresh basil
 ½ teaspoon salt
 ¼ teaspoon ground black pepper
 1 tablespoon olive oil
 1 14-ounce Italian bread shell (such as **Boboli** brand)
 1 cup shredded part-skim mozzarella cheese (4 ounces)
 2 plum tomatoes, halved lengthwise and sliced
 ¼ cup shredded fresh basil and/or fresh basil leaves

1. Preheat oven to 375°F. Coat an unheated large nonstick skillet with cooking spray. Preheat over medium heat. Add potatoes and garlic. Cook and stir about 4 minutes or until the vegetables are tender.

2. Meanwhile, in a small bowl, stir together egg, milk, the 1 tablespoon snipped basil, salt, and pepper.

3. Add oil to potato mixture in skillet; add egg mixture. Cook, without stirring, until mixture begins to set on the bottom and around the edge. Using a large spatula, lift and fold partially cooked egg mixture so uncooked portion flows underneath. Continue cooking about 2 minutes or until egg is set but still glossy and moist. Remove from heat.

4. To assemble, place bread shell on a large baking sheet or 12-inch pizza pan. Top with half of the shredded mozzarella cheese, the cooked egg mixture, the tomatoes, and the remaining cheese.

5. Bake about 10 minutes or until cheese is melted. Sprinkle with the ¼ cup shredded basil and/or basil leaves. Cut pizza into wedges. Makes 8 servings.

Scrambled Eggs with
Tomatoes and Peppers

Scrambled Eggs with Tomatoes and Peppers

Egg product and fat-free milk keep the fat content low.

PER SERVING: 114 cal., 4 g total fat (1 g sat. fat), 0 mg chol., 386 mg sodium, 7 g carb., 1 g fiber, 13 g pro. Exchanges: 2 lean meat, 0.5 vegetable, 1 fat. Carb choices: 0.5.

 1 tablespoon olive oil
 ½ cup chopped onion
 ½ cup chopped red or green sweet pepper
 ½ cup chopped, seeded tomato
 2 cups refrigerated or frozen egg product, thawed, or 8 eggs
 ⅓ cup fat-free milk
 ¼ teaspoon salt
 ⅛ teaspoon ground black pepper

1. In a large skillet, heat olive oil over medium heat. Add onion and sweet pepper; cook for 4 to 6 minutes or until tender, stirring occasionally. Stir in tomato.

2. Meanwhile, in a medium bowl, beat together eggs, milk, salt, and black pepper. Add egg mixture to onion mixture in skillet. Cook over medium heat, without stirring, until mixture begins to set on the bottom and around the edge.

3. With a spatula or a large spoon, gently lift and fold the partially cooked egg mixture so any uncooked egg portion flows underneath. Continue cooking over medium heat for 2 to 3 minutes or until the egg mixture is cooked through but still glossy and moist. Remove from heat. Serve warm. Makes 4 servings.

(egg substitutes)

Many recipes that call for eggs require the binding property found in the egg white. The white, primarily protein and water, is the main ingredient in most egg substitutes, or egg product. The yolk is omitted, along with most of the fat and cholesterol. Egg product can be used in many recipes that call for whole eggs. Or prepare your own substitute by using 2 egg whites for each whole egg called for in a recipe.

Breakfast Pizza

Asparagus-Zucchini Frittata

Not to worry if asparagus isn't in season. Just use a couple of packages of thawed frozen asparagus instead.

PER SERVING: 176 cal., 9 g total fat (3 g sat. fat), 353 mg chol., 527 mg sodium, 11 g carb., 3 g fiber, 15 g pro. Exchanges: 1.5 medium-fat meat, 2 vegetable. Carb choices: 1.

　　 Nonstick cooking spray
1½　 pounds fresh asparagus, trimmed and cut into 1-inch-long pieces
　1　 medium yellow sweet pepper, cut into strips
　⅓　 cup chopped onion
　¼　 cup bottled roasted red sweet peppers, drained and chopped
　1　 small zucchini, halved lengthwise and cut into ¼-inch-thick slices (about 1 cup)
　10　 eggs or 2 ½ cups refrigerated or frozen egg product, thawed
　1　 cup fat-free milk
　2　 tablespoons snipped fresh dill or ½ teaspoon dried dill
　1　 teaspoons salt
　½　 teaspoon ground black pepper
　　 Fresh dill sprigs (optional)

1. Preheat oven to 350°F. Coat a 3-quart rectangular baking dish with cooking spray; set aside.

2. In a large saucepan, bring about 1 inch of water to boiling. Add asparagus, sweet pepper strips, and onion. Return to boiling; reduce heat. Cover and simmer about 1 minute or until crisp-tender. Drain well. Stir in roasted red peppers. Evenly spread asparagus mixture in prepared baking dish. Layer zucchini slices on top.

3. In a large bowl, beat eggs with a rotary beater or wire whisk until combined. Beat in milk, snipped or dried dill, salt, and black pepper. Pour over vegetables in baking dish.

4. Bake, uncovered, for 40 to 45 minutes or until a knife inserted near center comes out clean. Let stand for 10 minutes before serving. If desired, garnish with dill sprigs. Makes 6 servings.

Asparagus-Zuchhini Frittata

Hash Brown Strata

A strata makes a perfect breakfast—
everything you need is in one dish.
Just as good: Mix ahead, chill, and bake in the morning.

PER SERVING: 162 cal., 5 g total fat (2 g sat. fat), 17 mg chol., 477 mg sodium, 15 g carb., 1 g fiber, 15 g pro. Exchanges: 1 starch, 2 very lean meat. Carb choices: 1.

Nonstick cooking spray
- 2 **cups loose-pack frozen diced hash brown potatoes with onion and peppers**
- 1 **cup broccoli florets**
- 3 **ounces turkey bacon or turkey ham, cooked and chopped or crumbled**
- ⅓ **cup evaporated fat-free milk**
- 2 **tablespoons all-purpose flour**
- 2 **8-ounce cartons refrigerated or frozen egg product, thawed, or 8 eggs, beaten**
- ½ **cup shredded reduced-fat cheddar cheese (2 ounces)**
- 1 **tablespoon snipped fresh basil or ½ teaspoon dried basil, crushed**
- ¼ **teaspoon ground black pepper**
- ⅛ **teaspoon salt**

1. Preheat oven to 350°F. Coat a 2-quart square baking dish with nonstick cooking spray. Spread hash brown potatoes and broccoli evenly in bottom of prepared baking dish; top with turkey bacon. Set aside.

2. In a medium bowl, slowly stir milk into flour. Stir in egg, half of the cheese, the basil, pepper, and salt; pour over vegetables.

3. Bake, uncovered, for 40 to 45 minutes or until a knife inserted near the center comes out clean. Sprinkle with remaining cheese. Let stand for 5 minutes before serving. Cut into triangles. Makes 6 servings.

Make-Ahead Directions: Prepare as directed through Step 2. Cover and chill for 4 to 24 hours. Preheat oven to 350°F. Continue as in Step 3.

Fresh Tomato Omelets with Mozzarella Cheese

Fresh Tomato Omelets with Mozzarella Cheese

To serve more, make the recipe two or three times. For a flavor change, substitute basil or thyme for the oregano.

PER SERVING: 103 cal., 2 g total fat (1 g sat. fat), 9 mg chol., 463 mg sodium, 4 g carb., 1 g fiber, 16 g pro. Exchanges: 0.5 vegetable, 2 very lean meat, 0.5 fat. Carb choices: 0.

- 1 **cup refrigerated or frozen egg product, thawed, or 4 eggs, beaten**
- ⅛ **teaspoon salt**
- ⅛ **teaspoon ground black pepper**
- **Nonstick cooking spray**
- 1 **teaspoon snipped fresh oregano or ¼ teaspoon dried oregano, crushed**
- 4 **medium tomato slices**
- ¼ **cup shredded mozzarella cheese (1 ounce)**
- **Small tomato, cut into wedges (optional)**

1. In a small bowl, stir together egg, salt, and pepper. Coat an unheated 8-inch nonstick skillet with nonstick cooking spray. Preheat skillet over medium heat.

2. Pour ½ cup of the egg mixture into the hot skillet. Immediately begin stirring egg mixture gently but continuously with a wooden or plastic spatula until mixture resembles small pieces of cooked egg surrounded by liquid egg. Stop stirring. Cook for 30 to 60 seconds more or until egg is set but shiny.

3. Sprinkle half of the fresh oregano or half of the dried oregano onto the eggs. Place 2 slices of tomato on top of one half of the egg mixture in skillet. Top with half of the shredded cheese.

4. Use a spatula to lift and fold the opposite edge of the omelet over tomatoes. Flip or slide omelet onto a warm plate; keep warm. Repeat with remaining egg mixture, oregano, tomato, and cheese. If desired top with tomato wedges. Makes 2 servings.

Vegetable Frittata and
Flaxseed Banana Muffins
(recipes, pages 15 and 17)

Quick Tip

Egg substitutes are great
to keep on hand and use
for many recipes. But
sometimes you might only
have eggs in the shell. When
a recipe calls for several
eggs or it needs a little
richness or color, use
2 egg whites and 1 whole
egg for every 2 eggs.

Spinach and Cheese Omelet

Vegetable Frittata

The frittata is a versatile dish. Add any vegetable-and-cheese combination that appeals to you.

PER SERVING: 141 cal., 8 g total fat (2 g sat. fat), 165 mg chol., 353 mg sodium, 5 g carb., 1 g fiber, 13 g pro. Exchanges: 0.5 vegetable, 2 lean meat, 0.5 fat. Carb choices: 0.

- 2 teaspoons olive oil
- ½ cup coarsely chopped broccoli florets
- ½ cup sliced fresh mushrooms
- ½ cup chopped carrot
- ¼ cup chopped onion
- 6 egg whites*
- 3 eggs*
- 2 tablespoons snipped fresh basil
- ¼ teaspoon salt
- ¼ teaspoon ground black pepper
- ⅓ cup shredded part-skim mozzarella cheese

1. Preheat broiler. In a medium broilerproof skillet, heat oil over medium heat. Add broccoli, mushrooms, carrot, and onion; cook for 7 to 8 minutes or until vegetables are crisp-tender, stirring occasionally. (If vegetables start to overbrown, reduce heat.)

2. Meanwhile, in a medium bowl, whisk together egg whites, eggs, basil, salt, and pepper. Pour egg mixture onto vegetables in skillet. Cook over medium heat.

3. As mixture sets, run a spatula around the edge of the skillet, lifting the egg mixture so the uncooked portion flows underneath. Continue cooking and lifting edge until the egg mixture is almost set and the surface is just slightly moist.

4. Sprinkle cheese onto egg mixture. Broil 4 inches from the heat about 2 minutes or until the top is light brown and the center is set. Let stand for 5 minutes before serving. Makes 4 servings.

*Test Kitchen Tip: If you like, you can substitute 1½ cups refrigerated or thawed frozen egg product for the egg whites and eggs.

Spinach and Cheese Omelet

A high-quality sharp cheddar adds the most flavor in the smallest quantity—and the fewest calories.

PER SERVING: 120 cal., 3 g total fat (2 g sat. fat), 10 mg chol., 438 mg sodium, 5 g carb., 1 g fiber, 16 g pro. Exchanges: 0.5 vegetable, 2 very lean meat, 0.5 fat. Carb choices: 0.

- Nonstick cooking spray
- 2 cups refrigerated or frozen egg product, thawed, or 8 eggs
- 2 tablespoons snipped fresh chives, Italian (flat-leaf) parsley, or chervil
- ⅛ teaspoon salt
- ⅛ teaspoon cayenne pepper
- ½ cup shredded reduced-fat sharp cheddar cheese
- 2 cups fresh baby spinach leaves or torn fresh spinach
- 1 recipe Red Pepper Relish (see recipe, below)

1. Lightly coat a 10-inch nonstick skillet with a flared side with cooking spray. Heat skillet over medium-high heat.

2. In a bowl, whisk together eggs, chives, salt, and cayenne pepper until frothy. Pour mixture into hot skillet. Immediately begin stirring eggs gently but continuously with a wooden spatula until mixture resembles small pieces of cooked egg surrounded by liquid. Discontinue stirring; cook for 30 to 60 seconds more or until egg is set but shiny. Sprinkle with cheese. Top with spinach and half of Red Pepper Relish. With a spatula, lift and fold one side of omelet over filling. Transfer to a warm platter. Top with remaining relish. Makes 4 servings.

Red Pepper Relish: In a small bowl, stir together ⅔ cup chopped red sweet pepper, 2 tablespoons finely chopped onion, 1 tablespoon cider vinegar, and ¼ teaspoon ground black pepper. Makes ¾ cup.

Raisin-Carrot Muffins

Wheat germ and carrots up the fiber in these
cakelike muffins. Buttermilk keeps them low in fat.

PER MUFFIN: 146 cal., 4 g total fat (1 g sat. fat), 14 mg chol., 168 mg sodium,
24 g carb., 2 g fiber, 4 g pro. Exchanges: 1 starch, 0.5 other carb., 0.5 fat.
Carb choices: 1.5.

PER MUFFIN WITH SUBSTITUTE: same as above, except 127 cal.,
19 g carb. Carb choices: 1.

- ⅔ cup golden raisins or dried currants
- ½ cup boiling water
- Nonstick cooking spray
- 1½ cups all-purpose flour
- ½ cup whole wheat flour
- ⅓ cup toasted wheat germ
- 1½ teaspoons baking powder
- ½ teaspoon baking soda
- ½ teaspoon salt
- ½ teaspoon ground cinnamon
- 1 egg
- 1¼ cups buttermilk
- ⅓ cup packed brown sugar or brown sugar substitute* equivalent to ⅓ cup brown sugar
- ¼ cup cooking oil
- 1 cup finely shredded carrots
- Ground cinnamon

1. Preheat oven to 400°F. In a small bowl, combine raisins and boiling water; set aside. Coat sixteen 2½-inch muffin cups with cooking spray or line with paper bake cups; set aside.

2. In a medium bowl, stir together all-purpose flour, whole wheat flour, wheat germ, baking powder, baking soda, salt, and the ½ teaspoon cinnamon. Make a well in the center.

3. In a small bowl, beat egg slightly; stir in buttermilk, brown sugar, and oil. Add all at once to flour mixture; stir just until moistened (the batter should be lumpy). Drain raisins. Gently fold raisins and carrots into batter. Spoon batter evenly into prepared muffin cups, filling each cup two-thirds full. Sprinkle tops with additional cinnamon.

4. Bake for 18 to 20 minutes or until golden. Cool in muffin cups on a wire rack for 5 minutes. Remove from cups. Serve warm. Makes 16 muffins.

*Sugar Substitutes: Choose from Sweet'N Low Brown or Sugar Twin Granulated Brown. Follow package directions to use product amount equivalent to ⅓ cup brown sugar.

Best-of-Bran Muffins

These muffins are stuffed with good things:
fiber-rich bran, flaxseeds, and canola oil.

PER MUFFIN: 146 cal., 6 g total fat (0 g sat. fat), 1 mg chol., 188 mg sodium,
23 g carb., 4 g fiber, 4 g pro. Exchanges: 1 starch, 0.5 carb.,
1 fat. Carb choices: 1.5.

- 3 cups whole bran cereal (not flakes)
- 1 cup tropical blend or regular mixed dried fruit bits or raisins
- ½ cup ground flaxseeds
- ½ cup canola oil or cooking oil
- 1 cup boiling water
- 2 cups buttermilk
- ½ cup refrigerated or frozen egg product, thawed, or 2 eggs, slightly beaten
- ¼ cup molasses
- 2¼ cups whole wheat flour
- ½ cup chopped walnuts (optional)
- 1 tablespoon sugar
- 2½ teaspoons baking soda
- Nonstick cooking spray

1. In a very large bowl, combine cereal, dried fruit, flaxseeds, and oil. Pour boiling water over mixture. Let stand for 5 minutes.

2. In a medium bowl, combine buttermilk, egg, and molasses; add to bran mixture. Stir to combine.

3. In a bowl, stir together flour, nuts (if using), sugar, and baking soda; add to bran mixture. Stir just until moistened (do not overmix). Let stand for 15 to 30 minutes.

4. Meanwhile, preheat oven to 400°F. Lightly coat twenty-four 2½-inch muffin cups with nonstick cooking spray. Spoon batter into prepared cups, filling each about three-fourths full. Bake 15 minutes or until a toothpick inserted in centers comes out clean. Cool in cups on wire racks for 5 minutes. Remove from cups. Serve warm. Makes 24 muffins.

Flaxseed Banana Muffins

With four grains, each muffin boasts 4 grams of heart-healthy fiber.

PER MUFFIN: 161 cal., 8 g total fat (1 g sat. fat), 18 mg chol., 117 mg sodium, 19 g carb., 4 g fiber, 6 g pro. Exchanges: 1.5 starch, 1.5 fat. Carb choices: 1.

PER MUFFIN WITH SUBSTITUTE: same as above, except 140 cal., 15 g carb. Exchanges: 1 starch. Carb choices: 1.

Nonstick cooking spray
¾ cup whole wheat flour
¼ cup gluten flour (wheat gluten)
¼ cup barley flour
¼ cup oat bran
2 tablespoons wheat bran
1 teaspoon baking powder
¼ teaspoon baking soda
¼ teaspoon salt
1 egg or ¼ cup refrigerated or frozen egg product, thawed
1 large very ripe banana, mashed (¾ cup)
½ cup buttermilk or sour milk*
⅓ cup sugar or sugar substitute** equivalent to ⅓ cup sugar
¼ cup cooking oil
1 teaspoon vanilla
⅓ cup flaxseeds
¼ cup chopped walnuts (optional)

1. Preheat oven to 400°F. Coat twelve 2½-inch muffin cups with nonstick cooking spray, or line with paper bake cups and coat insides of paper cups with nonstick cooking spray; set aside.

2. In a medium bowl, combine whole wheat flour, gluten flour, barley flour, oat bran, wheat bran, baking powder, baking soda, and salt. Make a well in the center; set aside.

3. In another medium bowl, beat egg with a whisk; whisk in mashed banana, buttermilk, sugar, oil, and vanilla. Add egg mixture all at once to flour mixture. Stir just until moistened (the batter should be lumpy). Stir in flaxseeds and, if desired, walnuts.

4. Spoon batter into prepared muffin cups, filling each cup two-thirds full.

5. Bake about 15 minutes or until a toothpick inserted in centers comes out clean. Cool in muffin cups on a wire rack for 5 minutes. Remove from cups. Serve warm. Makes 12 muffins.

*Test Kitchen Tip: To make ½ cup sour milk, place 1½ teaspoons lemon juice or vinegar in a glass measuring cup. Add enough fat-free milk to make ½ cup total liquid; stir. Let stand for 5 minutes.

**Sugar Substitutes: Choose from Splenda granular, Equal Spoonful or packets, or Sweet'N Low bulk or packets. Follow directions to use amount equivalent to ⅓ cup sugar.

Best-of-Bran Muffins

Tangerine Puckers

These mini muffins are sized just right for brunch.

PER MINI MUFFIN: 43 cal., 1 g total fat (0 g sat. fat), 0 mg chol., 59 mg sodium, 8 g carb., 0 g fiber, 1 g pro. Exchanges: 0.5 other carb. Carb choices: 0.5.

PER MINI MUFFIN WITH SUBSTITUTE: same as above, except 38 cal., 6 g carb.

Nonstick cooking spray
- 1 cup all-purpose flour
- 1½ teaspoons baking powder
- 2 tablespoons sugar or sugar substitute* equivalent to 2 tablespoons sugar
- ¼ teaspoon salt
- 2 tablespoons refrigerated or frozen egg product, thawed, or 1 egg white
- ½ cup fat-free milk
- 1 tablespoon cooking oil
- 1 teaspoon vanilla
- ½ cup fresh tangerine sections (2 to 3 tangerines), coarsely chopped

1. Preheat oven to 400°F. Lightly coat eighteen 1¾-inch muffin cups with nonstick spray; set aside.

2. In a medium bowl, stir together flour, baking powder, sugar, and salt. Make a well in the center of the flour mixture; set aside.

3. In a bowl, beat egg; stir in milk, oil, and vanilla. Add all at once to flour mixture. Using a fork, stir just until moistened (batter should be lumpy). Fold in the tangerine sections.

4. Divide batter among prepared cups, filling each almost full. Bake about 14 minutes or until golden.

5. Cool in muffin cups on a wire rack for 5 minutes. Remove from cups. Makes 18 mini muffins.

*Sugar Substitutes: Choose from Splenda granular, Equal Spoonful or packets, or Sweet'N Low bulk or packets. Follow package directions to measure the product amount equivalent to 2 tablespoons sugar.

Ginger Pear Muffins

Sprinkle on a little spiced oat bran for a streusellike topper.

PER MUFFIN: 149 cal., 7 g total fat (1 g sat. fat), 0 mg chol., 96 mg sodium, 19 g carb., 2 g fiber, 3 g pro. Exchanges: 1 starch, 1.5 fat. Carb choices: 1.

PER MUFFIN WITH SUBSTITUTE: same as above, except 136 cal., 16 g carb.

Nonstick cooking spray
- 1 cup all-purpose flour
- 1 cup quick-cooking rolled oats
- 3 tablespoons packed brown sugar or brown sugar substitute* equivalent to 3 tablespoons brown sugar
- 1½ teaspoons baking powder
- ½ teaspoon ground ginger
- ¼ teaspoon salt
- ¼ cup refrigerated or frozen egg product, thawed, or 1 egg
- ⅔ cup fat-free milk
- ⅓ cup cooking oil
- ¾ cup chopped, cored pear
- ¼ cup chopped walnuts (optional)
- 1 tablespoon oat bran
- ¼ teaspoon ground ginger

1. Preheat oven to 400°F. Lightly coat twelve 2½-inch muffin cups with cooking spray; set aside.

2. In a large bowl, stir together flour, rolled oats, brown sugar, baking powder, the ½ teaspoon ginger, and the salt. Make a well in the center.

3. In a small bowl, beat egg; stir in milk and oil. Add all at once to flour mixture. Using a fork, stir just until moistened (batter should be lumpy). Fold in chopped pear and, if desired, walnuts.

4. Divide batter among prepared muffin cups. Combine oat bran and the ¼ teaspoon ginger; sprinkle onto muffins. Bake for 18 to 20 minutes or until golden.

5. Cool muffins in muffin cups on a wire rack for 5 minutes. Remove from muffin cups; serve warm. Makes 12 muffins.

*Sugar Substitutes: Choose from 1½ teaspoons Sweet'N Low Brown or 3 tablespoons Sugar Twin Granulated Brown in place of the brown sugar.

(oat health notes)

Oats may help fight off many diseases, including these:

Diabetes: Studies show eating whole grains such as oats can significantly lower your risk of obesity and diabetes. What's more, consuming more whole grains can improve insulin sensitivity for people with insulin resistance or type 2 diabetes. That means insulin will respond more efficiently to high blood glucose levels. Oats and other fiber-rich foods help keep blood glucose stable throughout the day when eaten for breakfast.

Heart disease: Oats and oat products contain a type of fiber called beta-glucan, which has been shown to help lower cholesterol. Antioxidants in oats called avenanthramides help keep LDL (bad) cholesterol from oxidizing, especially when you consume oats with vitamin C. For an extra heart health benefit, eat a small orange or drink orange juice with your morning oats.

Cancer: Oats are a good source of selenium, which is involved in the DNA repair associated with reducing the risk of cancer, especially of the colon. They also help decrease asthma symptoms.

Ginger Pear Muffins

(smart spreads for breads)

Before you slather butter onto your toast or bread, think about some of the delicious alternatives.
By substituting some of the suggestions below in small amounts for traditional bread spreads, you
can slash some of the saturated fat or sugar from your diet. (Be aware that some reduced-fat products
may contain more sugar to enhance the flavor. Read the labels to check the number of carbohydrates.)

- Reduced-fat or fat-free options: peanut butter, cream cheese, margarine, Benecol (cholesterol-
  lowering spread).
- Reduced-sugar or low-calorie options: apple butter, spreadable fruit or fruit preserves,
  and fruit jellies.

Lemon-Nutmeg Scones

Blueberry-Oat Scones with Flaxseeds

Flaxseeds provide all eight essential amino acids and many nutrients, including omega-3 essential fatty acids. The tiny seeds may help lower cholesterol and blood glucose levels.

PER SCONE: 148 cal., 5 g total fat (3 g sat. fat), 10 mg chol., 133 mg sodium, 22 g carb., 2 g fiber, 4 g pro. Exchanges: 1.5 starch, 1 fat. Carb choices: 1.5.

PER SCONE WITH SUBSTITUTE: same as above, except 133 cal., 19 g carb. Exchanges: 1 starch. Carb choices: 1.

- 2 tablespoons flaxseeds, toasted
- 1½ cups all-purpose flour
- ½ cup rolled oats
- ¼ cup sugar or sugar substitute** equivalent to ¼ cup sugar
- 2 teaspoons baking powder
- ¼ teaspoon salt
- ¼ cup cold butter, cut into pieces
- 1 egg white
- 1 6-ounce carton plain fat-free or low-fat yogurt
- 1¼ cups fresh blueberries
- Fat-free milk
- Rolled oats and/or flaxseeds (optional)

1. Preheat oven to 400°F. Line a baking sheet with foil; set aside. Place the 2 tablespoons flaxseeds in a spice grinder; pulse until ground to a fine powder.

2. In a bowl, combine ground flaxseeds, flour, the ½ cup oats, the sugar, baking powder, and salt. Using a pastry blender, cut in butter until mixture resembles coarse crumbs. Make a well in the center of flour mixture; set aside. In a bowl, slightly beat egg white; stir in yogurt. Gently fold in berries. Add berry mixture all at once to flour mixture. With a fork, stir just until moistened.

3. Turn out dough onto a lightly floured surface. Knead by folding and gently pressing dough for 10 to 12 strokes or until nearly smooth. Pat or lightly roll dough into a 10-inch circle. Cut into 12 wedges; place 1 inch apart on baking sheet. Brush wedges with milk. If desired, sprinkle with oats and/or flaxseeds. Bake for 16 to 18 minutes or until golden. Serve warm. Makes 12 scones.

**Sugar Substitutes: Choose from Splenda granular, Equal Spoonful or packets, or Sweet'N Low bulk or packets. Follow the package directions to use the product amount equivalent to ¼ cup sugar.

Lemon-Nutmeg Scones

Try these first with the lemon yogurt, then next time substitute orange or peach yogurt for the lemon.

PER SCONE: 173 cal., 7 g total fat (3 g sat. fat), 16 mg chol., 206 mg sodium, 26 g carb., 2 g fiber, 5 g pro. Exchanges: 1 carb., 1 starch. Carb choices: 2.

PER SCONE WITH SUBSTITUTE: same as above, except 156 cal., 22 g carb. Exchanges: 0.5 carb., Carb choices: 1.5.

- **Nonstick cooking spray**
- 1¼ cups all-purpose flour
- ¾ cup oat bran
- 3 tablespoons sugar or sugar substitute* equivalent to 3 tablespoons sugar
- 2 teaspoons baking powder
- ¼ teaspoon baking soda
- ¼ teaspoon ground nutmeg
- ⅛ teaspoon salt
- ¼ cup butter
- 1 6-ounce carton lemon, orange, or peach low-fat yogurt with sweetener
- ¼ cup refrigerated or frozen egg product, thawed, or 1 egg

1. Preheat oven to 400°F. Lightly coat a baking sheet with nonstick spray; set aside.

2. In a medium bowl, stir together flour, oat bran, sugar, baking powder, baking soda, nutmeg, and salt. Using a pastry blender, cut in butter until crumbly. In a bowl, combine yogurt and egg; add all at once to flour mixture. Stir just until moistened.

3. Turn dough out onto a lightly floured surface. Knead by folding and gently pressing for 10 strokes. Lightly pat into a 6-inch circle. Cut dough into 8 wedges. Carefully separate wedges; place wedges about 2 inches apart on the prepared baking sheet.

4. Bake about 12 minutes or until scones are golden. Cool scones on the baking sheet on a wire rack for 5 minutes. Remove scones from the baking sheet. Serve warm. Makes 8 scones.

*Sugar Substitutes: Choose from Splenda granular, Equal Spoonful or packets, or Sweet'N Low bulk or packets. Follow package directions to measure the product amount equivalent to 3 tablespoons sugar.

Cranberry Whole Wheat Scones

A sprinkle of rolled oats decorates the tops
and adds a little fiber to these merry treats.

PER SCONE: 169 cal., 6 g total fat (3 g sat. fat), 15 mg chol., 172 mg sodium,
26 g carb., 2 g fiber, 4 g pro. Exchanges: 1 starch, 0.5 fruit, 0.5 carb.,
1 fat. Carb choices: 2.

PER SCONE WITH SUBSTITUTE: same as above, except 157 cal., 23 g carb.
Exchanges: 0 carb. Carb choices: 1.5.

1½   cups all-purpose flour
½   cup whole wheat flour
3   tablespoons sugar or sugar substitute* equivalent to
     3 tablespoons sugar
1½   teaspoons baking powder
1   teaspoon ground ginger or cinnamon
¼   teaspoon baking soda
¼   teaspoon salt
⅓   cup butter
½   cup refrigerated or frozen egg product, thawed, or
     2 eggs
⅓   cup buttermilk
¾   cup dried cranberries or currants
     Buttermilk
3   tablespoons rolled oats

1. Preheat oven to 400°F. In a large bowl, stir
together all-purpose flour, whole wheat flour, sugar,
baking powder, ginger, baking soda, and salt. Using a
pastry blender, cut in the butter until mixture resembles
coarse crumbs. Make a well in the center of flour mixture;
set aside.

2. In a small bowl, beat egg slightly; stir in the ⅓ cup
buttermilk and cranberries. Add buttermilk mixture
all at once to flour mixture. Stir just until moistened
(some of the dough may look dry).

3. Turn out dough onto a floured surface. Knead dough
for 10 to 12 strokes or until nearly smooth. Pat or lightly
roll dough to an 8-inch circle about ¾ inch thick. Brush
top with additional buttermilk; sprinkle with oats,
pressing gently into dough. Cut into 12 wedges.

4. Place dough wedges 1 inch apart on an ungreased
baking sheet. Bake for 13 to 15 minutes or until edges
are light brown. Serve warm. Makes 12 scones.

*Sugar Substitutes: Choose from Splenda granular, Equal
Spoonful or packets, or Sweet'N Low packets or bulk.
Follow package directions to use product amount
equivalent to 3 tablespoons sugar.

Mango Coffee Cake

If you can't find fresh mango, use a jar of mango slices
instead. You'll find them in the refrigerated area in the
produce section of your supermarket.

PER SERVING: 208 cal., 6 g total fat (1 g sat. fat), 0 mg chol., 73 mg sodium,
35 g carb., 3 g fiber, 4 g pro. Exchanges: 1 starch, 1½ carb., 1 fat. Carb
choices: 2.

PER SERVING WITH SUBSTITUTE: same as above, except 190 cal.,
30 g carb. Exchanges: 1 carb.

     Nonstick cooking spray
2   medium fresh mangoes
½   cup sugar or sugar substitute-sugar blend equivalent
     to ½ cup sugar*
¼   cup cooking oil
¾   cup fat-free milk
⅓   cup refrigerated or frozen egg product, thawed, or
     2 egg whites
⅔   cup all-purpose flour
½   cup whole wheat flour
2   teaspoons baking powder
½   teaspoon finely shredded lime peel
¼   teaspoon ground cardamom or ground allspice
1¼   cups quick-cooking rolled oats

1. Preheat oven to 375°F. Lightly coat a 9x1½-inch
round baking pan with nonstick cooking spray; set aside.
Seed, peel, and chop one of the mangoes; set aside. Seed,
peel, and slice the remaining mango; set aside.

2. In a large bowl, stir together sugar and oil. Add
milk and egg. Beat with an electric mixer on medium
speed for 1 minute. In a small bowl, combine all-purpose
flour, whole wheat flour, baking powder, lime peel, and
cardamom. Add to egg mixture; beat until combined.
Stir in chopped mango and oats. Spoon into prepared
pan. Arrange sliced mango on top of batter.

3. Bake for 35 to 40 minutes or until a toothpick inserted
near the center of the cake comes out clean. Cool in pan
on a wire rack for 30 minutes. Remove from pan. Serve
warm. Makes 10 servings.

*Test Kitchen Tip: If using a sugar substitute sugar blend,
we recommend Splenda Sugar Blend for Baking or Equal
Sugar Lite. Be sure to use package directions to determine
product amount equivalent to ½ cup sugar.

Mango Coffee Cake

Clockwise from top: Spiced Irish Oatmeal, Toasted Oat Muesli, and Double Oat Granola

Toasted Oat Muesli

You'll find flaxseeds, rich in omega-3 fatty acids, in the natural food aisle.

PER SERVING: 231 cal., 10 g total fat (3 g sat. fat), 2 mg chol., 57 mg sodium, 27 g carb., 5 g fiber, 10 g pro. Exchanges: 0.5 fruit, 1 starch, 0.5 fat-free milk, 1.5 fat. Carb choices: 1.5.

- 1½ **cups rolled oats**
- ½ **cup sliced almonds, coarsely chopped**
- 3 **tablespoons flaxseeds**
- ½ **cup dried banana chips and/or raisins**
- ½ **teaspoon ground allspice or ground cinnamon**
- 3½ **cups fat-free milk**

1. Preheat oven to 350°F. Place oats in a 15×10×1-inch baking pan. Bake for 8 minutes

2. Stir in almonds and flaxseeds. Bake for 8 to 10 minutes more or until oats are light brown and almonds are toasted, stirring once.

3. Cool in pan on a wire rack. Add banana chips and allspice; stir to combine. Serve with milk. Makes 7 (⅓-cup) servings.

Make-Ahead Directions: Cover and refrigerate for up to 2 weeks.

Double Oat Granola

Enjoy granola as a cereal with milk or yogurt or bake it into fruity bars for quick snacks.

PER SERVING: 175 cal., 6 g total fat (1 g sat. fat), 0 mg chol., 29 mg sodium, 27 g carb., 4 g fiber, 5 g pro. Exchanges: 1 starch, 1 carb., 0.5 fat. Carb choices: 2.

PER BAR: 93 cal., 4 g total fat (1 g sat. fat), 9 mg chol., 11 mg sodium, 13 g carb., 1 g fiber, 2 g pro. Exchanges: 0.5 starch, 0.5 carb., 0.5 fat. Carb choices: 1.

Nonstick cooking spray
2½ cups regular rolled oats
1 cup toasted oat bran cereal
½ cup toasted wheat germ
⅓ cup pecans, coarsely chopped
½ cup unsweetened applesauce
2 tablespoons honey
1 tablespoon cooking oil
¼ teaspoon ground cinnamon
⅓ cup snipped dried cranberries, snipped dried tart cherries, and/or dried blueberries

1. Preheat oven to 325°F. Lightly coat a 15×10×1-inch baking pan with nonstick cooking spray; set aside.

2. In a large bowl, stir together rolled oats, oat bran cereal, wheat germ, and pecans. In a small bowl, stir together applesauce, honey, oil, and cinnamon; pour over cereal mixture. Stir to mix evenly.

3. Spread granola evenly onto the prepared pan. Bake about 40 minutes or until golden brown, stirring every 10 minutes.

4. Stir dried fruit into granola. Spread on foil to cool. Makes 10 (½-cup) servings.

Apricot Granola Bars: Preheat oven to 325°F. Line an 8×8×2-inch baking pan with foil. Lightly coat with nonstick cooking spray. In a large bowl, combine 3 cups Double Oat Granola, ½ cup all-purpose flour, and ¼ cup snipped dried apricots. In a medium bowl, stir together 1 egg, ⅓ cup honey, ¼ cup cooking oil, and ½ teaspoon apple pie spice; stir into granola mixture until coated. Press into prepared pan. Bake about 25 minutes or until brown on edges. Cool on a wire rack. Use foil to remove from pan. Cut into bars. Makes 24 bars.

Make-Ahead Directions: Prepare granola or granola bars as directed. Store in an airtight container in a cool, dark place for up to 2 weeks.

Quick Tip

Fruity beverages labeled as punch, drink, or cocktail often contain added sugars and little fruit juice. For the most nutrition, fill your juice glass with 100-percent fruit juice. Keep portion size in mind—¼ cup of the unsweetened fruit juice equals 1 fruit exchange or 1 serving.

Spiced Irish Oatmeal

Steel-cut oats may also be called Irish, Scottish, or pinhead oats.

PER BAR: 158 cal., 2 g total fat (0 g sat. fat), 2 mg chol., 106 mg sodium, 27 g carb., 3 g fiber, 9 g pro. Exchanges: 0.5 fat-free milk, 1.5 starch. Carb choices: 2.

PER SERVING WITH SUBSTITUTE: same as above, except 149 cal., 24 g carb. Carb choices: 1.5.

3 cups water
1 cup steel-cut oats
1 tablespoon packed brown sugar or brown sugar substitute* equivalent to 1 tablespoon brown sugar
¼ teaspoon ground cinnamon
⅛ teaspoon salt
⅛ teaspoon ground allspice
Dash ground cloves or ground nutmeg
3 cups fat-free milk

1. In a 2-quart saucepan, combine water, oats, brown sugar, cinnamon, salt, allspice, and cloves.

2. Bring to boiling; reduce heat. Simmer, uncovered, for 10 to 15 minutes or until desired doneness and consistency, stirring occasionally. Serve with milk. Makes 6 (½-cup) servings.

*Sugar Substitutes: Use 1½ teaspoons Sweet'N Low Brown or 1 tablespoon Sugar Twin Granulated Brown for the brown sugar.

Good Morning Cereal Blend

Top this fiber-filled cereal blend with fat-free milk or yogurt for a satisfying breakfast.

PER SERVING: 196 cal., 2 g total fat (0 g sat. fat), 0 mg chol., 140 mg sodium, 46 g carb., 8 g fiber, 6 g pro. Exchanges: 3 starch. Carb choices: 3.

- **8 cups whole-bran cereal**
- **6 cups low-fat granola**
- **4 cups wheat-and-barley nugget cereal (such as Grape Nuts cereal)**
- **7 cups seven-grain-and-sesame cereal (such as Kashi Medley cereal)**
- **2 cups dried cranberries and/or raisins**

1. Combine cereals and cranberries. Cover and store cereal blend in airtight container for up to 2 weeks. Or seal in freezer bags; freeze for up to 3 months. Makes about 36 (¾-cup) servings.

Quick Tip

Yogurts that list "active yogurt cultures" or "living yogurt cultures" on the label help to replenish the so-called friendly bacteria in your intestines if the supply dwindles. This decrease in friendly bacteria occurs due to age, illness, or the use of medications, such as antibiotics.

Good Morning Cereal Blend

Tropical Fruit Smoothies

These do double duty as a quick breakfast
or a nutritious dessert.

PER SERVING: 103 cal., 0 g total fat (0 g sat. fat), 2 mg chol., 53 mg sodium,
22 g carb., 2 g fiber, 5 g pro. Exchanges: 0.5 fruit, 0.5 fat-free milk,
0.5 carb. Carb choices: 1.5.

- **1 6-ounce carton apricot-mango, orange-mango, piña colada, or pineapple fat-free yogurt with sweetener**
- **1 cup fat-free milk**
- **1 cup sliced fresh banana**
- **1 cup sliced fresh mango or refrigerated mango slices**
- **1 cup small ice cubes or crushed ice**
- **Sliced mango, lime wedges, or pineapple wedges (optional)**

1. In a blender, combine yogurt, milk, banana, and 1 cup sliced mango. Cover; blend until smooth. With blender running, add ice cubes through hole in lid, one at a time, until smooth. If desired, garnish with mango, lime, or pineapple. Makes 4 (1-cup) servings.

Papaya-Strawberry Soymilk Smoothies

Try mango-blueberry, banana-grape, or other duets.

PER SERVING: 97 cal., 1 g total fat (0 g sat. fat), 0 mg chol., 47 mg
sodium, 18 g carb., 2 g fiber, 3 g pro. Exchanges: 0.5 milk, 1 fruit.
Carb choices: 1.

- **1 cup vanilla-flavored soymilk**
- **½ cup orange juice**
- **1 cup chopped papaya**
- **½ cup frozen unsweetened whole strawberries**
- **2 tablespoons soy protein powder (optional)**
- **1 tablespoon honey (optional)**

1. In a blender, combine soymilk, orange juice, fruit, and, if desired, protein powder and honey. Cover and blend until mixture is smooth. Immediately pour into three glasses. Makes about 3 (1-cup) servings.

Strawberry-Banana Smoothies

Remember this recipe when you're short on time.

PER SERVING: 108 cal., 2 g total fat (0 g sat. fat), 2 mg chol., 30 mg sodium,
24 g carb., 4 g fiber, 4 g pro. Exchanges: 4 fruit. Carb choices: 2.

- **4 cups sliced fresh strawberries**
- **1 medium banana, sliced**
- **1 6-ounce carton vanilla low-fat yogurt**
- **1 cup ice cubes**
- **1 kiwifruit, peeled and sliced (optional)**

1. In a blender, combine strawberries, banana, and yogurt; cover and blend until smooth. With blender running, add ice cubes, one at a time, through the hole in the lid, until smooth. If desired, garnish each serving with kiwifruit. Makes 4 (1-cup) servings.

(high fiber)

Fiber is important in helping regulate blood glucose levels. And you need lots of it—about 35 grams a day. Why all the fiber? It helps you eat less, lose weight, and feel better. Fiber fills you up without filling you out, keeps your digestive system regulated, and helps lower your body's level of the "bad" cholesterol—LDL cholesterol. The best sources are whole grains, fruits, and vegetables. Include whole grain cereals, breads, and pastas and beans and legumes in your meal plans. If you're not used to eating a high-fiber diet, remember to gradually increase your intake of fiber-rich foods and to drink lots of water.

Lemon Breakfast Parfaits

Serve these lively layers of fruit and couscous for a smart start in the morning.

PER SERVING: 147 cal., 3 g total fat (1 g sat. fat), 7 mg chol., 61 mg sodium, 28 g carb., 4 g fiber, 5 g pro. Exchanges: 0.5 fruit, 1 starch, 0.5 fat. Carb choices: 2.

- ¾ cup fat-free milk
  Dash salt
- ⅓ cup whole wheat or regular couscous
- ½ cup lemon low-fat yogurt
- ½ cup light dairy sour cream
- 1 tablespoon honey
- ¼ teaspoon finely shredded lemon peel
- 3 cups assorted fresh fruit, such as sliced strawberries, kiwifruit, nectarine, or star fruit, and/or blueberries, or raspberries
  Chopped crystallized ginger (optional)
  Fresh mint (optional)

1. In a medium saucepan, bring milk and salt to boiling; stir in couscous. Simmer, covered, for 1 minute. Remove from heat; let stand for 5 minutes. Stir with a fork until fluffy. Cool.

2. In a small bowl, combine yogurt, sour cream, honey, and lemon peel; stir into couscous. In another bowl, combine desired fruit.

3. To serve, divide half of the fruit mixture among six parfait glasses. Spoon couscous mixture over fruit; top with remaining fruit. If desired, garnish with chopped crystallized ginger and mint. Makes 6 servings.

Lemon Breakfast Parfaits

Fruit and Yogurt Parfaits

Use kiwifruit and mango for
a green and gold combination.

PER SERVING: 181 cal., 4 g total fat (1 g sat. fat), 7 mg chol., 88 mg sodium, 30 g carb., 4 g fiber, 9 g pro. Exchanges: 1 fat-free milk, 0.5 fruit, 0.5 starch, 0.5 fat. Carb choices: 2.

- **1** medium fresh mango, peach, or nectarine or 2 medium kiwifruits
- **1** cup plain low-fat yogurt
- **½** teaspoon vanilla
- **½** cup bite-size shredded wheat biscuits, coarsely crushed
- **2** teaspoons sugar-free pancake and waffle syrup or light pancake and waffle syrup product
- **1** tablespoon sliced almonds, toasted
   Dash ground cinnamon

1. If desired, peel fruit; pit peach or nectarine. Chop fruit, reserving 2 wedges for garnish. Set aside.

2. Combine yogurt and vanilla. Spoon half of the yogurt mixture into two 8- to 10-ounce parfait glasses. Top with half of the crushed cereal, all of the chopped fruit, syrup, remaining yogurt mixture, and remaining crushed cereal. Sprinkle with almonds and cinnamon. Garnish each serving with a reserved fruit wedge. Makes 2 (¾-cup) servings.

Fruit-Filled Puff Pancakes

These puff pancakes deflate after baking to form a bowl just right for filling with fresh, colorful fruit.

PER SERVING: 163 cal., 5 g total fat (1 g sat. fat), 0 mg chol., 138 mg sodium, 26 g carb., 3 g fiber, 5 g pro. Exchanges: 1 carb., 1 fruit, 1 fat. Carb choices: 2.

  Nonstick cooking spray
¼ cup refrigerated or frozen egg product, thawed, or 1 egg
2 tablespoons all-purpose flour
2 tablespoons fat-free milk
2 teaspoons cooking oil
  Dash salt
1 tablespoon low-calorie orange marmalade spread
1 tablespoon orange juice or water
1 small banana, sliced
½ cup fresh blueberries, raspberries, and/or sliced strawberries

1. Preheat oven to 400°F. For pancakes, coat two 4- to 5-inch pie plates or foil tart pans or 10-ounce custard cups with nonstick spray. Set aside.

2. In a medium bowl, whisk together egg, flour, milk, oil, and salt until smooth. Divide batter among prepared pans. Bake about 25 minutes or until brown and puffed. Turn off oven; let stand in oven 5 minutes.

3. Meanwhile, in a small bowl, stir together marmalade and orange juice. Add banana and berries; stir gently to coat.

4. To serve, immediately after removing pancakes from oven, transfer to plates. Spoon fruit mixture into each pancake center. Makes 2 (1-pancake) servings.

Honey-Apple Pancakes

These pancakes are like breakfast apple pies.

PER 2 PANCAKES: 122 cal., 3 g total fat (0 g sat. fat), 26 mg chol., 163 mg sodium, 22 g carb., 1 g fiber, 3 g pro. Exchanges: 0.5 starch. Carb choices: 1.5.

1¼ cups all-purpose flour
2 teaspoons baking powder
¼ teaspoon salt
¼ teaspoon apple pie spice
⅛ teaspoon baking soda
1 beaten egg
¾ cup apple juice
2 tablespoons honey
1 tablespoon cooking oil
  Nonstick cooking spray
  Light or sugar-free pancake syrup (optional)

1. In a medium bowl, stir together flour, baking powder, salt, apple pie spice, and baking soda. Make a well in the center; set aside. In a bowl, stir together egg, apple juice, honey, and oil. Add egg mixture all at once to flour mixture; stir just until combined.

2. Lightly coat a heavy nonstick skillet with cooking spray. Heat over medium heat. For each pancake, pour ¼ cup of batter onto hot skillet spreading to a 4-inch diameter. Cook for 2 to 3 minutes or until pancakes have bubbly surfaces and edges are slightly dry. Turn; cook for 2 to 3 minutes more or until golden brown. If desired, serve with syrup. Makes eight 4-inch pancakes.

Fruit-Filled Puff Pancakes

Blueberry Buckwheat Pancakes

Buckwheat contains a phytochemical that might have a beneficial effect on blood glucose levels.

PER SERVING: 132 cal., 3 g total fat (1 g sat. fat), 2 mg chol., 244 mg sodium, 22 g carb., 3 g fiber, 6 g pro. Exchanges: 1 starch, 0.5 carb., 0.5 fat. Carb choices: 1.5.

½ **cup buckwheat flour**
½ **cup whole wheat flour**
1 **tablespoon sugar**
½ **teaspoon baking powder**
¼ **teaspoon baking soda**
¼ **teaspoon salt**
¼ **cup refrigerated or frozen egg product, thawed, or 1 egg**
1¼ **cups buttermilk or sour milk**
1 **tablespoon cooking oil**
¼ **teaspoon vanilla**
¾ **cup fresh or frozen blueberries, thawed**

1. In a medium bowl, stir together buckwheat flour, whole wheat flour, sugar, baking powder, baking soda, and salt. Make a well in center; set aside.

2. In a small bowl, beat egg slightly; stir in buttermilk, oil, and vanilla. Add buttermilk mixture all at once to flour mixture. Stir just until combined but still slightly lumpy. Stir in blueberries.

3. Heat a lightly greased griddle or heavy skillet over medium heat until a few drops of water sprinkled onto griddle dance across the surface. For each pancake, pour a scant ¼ cup batter onto hot griddle. Spread the batter into a circle that's about 4 inches in diameter.

4. Cook over medium heat until pancakes are brown, turning to cook second sides when pancake surfaces are bubbly and edges are slightly dry (1 to 2 minutes per side). Serve immediately or keep warm. Makes 6 (2-pancake) servings.

Oat Buttermilk
Pancakes

Oat Buttermilk Pancakes

Offer family and guests a refreshing option: sliced fresh fruit and fruit-flavored yogurt instead of syrup.

PER 2 PANCAKES: 189 cal., 5 g total fat (1 g sat. fat), 3 mg chol., 317 mg sodium, 28 g carb., 3 g fiber, 8 g pro. Exchanges: 1 starch, 1 carb., 0.5 fat. Carb choices: 2.

1¼ cups regular rolled oats
¾ cup all-purpose flour
½ cup whole wheat flour
1 tablespoon baking powder
¼ teaspoon salt
3 egg whites
2¼ cups buttermilk
2 tablespoons cooking oil
2 tablespoons honey (optional)
1 teaspoon vanilla
Nonstick cooking spray
Fresh strawberries (optional)
Light pancake and waffle syrup product (optional)

1. In a large bowl, stir together oats, all-purpose flour, whole wheat flour, baking powder, and salt. Make a well in the center; set aside.

2. In a medium bowl, use a fork to beat egg whites; stir in buttermilk, oil, honey (if using), and vanilla. Add all at once to flour mixture. Stir just until moistened (the batter should be lumpy). Cover; let stand at room temperature for 15 to 30 minutes.

3. Coat an unheated griddle or heavy skillet with nonstick cooking spray. Preheat griddle over medium-high heat.

4. For each pancake, pour about 1/4 cup of the batter onto the hot griddle or skillet. Spread the batter into a 4-inch circle.

5. Cook over medium heat for 4 to 6 minutes or until pancakes are golden, turning to cook second sides when pancakes have bubbly surfaces and the edges are slightly dry.

6. If desired, slice strawberries into fans; garnish pancakes with strawberry fans. Serve pancakes with syrup. Makes 8 (2-pancake) servings.

Walnut Waffles with Blueberry Sauce

Ground walnuts provide a light crunch and nutty flavor.

PER SERVING: 224 cal., 7 g total fat (1 g sat. fat), 3 mg chol., 359 mg sodium, 33 g carb., 4 g fiber, 8 g pro. Exchanges: 1 starch, 1 carb., 1.5 fat. Carb choices: 2.

1 cup all-purpose flour
1 cup whole wheat flour
¼ cup coarsely ground toasted walnuts
2 teaspoons baking powder
1 teaspoon baking soda
4 egg whites
2¼ cups buttermilk
2 tablespoons cooking oil
1 recipe Blueberry Sauce (see below)

1. In a medium bowl, stir together all-purpose flour, whole wheat flour, walnuts, baking powder, and soda.

2. In a bowl, beat egg whites with an electric mixer on medium speed until foamy. Stir in buttermilk and oil. Slowly add flour mixture, beating by hand until smooth. Preheat a lightly greased square or round waffle baker. Pour 1 cup batter (for round baker, use ²/₃ cup batter) onto grids of square waffle baker. Close lid. Bake according to manufacturer's directions. When done, use a fork to remove waffle. Repeat with remaining batter. Serve with Blueberry Sauce. Makes 8 (3-waffle) servings.

Blueberry Sauce: In a saucepan, combine 1 cup fresh or frozen blueberries, ¼ cup white grape juice, and 1 tablespoon honey. Heat just until bubbles form around edges. Cool. Transfer to a blender. Cover; blend until smooth. Stir in 1 cup fresh or frozen blueberries. Transfer to a serving container. Makes about 1²/₃ cups.

Walnut Waffles with Blueberry Sauce

Orange French Toast

If you top with sugar-free or light syrup, add those carbs to the total.

PER SERVING: 187 cal., 3 g total fat (0 g sat. fat), 1 mg chol., 250 mg sodium, 32 g carb., 8 g fiber, 12 g pro. Exchanges: 2 starch, 0.5 very lean meat. Carb choices: 1.5.

½ cup refrigerated or frozen egg product, thawed, or 2 eggs

½ cup fat-free milk

½ teaspoon finely shredded orange peel

¼ teaspoon vanilla

⅛ teaspoon ground cinnamon or nutmeg

8 slices whole grain bread

Nonstick cooking spray

Sugar-free or light pancake and waffle syrup product (optional)

Fresh blueberries and/or strawberries (optional)

1. In a shallow bowl, beat egg; stir in milk, orange peel, vanilla, and cinnamon. Dip bread slices into egg mixture, turning slices to coat both sides.

2. Coat an unheated large nonstick skillet or griddle with nonstick cooking spray. Preheat over medium heat. Place bread on hot skillet; cook for 4 to 6 minutes or until golden brown, turning once.

3. Serve warm. If desired, serve with syrup and garnish with berries. Makes 4 (2-slice) servings.

Orange French Toast

Quick Tip

Keep these on hand to feed a crowd quickly: whole grain freezer waffles; high-protein, low-carb cereals; ingredients for smoothies; a batch of homemade bran muffins (keep them in the freezer; thaw a few at a time); low-carb, multigrain bread; reduced-fat peanut butter; and sugar-free jelly.

Banana-Stuffed French Toast

Banana adds a delicious surprise to French toast.

PER SERVING: 210 cal., 4 g total fat (1 g sat. fat), 107 mg chol., 352 mg sodium, 34 g carb., 2 g fiber, 9 g pro. Exchanges: 1.5 starch, 0.5 carb., 0.5 medium-fat meat. Carb choices: 2.

Nonstick cooking spray

2 eggs or ½ cup refrigerated or frozen egg product, thawed

½ cup fat-free milk

½ teaspoon vanilla

⅛ teaspoon ground cinnamon

4 1-inch-thick slices French bread

⅔ cup thinly sliced banana

Sifted powdered sugar, light pancake and waffle syrup product, or maple syrup (optional)

1. Preheat the oven to 500°F. Line a baking sheet with foil; coat the foil with nonstick cooking spray. Set the baking sheet aside.

2. In a shallow bowl, combine eggs, milk, vanilla, and cinnamon. Beat with a wire whisk or rotary beater until mixed. Set aside.

3. Using a serrated knife, cut a pocket in each French bread slice, cutting horizontally from the top crust almost to, but not through, the bottom crust. Fill bread pockets with banana slices.

4. Dip the stuffed bread slices, one at a time, into egg mixture, coating both sides. Arrange the slices on the prepared baking sheet.

5. Bake slices, uncovered, for 10 to 12 minutes or until golden, turning once. If desired, sprinkle with powdered sugar or serve with syrup. Makes 4 (1-slice) servings.

Banana-Stuffed French Toast

(why bother with breakfast?)

There's no holiday from good nutrition! You already know that eating a healthful breakfast daily can help control your blood glucose. Here are three more reasons to start every day the right way.

1. Better performance. Breakfast eaters have a more positive attitude toward school and work, and they perform better. A Boston study showed that children who started eating breakfast raised their test scores significantly and were late or absent from school less frequently.

2. Better overall nutrition. People who eat breakfast are more likely to consume nutrients their bodies need. Skipping breakfast makes it hard to meet daily requirements for necessary nutrients.

3. Better weight control. Breakfast revs up your body's metabolic rate first thing in the morning, burning calories faster than if you skip it. Breakfast eaters maintain their weight more easily, too.

family-pleasing dinners

Thai Pork Stir-Fry

If you think tasty meals are hard to serve during the week, turn to these family-favorite dishes. From poultry and pork to beef or fish, our recipes will help you prepare healthful dinners on busy days in 30 minutes or less.

Thai Pork Stir-Fry

Grate or cut off as much ginger as you need, then freeze the leftover unpeeled fresh piece.

PER SERVING: 301 cal., 11 g total fat (3 g sat. fat), 71 mg chol., 206 mg sodium, 21 g carb., 3 g fiber, 28 g pro. Exchanges: 1 vegetable, 1 starch, 3 lean meat, 1 fat. Carb choices: 1.5.

- 2 tablespoons olive oil
- 1 tablespoon reduced-sodium soy sauce
- ½ teaspoon garlic powder
- ½ teaspoon ground cardamom
- ½ teaspoon chili powder
- ½ teaspoon ground black pepper
- ½ teaspoon finely chopped fresh ginger or ¼ teaspoon ground ginger
- 1½ pounds boneless pork loin, cut into bite-size strips
- 2 cups broccoli florets
- 1 cup thinly sliced carrots
- 1 cup cauliflower florets
- 2 tablespoons white vinegar
- 1 tablespoon curry powder
- 2 cups hot cooked brown rice

1. In a very large skillet, combine oil, soy sauce, garlic powder, cardamom, chili powder, pepper, and ginger. Add half of the pork.

2. Stir-fry pork over medium-high heat for 3 minutes. Using a slotted spoon, remove pork from skillet. Repeat with the remaining pork. Return all of the pork to the skillet.

3. Add broccoli, carrots, cauliflower, vinegar, and curry powder to pork mixture. Bring to boiling; reduce heat. Cover and simmer pork and vegetables for 3 to 5 minutes or until vegetables are crisp-tender, stirring occasionally. Serve over hot cooked brown rice. Makes 6 servings (1 cup stir-fry and ⅓ cup rice each).

(label lingo)

To keep your nutrition goals in check, learn to read labels. The "nutrition facts" label helps you track how much fat, saturated fat, cholesterol, sodium, fiber, and important nutrients you eat. The label also lists the number of calories and grams of carbohydrates, protein, and fat in a serving. You can use these numbers to calculate exchanges. Some food manufacturers list exchanges on the package. All recipes in this book also list nutrition facts and exchanges. Supermarkets often display nutrition information for fresh meat, poultry, seafood, vegetables, and fruits on posters or offer take-home brochures for consumers.

Pork Chops with Red Cabbage and Pears

Cranberry Pork Loin Chops

Pork Chops with Red Cabbage and Pears

The sweet-and-sour cabbage pairs deliciously with braised chops.

PER SERVING: 239 cal., 4 g total fat (1 g sat. fat), 70 mg chol., 323 mg sodium, 20 g carb., 4 g fiber, 30 g pro. Exchanges: 1 vegetable, 0.5 fruit, 0.5 carb., 4 very lean meat. Carb choices: 1.

PER SERVING WITH SUBSTITUTE: same as above, except 222 cal., 15 g carb. Exchanges: 0 carb. Carb choices: 0.

- ¼ cup cider vinegar
- 2 tablespoons packed brown sugar or brown sugar substitute* equivalent to 2 tablespoons brown sugar
- ½ teaspoon dried sage, crushed
- 6 small pork loin chops,** cut ½ inch thick (about 2 pounds total)
- ½ teaspoon dried thyme, crushed
- ¼ teaspoon salt
- ⅛ teaspoon ground black pepper
- 2 teaspoons canola oil
- 6 cups coarsely shredded red cabbage
- 1 cup sliced onion
- 2 medium pears, cored and sliced
  Snipped fresh sage and/or thyme (optional)

1. In a small bowl, combine cider vinegar, brown sugar, and ¼ teaspoon of the sage. Reserve 1 tablespoon of the mixture; set aside.

2. Sprinkle chops with dried thyme, salt, remaining ¼ teaspoon sage, and pepper. In a large skillet, heat oil over medium-high heat. Add chops. Cook for 6 to 8 minutes or until pork is slightly pink in the center and juices run clear (160°F), turning pork chops once halfway through cooking and brushing with 1 tablespoon vinegar mixture for the last 1 minute of cooking. Remove pork chops from skillet; cover and keep warm.

3. Add red cabbage and onion to skillet. Cook and stir over medium-high heat for 6 minutes. Add the reserved vinegar mixture and pears to skillet. Bring to boiling; reduce heat. Cover and simmer for 5 minutes. Top with pork chops; heat through. If desired, sprinkle chops with fresh sage and/or thyme. Makes 6 servings (1 chop and scant 1 cup cabbage mixture each).

***Sugar Substitutes:** Choose from Sweet'N Low Brown or Sugar Twin Granulated Brown. Follow package directions to use product amount equivalent to 2 tablespoons brown sugar.

****Test Kitchen Tip:** To keep the sodium in this dish in check, look for natural pork, not enhanced pork.

Cranberry Pork Loin Chops

Ladle the tangy orange-and-cranberry sauce onto broiled or grilled chicken and fish, too.

PER SERVING: 285 cal., 7 g total fat (2 g sat. fat), 89 mg chol., 172 mg sodium, 21 g carb., 1 g fiber, 31 g pro. Exchanges: 1.5 carb., 4 lean meat. Carb choices: 1.5.

- Nonstick cooking spray
- 4 boneless pork loin chops, cut ½ inch thick (about 1¼ pounds total)
- ½ cup canned whole cranberry sauce
- 2 tablespoons frozen orange juice concentrate, thawed
- 1 tablespoon honey
- ¼ teaspoon ground ginger
- ⅛ teaspoon ground nutmeg

1. Lightly coat an unheated large nonstick skillet with cooking spray. Preheat over medium-high heat. Sprinkle all sides of the chops with ⅛ teaspoon *salt* and ⅛ teaspoon ground *black pepper*. Add chops to hot skillet; reduce heat to medium. Cook for 8 to 10 minutes or until done (160°F), turning once. Remove chops from skillet; cover to keep warm.

2. Meanwhile, combine cranberry sauce, juice concentrate, honey, ginger, and nutmeg. Add mixture to same skillet. Cook and stir for 1 to 2 minutes or until slightly thickened. Serve over chops. Makes 4 servings.

Adobo Pork Chops

Adobo is the Spanish word for seasoning or marinade. This chili-spiced version also has a smidgen of cinnamon.

PER SERVING: 189 cal., 7 g total fat (2 g sat. fat), 71 mg chol., 170 mg sodium, 3 g carb., 0 g fiber, 25 g pro. Exchanges: 4 very lean meat, 1 fat. Carb choices: 0.

- 6 boneless pork top loin chops, cut ¾ inch thick
- 2 tablespoons packed brown sugar
- 2 tablespoons olive oil
- 2 tablespoons orange juice
- 2 tablespoons snipped fresh cilantro
- 1 tablespoon red wine vinegar or cider vinegar
- 2 teaspoons chili powder
- 1 teaspoon ground cumin
- 1 teaspoon dried oregano, crushed
- ¼ teaspoon cayenne pepper (optional)
- ¼ teaspoon ground cinnamon
- 3 cloves garlic, minced
- ½ teaspoon salt

1. Place chops in resealable plastic bag set in a shallow dish. In a bowl, combine remaining ingredients; pour over chops. Seal bag; turn to coat. Marinate in refrigerator for 2 to 24 hours.

2. Drain chops; discard marinade. Grill on rack of an uncovered grill directly over medium heat for 12 to 15 minutes or until medium doneness (160°F), turning once. Makes 6 servings.

Adobo Pork Chops

Pork Medaillons with Lemon-Pecan Spinach

Zippy spinach replaces the usual starchy vegetable.

PER SERVING: 213 cal., 10 g total fat (2 g sat. fat), 73 mg chol., 318 mg sodium, 5 g carb., 3 g fiber, 27 g pro. Exchanges: 1 vegetable, 3.5 lean meat, 0.5 fat. Carb choices: 0.

- 1 pound pork tenderloin, cut crosswise into 8 slices
- ¼ teaspoon salt
- ¼ teaspoon coarsely ground black pepper
- 1 tablespoon canola oil or margarine
- 2 tablespoons lemon juice
- ⅛ teaspoon bottled hot pepper sauce
- 1 10-ounce package frozen chopped spinach, thawed and well-drained
- 2 green onions, sliced
- 2 tablespoons chopped pecans
- 1 tablespoon snipped fresh parsley
- ⅛ teaspoon salt
  Lemon slices, halved (optional)

1. If necessary, press each pork tenderloin slice to 1-inch thickness. Sprinkle pork slices lightly with the ¼ teaspoon salt and pepper.

2. In a large skillet, heat oil over medium-high heat. Add pork slices; cook for 6 to 8 minutes or until pork is slightly pink in the center (160°F), turning once halfway through cooking. Remove pork from skillet, reserving drippings in the skillet. Cover pork and keep warm.

3. Stir lemon juice and hot pepper sauce into reserved drippings in skillet. Stir in spinach, green onions, pecans, parsley, and the ⅛ teaspoon salt. Cook over low heat until spinach mixture is heated through.

4. Place spinach mixture on a platter; arrange pork slices on top. If desired, garnish with lemon slices. Makes 4 servings.

Quick Tip

Some cuts of pork compare favorably with the white meat of chicken. A 3-ounce portion of roasted pork tenderloin, for example, has 139 calories and 4 grams of fat. The same size portion of roasted chicken (breast meat, no skin) has 142 calories and 3 grams of fat.

Pork Medaillons with
Lemon-Pecan Spinach

Sesame Orange Beef

For a triple hit of orange bliss, use orange juice, peel, and slices in this lighter version of the Asian classic.

PER SERVING: 348 cal., 10 g total fat (2 g sat. fat), 52 mg chol., 341 mg sodium, 41 g carb., 6 g fiber, 24 g pro. Exchanges: 1 vegetable, 1 fruit, 1.5 starch, 2.5 lean meat. Carb choices: 3.

- 8 ounces fresh green beans, halved crosswise
- 2 teaspoons sesame seeds
- ½ teaspoon finely shredded orange peel
- ½ cup orange juice
- 2 tablespoons reduced-sodium soy sauce
- 1 tablespoon toasted sesame oil
- 1 teaspoon cornstarch
- Nonstick cooking spray
- ½ cup bias-sliced green onions
- 1 tablespoon grated fresh ginger
- 2 cloves garlic, minced
- 1 teaspoon cooking oil
- 12 ounces boneless beef sirloin steak, thinly sliced
- 2 cups hot cooked brown rice
- 2 oranges, peeled and thinly sliced crosswise or sectioned

1. In a covered medium saucepan, cook green beans in a small amount of boiling water for 6 to 8 minutes or until crisp-tender. Drain; set aside.

2. Meanwhile, in a small skillet, toast sesame seeds over medium heat for 1 to 2 minutes, stirring frequently. Set aside.

3. For sauce, in a small bowl, combine orange peel, orange juice, soy sauce, toasted sesame oil, and cornstarch; set aside.

4. Coat an unheated large nonstick skillet with cooking spray. Preheat over medium-high heat. Add green onions, ginger, and garlic to hot skillet; cook and stir for 1 minute. Add the precooked green beans; cook and stir for 2 minutes. Remove vegetables from skillet.

5. Carefully add cooking oil to the hot skillet. Add beef; cook and stir about 3 minutes or until desired doneness. Remove beef from skillet.

6. Stir sauce; add to skillet. Cook and stir until thickened and bubbly; cook and stir for 2 minutes more. Return beef and vegetables to skillet. Heat through, stirring to coat all ingredients with sauce.

7. Serve beef mixture over hot cooked brown rice. Top with orange slices; sprinkle with toasted sesame seeds. Makes 4 servings (¾ cup meat and ½ cup rice each).

Herbed Steak with Balsamic Sauce

The sweet flavor of balsamic vinegar is the star of the sauce.

PER SERVING: 214 cal., 11 g total fat (4 g sat. fat), 74 mg chol., 279 mg sodium, 2 g carb., 0 g fiber, 25 g pro. Exchanges: 3.5 lean meat, 0.5 fat. Carb choices: 0.

- 1 teaspoon cracked black pepper
- 2 teaspoons dried Italian seasoning, crushed
- 1 teaspoon garlic powder
- ¼ teaspoon salt
- 1 tablespoon olive oil
- 2 boneless beef top loin steaks, cut ¾ inch thick
- ½ cup reduced-sodium beef broth
- 1 tablespoon balsamic vinegar
- 1 tablespoon butter
- 2 tablespoons snipped fresh flat-leaf parsley

1. In a small bowl, combine pepper, Italian seasoning, garlic powder, and salt. Sprinkle evenly over both sides of each steak; rub in with your fingers.

2. In a heavy large skillet, heat oil over medium-low to medium heat. Add steaks; cook until desired doneness, turning once halfway through cooking time. Allow 10 to 13 minutes for medium-rare doneness (145°F) to medium doneness (160°F). Remove steaks from skillet, reserving drippings in skillet. Keep steaks warm.

3. Add broth and vinegar to skillet; stir to scrape up any browned bits from bottom of skillet. Bring to boiling. Boil gently, uncovered, about 4 minutes or until sauce is reduced by half. Remove from heat; stir in butter.

4. Divide sauce among four dinner plates. Cut each steak in half. Place a piece of meat on top of sauce on each plate; sprinkle with parsley. Makes 4 servings.

Ginger Beef Stir-Fry

Add more color by using orange or
yellow sweet pepper strips in addition to the red.

PER SERVING: 274 cal., 7 g total fat (1 g sat. fat), 32 mg chol., 552 mg sodium, 34 g carb., 5 g fiber, 20 g pro. Exchanges: 1.5 vegetable, 1.5 starch, 2 very lean meat, 1 fat. Carb choices: 2.

- **8   ounces beef top round steak**
- **½   cup reduced-sodium beef broth**
- **3   tablespoons reduced-sodium soy sauce**
- **2½ teaspoons cornstarch**
- **2   to 3 teaspoons grated fresh ginger**
- **Nonstick cooking spray**
- **1½ cups sliced fresh mushrooms**
- **1   medium carrot, thinly bias-sliced**
- **3   cups small broccoli florets or 1 pound fresh asparagus spears, trimmed and cut into 2-inch pieces**
- **1   small red sweet pepper, seeded and cut into ¼-inch strips**
- **1   tablespoon cooking oil**
- **2   green onions, bias-sliced into 2-inch pieces**
- **2   cups hot cooked brown rice**

1. If desired, partially freeze beef for easier slicing. Trim fat from beef. Thinly slice beef across the grain into bite-size strips; set aside. For sauce, in a small bowl, stir together beef broth, soy sauce, cornstarch, and ginger; set aside.

2. Lightly coat an unheated wok or large nonstick skillet with cooking spray. Preheat over medium-high heat. Add mushrooms and carrot; stir-fry for 2 minutes. Add broccoli and sweet pepper; stir-fry about 2 minutes or until vegetables are crisp-tender. Remove vegetables from wok.

3. Carefully add oil to wok. Add beef; stir-fry for 2 to 3 minutes or until desired doneness. Push beef from center of wok. Stir sauce; add to center of wok. Cook and stir until thickened and bubbly.

4. Return vegetables to wok. Add green onions. Stir ingredients to coat with sauce; heat through. Serve warm over hot cooked brown rice. Makes 4 servings (1 cup beef mixture and ½ cup rice each).

Ginger Beef Stir-Fry

(lighten up!)

Use these strategies for more healthful meals.

1. **Choose** cuts of meat with the words "round" or "loin" in the name (for example, ground round or pork tenderloin), skinless poultry, fish, and dry beans, peas, and lentils.

2. **Buy** fat-free and low-fat milk and yogurt. Taste-test various brands of reduced-fat cheeses to find ones you like.

3. **Stock up** on low-fat snacks such as pretzels, air-popped popcorn, flavored rice cakes, and baked bagel chips.

4. **Choose** soft-style margarines with liquid vegetable oil as the first ingredient. Tub or liquid margarines have less saturated fat than stick margarines.

5. **Try** reduced-fat or fat-free sour cream, cream cheese, mayonnaise, salad dressing, margarine, and tartar sauce.

6. **Select** frozen vegetables that have no butter or sauces.

7. **Look for** reduced-sodium Worcestershire and soy sauces; canned broth, beans, and soups; bouillon cubes; lunch meats; bacon; and ham.

8. **Choose** whole grain breads and crackers to boost fiber.

9. **Bake,** broil, grill, poach, steam, or microwave foods instead of frying.

10. **Sauté** foods in cooking spray, low-sodium broth, or fruit juice.

Bistro Beef Steak with Wild Mushrooms

Bistro Beef Steak with Wild Mushrooms

Herbes de Provence is a French blend of eight different dried herbs.

PER SERVING: 206 cal., 8 g total fat (2 g sat. fat), 66 mg chol., 291 mg sodium, 4 g carb., 1 g fiber, 27 g pro. Exchanges: 0.5 vegetable, 3 lean meat, 0.5 fat. Carb choices: 0.

- 3 cloves garlic, minced
- 1 teaspoon herbes de **Provence**
- ½ teaspoon ground black pepper
- ¼ teaspoon salt
- 3 8-ounce boneless beef top loin steaks, cut ¾ inch thick
- 1 tablespoon olive oil
- ⅓ cup finely chopped shallots
- 2 cloves garlic, minced
- 8 ounces assorted fresh wild mushrooms (oyster, cremini, and/or shiitake), sliced*
- ¼ cup dry sherry (optional)
- 1 14-ounce can reduced-sodium beef broth
- 1 tablespoon cornstarch
- 1 teaspoon herbes de **Provence**

1. Preheat broiler. In a small bowl, combine the 3 cloves garlic, the 1 teaspoon herbes de Provence, pepper, and salt. Sprinkle onto steaks; rub in garlic mixture with your fingers.

2. Place steaks on the unheated rack of a broiler pan. Broil 3 to 4 inches from heat for 9 to 11 minutes for medium-rare to medium doneness (145°F to 160°F), turning once.

3. Meanwhile, in a large nonstick skillet, heat oil over medium-high heat. Add shallots and the 2 cloves garlic; cook for 1 to 3 minutes or until shallots are tender. Add mushrooms; cook for 6 to 7 minutes or until mushrooms are tender and any liquid evaporates, stirring occasionally. Remove from heat. If desired, stir in sherry. Return mixture to boiling. Cook for 30 to 60 seconds or until liquid evaporates.

4. In a medium bowl, stir together broth, cornstarch, and the 1 teaspoon herbes de Provence. Stir broth mixture into mushroom mixture in skillet. Cook and stir over medium heat until thickened and bubbly. Cook and stir for 2 minutes more.

5. Cut steaks in half; serve with mushroom mixture. Makes 6 servings (one 4-ounce steak and ⅓ cup sauce each).

***Test Kitchen Tip:** Remove stems from the oyster and shiitake mushrooms before slicing.

Steak with Chutney Sauce

Chutney is a sweet and spicy condiment used in Indian cooking. Look for mango chutney with other condiments or the foreign foods in the supermarket.

PER SERVING: 269 cal., 8 g total fat (3 g sat. fat), 46 mg chol., 173 mg sodium, 22 g carb., 1 g fiber, 25 g pro. Exchanges: 3.5 lean meat, 0.5 fruit, 1 other carb. Carb choices: 1.5.

- 1 1½-pound beef flank steak
- ⅔ cup pineapple juice
- ⅓ cup mango chutney
- 1 tablespoon rum or pineapple juice
- 1 tablespoon rice vinegar
- 1 clove garlic, minced
- ¼ teaspoon salt
- ¼ cup golden raisins
- 1 teaspoon cornstarch
- Mango slices (optional)
- Fresh parsley sprigs (optional)

1. Trim fat from steak. Score both sides in a diamond pattern, making shallow diagonal cuts 1 inch apart.

2. For marinade, combine juice, chutney, rum, rice vinegar, garlic, and salt. Place steak in a resealable plastic bag set in a shallow dish. Add marinade; seal bag. Marinate steak in the refrigerator for 2 to 24 hours, turning bag occasionally.

3. Drain steak, reserving marinade. Grill steak on rack of an uncovered grill directly over medium heat for 17 to 21 minutes or until medium doneness (160°F), turning once.

4. Meanwhile, for the sauce, pour reserved marinade into a saucepan; stir in raisins and cornstarch. Cook and stir until thickened and bubbly; cook and stir for 2 minutes more.

5. To serve, thinly slice steak diagonally across the grain. Serve with sauce. If desired, garnish with mango slices and parsley. Makes 6 servings (one 4-ounce steak and scant 1 cup sauce each).

Indian Beef Patties with Cucumber Yogurt Sauce

A tangy cucumber sauce complements the patties.

PER SERVING: 241 cal., 12 g total fat (5 g sat. fat), 75 mg chol., 377 mg sodium, 8 g carb., 1 g fiber, 24 g pro. Exchanges: 0.5 milk, 2.5 medium-fat meat, 0.5 vegetable. Carb choices: 0.5.

½ cup finely chopped onion
4 tablespoons finely chopped, seeded fresh jalapeño pepper*
2 tablespoons snipped fresh mint
1 teaspoon ground cumin
2 cloves garlic, minced
½ teaspoon salt
1 pound lean ground beef
4 slices Indian flatbread (optional)
1 recipe Cucumber Yogurt Sauce (see recipe, below)

1. In a medium bowl, combine onion, jalapeño pepper, mint, cumin, garlic, and salt. Add ground meat; mix well. Form into four ¾-inch-thick patties.

2. Grill on rack of an uncovered grill directly over medium heat for 14 to 18 minutes or until done (160°F), turning once. If desired, serve on flatbread. Top with Cucumber Yogurt Sauce. Makes 4 servings.

Cucumber Yogurt Sauce: In a small bowl, combine 1 cup plain low-fat yogurt and ⅔ cup chopped, seeded cucumber. Cover and chill until serving time.

*Test Kitchen Tip: Because chile peppers contain volatile oils that can burn skin and eyes, avoid direct contact with them. When working with peppers, wear plastic gloves. If you do touch the peppers, wash your hands and nails well.

Deviled Roast Beef

For the mustard lover in your midst, here's a "deviled" beef dish that is simply delicious.

PER SERVING: 217 cal., 9 g total fat (3 g sat. fat), 78 mg chol., 342 mg sodium, 5 g carb., 0 g fiber, 28 g pro. Exchanges: 3 lean meat 1 vegetable. Carb choices: 0.5.

1 2- to 2 ½-pounds beef eye of round roast
¼ cup Dijon-style mustard
¼ teaspoon coarsely ground pepper
2 cups sliced fresh mushrooms
1 cup beef broth
1 small onion, cut into thin wedges
¼ cup water
2 cloves garlic, minced
1 teaspoon Worcestershire sauce
¼ teaspoon dried thyme, crushed
½ cup fat-free milk
3 tablespoons all-purpose flour

1. Preheat oven to 325°F. Trim fat from beef. In a small bowl, stir together 2 tablespoons of Dijon-style mustard and the pepper; rub onto beef. Place beef on a rack in a shallow roasting pan. Insert a meat thermometer. Roast until thermometer registers 140° for medium-rare (1½ to 2 hours) or 155° for medium (1¾ to 2¼ hours). Cover with foil; let stand for 15 minutes before carving. (The temperature of the meat will rise 5° during standing.)

2. Meanwhile, for sauce, in a medium saucepan combine mushrooms, broth, onion, water, garlic, Worcestershire sauce, and thyme. Bring to boiling; reduce heat. Simmer, covered, about 5 minutes or until vegetables are tender. In a small bowl, stir together milk and remaining mustard; gradually stir into flour. Add to mushroom mixture in saucepan. Cook and stir over medium heat until thickened and bubbly. Cook and stir for 1 minute more.

3. To serve, thinly slice beef across the grain. Arrange on a serving platter. Spoon some of the sauce over beef. Pass remaining sauce. Makes 8 to 10 servings.

(shed the skin)

Leaving the skin on chicken during cooking helps to add flavor and keeps moistness in the meat. The meat doesn't absorb much of the fat from the skin. However, because the skin contains a lot of fat (8 grams of fat with skin versus 3 grams of fat without skin for a 3-ounce portion), removing it before eating chicken significantly lowers the fat and calories (193 calories with skin versus 142 without skin for a 3-ounce portion).

Ginger Chicken with Rice Noodles

Ginger Chicken with Rice Noodles
This flavorful dish is as tasty as any restaurant version.
PER SERVING: 396 cal., 13 g total fat (2 g sat. fat), 82 mg chol., 369 mg sodium, 32 g carb., 3 g fiber, 37 g pro. Exchanges: 2 starch, 4.5 very lean meat, 0.5 vegetable, 1.5 fat. Carb choices: 2.

- ¼ cup finely chopped green onions
- 1 tablespoon grated fresh ginger
- 6 cloves garlic, minced
- 2 teaspoons olive oil
- ¼ teaspoon salt
- 4 skinless, boneless chicken breast halves (about 20 ounces total)
- 4 ounces dried rice noodles
- 1 cup chopped carrots
- 1 teaspoon finely shredded lime peel
- 2 tablespoons lime juice
- 4 teaspoons olive oil
- 2 to 4 tablespoons snipped fresh cilantro
- ¼ cup coarsely chopped peanuts

1. For rub, in a small bowl, combine green onions, ginger, garlic, the 2 teaspoons oil, and salt. Sprinkle evenly onto chicken; rub in with your fingers.

2. Grill chicken on the rack of an uncovered grill directly over medium heat for 12 to 15 minutes or until tender and no longer pink (170°F), turning once.

3. Meanwhile, in a large saucepan, cook noodles and carrots in a large amount of boiling water for 3 to 4 minutes or just until noodles are tender; drain. Rinse with cold water; drain again. Using kitchen shears, snip noodles into bite-size lengths.

4. In a medium bowl, stir together lime peel, lime juice, and the 4 teaspoons oil. Add noodle mixture and cilantro; toss gently to coat. Divide noodle mixture among four bowls. Thinly slice chicken diagonally; arrange on noodle mixture. Top with peanuts. Makes 4 servings.

Make-Ahead Directions: Rub chicken as directed in Step 1. Cover and chill for up to 24 hours. Prepare as directed in Steps 2 through 4.

Penne with Chicken and Broccoli

Penne with Chicken and Broccoli

Light mayonnaise keeps the fat and calories low.

PER SERVING: 309 cal., 9 g total fat (1 g sat. fat), 48 mg chol., 399 mg sodium, 30 g carb., 4 g fiber, 26 g pro. Exchanges: 0.5 vegetable, 2 starch, 2.5 very lean meat, 1 fat. Carb choices: 2.

- 8 ounces dried whole grain penne pasta
- 3 cups broccoli florets
- 4 skinless, boneless chicken breast halves (1 to 1¼ pounds total), cut into bite-size pieces
- 1 teaspoon adobo seasoning
- 2 tablespoons olive oil, margarine, or butter
- 1 clove garlic, minced
- ¼ cup light mayonnaise or salad dressing
- ⅛ teaspoon ground black pepper
- 2 tablespoons finely shredded Parmesan cheese

1. Cook pasta according to package directions, adding broccoli the last 5 minutes; drain. Return to pan.

2. Meanwhile, in a medium bowl, combine chicken and adobo seasoning; toss gently to coat.

3. In a large skillet, heat oil over medium-high heat. Add garlic; cook for 30 seconds. Add chicken; cook for 3 to 4 minutes or until chicken is no longer pink, stirring occasionally.

4. Add chicken to pasta mixture in pan. Stir in mayonnaise and pepper. Cook over low heat until heated through, stirring often.

5. To serve, top pasta mixture with Parmesan. Makes 6 (1⅔-cup) servings.

Jerk Chicken Breasts

The skinless chicken breast halves reduce the fat.

PER SERVING: 180 cal., 3 g total fat (1 g sat. fat), 88 mg chol., 283 mg sodium, 2 g carb., 0 g fiber, 35 g pro. Exchanges: 5 very lean meat. Carb choices: 0.

- 6 skinless, boneless chicken breast halves (about 2 pounds total)
- 4 teaspoons Jamaican jerk seasoning
- 8 cloves garlic, minced
- 2 teaspoons snipped fresh thyme or ½ teaspoon dried thyme, crushed
- 2 teaspoons finely shredded lemon peel
- 2 tablespoons lemon juice
   Olive oil cooking spray or 2 teaspoons olive oil
   Lemon wedges (optional)

1. Place a chicken breast half between two sheets of plastic wrap; pound gently with the flat side of a meat mallet to an even ½-inch thickness. Repeat with remaining chicken.

2. In a small bowl, combine jerk seasoning, garlic, thyme, and lemon peel. Brush chicken breasts with lemon juice. Sprinkle seasoning mixture evenly onto chicken; rub in with your fingers. Place chicken in a resealable plastic bag; seal bag. Chill in the refrigerator until ready to cook.

3. Coat a cold grill rack with cooking spray. Grill chicken on rack of an uncovered grill directly over medium heat for 6 to 10 minutes or until tender and no longer pink, turning once halfway through grilling. To serve, slice chicken; if desired, serve with lemon wedges. Makes 6 servings.

Broiling Directions: Preheat broiler. Coat the unheated rack of the broiler pan with cooking spray. Place chicken on the rack in the broiler pan. Broil 3 to 4 inches from heat for 6 to 10 minutes or until chicken is tender and no longer pink, turning once halfway through broiling.

Make-Ahead Directions: Prepare chicken as directed through Step 2. Cover and chill for up to 24 hours. Grill or broil as directed.

Jerk Chicken Breasts

Bangkok Stir-Fry

Don't be put off by the aroma of fish sauce. It adds an undetectable yet characteristic flavor to the dish.

PER SERVING: 327 cal., 3 g total fat (1 g sat. fat), 49 mg chol., 541 mg sodium, 49 g carb., 5 g fiber, 26 g protein. Exchanges: 2.5 starch, 0.5 fruit, 2.5 very lean meat, 1 vegetable. Carb choices: 3.

- 2 tablespoons fish sauce (nam pla)
- 1 tablespoon lime juice
- 2 teaspoons minced fresh lemongrass or 1 teaspoon finely shredded lemon peel
  Nonstick cooking spray
- 1 large red onion, cut in thin wedges (1½ cups)
- 3 cloves garlic, minced
- 1 small cucumber, cut into thin bite-size strips (1 cup)
- ¼ of a pineapple, peeled, cored, and cut into ¼-inch wedges
- 1 or 2 fresh jalapeño chile peppers, seeded and finely chopped*
- 12 ounces skinless, boneless chicken breast halves, cut into thin bite-size strips
- 1 cup sugar snap pea pods, trimmed
- 2 cups hot cooked brown, jasmine, or basmati rice
  Snipped fresh cilantro or parsley (optional)

1. For sauce, in a small bowl, stir together fish sauce, lime juice, and lemongrass; set aside.

2. Coat an unheated large nonstick skillet or wok with cooking spray. Preheat skillet over medium-high heat. Add onion and garlic to hot skillet; cook and stir for 2 minutes. Add cucumber, pineapple, and chile peppers. Cook and stir for 2 minutes more. Remove from skillet.

3. Add chicken to skillet. Cook and stir for 2 to 3 minutes or until chicken is tender and no longer pink. Return onion mixture to skillet; add pea pods. Add sauce. Cook and stir about 1 minute or until heated through. Serve immediately over hot rice. If desired, sprinkle with snipped cilantro. Makes 4 (1-cup) servings.

*Test Kitchen Tip: Because chile peppers contain volatile oils that can burn your skin and eyes, avoid direct contact with them as much as possible. When working with them, wear plastic or rubber gloves. If your bare hands do touch the peppers, wash your hands and nails well.

Bangkok Stir-Fry

Chicken with Broccoli and Garlic

Though moist and juicy chicken thighs contain more fat than white meat does, this dish retains its low-cal status. Broccoli slaw and pecans boost the flavor.

PER SERVING: 270 cal., 10 g total fat (2 g sat. fat), 68 mg chol., 392 mg sodium, 24 g carb., 3 g fiber, 23 g pro. Exchanges: 2 vegetable, 1 carb., 2.5 medium-fat meat, 0.5 fat. Carb choices: 1.5.

- ¼ cup all-purpose flour
- ¼ teaspoon salt
- ¼ teaspoon ground black pepper
- 4 medium skinless, boneless chicken thighs (about 12 ounces total), trimmed of fat
- 1 tablespoon olive oil
- 6 cloves garlic, minced (about 1 tablespoon)
- 1 cup reduced-sodium chicken broth
- 3 tablespoons white wine vinegar
- 1 tablespoon honey
- 1 16-ounce package shredded broccoli (broccoli slaw mix)
- 2 tablespoons coarsely chopped pecans

1. In a plastic bag, combine flour, salt, and pepper. Add chicken; seal bag. Shake to coat.

2. In a large skillet, cook chicken in hot oil over medium heat for 10 to 12 minutes or until chicken is tender and no longer pink (180°F), turning once. Transfer chicken to plate; cover and keep warm.

3. Add garlic to skillet. Cook and stir for 15 seconds. Add broth, vinegar, and honey. Bring to boiling; reduce heat. Simmer, uncovered, for 5 minutes. Stir in broccoli. Return to boiling; reduce heat. Simmer, covered, for 8 to 10 minutes more or until broccoli is crisp-tender. Stir in pecans. Serve broccoli mixture with chicken. Makes 4 servings (1 thigh and 1 cup broccoli each).

Summer Chicken and Mushroom Pasta

Healthy doses of garlic and white wine enlighten this herbed mushroom and pasta combination. Light and fresh, it is perfect for dinner on a warm summer evening.

PER SERVING: 299 cal., 8 g total fat (2 g sat. fat), 37 mg chol., 249 mg sodium, 33 g carb., 2 g fiber, 22 g pro. Exchanges: 1.5 starch, 1.5 very lean meat, 2 vegetable, 1 fat. Carb choices: 2.

- 8 ounces dried penne pasta
- 12 ounces skinless, boneless chicken breast halves, cut into bite-size strips
- ¼ teaspoon salt
- ⅛ teaspoon freshly ground black pepper
- 2 tablespoons olive oil or cooking oil
- 3 large cloves garlic, minced
- 3 cups sliced fresh mushrooms
- 1 medium onion, thinly sliced
- ½ cup chicken broth
- ¼ cup dry white wine
- 1 cup cherry tomatoes, halved
- ¼ cup shredded fresh basil
- 3 tablespoons snipped fresh oregano
- ¼ cup shaved Parmesan cheese
- ⅛ teaspoon freshly ground black pepper

1. Cook pasta in boiling, lightly salted water according to package directions; drain. Return pasta to saucepan; cover and keep warm.

2. Meanwhile, sprinkle chicken with salt and ⅛ teaspoon pepper. In a large skillet, heat 1 tablespoon of the oil over medium-high heat. Add chicken and garlic. Cook and stir for 3 to 4 minutes or until chicken is tender and no longer pink. Remove chicken from skillet; cover and keep warm.

3. Add remaining oil to skillet. Add mushrooms and onion; cook just until tender, stirring occasionally. Carefully add chicken broth and white wine. Bring to boiling; reduce heat. Boil gently, uncovered, about 2 minutes or until liquid is reduced by half. Remove skillet from heat.

4. Add cooked pasta, chicken, cherry tomatoes, basil, and oregano to mushroom mixture; toss gently to coat. Transfer chicken mixture to a serving dish; sprinkle with Parmesan cheese and ⅛ teaspoon pepper. Serve immediately. Makes 6 servings.

Feta-Stuffed Chicken Breasts

Even the kids love the feta cheese, tomato, and basil filling.

PER SERVING: 168 cal., 5 g total fat (2 g sat. fat), 75 mg chol., 221 mg sodium, 1 g carb., 0 g fiber, 29 g pro. Exchanges: 4 very lean meat, 2 fat. Carb choices: 0.

- 1 tablespoon snipped dried tomatoes (not oil-packed)
- 4 skinless, boneless chicken breast halves (1 to 1½ pounds total)
- ¼ cup crumbled feta cheese (1 ounce)
- 2 tablespoons fat-free cream cheese (1 ounce), softened
- 2 teaspoons snipped fresh basil or ½ teaspoon dried basil, crushed
- ⅛ teaspoon ground black pepper
- 1 teaspoon olive oil or cooking oil
  Fresh basil sprigs (optional)

1. In a small bowl, pour enough boiling water over the tomatoes to cover. Let stand for 10 minutes. Drain and pat dry; set aside.

2. Using a sharp knife, cut a pocket in each chicken breast by cutting horizontally through the thickest portion to, but not through, the opposite side. Set aside.

3. In a small bowl, combine drained tomatoes, feta cheese, cream cheese, and snipped or dried basil. Spoon about 1 rounded tablespoon into each pocket. If necessary, secure the openings with wooden toothpicks. Sprinkle with pepper.

4. In a large nonstick skillet, cook chicken in hot oil over medium-high heat for 12 to 14 minutes or until tender and no longer pink, turning once (reduce heat if necessary to prevent overbrowning). Serve warm. If desired, garnish with basil sprigs. Makes 4 servings.

Garlic and Mint Chicken Breasts

Mint adds a wonderful fresh flavor to this easy dish.

PER SERVING: 202 cal., 6 g total fat (1 g sat. fat), 82 mg chol., 229 mg sodium, 2 g carb., 0 g fiber, 34 g pro. Exchanges: 4.5 very lean meat, 1 fat. Carb choices: 0.

- 4 skinless, boneless chicken breast halves (1¼ to 1½ pounds total)
- ½ cup fresh mint
- 1 tablespoon lemon juice
- 1 tablespoon olive oil
- 1 tablespoon reduced-sodium soy sauce
- 4 cloves garlic
- 1 teaspoon chili powder
- ¼ teaspoon ground black pepper
- 2 cups hot cooked couscous (optional)
  Grilled green onions* (optional)
  Fresh mint (optional)

1. Place chicken in a resealable plastic bag set in a shallow dish.

2. For marinade, in a blender, combine the ½ cup mint, lemon juice, oil, soy sauce, garlic, chili powder, and pepper. Cover; blend until smooth. Pour over chicken. Seal bag; turn to coat. Marinate in the refrigerator for 4 hours, turning the bag occasionally.

3. Drain chicken, discarding marinade. Grill on rack of an uncovered grill directly over medium heat for 12 to 15 minutes or until tender and no longer pink (170°F), turning once. If desired, serve over couscous with onions; top with mint. Makes 4 servings.

*Test Kitchen Tip: To grill, place green onions on edge of grill the last 2 minutes of grilling chicken.

Feta-Stuffed Chicken Breasts

(lunches outside of the box)

Do you suffer from S.O.S. Syndrome? You know, the Same Old Sandwich. Packing a lunch gives you control over what you're eating, but it's no fun when lunch is as drab as the brown bag it comes in. Why not get a jump on making lunch interesting by fixing it in advance? Simply prepare and chill Curried Chicken Couscous as directed (see recipe, below) in a microwave-safe container. At lunchtime, just pop the container in the microwave oven to reheat. You'll be the envy of the lunch bunch when you heat up your satisfying meal. Even better, you'll know it's healthful, too.

Curried Chicken Couscous

Curried Chicken Couscous

This recipe is great for those busy nights when your family is on the go and everyone needs to eat at different times. Keep it in your freezer in individual serving bowls.

PER SERVING: 303 cal., 3 g total fat (1 g sat. fat), 59 mg chol., 365 mg sodium, 39 g carb., 3 g fiber, 27 g pro. Exchanges: 0.5 vegetable, 0.5 other carb., 2 starch, 3 very lean meat. Carb choices: 2.5.

Nonstick cooking spray
⅔ **cup chopped onion**
2 **teaspoons curry powder**
1⅓ **cups water**
⅔ **cup quick-cooking couscous**
2 **cups cubed cooked chicken breast (about 5 ounces)**
⅔ **cup loose-pack frozen peas**
½ **cup fat-free mayonnaise or salad dressing**
½ **cup chopped red sweet pepper**
¼ **cup bottled mango chutney**

1. Lightly coat four 1½- to 2-cup microwave-safe bowls or mugs with cooking spray. Set aside. Lightly coat an unheated medium skillet with cooking spray.

2. Preheat skillet over medium heat. Add onion; cook and stir until crisp-tender. Stir in curry powder; cook for 1 minute more. Add the water and couscous to skillet; bring to boiling. Remove from heat.

3. Stir in chicken, peas, mayonnaise, sweet pepper, and chutney. Divide among the coated bowls or mugs. Wrap tightly with foil; place in a freezer bag, seal, and freeze for up to 2 months.

4. To serve, remove foil; cover with vented plastic wrap. Microwave on 70 percent power (medium-high) about 3 minutes or until heated through, stirring once. Makes 4 (1¼-cup) servings.

Asparagus-Stuffed Turkey Rolls

If you need an impressive entrée in a hurry, this recipe is the answer.

PER SERVING: 142 cal., 2 g fat (1 g sat. fat), 68 mg chol., 271 mg sodium, 3 g carb., 1 g fiber, 28 g pro. Exchanges: 0.5 vegetable, 4 very lean meat. Carb choices: 0.

  2 **turkey breast tenderloins (about 1 pound total)**
 16 **thin fresh asparagus spears**
     Nonstick cooking spray
 ½ **cup reduced-sodium chicken broth**
  2 **tablespoons lemon juice**
 ¼ **teaspoon salt**
 ⅛ **teaspoon ground black pepper**

1. Split each turkey breast tenderloin in half horizontally to form a total of 4 turkey steaks. Place each steak between two pieces of plastic wrap. Using the flat side of a meat mallet, lightly pound turkey to ¼-inch thickness. Trim asparagus spears, breaking off woody ends. Arrange 4 asparagus spears on the short end of each turkey piece. Roll up turkey. If necessary, secure with wooden toothpicks.

2. Coat an unheated large nonstick skillet with cooking spray. Preheat skillet over medium heat. Cook turkey rolls in hot skillet until browned, turning to brown evenly. Add broth, lemon juice, salt, and pepper. Bring to boiling; reduce heat. Cover and simmer for 8 to 10 minutes or until turkey is no longer pink.

3. Transfer turkey to serving platter; discard toothpicks. Cover and keep warm. Boil liquid in skillet, uncovered, for 2 to 3 minutes or until reduced to ½ cup. Spoon over turkey. Makes 4 servings.

Mediterranean Tostadas

Make the hummus and chicken the day before. The next day, you'll have a great lunch ready to go.

PER SERVING: 413 cal., 7 g total fat (1 g sat. fat), 82 mg chol., 676 mg sodium, 45 g carb., 8 g fiber, 42 g pro. Exchanges: 3 starch, 4 very lean meat. Carb choices: 3.

  1 **tablespoon olive oil**
  1 **teaspoon lemon juice**
 ¼ **teaspoon paprika**
     Dash salt
     Dash freshly ground black pepper
  4 **medium skinless, boneless chicken breast halves**
  2 **whole wheat pita bread rounds, split and toasted**
  1 **recipe Hummus (see recipe, below)**
 ¾ **cup coarsely chopped tomato**
 ½ **cup chopped cucumber**
     Fresh cilantro (optional)
     Plain fat-free yogurt (optional)

1. Preheat broiler. In a small bowl, combine oil, lemon juice, paprika, salt, and pepper; set aside.

2. Place chicken on the unheated rack of a broiler pan. Brush both sides of chicken with the oil mixture. Broil 4 to 5 inches from heat for 10 to 12 minutes or until chicken is tender and no longer pink (170°F), turning once. Cool chicken slightly; coarsely chop chicken.

3. To serve, spread Hummus over the toasted pita halves. Top with the chicken, tomato, and cucumber. If desired, garnish with cilantro and serve with yogurt. Makes 4 servings.

Hummus: In a blender or food processor, combine one 15-ounce can garbanzo beans, rinsed and drained; ½ cup chopped fresh cilantro; 3 tablespoons lemon juice or lime juice; 3 tablespoons water; 2 cloves garlic, peeled and halved; ⅛ teaspoon salt; and a dash bottled hot pepper sauce. Cover and blend or process until smooth. Refrigerate until ready to serve. Makes about 1⅓ cups.

To make meal preparation easier, look for cut-up vegetables in the salad bar of your supermarket. No salad bar? Most supermarkets carry packaged stir-fry vegetables. Use them in salads, casseroles, slow-cooker recipes, and—of course—stir-fries.

Indian-Spiced Turkey Tenderloins

Too cold outside to grill? Use the broiling directions instead.

PER SERVING: 158 cal., 3 g total fat (1 g sat. fat), 73 mg chol., 502 mg sodium, 2 g carb., 1 g fiber, 28 g pro. Exchanges: 4 very lean meat, 0.5 fat. Carb choices: 0.

2 turkey breast tenderloins (about 1 pound total)
1½ teaspoons ground cumin
1½ teaspoons coriander seeds, crushed
1 teaspoon finely shredded lime peel
¾ teaspoon salt
¾ teaspoon ground ginger
¼ to ½ teaspoon crushed red pepper
¼ cup light dairy sour cream
1 tablespoon lime juice

1. Split each turkey tenderloin in half horizontally to form a total of 4 turkey steaks; set aside. In a small bowl, combine cumin, coriander seeds, lime peel, salt, ginger, and crushed red pepper. Set aside ¼ teaspoon of the cumin mixture. Sprinkle remaining cumin mixture over the turkey steaks; rub in with your fingers.

2. Place turkey steaks on the rack of an uncovered grill directly over medium heat. Grill for 12 to 15 minutes or until no longer pink (170°F), turning once halfway through grilling time.

3. Meanwhile, in a small bowl, combine sour cream, lime juice, and reserved cumin mixture. Serve sauce with grilled turkey steaks. Makes 4 servings.

To Broil: Coat the unheated rack of a broiler pan with cooking spray. Place turkey steaks on prepared rack; broil 4 to 5 inches from heat for 8 to 10 minutes or until no longer pink (170°F), turning once halfway through broiling time.

Turkey Tetrazzini

Evaporated fat-free milk gives this Alfredo-style dish just-like-cream flavor without the fat.

PER SERVING: 202 cal., 2 g total fat (1 g sat. fat), 24 mg chol., 253 mg sodium, 32 g carb., 2 g fiber, 17 g pro. Exchanges: 0.5 vegetable, 0.5 milk, 1.5 starch, 1 very lean meat. Carb choices: 2.

4 ounces dried whole wheat spaghetti
2 cups sliced fresh cremini, stemmed shiitake, or button mushrooms
¾ cup chopped red and/or green sweet pepper
½ cup cold water
3 tablespoons all-purpose flour
1 12-ounce can evaporated fat-free milk (1½ cups)
½ teaspoon instant chicken bouillon granules
⅛ teaspoon salt
⅛ teaspoon ground black pepper
Dash ground nutmeg
1 cup chopped cooked turkey breast or chicken breast (about 5 ounces)
¼ cup finely shredded Parmesan cheese (1 ounce)
2 tablespoons snipped fresh parsley
Nonstick cooking spray
Fresh parsley (optional)

1. Preheat oven to 400°F. Cook the spaghetti according to package directions, except omit the cooking oil and only lightly salt the water. Drain well.

2. Meanwhile, in a covered large saucepan, cook the mushrooms and sweet pepper in a small amount of boiling water for 3 to 6 minutes or until the vegetables are tender. Drain well; return to saucepan.

3. In a screw-top jar, combine the ½ cup cold water and flour; cover and shake until well-mixed. Stir flour mixture into the vegetable mixture in saucepan. Stir in evaporated milk, bouillon granules, salt, black pepper, and nutmeg. Cook and stir until thickened and bubbly. Stir in the cooked spaghetti, cooked turkey, Parmesan cheese, and the 2 tablespoons parsley.

4. Lightly coat a 2-quart square baking dish with cooking spray. Spoon spaghetti mixture into dish. Bake, covered, for 10 to 15 minutes or until heated through. If desired, garnish each serving with additional parsley. Makes 6 (about 1-cup) servings.

(turkey talk)

Turkey white meat is naturally low in fat. It has a slightly heartier taste than chicken and is versatile enough to be used as a substitute in place of higher-fat meats. Like all meats, turkey is a good source of iron, zinc, and vitamin B_{12}. If you only think of turkey at holidays, think again—whether you broil it, bake it, or grill it, turkey is a versatile meat for any time of year.

Turkey Tetrazzini

Sage and Cream Turkey Fettuccine

Fat-free sour cream adds richness
while keeping fat in check.

PER SERVING: 312 cal., 2 g total fat (0 g sat. fat), 60 mg chol., 478 mg sodium, 43 g carb., 2 g fiber, 30 g pro. Exchanges: 2.5 starch, 3 very lean meat, 1 vegetable. Carb choices: 3.

- **6 ounces dried spinach and/or plain fettuccine**
- **⅔ cup fat-free or light dairy sour cream**
- **4 teaspoons all-purpose flour**
- **½ cup reduced-sodium chicken broth**
- **2 teaspoons snipped fresh sage or 1 teaspoon dried sage, crushed**
- **¼ teaspoon ground black pepper**
- **Nonstick cooking spray**
- **12 ounces turkey breast tenderloin steak, cut into bite-size strips**
- **½ teaspoon salt**
- **2 cups sliced fresh mushrooms**
- **4 green onions, sliced**
- **2 cloves garlic, minced**
- **Fresh sage sprigs (optional)**

1. Cook fettuccine according to package directions; drain and set aside.

2. Meanwhile, in a small bowl, stir together sour cream and flour. Gradually stir in broth until smooth. Stir in snipped sage and pepper; set aside.

3. Coat an unheated 8-inch skillet with cooking spray. Preheat over medium-high heat. Sprinkle turkey with salt. Add turkey, mushrooms, green onions, and garlic to hot skillet. Cook and stir about 3 minutes or until turkey is no longer pink.

4. Stir sour cream mixture into turkey mixture. Cook and stir until thickened and bubbly. Cook and stir for 1 minute more.

5. Serve turkey over pasta. If desired, garnish with sage sprigs. Makes 4 servings.

Turkey Scaloppine with Peppers

A squeeze of lime adds refreshing flavor to this zesty dish.

PER SERVING: 146 cal., 2 g total fat (0 g sat. fat), 51 mg chol., 202 mg sodium, 10 g carb., 1 g fiber, 21 g pro. Exchanges: 0.5 carb., 3 very lean meat. Carb choices: 1.

- **1 12-ounce turkey breast tenderloin**
- **½ cup thinly sliced leek**
- **¼ cup thinly sliced red sweet pepper**
- **1 tablespoon thinly sliced fresh serrano or Anaheim chile pepper***
- **¼ teaspoon salt**
- **⅓ cup all-purpose flour**
- **Nonstick cooking spray**
- **Lime wedges**

1. Cut turkey tenderloin crosswise into 4 pieces; place each piece between two pieces of plastic wrap. Using the flat side of a meat mallet, lightly pound to ¼-inch thickness; remove top piece of plastic wrap. Sprinkle leek, sweet pepper, chile pepper, and salt on both sides of turkey; cover with plastic wrap. Lightly pound to ⅛-inch thickness; remove plastic wrap. Coat with flour, shaking off any excess.

2. Coat an unheated large nonstick skillet with cooking spray. Preheat skillet over medium-high heat. Cook turkey in hot skillet for 6 to 8 minutes or until no longer pink, turning once halfway through cooking time (reduce heat if necessary to prevent overbrowning). Serve with lime wedges. Makes 4 servings.

*Test Kitchen Tip: Because chile peppers contain volatile oils that can burn your skin and eyes, avoid direct contact with them as much as possible. When working with chile peppers, wear plastic or rubber gloves. If your hands do touch the peppers, wash your hands and nails well.

Basil-Buttered Salmon

Use the leftover basil-and-butter mixture
to season vegetables.

PER SERVING: 294 cal., 19 g total fat (5 g sat. fat), 94 mg chol., 113 mg sodium, 0 g carb., 0 g fiber, 28 g pro. Exchanges: 4 very lean meat, 1.5 fat. Carb choices: 0.

- **4** fresh or frozen skinless salmon, halibut, or sea bass fillets (about 1¼ pounds total)
- **½** teaspoon salt-free lemon-pepper seasoning
- **2** tablespoons butter, softened
- **1** teaspoon snipped fresh lemon basil, regular basil, or dill, or ¼ teaspoon dried basil or dill, crushed
- **1** teaspoon snipped fresh parsley or cilantro
- **¼** teaspoon finely shredded lemon peel or lime peel

1. Thaw fish, if frozen. Rinse fish; pat dry with paper towels. Sprinkle with lemon-pepper seasoning.

2. Place fish on the greased unheated rack of a broiler pan. Turn under any thin portions to make a uniform thickness. Broil 4 inches from heat for 5 minutes. Carefully turn fish. Broil for 3 to 7 minutes more or until fish flakes easily when tested with a fork.

3. Meanwhile, in a small bowl, stir together butter, basil, parsley, and lemon peel. To serve, spoon 1 teaspoon of the butter mixture on top of each fish piece. Cover and chill remaining mixture for another use. Makes 4 servings.

Grilling Directions: Place fish on the greased rack of an uncovered grill directly over medium heat. Grill for 8 to 12 minutes or until fish flakes easily when tested with a fork, carefully turning once halfway through grilling.

Basil-Buttered Salmon

Grilled Sea Bass with Tomatoes

Rub the fish with a garlic and ginger sesame oil mixture before grilling and smother it with a tomato-onion-hot pepper medley.

- **4** **6-ounce fresh or frozen sea bass or halibut fillets, ¾ to 1 inch thick**
- **4** **cloves garlic, minced**
- **1** **tablespoon grated fresh ginger**
- **2** **teaspoons toasted sesame oil**
- **¾** **teaspoon salt**
- **½** **teaspoon ground cardamom**
- **4** **teaspoons lemon juice**
- **1** **medium red onion, sliced ¼ inch thick**
- **1** **tablespoon olive oil**
- **2** **fresh jalapeño peppers,* seeded and finely chopped (about 3 tablespoons)**
- **3** **small yellow or red tomatoes, halved and cut into wedges**
- **1** **tablespoon snipped fresh oregano**
- **¾** **teaspoon snipped fresh thyme**
- **¼** **teaspoon black pepper**

1. Thaw fish, if frozen. Rinse fish; pat dry with paper towels. Set aside.

2. For paste, stir together half of the garlic, the ginger, sesame oil, ½ teaspoon of the salt, and the cardamom. With your fingers, rub both sides of fish evenly with mixture. Cover and chill for 15 minutes. Measure thickness of fish. Drizzle lemon juice over fish.

3. Grill fish on the greased rack of an uncovered grill directly over medium heat for 4 to 6 minutes per ½-inch thickness or until fish flakes easily when tested with a fork, turning once halfway through grilling time.

4. Meanwhile, in a large heavy skillet, cook onion slices in hot olive oil over medium-high heat until tender, stirring frequently. Add remaining garlic and the jalapeño peppers; continue cooking until onions are golden. Add tomatoes, oregano, thyme, black pepper, and remaining ¼ teaspoon salt. Stir gently until heated through.

5. To serve, place fish on a serving platter; top with the tomato-onion mixture. Makes 4 servings.

*Test Kitchen Tip: Because chile peppers contain volatile oils that can burn your skin and eyes, avoid direct contact with them as much as possible. When working with chile peppers, wear plastic or rubber gloves. If your hands do touch the peppers, wash your hands and nails well.

Grouper with Red Pepper Sauce

Serve fish on a bed of steamed mixed vegetables.

PER SERVING: 197 cal., 8 g total fat (1 g sat. fat), 42 mg chol., 245 mg sodium, 9 g carb., 2 g dietary fiber, 23 g pro. Exchanges: 1.5 vegetable, 3 very lean meat, 1 fat. Carb choices: 0.5.

- 4 4-ounce fresh or frozen skinless grouper fillets, ½ to 1 inch thick
- 1 cup chopped red sweet pepper
- 4 teaspoons butter
- 2 medium tomatoes, peeled, seeded, and chopped
- 1 teaspoon sugar
- 1 teaspoon red wine vinegar
- ¼ teaspoon salt
- ⅛ teaspoon garlic powder
-   Dash cayenne pepper
- 2 tablespoons lemon juice
- 4 teaspoons olive oil
- ¼ teaspoon dried rosemary, crushed

1. Thaw fish, if frozen; set aside. For sauce, in a small saucepan, cook sweet pepper in hot butter over medium heat until tender. Stir in tomatoes, sugar, vinegar, salt, garlic powder, and cayenne pepper. Cook for 5 minutes more, stirring occasionally. Remove from heat; cool slightly. Transfer mixture to a blender. Cover and blend until smooth. Return to saucepan.

2. Rinse fish; pat dry with paper towels. In a small bowl, combine lemon juice, oil, and rosemary. Brush both sides of fish with lemon mixture.

3. Place fish in a greased wire grill basket, tucking under any thin edges to make a uniform thickness. Place basket on the rack of an uncovered grill directly over medium heat. Grill until fish flakes easily when tested with a fork, turning basket once. (Allow 4 to 6 minutes per ½-inch thickness of fish.)

4. Meanwhile, heat sauce over low heat. Serve the sauce with fish. Makes 4 servings.

To Broil: Place fish on the greased unheated rack of a broiler pan, tucking under any thin edges. Broil about 4 inches from heat. (Allow 4 to 6 minutes per ½-inch thickness of fish.) If fish is 1 inch thick, turn once during broiling.

Curried Seafood with Linguine

Fusion is fun—the pasta may be Italian, but the flavors are Asian.

PER SERVING: 307 cal., 9 g total fat (1 g sat. fat), 42 mg chol., 270 mg sodium, 41 g carb., 3 g fiber, 17 g pro. Exchanges: 2 starch, 1 very lean meat, 1.5 fat, 2 vegetable. Carb choices: 3.

- 4 ounces fresh or frozen medium shrimp in shells
- 4 ounces fresh or frozen sea scallops
- 1½ to 2 teaspoons curry powder
- 6 ounces dried linguine or spaghetti
- ⅓ cup apricot nectar
- 1 tablespoon reduced-sodium soy sauce
- 1 teaspoon cornstarch
- ¼ teaspoon ground ginger
- 2 tablespoons cooking oil
- 1 cup sliced fresh mushrooms
- ½ cup thinly sliced carrot
- 3 cups chopped bok choy
- 2 green onions, bias-sliced into 1-inch pieces

1. Thaw shrimp and scallops, if frozen. Peel and devein shrimp, leaving tails intact if desired. Halve large scallops. Rinse shrimp and scallops; pat dry with paper towels. In a bowl, toss seafood with curry powder.

2. Cook pasta according to package directions; drain. Cover and keep warm.

3. Meanwhile, in a small bowl, stir together nectar, soy sauce, cornstarch, and ginger; set aside.

4. In a large skillet, heat 1 tablespoon of the oil over medium-high heat. Add mushrooms and carrot; cook and stir for 2 minutes. Add bok choy and green onions; cook and stir for 2 minutes. Remove from skillet.

5. Add remaining 1 tablespoon oil and seafood to skillet. Cook and stir for 2 to 3 minutes or until opaque; push from center. Stir apricot nectar mixture; add to center. Cook and stir until thickened and bubbly. Return vegetables to skillet; stir to coat. Cover and cook for 1 minute.

6. To serve, spoon seafood mixture over hot cooked pasta. Makes 4 servings.

Catfish with Black Bean and Avocado Relish

Parmesan Baked Fish

This five-ingredient dish is quick to fix and delicious to eat.

PER SERVING: 169 cal., 10 g total fat (2 g sat. fat), 23 mg chol., 247 mg sodium, 1 g carb., 0 g fiber, 18 g pro. Exchanges: 2.5 lean meat, 0.5 fat. Carb choices: 0.

  4 **4-ounce fresh or frozen skinless salmon or other firm fish fillets, about 1 inch thick**
  ¼ **cup light mayonnaise or salad dressing**
  2 **tablespoon grated Parmesan cheese**
  1 **tablespoon snipped fresh chives or sliced green onion**
  1 **teaspoon Worcestershire sauce**

1. Thaw fish, if frozen. Preheat oven to 450°F. Rinse fish; pat dry with paper towels. Set aside.

2. In small bowl, stir together mayonnaise, Parmesan cheese, chives, and Worcestershire sauce. Spread mayonnaise mixture over fish. Place in greased 2-quart square or rectangular baking dish.

3. Bake for 8 to 12 minutes or until fish flakes easily with a fork. Makes 4 servings.

Catfish with Black Bean and Avocado Relish

Another time, try the relish on halibut, orange roughy, or tuna.

PER SERVING: 273 cal., 15 g total fat (3 g sat. fat), 53 mg chol., 337 mg sodium, 14 g carb., 6 g fiber, 23 g pro. Exchanges: 0.5 starch, 3 very lean meat, 0.5 vegetable, 2.5 fat. Carb choices: 0.5.

  6 **4-ounce fresh or frozen catfish fillets, ½ inch thick**
  1 **teaspoon finely shredded lime peel**
  3 **tablespoons lime juice**
  2 **tablespoons snipped fresh cilantro**
  2 **tablespoons snipped fresh oregano**
  2 **tablespoons finely chopped green onion**
  1 **tablespoon olive oil**
  ¼ **teaspoon salt**
  ¼ **teaspoon cayenne pepper**
  1 **15-ounce can black beans, rinsed and drained**
  1 **medium avocado, halved, seeded, peeled, and diced**
  1 **medium tomato, chopped**
    Lime wedges

1. Thaw fish, if frozen. Rinse fish; pat dry with paper towels. Cover and chill until ready to use.

2. For relish, in a small bowl, combine lime peel, lime juice, cilantro, oregano, green onion, oil, salt, and cayenne pepper. In a medium bowl, stir together beans, avocado, and tomato; stir in half of the cilantro mixture. Cover and chill relish until serving time.

3. Grill fish on the greased rack of an uncovered grill directly over medium heat for 4 to 6 minutes or until fish flakes easily when tested with a fork, turning and brushing fish once with the remaining cilantro mixture halfway through grilling.

4. Discard remaining cilantro mixture. Serve fish with relish and lime wedges. Makes 6 servings.

Quick Tip

One of the most exciting nutritional facts about fish regards omega-3 fatty acids. Fatty fish from cold-water regions, such as salmon, tuna, mackerel, and sardines, contain this kind of fat. These healthful fats reduce the risk of heart disease.

(scallop tips)

There are two basic types of scallops: sea and bay. Bays are smaller and can be tastier, except they're more likely to become overcooked. When purchasing scallops, avoid those that smell fishy or sour, both signs that they aren't fresh. Be aware that a stark bleached-white color or excessive milky liquid in the display tray can be a sign the scallops have been treated heavily with sodium tripolyphosphate (STP). While STP is useful to help bind natural moisture to seafood during the freezing and thawing process, it can be overused and cause scallops to soak up additional water.

**Scallops with
Anise-Orange Tapenade**

Scallops with Anise-Orange Tapenade

The licoricelike flavor of anise and the hint of orange add a bright note to traditional olive relish.

PER SERVING: 145 cal., 3 g total fat (0 g sat. fat), 47 mg chol., 353 mg sodium, 5 g carb., 1 g fiber, 24 g pro. Exchanges: 3.5 very lean meat, 0.5 fat. Carb choices: 0.

- 12 fresh or frozen sea scallops (about 1¼ pounds total)
- ⅓ cup pitted kalamata olives, coarsely chopped
- 1 green onion, sliced
- ½ teaspoon finely shredded orange peel
- 2 teaspoons orange juice
- ¼ teaspoon anise seeds, crushed
- ⅛ teaspoon cayenne pepper
- Nonstick cooking spray
- Finely shredded orange peel (optional)

1. Thaw scallops, if frozen. Rinse scallops; pat dry with paper towels. Set aside.

2. For tapenade, in a small bowl, combine olives, green onion, the ½ teaspoon orange peel, orange juice, anise seeds, and cayenne pepper.

3. Coat an unheated large nonstick skillet with cooking spray. Preheat over medium-high heat. Add scallops; cook for 3 to 6 minutes or until scallops are opaque, turning once. Serve warm with tapenade. If desired, top with orange peel. Makes 4 servings.

Szechwan Shrimp

When you see the word "Szechwan,"
you can expect the dish to pack a little heat.

PER SERVING: 249 cal., 5 g total fat (1 g sat. fat), 129 mg chol., 372 mg sodium, 30 g carb., 0 g fiber, 19 g pro. Exchanges: 2 very lean meat, 2 starch, 0.5 fat. Carb choices: 2.

- 1 pound fresh or frozen medium shrimp in shells
- 3 tablespoons water
- 2 tablespoons ketchup
- 1 tablespoon reduced-sodium soy sauce
- 1 tablespoon rice wine, dry sherry, or water
- 2 teaspoons cornstarch
- 1 teaspoon honey
- 1 teaspoon grated fresh ginger or ¼ teaspoon ground ginger
- ½ teaspoon crushed red pepper
- ½ cup sliced green onions
- 4 cloves garlic, minced
- 1 tablespoon peanut oil or cooking oil
- 2 cups rice noodles or hot cooked rice
- 2 small fresh red chile peppers (such as Fresno or Thai),* sliced (optional)

1. Thaw shrimp, if frozen. Peel and devein shrimp. Rinse shrimp; pat dry with paper towels. Set aside.

2. For sauce, in a small bowl, stir together the 3 tablespoons water, ketchup, soy sauce, rice wine, cornstarch, honey, ground ginger (if using), and crushed red pepper. Set aside.

3. In a wok or large skillet, cook and stir green onions, garlic, and fresh ginger (if using) in hot peanut oil over medium-high heat for 30 seconds. Add shrimp. Cook and stir for 2 to 3 minutes or until shrimp are pink; push to side of wok.

4. Stir sauce; add to center of wok. Cook and stir until thickened and bubbly. Cook and stir for 2 minutes more. Serve with rice noodles or rice. If desired, garnish with chile peppers. Makes 4 servings.

*Test Kitchen Tip: Because chile peppers contain volatile oils that can burn your skin and eyes, avoid direct contact with them as much as possible. When working with chile peppers, wear plastic or rubber gloves. If your bare hands do touch the peppers, wash your hands and nails well.

Szechwan Shrimp

Creole-Style Shrimp and Grits

Creole cooking is a New Orleans specialty that reflects the influences of French, Spanish, and African cuisines.

PER SERVING: 241 cal., 6 g total fat (1 g sat. fat), 129 mg chol., 387 mg sodium, 25 g carb., 2 g fiber, 22 g pro. Exchanges: 1 starch, 2 very lean meat, 2 vegetable, 1 fat. Carb choices: 1.5.

- 1 pound fresh or frozen medium shrimp in shells
- ½ cup quick-cooking yellow grits
- 12 ounces fresh asparagus, trimmed and bias-sliced into 2-inch pieces
- 1 medium red sweet pepper, cut into ½-inch squares
- ½ cup chopped onion
- 2 cloves garlic, minced
- 1 tablespoon olive oil
- 2 tablespoons all-purpose flour
- 2 teaspoons salt-free Creole seasoning
- ¾ cup reduced-sodium chicken broth
- ¼ teaspoon salt
- ¼ teaspoon ground black pepper

1. Thaw shrimp, if frozen. Peel and devein shrimp, leaving tails intact if desired. Rinse shrimp; pat dry. Make grits according to package directions; keep grits warm.

2. Meanwhile, in a large skillet, cook asparagus, sweet pepper, onion, and garlic in hot oil until tender.

3. Stir flour and Creole seasoning into vegetable mixture; add broth all at once. Cook and stir until thickened and bubbly; reduce heat.

4. Stir in shrimp, salt, and black pepper. Cover and cook for 1 to 3 minutes or until shrimp are pink, stirring once. Serve warm over grits. Makes 4 servings.

Garden-Style Ravioli

Convenient purchased ravioli makes cooking dinner a breeze. Vary the vegetables to your own liking.

PER SERVING: 278 cal., 9 g total fat (3 g sat. fat), 26 mg chol., 379 mg sodium, 39 g carb., 2 g fiber, 13 g pro. Exchanges: 2 starch, 0.5 lean meat, 1.5 vegetable, 1 fat. Carb choices: 2.5

1 9-ounce package refrigerated light cheese ravioli
1 tablespoon olive oil
2 medium red and/or green sweet peppers, cut into chunks
1 medium carrot, cut into long, thin strips
1 small onion, chopped
2 cloves garlic, minced
1 medium tomato, chopped
¼ cup reduced-sodium chicken broth
1 tablespoon snipped fresh tarragon or 1 teaspoon dried tarragon, crushed, or 3 tablespoons snipped fresh basil or 2 teaspoons dried basil, crushed
Jalapeño pepper (optional)
Fresh tarragon or basil sprig (optional)

1. Cook ravioli according to package directions, except omit any oil or salt. Drain; return to hot pan.

2. Meanwhile, in a large nonstick skillet, heat oil over medium heat. Add sweet peppers, carrot, onion, and garlic; cook about 5 minutes or until tender. Stir in tomato, broth, and snipped tarragon. Cook and stir about 2 minutes or until heated through.

3. Add sweet pepper mixture to cooked ravioli in pan; toss gently to combine. If desired, garnish with a jalapeño pepper and a tarragon sprig. Makes 4 (1-cup) servings.

Garden-Style Ravioli

Quick Tip

Lentils, a member of the legume family, are a good source of vegetable protein. Cooked lentils have a beanlike texture and a mild, nutty flavor. For a break from meat, lentils provide a hearty meatless meal. Store lentils, tightly wrapped, in a cool, dry place for up to one year.

Summer Vegetable Pilaf

Summer Vegetable Pilaf

The essences of lemon and fresh basil heighten the flavors of garden-fresh summer vegetables in this lentil-and-rice pilaf.

PER SERVING: 275 cal., 6 g total fat (2 g sat. fat), 8 mg chol., 495 mg sodium, 44 g carb., 11 g fiber, 12 g pro. Exchanges: 1.5 vegetable, 2.5 starch, 1 fat. Carb choices: 3.

- 1 14½-ounce can vegetable broth
- 1 medium onion, chopped
- ½ cup dry lentils, drained and rinsed
- ½ cup uncooked long grain white rice
- ¼ cup water
- 1 teaspoon finely shredded lemon peel
- 1½ cups small fresh broccoli florets, sliced zucchini or yellow summer squash, and/or fresh snow or sugar snap pea pods
- 1 medium carrot, cut into thin strips
- ½ small eggplant, peeled and diced
- 2 cloves garlic, minced
- 2 teaspoons olive oil
- 3 plum tomatoes, chopped
- ¼ cup snipped fresh basil
- ¼ cup finely shredded **Asiago or Parmesan cheese (1 ounce)**

1. In a 3-quart saucepan, combine broth, onion, lentils, uncooked rice, the water, and lemon peel. Bring to boiling; reduce heat. Simmer, covered, for 20 minutes, adding broccoli and carrot during the last 3 to 5 minutes of cooking.

2. Meanwhile, in a 10-inch skillet, cook the eggplant and garlic in hot oil over medium heat until the eggplant is soft, about 5 minutes.

3. Remove lentil mixture from heat; let stand, covered, for 5 minutes. Carefully stir in the eggplant mixture, tomatoes, and basil. To serve, sprinkle with cheese. Makes 4 (1¼-cup) servings.

Mushroom and Asparagus Fettuccine

Rich in protein, earthy mushrooms substitute for meat in this colorful pasta dish.

PER SERVING: 319 cal., 8 g total fat (1 g sat. fat), 1 mg chol., 255 mg sodium, 54 g carb., 3 g fiber, 15 g pro. Exchanges: 3 starch, 1.5 vegetable, 1 fat. Carb choices: 3.5.

- 8 ounces dried whole wheat fettuccine or linguine
- 8 ounces fresh asparagus, trimmed and cut into 1½-inch pieces
-    Nonstick cooking spray
- 3 cups sliced fresh cremini, shiitake, or button mushrooms
- 1 medium leek, thinly sliced, or ½ cup chopped onion
- 3 cloves garlic, minced
- ⅓ cup vegetable broth
- ¼ cup evaporated fat-free milk
- 1 tablespoon finely shredded fresh basil or 1 teaspoon dried basil, crushed
- 1 tablespoon snipped fresh oregano or 1 teaspoon dried oregano, crushed
- ¼ teaspoon salt
- ⅛ teaspoon ground black pepper
- 3 plum tomatoes, chopped
- ¼ cup pine nuts, toasted
-    Finely shredded Parmesan cheese (optional)

1. Cook fettuccine or linguine according to package directions, adding asparagus for the last 1 to 2 minutes of the cooking time; drain. Return pasta mixture to saucepan; cover and keep warm.

2. Meanwhile, coat an unheated large nonstick skillet with cooking spray. Preheat over medium-high heat. Add mushrooms, leek, and garlic to hot skillet. Cover and cook for 4 to 5 minutes or until tender, stirring occasionally. Stir in vegetable broth, evaporated milk, dried basil (if using), dried oregano (if using), salt, and pepper. Bring to boiling. Boil gently, uncovered, for 4 to 5 minutes or until mixture is slightly thickened. Stir in tomatoes, fresh basil (if using), and fresh oregano (if using); heat through.

3. Spoon mushroom mixture over pasta mixture; gently toss to coat. Sprinkle with pine nuts and, if desired, Parmesan cheese. Serve immediately. Makes about 4 (1¼-cup) servings.

Pasta with Ricotta and Vegetables

Pasta with Ricotta and Vegetables

Serve this colorful pasta dish with a simple mixed-greens salad.

PER SERVING: 361 cal., 9 g total fat (2 g sat. fat), 17 mg chol., 408 mg sodium, 55 g carb., 7 g fiber, 16 g pro. Exchanges: 1.5 vegetable, 3 starch, 1 lean meat, 0.5 fat. Carb choices: 4.

- 8 ounces dried cut ziti or penne pasta
- 2½ cups broccoli florets
- 1½ cups 1-inch pieces fresh asparagus
- 1 cup ricotta cheese
- ¼ cup shredded fresh basil
- 1 tablespoon snipped fresh thyme
- 1 tablespoon balsamic vinegar
- 1 tablespoon olive oil
- 1 clove garlic, minced
- ½ teaspoon salt
- ½ teaspoon ground black pepper
- 1⅓ cups chopped, seeded red and/or yellow tomatoes
  Shaved Parmesan or Romano cheese (optional)
  Fresh thyme sprigs (optional)

1. Cook pasta according to package directions, adding broccoli and asparagus for the last 3 minutes of cooking time. Drain well. Return pasta mixture to hot pan; cover and keep warm.

2. Meanwhile, in a large bowl, combine ricotta cheese, basil, snipped thyme, balsamic vinegar, oil, garlic, salt, and pepper. Gently stir in tomatoes.

3. Add drained pasta mixture to tomato mixture; toss gently to combine. Top with Parmesan cheese. If desired, garnish with thyme sprigs. Makes 4 (2-cup) servings.

Crispy Tofu and Vegetables

The contrast of the crispy, crunchy coating and
silken interior of these tofu cutlets
may convert the most avowed meat lover.

PER SERVING: 198 cal., 10 g total fat (1 g sat. fat), 0 mg chol., 410 mg
sodium, 14 g carb., 3 g fiber, 16 g pro. Exchanges: 1.5 vegetable,
0.5 starch, 1 lean meat, 1 fat. Carb choices: 1.

1 **10.5-ounce package light extra-firm tofu
   (fresh bean curd), drained**
3 **tablespoons reduced-sodium soy sauce**
8 **green onions**
2 **cups snow pea pods, strings and tips removed**
1 **tablespoon toasted sesame oil**
1 **teaspoon grated fresh ginger or ½ teaspoon ground
   ginger**
1 **clove garlic, minced**
1 **red sweet pepper, seeded and cut into long,
   thin strips**
1 **yellow sweet pepper, seeded and cut into long,
   thin strips**
3 **tablespoons cornmeal**
1 **tablespoon white or black sesame seeds, toasted
   (optional)**

1. Cut tofu crosswise into 8 slices. Arrange slices in
one layer on a large plate or jelly-roll pan. Pour soy sauce
over tofu; turn slices to coat and let stand for 1 hour.

2. Meanwhile, cut root ends off green onions. Cut off
dark green portion of onions, leaving 3 inches of white
and light green. Cut green onions in half lengthwise,
forming 16 long strips. Set aside. Cut pea pods in half
lengthwise. Set aside.

3. Pour oil into a large nonstick skillet. Preheat over
medium-high heat. Stir-fry fresh ginger (if using) and
garlic for 30 seconds. Add sweet pepper strips and stir-
fry for 1 minute. Add green onions and pea pods; stir-fry
for 2 to 3 minutes more or until crisp-tender.

4. Drain tofu, reserving soy sauce. Stir reserved soy
sauce and, if using, ground ginger into cooked vegetables;
transfer vegetable mixture to a serving platter. Cover and
keep warm. Carefully dip tofu slices in cornmeal to lightly
coat both sides. Cook in same skillet for 3 minutes on each
side or until crisp and hot, using a spatula to turn carefully.
(You may need to cook tofu slices in two batches; do not
crowd skillet.) Serve tofu slices with vegetables. If desired,
sprinkle with sesame seeds. Makes 4 servings (2 slices
tofu plus 1 cup vegetables each).

Ratatouille over Polenta

Purchased polenta complements this entrée.
Look for it in the produce section of your supermarket
or with the refrigerated tortillas.

PER SERVING: 260 cal., 8 g total fat (1 g sat. fat), 9 mg chol., 576 mg sodium,
38 g carb., 5 g fiber, 10 g pro. Exchanges: 1 vegetable, 2 starch, 1 fat.
Carb choices: 2.5.

1 **16-ounce tube refrigerated cooked polenta**
1 **small green sweet pepper, seeded and cut into
   thin strips**
1 **small onion, thinly sliced**
1 **clove garlic, minced**
1 **tablespoon cooking oil**
½ **small eggplant, cut into ½-inch pieces**
1 **large yellow summer squash or zucchini, sliced**
1 **large tomato, cut into wedges**
1 **cup small pattypan squash, quartered**
1 **tablespoon snipped fresh basil**
3 **tablespoons snipped fresh parsley**
   Shredded Parmesan cheese (optional)

1. Cut polenta into 8 to 12 slices and heat according to
package directions. Cover and keep warm.

2. For ratatouille, in a 4-quart saucepan, cook the
sweet pepper, onion, and garlic in hot oil over medium
heat for 5 minutes, stirring frequently. Add the eggplant;
cook for 5 minutes more, stirring frequently. Stir in
summer squash, tomato, pattypan squash, basil,
⅛ teaspoon *salt,* and ⅛ teaspoon ground *black pepper*.
Cook, covered, for 5 to 7 minutes more or until vegetables
are tender, stirring occasionally. Stir in parsley.

3. To serve, place 2 slices of polenta each on four to
six dinner plates. Spoon warm ratatouille over each
serving. If desired, sprinkle with Parmesan cheese.
Makes 4 to 6 servings.

Crispy Tofu
and Vegetables

company-
worthy meals

Pork Medallions with Pear Sauce

For your family feast, choose your bird by the number at your table—roast turkey for a big group or Cornish game hen for a smaller gathering. If pork is your pick, we have that, too. If fish is more your kind of dish, try one of our salmon recipes for your next special dinner.

Pork Medallions with Pear Sauce

A fragrant sauce featuring pears, dried cherries, maple syrup, and white wine sweetens tender pork medallions scented with rosemary and thyme.

PER SERVING: 255 cal., 7 g total fat (2 g sat. fat), 60 mg chol., 179 mg sodium, 29 g carb., 3 g fiber, 19 g pro. Exchanges: 1 fruit, 1.5 lean meat. Carb choices: 2.

- 1 12- to 16-ounce pork tenderloin
- 2 teaspoons snipped fresh rosemary or ½ teaspoon dried rosemary, crushed
- 1 teaspoon snipped fresh thyme or ¼ teaspoon dried thyme, crushed
- ¼ teaspoon salt
- ¼ teaspoon black pepper
- 1 tablespoon olive oil or cooking oil
- 2 medium pears, peeled and coarsely chopped
- ¼ cup pure maple syrup or maple-flavored syrup
- 2 tablespoons dried tart red cherries, halved
- 2 tablespoons dry white wine or apple juice

1. Trim fat from meat. Cut meat into ¼-inch slices. In a medium bowl, combine rosemary, thyme, salt, and pepper. Add meat slices; toss to coat.

2. In a large skillet, cook meat slices, half at a time, in hot oil for 2 to 3 minutes or until meat is slightly pink in the center, turning once. Remove meat from skillet; set aside.

3. In the same skillet, combine pears, maple syrup, dried cherries, and white wine. Bring to boiling; reduce heat. Boil gently, uncovered, about 3 minutes or just until pears are tender.

4. Return meat to skillet with pears; heat through. To serve, use a slotted spoon to transfer meat to a warm serving platter. Spoon the pear mixture over meat. Makes 4 servings.

Mustard-Maple Pork Roast

Maple syrup, orange peel, and mustard add captivating flavor to the glaze for this succulent and impressive roast.

PER SERVING: 284 cal., 9 g total fat (3 g sat. fat), 62 mg chol., 303 mg sodium, 22 g carb., 3 g fiber, 28 g pro. Exchanges: ½ vegetable, 1½ starch, 3 lean meat. Carb choices: 1.5.

- 1   2- to 2½- pound boneless pork top loin roast (single loin)
- 2   tablespoons Dijon-style mustard
- 1   tablespoon sugar-free maple-flavored syrup
- 2   teaspoons dried sage, crushed
- 1   teaspoon finely shredded orange peel
- ¼   teaspoon ground black pepper
- ⅛   teaspoon salt
- 20   to 24 tiny new potatoes, 1½ to 2 inches in diameter (about 1¾ pounds)*
- 1   1-pound package peeled fresh baby carrots
- 1   tablespoon olive oil
- ¼   teaspoon salt

1. Preheat oven to 325°F. Trim fat from roast. Place roast, fat side up, on a rack in a shallow roasting pan. In a small bowl, stir together mustard, syrup, sage, orange peel, pepper, and the ⅛ teaspoon salt. Spoon mixture onto roast, spreading evenly over the top. Insert an oven-going meat thermometer into center of roast. Roast for 30 minutes.

2. Meanwhile, peel a strip of skin from the center of each potato. In a 4-quart Dutch oven, cook potatoes, covered, in enough lightly salted boiling water to cover

for 5 minutes. Add carrots; cook for 5 minutes more. Drain. Return to saucepan. Add olive oil and the ¼ teaspoon salt; toss gently to coat.

3. Place potato mixture in roasting pan around roast. Roast for 45 minutes to 1 hour more or until meat thermometer registers 155°F. Remove roast from oven; cover tightly with foil. Let stand for 15 minutes before slicing. (The temperature of the meat after standing should be 160°F.) Makes 8 servings.

*Test Kitchen Tip: If your potatoes are larger, use fewer potatoes to make 1¾ pounds. Cut large potatoes in half.

Chili-Glazed Pork Roast

For presentation and to control portions, plate the roast and vegetables in the kitchen.

PER SERVING: 134 cal., 4 g total fat (2 g sat. fat), 50 mg chol., 37 mg sodium, 2 g carb., 0 g fiber, 20 g pro. Exchanges: 3 very lean meat, 0.5 fat. Carb choices: 0.

- 1   tablespoon packed brown sugar
- 1   tablespoon snipped fresh thyme or 1 teaspoon dried thyme, crushed
- 1   teaspoon chili powder
- 1   teaspoon snipped fresh rosemary or ¼ teaspoon dried rosemary, crushed
- ⅛   teaspoon cayenne pepper
- 1   2- to 2½-pound boneless pork top loin roast (single loin)
-   Fresh rosemary sprigs (optional)

1. Preheat oven to 325°F. In a small bowl, combine brown sugar, thyme, chili powder, snipped fresh rosemary, and cayenne pepper. Sprinkle sugar mixture evenly onto roast; rub in with your fingers.

2. Place pork roast on a rack in a shallow roasting pan. Insert an oven-going meat thermometer into center. Roast for 1¼ to 1½ hours or until thermometer reads 155°F.

3. Cover roast with foil; let stand for 15 minutes. (The temperature of the meat after standing should be 160°F.) Slice before serving. If desired, garnish with rosemary sprigs. Makes 8 to 10 servings.

Make-Ahead Directions: Prepare roast as directed through Step 1. Cover and chill for up to 24 hours. Preheat oven to 325°F. Continue as directed in Step 2.

Mustard-Maple Pork Roast

Pork Spirals with Red Pepper Sauce

Pork Spirals with Red Pepper Sauce

These pork spirals will garner requests for seconds from guests. The red pepper sauce is versatile enough for chicken, beef, or fish.

PER SERVING: 176 cal., 7 g total fat (2 g sat. fat), 62 mg chol., 146 mg sodium, 6 g carb., 1 g fiber, 22 g pro. Exchanges: 0.5 Starch, 2.5 lean meat, 1 fat. Carb choices: 0.5.

1 **12-ounce pork tenderloin**
1 **cup loosely packed fresh spinach leaves, stems removed**
⅓ **cup finely chopped fresh mushrooms**
¼ **cup snipped fresh basil**
2 **tablespoons fine dry bread crumbs**
1 **tablespoon finely shredded Parmesan cheese**
1 **slightly beaten egg white**
1 **tablespoon olive oil**
   Black pepper
½ **of a 7-ounce jar roasted red sweet peppers, drained**
1 **teaspoon red or white wine vinegar**
1 **clove garlic**
   Dash salt

1. Trim fat from meat. Using a sharp knife, make a lengthwise cut along the center of the tenderloin, cutting to, but not through, the opposite side. Spread meat open. Place meat between two pieces of plastic wrap. Working from center to the edges, use flat side of a meat mallet to pound meat into an 11×7-inch rectangle. Remove plastic. Fold in the narrow ends as necessary to make an even rectangle.

2. Stack spinach leaves on top of each other; slice crosswise into thin strips. In a medium bowl, stir together spinach, mushrooms, basil, bread crumbs, Parmesan cheese, and egg white. Spread evenly over pork. Starting at one of the short sides, roll up. Tie with 100-percent-cotton string at 1½-inch intervals. Brush surface of meat with 1 teaspoon of the olive oil; sprinkle with pepper.

3. Arrange medium-hot coals around a drip pan. Test for medium heat above pan. Place meat on grill rack over pan. Cover; grill for 25 to 30 minutes or until a meat thermometer inserted in the center registers 155°F. Remove from grill. Cover with foil; let stand for 10 minutes. (The temperature of the meat after standing should be 160°F.)

4. Meanwhile, for sauce, in a food processor combine roasted peppers, remaining 2 teaspoons olive oil, wine vinegar, garlic, and salt. Cover and process until smooth. Transfer sauce to a small saucepan; cook over medium heat until heated through. To serve, remove strings from pork. Slice pork; serve with sauce. Makes 4 servings.

Pork Diane

Worcestershire sauce, Dijon mustard, and a double dose of lemon—lemon juice and lemon-pepper seasoning—add zest to this pork loin, perfect for a small gathering.

PER SERVING: 131 cal., 5 g total fat (2 g sat. fat), 55 mg chol., 377 mg sodium, 1 g carb., 0 g fiber, 19 g pro. Exchanges: 3 very lean meat, ½ fat. Carb choices: 0.

- **1 tablespoon Worcestershire sauce**
- **1 teaspoon lemon juice**
- **1 teaspoon Dijon-style mustard**
- **4 3-ounce boneless pork top loin chops, cut ¾ to 1 inch thick**
- **½ to 1 teaspoon lemon-pepper seasoning**
- **1 tablespoon butter or margarine**
- **1 tablespoon snipped fresh chives, parsley, or oregano**

1. For sauce, in a small bowl, stir together 1 tablespoon *water*, Worcestershire sauce, lemon juice, and mustard; set aside.

2. Trim fat from chops. Sprinkle both sides of each chop with lemon-pepper seasoning. In a 10-inch skillet melt butter over medium heat. Add chops and cook for 8 to 12 minutes or until pork juices run clear (160°F), turning once halfway through cooking time. Remove from heat. Transfer pork chops to a platter; cover and keep warm.

3. Pour sauce into skillet; stir to scrape up any crusty browned bits from bottom of skillet. Serve sauce over chops. Sprinkle with chives. Makes 4 servings.

Pork Diane

Menu

Pork Diane *(opposite)*

Roasted Vegetable
Couscous *(page 228)*

Light and Luscious
Pumpkin Pie
(page 323)

Roast Pork Loin Stuffed with Andouille and Crawfish

Andouille is a smoked pork sausage used in Cajun cooking.

PER SERVING: 305 cal., 11 g total fat (4 g sat. fat), 84 mg chol., 388 mg sodium, 9 g carb., 2 g fiber, 34 g pro. Exchanges: 0.5 starch, 4.5 meat. Carb choices: 0.5.

- 4 **ounces (cooked) andouille or smoked turkey sausage, chopped**
- 1 **tablespoon olive oil**
- 4 **ounces fresh or frozen peeled crawfish tails, thawed**
- 1 **small onion, thinly sliced**
- 1 **stalk celery, thinly sliced**
- 3 **cups dried cubed whole wheat bread (about 5 slices)**
- ¼ **to ½ cup water**
- 1 **3½- to 4-pound boneless pork top loin roast (single loin)**
- ¼ **teaspoon ground black pepper**
- 2 **small white and/or red onions, cut into wedges**
- 2 **medium carrots, sliced**
- 2 **stalks celery, sliced ½ inch thick**
- ½ **cup bourbon or reduced-sodium beef broth**
- 2 **tablespoons tomato paste**
- 4 **cloves garlic, minced**
- 2 **cups reduced-sodium chicken broth**
- 5 **sprigs fresh thyme**
- ½ **sprig fresh rosemary**

1. For stuffing, in a saucepan, cook sausage in hot oil for 2 minutes. Add crawfish, sliced onion, and celery; cook until tender. Add bread. Stir in water to moisten.

2. Preheat oven to 325°F. Trim fat from pork. Butterfly meat by making a lengthwise cut down the center to within ½ inch of other side; spread open. Starting in "V" of first cut, cut horizontally from center to ½ inch of other side. Repeat on opposite side; spread open. Cover with plastic wrap; pound pork until ½ inch thick (about a 15×9-inch rectangle).

3. Spread stuffing evenly onto pork, leaving 1 inch on each long side. Starting from a long side, roll into a spiral. Using 100-percent-cotton string, tie loin at even intervals until evenly shaped and tied. Sprinkle with pepper.

4. In a large roasting pan, combine onion wedges, carrots, and ½-inch celery slices; place a rack over the vegetables. Place roast on top of rack (tuck vegetables under the roast). Insert an oven-going meat thermometer into center of roast. Roast for 2 to 2½ hours or until thermometer registers 155°F.

5. Remove roast and vegetables from pan, reserving drippings. Cover; let stand for 10 to 15 minutes. (The temperature of roast after standing should be 160°F.)

6. Meanwhile, for sauce, stir bourbon into reserved drippings in pan, scraping to loosen browned bits. Transfer to a saucepan. Stir in tomato paste and garlic. Bring to boiling; reduce heat. Simmer, uncovered, for 3 to 4 minutes or until thickened, stirring constantly. Stir in broth, thyme, and rosemary. Bring to boiling; reduce heat. Simmer, uncovered, for 10 minutes. Discard thyme and rosemary. Cool slightly. Pour into a food processor; cover and process until nearly smooth.

7. To serve, cut meat into ½- to ¾-inch slices. Serve meat and vegetables with sauce. Makes 12 servings.

Roast Rack of Lamb

Roast Rack of Lamb

Dried lavender, rosemary, garlic, dried cranberries, and bread crumbs coat this celebratory lamb roast. Look for dried lavender at health food stores or online.

PER SERVING: 212 cal., 11 g total fat (3 g sat. fat), 36 mg chol., 255 mg sodium, 9 g carb., 1 g fiber, 11 g pro. Exchanges: 0.5 starch, 1.5 lean meat, 1 fat. Carb choices: 0.5.

- 2 **1-pound French-style lamb rib roasts (each rack about 8×4 ×1½-inches, 8 ribs)**
- 1 **cup Merlot or other dry red wine**
- 2 **cloves garlic, minced**
- 1 **teaspoon freshly grated nutmeg or ½ teaspoon ground nutmeg**
- 3 **tablespoons olive oil**
- 1 **tablespoon butter**
- 1 **tablespoon snipped fresh rosemary**
- 2 **cups soft whole wheat bread crumbs**
- 3 **tablespoon dried cranberries**
- 1 **tablespoon dried lavender (optional)**
- ½ **teaspoon salt**
- ½ **teaspoon ground black pepper**

1. Peel off the lamb's layer of fell (membrane) and fat, if present, down to silver skin. Place roast in a large resealable plastic bag in a shallow dish. Add wine, 1 clove garlic, and nutmeg. Seal bag. Marinate in refrigerator for 4 to 24 hours, turning bag occasionally.

2. In a medium skillet, heat 1 tablespoon of the oil and 1 tablespoon butter over medium heat. Add rosemary and remaining garlic; cook for 1 minute. Add crumbs; cook and stir 3 minutes. Remove from heat. Add cranberries, lavender (if desired), salt, and pepper. Stir in remaining oil.

3. Preheat oven to 450°F. Remove lamb from marinade, reserving marinade. Place lamb, bone side down, in a shallow roasting pan lined with foil. Pat crumb mixture evenly onto lamb. Pour reserved marinade into pan.

4. Roast, uncovered, for 25 to 30 minutes or until meat thermometer registers 140°F (medium rare) or 155°F (medium). To prevent overbrowning, cover loosely with foil for last 5 minutes of roasting. (If roast is thicker than above dimensions, increase roasting time by 10 to 15 minutes and cover sooner.) Let stand for 15 minutes. Makes 8 servings.

(love that lamb)

When buying lamb, use the color as the guide. The darker the color, the older the animal. The cuts most often found at the supermarket include leg of lamb, rack of lamb, chops, and loin. These cuts can be cooked by roasting, broiling, sautéing, or grilling. It's best to serve these cuts rare or medium rare. Chops from the shoulder are best cooked by braising to tenderize them. Less tender cuts of lamb, such as those from the shoulder, breast, or shank, are also best if marinated before cooking.

Roasted Leg of Lamb with Red Wine-Shallot Sauce

Add mixed vegetables to the pan the last hour of roasting.

PER SERVING: 232 cal., 7 g total fat (3 g sat. fat), 86 mg chol., 313 mg sodium, 8 g carb., 0 g fiber, 26 g pro. Exchanges: 0.5 starch, 3 lean meat. Carb choices. 0.5.

Roasted Leg of Lamb with Red Wine-Shallot Sauce

- 1 4-pound leg of lamb
- 1 teaspoon lemon-pepper seasoning
- 1 sprig fresh rosemary
- 6 cloves garlic, quartered lengthwise
- ½ cup thinly sliced shallots
- 2 tablespoons butter
- ¼ cup seedless red raspberry preserves
- 1½ cups dry red wine
- ½ teaspoon finely shredded lemon peel
- ½ teaspoon salt
- ⅛ teaspoon ground black pepper

1. Preheat oven to 325°F. Trim fat from meat. Using a small knife, cut ½-inch-wide pockets about 1 inch deep in the meat at 1-inch intervals. Place meat, fat side up, on a rack in a shallow roasting pan. Season with lemon-pepper seasoning. Pull small bunches of leaves from the rosemary sprig. Push slivers of garlic and rosemary leaves into the pockets in the meat. Insert a meat thermometer in thickest portion of meat.

2. Roast lamb, uncovered, for 2 to 2¼ hours or until meat thermometer registers 140°F for medium-rare doneness or 155°F for medium doneness. Cover and let stand 15 minutes before carving. (The meat's temperature will rise 5° during standing time.)

3. Meanwhile, for sauce, in a saucepan, cook shallots in 1 tablespoon of the butter over medium heat until tender. Stir in preserves until melted. Stir in wine. Bring to boiling. Boil gently, uncovered, for 15 minutes or until reduced to 1⅓ cups. Whisk in remaining 1 tablespoon butter. Remove from heat. Stir in lemon peel, salt, and pepper. Serve warm with lamb. Makes 10 to 12 servings.

Garlic Chicken with Sweet Potatoes

Garlic Chicken with Sweet Potatoes

Whole garlic cloves become mellow
and buttery soft when roasted.

PER SERVING: 393 cal., 12 g total fat (2 g sat. fat), 119 mg chol., 481 mg sodium, 30 g carb., 4 g fiber, 40 g pro. Exchanges: 2 starch, 4.5 lean meat. Carb choices: 2.

- **3 heads garlic**
- **2 tablespoons olive oil**
- **1½ tablespoons snipped fresh rosemary**
- **1 teaspoon ground black pepper**
- **½ teaspoon salt**
- **1 3- to 3½-pound whole roasting chicken**
- **3 medium sweet potatoes (1½ to 1¾ pounds), peeled and cut into 1-inch pieces**
- **1 large sweet onion (such as Vidalia, Maui, or Walla Walla), cut into wedges**

1. Preheat oven to 375° F. Separate the cloves of garlic (you should have about 30 cloves) and peel. Mince 4 cloves. Set aside remaining garlic cloves.

2. In a small bowl, combine minced garlic with 1 tablespoon of the olive oil, 1 tablespoon of the rosemary, the pepper, and ¼ teaspoon of the salt. Rub minced garlic mixture onto chicken.

3. Place 6 garlic cloves into the cavity of the chicken. Tie legs to tail. Twist wing tips under back. Place on a rack in a shallow roasting pan. Insert oven-going meat thermometer into center of an inside thigh muscle. Do not allow thermometer tip to touch bone. Roast, uncovered, for 1½ to 1¾ hours or until drumsticks move easily in their sockets and meat thermometer registers 180°F.

4. Meanwhile, place sweet potatoes, onion wedges, remaining garlic cloves, ½ tablespoon of the rosemary, and ¼ teaspoon of the salt in a 13×9×2-inch baking pan. Drizzle vegetable mixture with remaining 1 tablespoon olive oil; toss to coat. Place in oven on a separate rack and roast, uncovered, for 50 to 60 minutes or until tender, stirring every 15 minutes.

5. Remove chicken from oven. Cover loosely with foil and let stand 15 minutes before carving. Serve chicken with vegetables. Carve chicken, discarding skin before serving. Makes 4 to 6 servings.

Tomato Pesto Chicken Rolls

You can make these rolls up to 24 hours ahead.
Prepare as directed through Step 3; cover and chill.

PER SERVING: 254 cal., 8 g total fat (2 g sat. fat), 79 mg chol., 326 mg sodium, 8 g carb., 1 g fiber, 36 g pro. Exchanges: 1 vegetable, 5 very lean meat, 1 fat. Carb choices: 0.5.

- **Nonstick cooking spray**
- **6 skinless, boneless chicken breast halves (about 1½ pounds total)**
- **⅛ teaspoon ground black pepper**
- **½ of an 8-ounce tub fat-free cream cheese**
- **2 tablespoons purchased dried tomato pesto**
- **2 tablespoons olive oil**
- **⅓ cup seasoned fine dry bread crumbs**
- **1 pound fresh asparagus spears**

1. Preheat oven to 400°F. Lightly coat a 9×9×2-inch baking pan and a shallow roasting pan with nonstick cooking spray; set aside.

2. Place each chicken breast half between 2 pieces of plastic wrap. Using the flat side of a meat mallet, pound each breast half until ¼ inch thick. Remove and discard the plastic wrap. Sprinkle chicken with pepper.

3. For filling, in a small bowl, stir together cream cheese and tomato pesto. Place 2 tablespoons of the filling in the center of each breast. Fold in sides and roll up. Secure rolls with wooden toothpicks. Brush chicken pieces, using 1 tablespoon of the oil; roll in crumbs.

4. Place chicken rolls, seam sides down, in the prepared baking pan. Bake, uncovered, for 10 minutes.

5. Meanwhile, snap off and discard woody bases from asparagus. If desired, scrape off scales. Toss asparagus with remaining 1 tablespoon oil; arrange in prepared roasting pan. Place in oven alongside chicken.

6. Bake, uncovered, for 15 to 20 minutes more or until asparagus is crisp-tender and the chicken is no longer pink (170°F). Makes 6 servings.

Roast Tarragon Chicken

Start out roasting just the chicken, then add the shallots to the pan and roast a little longer. Finally, add the tomatoes and roast until the chicken tests done with an instant-read thermometer.

PER SERVING: 209 cal., 8 g total fat (2 g sat. fat), 86 mg chol., 198 mg sodium, 6 g carb., 1 g fiber, 28 g pro. Exchanges: 3.5 very lean meat, 1 vegetable, 1 fat. Carb choices: 0.5.

  2   tablespoons olive oil
2½   teaspoons dried tarragon, crushed
  2   cloves garlic, minced
  ½   teaspoon ground black pepper
  ¼   teaspoon salt
  1   pound cherry tomatoes
  8   small shallots
2½ to 3 pounds meaty chicken pieces (breasts, thighs, and drumsticks)

1. Preheat oven to 375°F. In a medium bowl, stir together olive oil, tarragon, garlic, pepper, and salt. Add tomatoes and shallots; toss gently to coat. Use a slotted spoon to remove tomatoes and shallots from bowl, reserving the olive oil mixture. Set vegetables aside.

2. Remove skin from chicken. Place chicken in a shallow roasting pan. Brush chicken with the reserved olive oil mixture.

3. Roast chicken for 20 minutes. Add shallots; roast for 15 minutes. Add tomatoes; roast for 10 to 12 minutes more or until chicken is no longer pink (170°F for breasts; 180°F for thighs and drumsticks) and vegetables are tender. Makes 6 servings.

Roast Tarragon Chicken

Menu

Lemon Chicken *(below)*

Spanish Rice with Pigeon Peas *(page 232)*

Green beans with almonds

Cranberry-Walnut Whole Wheat Rolls *(page 286)*

Lemon Chicken

The bread-crumb coating thickens the sauce.

PER SERVING: 254 cal., 8 g total fat (2 g sat. fat), 66 mg chol., 639 mg sodium, 15 g carb., 1 g fiber, 29 g pro. Exchanges: 1 starch, 3.5 very lean meat, 1.5 fat. Carb choice: 1.

  4   skinless, boneless chicken breast halves (1 to 1¼ pounds)
  ¼   cup fat-free milk
  ⅔   cup fine dry bread crumbs
  1   teaspoon adobo seasoning
  2   tablespoons margarine or cooking oil
1¾   cups water
  1   clove garlic, minced
  1   lemon, halved crosswise
  1   tablespoon snipped fresh parsley
      Shredded lemon peel (optional)

1. Split chicken halves in half horizontally. Place milk in a shallow bowl. In a shallow dish, combine crumbs and adobo seasoning. Dip chicken into milk, then into crumb mixture, turning to coat evenly.

2. In a large nonstick skillet, cook chicken in hot margarine over medium heat about 5 minutes or until brown, turning occasionally.

3. Add the water and garlic. Squeeze juice from one lemon half onto chicken. Bring to boiling; reduce heat. Simmer, uncovered, about 15 minutes or until thickened, stirring often. Slice remaining lemon half.

4. To serve, top with parsley and, if desired, lemon peel. Serve with lemon slices. Makes 4 servings.

Lemon Chicken
and Spanish Rice
with Pigeon Peas

**Cilantro Chicken
with Peanuts**

Cilantro Chicken with Peanuts

If you choose to serve this dish over rice instead of
cabbage, add 1½ starch exchanges per serving.

PER SERVING: 231 cal., 10 g total fat (2 g sat. fat), 66 mg chol., 347 mg
sodium, 6 g carb., 4 g fiber, 30 g prot. Exchanges: 4 very lean meat,
1 vegetable, 1.5 fat. Carb choices: 0.5.

- **8 ounces skinless, boneless chicken breast halves, cut
  into 1-inch strips**
- **1 teaspoon cooking oil**
- **2 teaspoon reduced-sodium soy sauce**
- **1 teaspoon rice vinegar**
- **½ teaspoon toasted sesame oil**
- **¼ teaspoon crushed dried red chile pepper**
- **¾ cup fresh cilantro leaves**
- **2 cups finely shredded Chinese cabbage**
- **2 tablespoons dry-roasted peanuts, coarsely chopped**

1. In medium nonstick skillet, cook and stir chicken
in hot cooking oil over medium-high heat for 3 to
4 minutes or until chicken is tender and no longer pink.

2. Add soy sauce, vinegar, sesame oil, and crushed red
pepper. Cook and stir for 1 minute more. Remove from
heat. Stir in the cilantro.

3. To serve, spoon chicken mixture over cabbage and
sprinkle with peanuts. Makes 2 servings.

Moroccan Chicken

Serve this cumin-scented chicken on a bed
of couscous and chopped zucchini and carrot.

PER SERVING: 251 cal., 9 g total fat (2 g sat. fat), 92 mg chol., 121 mg
sodium, 11 g carb., 0 g fiber, 30 g pro. Exchanges: 4 very lean meat,
1 carb., 1 fat. Carb choices: 1.

- 2 pounds meaty chicken pieces (breast halves, thighs, and drumsticks), skinned
- 2 teaspoons finely shredded orange peel (set aside)
- ½ cup orange juice
- 1 tablespoon olive oil
- 1 tablespoon grated fresh ginger
- 1 teaspoon paprika
- 1 teaspoon ground cumin
- ½ teaspoon ground coriander
- ¼ teaspoon crushed red pepper
- ⅛ teaspoon salt
- 2 tablespoons honey
- 2 teaspoons orange juice

1. Place the chicken pieces in a large resealable plastic bag set in a deep bowl. Set aside.

2. For marinade, in a small bowl, stir together the ½ cup orange juice, the olive oil, ginger, paprika, cumin, coriander, red pepper, and salt; pour over chicken. Seal bag; turn bag to coat chicken. Marinate in the refrigerator for 4 to 24 hours, turning bag occasionally.

3. Meanwhile, for glaze, in a small bowl, stir together orange peel, honey, and the 2 teaspoons orange juice.

4. Drain chicken, discarding the marinade. Preheat oven to 375°F. In a shallow baking dish, arrange the chicken, meaty sides up. Bake for 45 to 55 minutes or until chicken is done (170°F for breast halves; 180°F for thighs and drumsticks), brushing often with glaze the last 10 minutes of baking. Makes 4 servings.

Grilling Directions: Marinate chicken and prepare glaze as directed in Steps 1 through 3. Prepare grill for indirect grilling. Test for medium heat above pan. Arrange chicken pieces, meaty sides up, on lightly greased grill rack over drip pan. Cover and grill for 50 to 60 minutes or until chicken is done (170°F for breast halves; 180°F for thighs and drumsticks), brushing often with glaze the last 10 minutes of grilling.

Cornish Game Hen with Roasted Root Vegetables

Leave the peel on the potatoes and carrots for
a little extra fiber and a little less work.

PER SERVING: 345 cal., 12 g total fat (2 g sat. fat), 133 mg chol., 399 mg
sodium, 27 g carb., 5 g fiber, 32 g pro. Exchanges: 1 vegetable,
1.5 starch, 3.5 lean meat. Carb choices: 1.5.

- 1 medium carrot, cut into large chunks
- 1 medium russet potato, cut into large chunks
- 1 medium parsnip or turnip, peeled and cut into chunks
- 1 small onion, cut into wedges
- 1 tablespoon olive oil
- 1 tablespoon balsamic vinegar
- 1 Cornish game hen or poussin (about 1½ pounds)
- 2 cloves garlic, minced
- 2 teaspoons snipped fresh rosemary or ½ teaspoon dried rosemary, crushed
- ¼ teaspoon salt
- ⅛ teaspoon ground black pepper

1. Preheat oven to 400°F. In a large bowl, combine carrot, potato, parsnip, and onion. Add oil and balsamic vinegar; toss gently to coat. Spread in a 9×9×2-inch baking pan; cover with foil. Roast for 30 minutes.

2. Meanwhile, gently separate the skin from the breast and the tops of drumsticks by slipping a paring knife or your fingers between the skin and meat to make 2 pockets that extend all the way to the neck cavity and the drumsticks.

3. In a small bowl, combine garlic, rosemary, salt, and pepper. Rub 2 teaspoons of the fresh rosemary mixture (or ½ teaspoon dried rosemary mixture) under skin onto breast and drumstick meat. Using 100-percent-cotton string, tie drumsticks to tail; tie wing tips to body. Rub remaining rosemary mixture onto the skin. If desired, insert a meat thermometer into the center of an inside thigh muscle, making sure it does not touch fat or bone.

4. Reduce oven temperature to 375°F. Stir vegetables. Place hen, breast side up, in baking pan with vegetables. Roast vegetables and hen, uncovered, for 1 to 1¼ hours or until vegetables are tender, hen juices run clear, and the thermometer registers 180°F, stirring vegetables once or twice during roasting.

5. Remove string from hen. Cover with foil; let stand for 10 minutes. To serve hen, use kitchen shears or a long heavy knife to carefully cut hen in half lengthwise. Remove skin and discard. Serve with vegetables. Makes 2 servings.

Turkey Piccata

(10 twists on citrus)

Add zest to holiday meals and snacks with these citrus ideas.

1. **Serve lycopene-rich** cara cara oranges and finely shredded lime peel with light vanilla yogurt for dessert.
2. **Showcase** the intense flavor of anthocyanin-rich blood oranges by tossing segments into salsas and chutneys.
3. **Add tangerine or tangelo** segments to tuna or spinach salads for contrasts in color and flavor. The vitamin C-rich citrus helps you absorb the iron from the spinach.
4. **Partner grapefruit** or pummelo segments with avocado and your favorite greens for a refreshing salad.
5. **Simmer kumquats** to make marmalade or a tangy sauce for meat, poultry, fish, or tofu.
6. **Squeeze fresh lemon** or lime juice into marinades.
7. **Substitute lemon or lime** juice for some or all of the salt in sauces and soups.
8. **Stir up a dressing** of lime or lemon juice, a bit of zest, and olive oil to brighten the flavors of salads, steamed vegetables, or grilled meat.
9. **Enjoy the pleasant taste** of fresh lemon, lime, or orange slices or wedges in a glass of water, lemonade, or tea.
10. **Grate lemon or lime zest** into soups or risotto for flavor.

Stuffed Turkey Tenderloins

As guests savor these moist cayenne pepper-crusted turkey tenderloins, they'll delight in the tangy spinach-and-goat cheese filling tucked inside.

PER SERVING: 254 cal., 10 g fat (4 g sat. fat), 95 mg chol., 478 mg sodium, 1 g carb., 2 g fiber, 38 g pro. Exchanges: 5.5 very lean meat, 1.5 fat. Carb choices: 0.

- 4 **10- to 12-ounce turkey breast tenderloins**
- 4 **cups chopped fresh spinach leaves**
- 6 **ounces semisoft goat cheese (chèvre) or feta cheese, crumbled (about 1½ cups)**
- ½ **teaspoon ground black pepper**
- 2 **tablespoons olive oil**
- 2 **teaspoons paprika**
- 1 **teaspoon salt**
- ¼ **teaspoon cayenne pepper**

1. Make a pocket in each turkey breast tenderloin by cutting lengthwise from one side almost to, but not through, the opposite side; set aside.

2. In a large bowl, combine spinach, cheese, and black pepper. Spoon spinach mixture into pockets, dividing evenly. To hold in stuffing, tie 100-percent-cotton kitchen string around each tenderloin in 3 or 4 places.

3. In a small bowl, combine oil, paprika, salt, and cayenne pepper; brush evenly onto tenderloins. Wrap meat in plastic wrap. Refrigerate for 4 to 24 hours.

4. Preheat oven to 375°F. Unwrap turkey and place in a shallow roasting pan. Roast about 40 minutes or until done (170°F). Remove and discard strings; slice turkey tenderloins crosswise. Makes 8 servings.

Turkey Piccata

A piccata in Italy is usually pan-fried veal in a lemon sauce. We used lean turkey and less flour and oil.

PER SERVING: 148 cal., 3 g total fat (0 g sat. fat), 57 mg chol., 323 mg sodium, 5 g carb., 0 g fiber, 24 g pro. Exchanges: 3.5 very lean meat, 0.5 fat. Carb choices: 0.

- 1 **turkey breast tenderloin (13 to 15 ounces)**
- 2 **tablespoons all-purpose flour**
- ¼ **teaspoon salt**
- ¼ **teaspoon ground black pepper**
- 2 **teaspoons olive oil**
- 1 **cup reduced-sodium chicken broth**
- 2 **teaspoons finely shredded lemon peel**
- 2 **tablespoons lemon juice**
- 2 **cloves garlic, minced**
- ½ **teaspoon dry mustard**
- ¼ **cup sliced green onions**
  Lemon peel strips (optional)
  Sliced green onions (optional)
  Thin lemon slices (optional)

1. Split turkey breast tenderloin in half horizontally; cut each half crosswise to make 4 portions. Place each portion between 2 pieces of plastic wrap. Lightly pound turkey to about ⅜-inch thickness. Remove plastic wrap. In a shallow dish, combine flour, ⅛ teaspoon of the salt, and pepper. Evenly coat turkey with flour mixture; shake off excess flour mixture.

2. In a large nonstick skillet, heat oil over medium-high heat. Add turkey; cook about 6 minutes or until brown, turning once to brown evenly. Add broth, peel, lemon juice, garlic, dry mustard, and remaining ⅛ teaspoon salt to skillet. Bring to boiling; reduce heat. Simmer, uncovered, about 10 minutes or until turkey is no longer pink and liquid is slightly reduced.

3. Add green onions. Cook for 2 minutes more. To serve, if desired, top turkey with lemon peel strips, additional green onions, and lemon slices. Serve with some of the cooking liquid. Makes 4 servings.

Roast Herbed Turkey

If you choose to stuff the bird, the roasting time will increase. Roast the bird until the temperature of the stuffing reaches at least 165°F.

PER SERVING: 295 cal., 9 g total fat (3 g sat. fat), 172 mg chol., 165 mg sodium, 2 g carb., 0 g fiber, 48 g pro. Exchanges: 7 very lean meat, 1 fat. Carb choices: 0.

- 1 10- to 12-pound turkey
- 3 tablespoons snipped fresh sage or 1 tablespoon dried sage, crushed
- ½ teaspoon salt
- ½ teaspoon ground black pepper
- 1 recipe Spiced Sweet Potato Stuffing (optional) (see recipe, page 232)
- 1 tablespoon olive oil
- 1 orange
- 1 tablespoon honey
-   Oranges, halved (optional)
-   Fresh sage leaves (optional)

1. Rinse turkey cavity; pat dry with paper towels. Season the cavity with 1 tablespoon sage, salt, and pepper. If desired, lightly pack in Spiced Sweet Potato Stuffing.

2. Preheat oven to 325°F. Pull turkey's neck skin to back; fasten with a skewer. Tuck ends of drumsticks under band of skin across the tail. If the band of skin is not present, tie drumsticks securely to tail with 100-percent-cotton string. Twist wing tips under back.

3. Place turkey, breast side up, on a rack in a shallow roasting pan. Brush with olive oil. Insert an oven-going meat thermometer into the center of one of the inside thigh muscles, making sure the thermometer does not touch the bone. Roast for 2¾ to 3 hours or until meat thermometer registers 180°F and center of stuffing (if using) registers 165°F.

4. Halve and juice orange. In a small bowl, combine orange juice, honey, and remaining 2 tablespoons snipped sage. Brush onto turkey. Cover turkey with foil; let stand for 15 minutes before carving. If desired, garnish with orange halves and sage leaves. Makes 16 servings.

Menu

Herbed-Lemon Turkey with Wild Mushroom Gravy

Cheesy Cauliflower
(page 223)

Rice pilaf

Creamy Lime Mousse
(page 336)

Herbed-Lemon Turkey

A luscious dried cherry and sage mixture is nestled just beneath the skin of the turkey for a burst of flavor.

PER SERVING: 224 cal., 6 g fat (1 g sat. fat), 105 mg chol., 73 mg sodium, 4 g carb., 0 g fiber, 36 g pro. Exchanges: 5 very lean meat, 1 fat. Carb choices: 0.

- ½ cup dried cherries
- 2 tablespoons olive oil
- 1½ teaspoons snipped fresh sage or ½ teaspoon dried sage, crushed.
- 1 4½- to 5-pound whole turkey breast (bone-in)
- 1 lemon, quartered
- 1 medium onion, quartered
-   Wild Mushroom Gravy (optional) (see recipe, page 87)

1. Preheat oven to 325°F. In a blender or food processor combine cherries, 1 tablespoon olive oil, and sage. Cover; blend or process just until cherries are finely chopped.

2. Slip your fingers between the skin and meat of turkey breast to loosen skin. Lift skin and, using a spatula, carefully spread cherry mixture directly onto breast. Place turkey on a rack in a shallow roasting pan. Place lemon and onion quarters underneath turkey on rack. Insert an oven-going thermometer into breast, making sure the thermometer does not touch the bone. Brush with remaining 1 tablespoon oil.

3. Roast turkey, uncovered, in preheated oven for 1½ to 2¼ hours or until thermometer registers 170°F, covering with foil the last 45 minutes of roasting to prevent overbrowning. Cover and let stand for 15 minutes before carving. Makes 12 servings.

Herbed-Lemon Turkey with Wild Mushroom Gravy

Wild Mushroom Gravy

This exotic mushroom gravy is a no-fat addition to your holiday meal.

PER SERVING: 40 cal., 0 g fat (0 g sat. fat), 0 mg chol., 103 mg sodium, 9 g carb., 1 g fiber, 1 g pro. Exchanges: 0.5 carb. Carb choices: 0.5.

Nonstick cooking spray
4 ounces shallots, peeled and coarsely chopped (about 1 cup)
1½ cups sliced fresh exotic mushrooms (such as oyster, shiitake, and/or crimini) or sliced fresh button mushrooms
1 14-ounce can reduced-sodium chicken broth
¼ cup all-purpose flour
2 teaspoons balsamic vinegar
1 teaspoon snipped fresh oregano or marjoram or ¼ teaspoon dried oregano or marjoram, crushed
Dash ground black pepper

1. Lightly coat an unheated medium saucepan with cooking spray. Add shallots; cook and stir over medium heat about 6 minutes or until shallots are tender and golden brown. Add mushrooms; cook for 4 minutes more.
2. Stir together ½ cup of the broth and the flour; add to saucepan. Add remaining broth, the balsamic vinegar, and dried herb, if using. Cook and stir until thickened and bubbly; cook and stir for 1 minute more. Stir in fresh herb, if using. Season with pepper. Serve with turkey. Makes 12 (3-tablespoon) servings.

Beef Braciole

Beef Braciole

Braciole are stuffed beef rolls.

PER SERVING: 162 cal., 6 g total fat (2 g sat. fat), 148 mg chol., 359 mg sodium, 4 g carb., 1 g fiber, 21 g pro. Exchanges: 0.5 vegetable, 3 lean meat. Carb choices: 0.

　Nonstick cooking spray
2　pounds boneless beef eye round roast
¼　teaspoon salt
¼　teaspoon ground black pepper
6　hard-cooked eggs, peeled and chopped
¼　cup grated Romano cheese
3　cloves garlic, minced
2　tablespoons snipped fresh parsley
1　tablespoon snipped fresh oregano or 1 teaspoon dried oregano, crushed
¼　teaspoon salt
¼　teaspoon ground black pepper
½　cup water
3　cups reduced-sodium pasta sauce or three 8-ounce cans no-salt-added tomato sauce plus 2 teaspoons dried Italian seasoning, crushed, and ¼ teaspoon salt

1. Coat a 3-quart rectangular baking dish with nonstick cooking spray; set aside.

2. Trim fat from beef. Cut meat crosswise into 12 slices, each about ½ inch thick. Place each slice between 2 pieces of plastic wrap. Working from the center to the edges, gently pound meat with the flat side of a meat mallet to about ⅛-inch thickness. Sprinkle meat with ¼ teaspoon salt and ¼ teaspoon pepper.

3. Preheat oven to 375°F. For filling, in a medium bowl, combine chopped eggs, Romano cheese, garlic, parsley, oregano, ¼ teaspoon salt, and ¼ teaspoon pepper.

4. Spoon a scant ¼ cup of the filling onto each beef slice. Roll up. Secure each beef roll-up with a wooden toothpick.

5. Pour the water into the prepared baking dish. Arrange beef roll-ups in the dish. Cover with foil. Bake about 1¼ hours or until beef is tender.

6. Meanwhile, in a medium saucepan, heat pasta sauce over medium heat. (Or in a medium saucepan, combine canned tomato sauce, Italian seasoning, and ¼ teaspoon salt; heat through over medium heat.)

7. For each serving, spoon warm sauce onto a dinner plate. Using a slotted spoon, transfer a beef roll-up to each plate. Drizzle with a little cooking liquid. Top with additional tomato sauce. Makes 12 servings.

Menu

Beef Braciole *(at right)*

Broccoli Rabe with Garlic *(page 227)*

Thyme-Roasted Parsnips and Carrots *(page 227)*

Potato Parker House Rolls *(page 299)*

Salmon with Rosemary

Roast the peppers and tomatoes to concentrate their sweetness in this colorful holiday pasta dish.

PER SERVING: 319 cal., 19 g total fat (3 g sat. fat), 66 mg chol., 219 mg sodium, 10 g carb., 2 g fiber, 24 g pro. Exchanges: 1.5 veg. 3 lean meat, 2 fat. Carb choices: 0.5.

- 1 pound fresh or frozen skinless salmon fillets, cut into 5 pieces
- 2 medium yellow and/or green sweet peppers, cut into 1-inch pieces
- 8 ounces cherry tomatoes, halved (1½ cups)
- 2 tablespoons olive oil
- 1 tablespoon snipped fresh rosemary or 1 teaspoon dried rosemary, crushed
- ¼ teaspoon ground black pepper
- 2 tablespoons dry white wine
- 2 tablespoons balsamic vinegar
- 6 ounces dried whole grain pasta (such as linguine, fettuccine, or penne) (optional)
- ⅓ cup snipped fresh basil

1. Thaw salmon, if frozen. Rinse sal[...] paper towels. Set aside. Preheat the ove[...]

2. In a 15×10×1-inch baking pan, combin[...] pepper pieces and tomatoes. Drizzle with olive oil and sprinkle with half of the rosemary, ¼ teaspoon salt, and the black pepper. Toss to coat. Roast, uncovered, for 20 minutes.

3. Remove pan from oven. Stir wine and balsamic vinegar into vegetable mixture. Add salmon pieces to pan and turn to coat with wine mixture. Return to oven and roast about 10 minutes more or until salmon flakes easily when tested with a fork.

4. Meanwhile, cook pasta according to package directions; drain and keep warm.

5. To serve, if desired, divide pasta among 4 plates. Top pasta with vegetable mixture and sprinkle with basil. Place salmon on vegetables and sprinkle with remaining rosemary. Makes 5 servings.

Salmon with Rosemary

Salmon with Asparagus and Mushrooms

(fish for thought)

Serving fish for special occasions adds healthful variety to your menus. Not only does it taste good, but fish is a good source of high-quality protein and good-for-you fats. The fat in fish is mostly polyunsaturated and monounsaturated, unlike the saturated fat found in meat. Fish also has omega-3, polyunsaturated fatty acids thought to be beneficial in reducing blood clots, lowering LDL "bad" blood cholesterol levels, and reducing the risk of heart disease. Fish that are especially high in omega-3 fatty acids include sardine, herring, mackerel, Atlantic bluefish, tuna, salmon, pilchard, butterfish, and pompano.

Salmon with Asparagus and Mushrooms

Very few foods naturally contain vitamin D. The salmon and mushrooms in this recipe give you a double dose.

PER SERVING: 371 cal., 20 g total fat (4 g sat. fat), 67 mg chol., 289 mg sodium, 12 g carb., 3 g fiber, 28 g pro. Exchanges: 1.5 vegetable, 0.5 carb., 3.5 lean meat, 2.5 fat. Carb choices: 1.

4 fresh or frozen skinless salmon fillets, cut about 1 inch thick (about 1 pound total)
¼ teaspoon kosher salt
   Ground black pepper
2 tablespoons olive oil
2 cups sliced assorted fresh mushrooms (such as button, cremini, and/or stemmed shiitake)
1 cup chopped onion
6 cloves garlic, minced (1 tablespoon)
1 tablespoon chopped fresh thyme or dried thyme, crushed
1 cup dry white wine
1 cup clam juice, fish stock, chicken stock, or reduced-sodium chicken broth
2 cups 1½-inch-long pieces of asparagus
1 cup cherry tomatoes, halved
1 tablespoon chopped fresh flat-leaf parsley
1 teaspoon lemon juice
   Fresh thyme sprigs (optional)

1. Thaw fish, if frozen. Rinse fish; pat dry with paper towels. Measure thickness of fish fillets. Season fish with kosher salt and pepper. Set aside.

2. In a large skillet, heat 1 tablespoon of the olive oil over medium heat. Add mushrooms; cook about 5 minutes or until golden. Add onion, garlic, and thyme; cook until mushrooms are tender, stirring occasionally. Add wine. Bring to boiling; reduce heat. Simmer, uncovered, about 15 minutes or until liquid is reduced to ¼ cup. Add clam juice. Return to boiling; reduce heat. Simmer, uncovered, 15 minutes more or until liquid is reduced to ¾ cup.

3. Add asparagus. Cover; cook about 3 minutes or until asparagus is crisp-tender. Stir in tomatoes, parsley, and lemon juice. Season to taste with kosher salt and pepper. Transfer to a platter and keep warm.

4. In the same skillet, heat remaining 1 tablespoon olive oil over medium heat. Add salmon; cook for 4 to 6 minutes per ½-inch thickness of salmon or until salmon flakes easily when tested with a fork, turning once. Serve salmon over vegetable mixture. If desired, garnish with fresh thyme. Makes 4 servings.

Salmon with Apricot Sauce

Hot pepper sauce helps give the salmon a zesty zap of flavor.

PER SERVING: 304 cal., 8 g total fat (1 g sat. fat), 73 mg chol., 260 mg sodium, 27 g carb., 2 g fiber, 29 g pro. Exchanges: 1.5 other carb., 1 fruit, 4 very lean meat, 1 fat. Carb choices: 2.

4 fresh or frozen salmon or halibut steaks, cut ¾ inch thick
4 fresh apricots, pitted, or 8 dried apricot halves
½ cup apricot nectar
⅓ cup apricot preserves
3 tablespoon sliced green onion
1½ teaspoon snipped fresh oregano or ½ teaspoon dried oregano, crushed
⅛ teaspoon salt
   Few dashes bottled hot pepper sauce
1 tablespoon olive oil
1 to 2 teaspoons bottled hot pepper sauce
   Fresh oregano sprigs (optional)

1. Thaw fish, if frozen. Rinse fish; pat dry. Set aside. Cut up fresh apricots; set aside. (Or halve dried apricots; cover with boiling water. Let stand until needed; drain well before using.)

2. For sauce, in small saucepan, combine apricot nectar, preserves, green onion, oregano, and salt. Bring just to boiling, stirring often; reduce heat. Boil gently, uncovered, about 8 minutes or until slightly thickened. Reserve ¼ cup of the sauce to brush on fish. In small bowl, combine remaining sauce, apricots, and few dashes hot pepper sauce. Cover and keep warm.

3. In small bowl, stir together oil and 1 to 2 teaspoons hot pepper sauce. Brush both sides of fish with oil mixture. Sprinkle lightly with ground black pepper and additional salt.

4. Place fish on greased rack of uncovered grill directly over medium heat. Grill for 6 to 9 minutes or until fish flakes easily with fork, turning once halfway through grilling and brushing with reserved sauce during last 2 to 3 minutes. Discard any remaining sauce. Serve fish with sauce. If desired, garnish with fresh oregano sprigs. Makes 4 servings.

Spice-Rubbed Salmon with Tropical Rice

Salmon is one of the richest sources of heart-healthy omega-3 fatty acids.

PER SERVING: 366 cal., 13 g total fat (3 g sat. fat), 66 mg chol., 155 mg sodium, 35 g carb., 3 g fiber, 26 g pro. Exchanges: 0.5 fruit, 2 starch, 3 lean meat. Carb choices: 2.

PER SERVING WITH SUBSTITUTE: same as above, except 353 cal., 154 mg sodium, 32 g carb.

- 1 1-pound fresh or frozen skinless salmon fillet
  Nonstick cooking spray
- 1 tablespoon coriander seeds, coarsely crushed*
- 1 tablespoon packed brown sugar or brown sugar substitute** equivalent to 1 tablespoon brown sugar
- 1 teaspoon lemon-pepper seasoning
- 1 recipe Tropical Rice (see recipe, right)
  Lemon wedges (optional)
  Fresh cilantro (optional)

1. Thaw salmon, if frozen. Spray a shallow baking pan with nonstick cooking spray. Preheat oven to 450°F. Rinse salmon; pat dry with paper towels. Measure the thickness of the salmon. Place salmon in the prepared pan.

2. In a small bowl, stir together coriander seeds, brown sugar, and lemon-pepper seasoning. Sprinkle fish with mixture; using fingers press seasoning slightly.

3. Bake fish for 4 to 6 minutes per ½-inch thickness or until it flakes easily when tested with a fork.

4. Serve salmon with Tropical Rice. If desired, garnish with lemon wedges and fresh cilantro. Makes 4 servings (1 piece of salmon plus ½ cup rice).

Tropical Rice: In a medium bowl, stir together 2 cups hot cooked brown rice; 1 seeded, peeled, and chopped mango; 1 tablespoon snipped fresh cilantro; and 1 teaspoon finely shredded lemon peel. Serve warm.

*Test Kitchen Tip: If you don't have coriander seeds to crush for the fish coating, substitute 1 tablespoon sesame seeds (toasted, if desired) and ¼ teaspoon ground cumin.

**Sugar Substitutes: Choose from Sweet'N Low Brown or Sugar Twin Granulated Brown. Follow the package directions to use the product amount that's equivalent to 1 tablespoon brown sugar.

Pecan-Crusted Fish with Peppers and Squash

Pecans and cornmeal combine for a satisfying crunch that makes this fish stand out from any fried variety. Serve it with the colorful vegetables that bake alongside the fish.

PER SERVING: 358 cal., 18 g total fat (3 g sat. fat), 53 mg chol., 481 mg sodium, 26 g carb., 4 g fiber, 24 g pro. Exchanges: 1.5 vegetable, 1 starch, 2.5 very lean meat, 3 fat. Carb choices: 2.

- 1 pound fresh or frozen skinless catfish fillets, white fish, or orange roughy, cut ½ inch thick
  Nonstick cooking spray
- ½ cup yellow cornmeal
- ⅓ cup finely chopped pecans
- ½ teaspoon salt
- ¼ cup all-purpose flour
- ¼ teaspoon cayenne pepper
- ¼ cup refrigerated or frozen egg product, thawed, or 1 egg
- 1 tablespoon water
- 2 small red and/or orange sweet peppers, seeded and cut into wedges
- 1 medium zucchini, bias-sliced ½ inch thick
- 1 medium yellow summer squash, bias-sliced ½ inch thick
- 2 teaspoons cooking oil
- ¼ teaspoon seasoned salt
  Lemon wedges (optional)

Spice-Rubbed Salmon with Tropical Rice

Pecan-Crusted Fish with Peppers and Squash

1. Preheat oven to 425°F. Thaw fish, if frozen. Rinse fish; pat dry with paper towels. Cut fish into 3- to 4-inch pieces; set aside. Line a 15×10×1-inch baking pan with foil. Coat foil with cooking spray; set aside.

2. In a shallow dish, stir together cornmeal, pecans, and salt. In another dish, stir together flour and cayenne. In a small bowl, whisk egg and water. Dip each fish piece into flour mixture, shaking off excess. Dip fish into egg mixture, then into pecan mixture. Place in prepared pan.

3. In a large bowl, combine sweet peppers, zucchini, and squash. Add oil and seasoned salt; toss gently to coat. Arrange vegetables next to fish, overlapping as needed to fit.

4. Bake, uncovered, for 20 to 25 minutes or until fish flakes easily when tested with a fork and vegetables are crisp-tender. If desired, serve with lemon wedges. Makes 4 servings.

Menu

Provençal Fish Fillets
(at right)

Steamed green beans

Mixed greens salad

Whole wheat rolls

Provençal Fish Fillets

(cook fish right)

Minutes count when cooking fish. Weigh dressed fish or use a ruler to measure the thickness of the fillets and steaks in order to better estimate when to check for doneness. Properly cooked fish is opaque, flakes when tested with a fork, and readily comes away from the bones; the juices should be a milky white. Methods for cooking fish include baking, broiling, frying, microwaving, poaching, and grilling.

Provençal Fish Fillets

Cooks and their guests in Provence, France have long benefited from heart-healthy olives, tomatoes, and fish.

PER SERVING: 161 cal., 5 g total fat (1 g sat. fat), 48 mg chol., 292 mg sodium, 7 g carb., 2 g fiber, 21 g pro. Exchanges: 1 vegetable, 3 very lean meat, 1 fat. Carb choices: 0.5.

 4 4-ounce fresh or frozen skinless cod, catfish, pollock, or tilapia fillets, cut $\frac{1}{2}$ to 1 inch thick
 1 tablespoon olive oil
 1 medium onion, thinly sliced
 2 cloves garlic, minced
 1 $14\frac{1}{2}$-ounce can whole tomatoes, drained and chopped
 8 oil-cured Greek olives, pitted and halved, or 8 pitted ripe olives, halved
 2 teaspoons snipped fresh thyme or $\frac{1}{2}$ teaspoon dried thyme, crushed
 1 teaspoon capers, drained
    Nonstick cooking spray
    Fresh thyme sprigs (optional)

1. Thaw fish, if frozen. Rinse fish under cold water; pat dry with paper towels. Measure thickness of fish. Set fish aside.

2. For sauce, in a small saucepan, heat oil over medium heat. Add onion and garlic; cook about 5 minutes or until tender, stirring occasionally. Add tomatoes, olives, the snipped or dried thyme, and capers. Heat to boiling; reduce heat to medium. Simmer, uncovered, about 10 minutes or until most of the liquid has evaporated.

3. Meanwhile, preheat broiler. Spray unheated rack of a broiler pan with cooking spray. Place fish on rack, tucking under any thin edges. Broil 3 to 4 inches from heat for 4 to 6 minutes per $\frac{1}{2}$-inch thickness or until fish flakes easily, turning once if fillets are 1 inch thick. Serve with sauce. If desired, garnish with fresh thyme sprigs. Makes 4 servings.

Ginger-Marinated Sea Bass

You'll love how easy this sweet-spicy-salty marinade is to make for last-minute guests.

PER SERVING: 193 cal., 3 g total fat (1 g sat. fat), 69 mg chol., 556 mg sodium, 6 g carb., 0 g fiber, 33 g pro. Exchanges: 4 very lean meat, 1 carb. Carb choices: 0.5.

 4 6-ounce fresh or frozen sea bass or halibut steaks, cut 1 inch thick
 $\frac{1}{4}$ cup light teriyaki sauce
 2 tablespoons lemon juice
 1 tablespoon grated fresh ginger
 2 teaspoons brown sugar
 $\frac{1}{8}$ teaspoon cayenne pepper
 2 cloves garlic, minced
    Nonstick cooking spray
    Fresh cilantro sprigs (optional)

1. Thaw fish, if frozen. Rinse fish; pat dry with paper towels. Place fish in a shallow nonmetallic dish. For marinade, in a small bowl, combine teriyaki sauce, lemon juice, ginger, brown sugar, cayenne pepper, and garlic. Pour onto fish; turn fish to coat. Cover and marinate in the refrigerator for 1 to 2 hours, turning fish occasionally. Drain fish, reserving marinade.

2. Coat the unheated rack of a broiler pan with cooking spray. Place fish on the prepared rack. Broil about 4 inches from the heat for 8 to 12 minutes or until fish flakes easily when tested with a fork, turning and brushing once with reserved marinade. Discard any remaining marinade. If desired, garnish with cilantro. Makes 4 servings.

Fish with Tangerine Relish

Here's an alternative to the traditional turkey with cranberry relish.

PER SERVING: 175 cal., 4 g total fat (1 g sat. fat), 36 mg chol., 161 mg sodium, 11 g carb., 1 g fiber, 24 g pro. Exchanges: 0.5 fruit, 3.5 very lean meat, 0.5 fat. Carb choices: 1.

- **6** 4-ounce fresh or frozen skinless halibut, cod, sole, or other white fish fillets
- **¼** teaspoon salt
- **¼** teaspoon ground black pepper
- **⅓** cup orange juice
- **¼** cup finely chopped red onion or shallot
- **2** teaspoons white balsamic vinegar or balsamic vinegar
- **1** teaspoon snipped fresh tarragon or rosemary or ½ teaspoon dried tarragon or rosemary, crushed
- **1** teaspoon olive oil
- **1** clove garlic, minced
- **Dash** bottled hot pepper sauce
- **Nonstick** cooking spray
- **4** medium tangerines
- **2** tablespoons snipped fresh parsley
- **6** cups torn mixed salad greens (optional)

1. Thaw fish fillets, if frozen. Preheat broiler. Rinse fish; pat dry with paper towels. Sprinkle with salt and black pepper. Measure thickness of fish; set aside.

2. In a small saucepan, combine orange juice, onion, balsamic vinegar, tarragon, oil, garlic, and hot pepper sauce. Bring to boiling; reduce heat. Simmer, uncovered, for 5 to 6 minutes or until reduced to about ⅓ cup. Remove from heat. Remove 2 tablespoons of the liquid; set both mixtures aside.

3. Coat the unheated rack of a broiler pan with nonstick cooking spray. Place fish fillets on rack. Brush both sides of each fillet with the reserved 2 tablespoons liquid. Turn under any thin portions of fish to make uniform thickness. Broil 4 inches from the heat for 4 to 6 minutes per ½-inch thickness or until fish flakes easily with a fork.

4. Meanwhile, for tangerine relish, peel tangerines and separate into segments. Remove seeds and cut up tangerine segments into bite-size pieces. In a small bowl, combine tangerines, the remaining orange juice mixture, and the parsley.

5. To serve, place fish on greens, if using. Spoon tangerine relish onto fish. Makes 6 servings.

Catfish with Red Pepper Sauce

Catfish has a mild flavor and firm flesh. Grill or broil the fillets and serve with our vitamin C-loaded sauce.

PER SERVING: 234 cal., 16 g total fat (3 g sat. fat), 53 mg chol., 355 mg sodium, 5 g carb., 2 g fiber, 19 g pro. Exchanges: 0.5 vegetable, 2.5 lean meat, 1.5 fat. Carb choices: 0.

- **4** 4-ounce fresh or frozen skinless catfish fillets, cut ½ to 1 inch thick
- **1** recipe Red Pepper Sauce (see recipe, below)
- **2** tablespoons red wine vinegar
- **1** tablespoon olive oil
- **¼** teaspoon dried rosemary, crushed
- **¼** teaspoon salt
- **⅛** teaspoon ground black pepper
- **Nonstick** cooking spray

1. Thaw fish, if frozen. Prepare Red Pepper Sauce. Preheat broiler.

2. Rinse fish; pat dry with paper towels. Measure thickness. In a small bowl, combine vinegar, olive oil, and rosemary. Brush both sides of fish fillets with vinegar mixture. Sprinkle fish with salt and black pepper.

3. Coat the unheated rack of a broiler pan with nonstick cooking spray. Place fish on rack, tucking under any thin edges. Broil 3 to 4 inches from heat for 4 to 6 minutes per ½-inch thickness or until fish flakes easily, turning once if fish is 1 inch thick. Serve with warm Red Pepper Sauce. Makes 4 servings.

Red Pepper Sauce: In a small saucepan, heat 1 tablespoon olive oil over medium heat. Add 1 cup chopped red sweet pepper; cook until tender, stirring occasionally. Stir in 2 peeled, seeded, and chopped tomatoes; 1 teaspoon vinegar; ¼ teaspoon salt; ¼ teaspoon garlic powder; and a dash cayenne pepper. Cook for 5 minutes more, stirring often. Transfer mixture to a food processor or blender. Cover and process until nearly smooth. Return to pan; cover and keep warm.

Grilling Directions: Spray a grill basket with nonstick cooking spray. Place fish in basket, tucking under any thin edges. Place basket on the rack of an uncovered grill directly over medium coals. Grill for 4 to 6 minutes per ½-inch thickness of fish or until fish flakes easily when tested with a fork, turning basket once if fillets are 1 inch thick.

Basil-Lemon Shrimp Linguine

Look for high-fiber or whole grain pasta for more fiber.

PER SERVING: 336 cal., 6 g total fat (1 g sat. fat), 172 mg chol., 463 mg sodium, 39 g carb., 4 g fiber, 31 g pro. Exchanges: 1 vegetable, 2 starch, 3 very lean meat, 1 fat. Carb choices: 2.5.

- **1** pound fresh or frozen large shrimp in shells
- **6** ounces dried linguine
- **¼** teaspoon salt
- **8** ounces fresh asparagus spears, trimmed and cut diagonally into 2-inch pieces
- Nonstick cooking spray
- **2** cloves garlic, minced
- **1** cup thin yellow, red, and/or green sweet pepper strips
- **¼** cup snipped fresh basil or 1 tablespoon dried basil, crushed
- **1** teaspoon finely shredded lemon peel
- **¼** teaspoon salt
- **¼** teaspoon ground black pepper
- **¼** cup sliced green onions
- **2** tablespoons lemon juice
- **1** tablespoon olive oil
- Lemon wedges (optional)

1. Thaw shrimp, if frozen. Peel shrimp; devein, leaving tails intact. Rinse well.

2. Cook pasta according to the package directions, except use ¼ teaspoon salt and add asparagus the last 3 minutes of cooking; drain.

3. Meanwhile, lightly coat a large nonstick skillet with cooking spray. Heat over medium heat. Add garlic; cook and stir for 15 seconds. Add pepper strips; cook and stir for 2 minutes or until crisp-tender. Add shrimp, dried basil (if using), lemon peel, remaining ¼ teaspoon salt, and pepper. Cook and stir for 3 minutes or until shrimp turn pink. Remove from heat.

4. Add shrimp mixture to pasta mixture. Add fresh basil (if using), green onions, lemon juice, and oil; toss gently to coat. If desired, serve with lemon wedges. Makes 4 (2-cup) servings.

Curried Shrimp

For a taste of Thailand, this trendy shrimp dish has a flavorful coconut milk sauce.

PER SERVING: 154 cal., 3 g total fat (1 g sat. fat), 129 mg chol., 284 mg sodium, 11 g carb., 2 g fiber, 19 g pro. Exchanges: 1 vegetable, 2.5 very lean meat, 0.5 fat. Carb choices: 1.

1 **pound fresh or frozen large shrimp**
1 **teaspoon olive oil**
1 **cup chopped onion**
1 **tablespoon grated fresh ginger**
½ **teaspoon curry powder**
½ **teaspoon ground cumin**
¼ **teaspoon cayenne pepper**
6 **ounces fresh pea pods, trimmed and halved lengthwise (2 cups)**
¼ **cup orange juice**
3 **tablespoons unsweetened light coconut milk**
¼ **teaspoon salt**
Cooked whole wheat couscous (optional)*
½ **cup snipped fresh cilantro**

1. Thaw shrimp, if frozen. Peel and devein; rinse and pat dry. Set aside.

2. In a large nonstick skillet, heat olive oil over medium heat. Add onion; cook and stir about 5 minutes or until tender. Add ginger, curry powder, cumin, and cayenne pepper; cook and stir for 1 minute. Add shrimp and peas, stirring to coat with the spices. Cook and stir about 3 minutes or until shrimp are opaque. Stir in orange juice, coconut milk, and salt; heat through.

3. If desired, serve shrimp mixture with couscous. Top each serving with cilantro. Makes 4 servings.

*To cook couscous: In a medium saucepan, bring 1½ cups water to boiling. Stir in 1 cup whole wheat couscous; cover and remove from heat. Let stand for 5 minutes.

Menu

Curried Shrimp *(at left)*

Couscous

Mixed fruit salad

Frozen low-fat yogurt

Soy-Lime Scallops with Leeks

This time-saving meal is great for an indoor grill.

PER SERVING: 130 cal., 1 g total fat (0 g sat. fat), 37 mg chol., 478 mg sodium, 9 g carb., 1 g fiber, 20 g pro. Exchanges: 0.5 carb., 2.5 very lean meat, 0.5 vegetable. Carb choices: 0.5.

1 **pound fresh or frozen sea scallops**
¼ **cup reduced-sodium soy sauce**
¼ **cup rice vinegar**
4 **baby leeks or 2 leeks cut in half lengthwise**
8 **medium green scallions, red scallions, or green onions**
1 **medium lime, halved**

1. Thaw scallops, if frozen. Rinse scallops; pat dry with paper towels. For marinade, in a small bowl, combine soy sauce and rice vinegar; set aside.

2. Trim root ends and green tops of leeks. Rinse leeks thoroughly to remove any grit.

3. Place leeks, scallops, and scallions in a resealable plastic bag set in a shallow dish. Add marinade to bag. Seal bag; turn to coat scallops and vegetables. Marinate in refrigerator for 30 minutes.

4. Remove scallops, leeks, and scallions from bag. Discard marinade. Place leeks, scallops, scallions, and lime halves (cut sides down) on the rack of an uncovered grill directly over medium heat. Grill for 8 to 10 minutes or until scallops are opaque, turning scallops and vegetables occasionally. Remove scallions from grill rack before they overbrown.

5. To serve, transfer leeks and scallions to 4 dinner plates. Top with scallops. Using grilling tongs, remove limes from grill; squeeze over scallops. Makes 4 servings.

Soy-Lime Scallops with Leeks

(so-called shellfish)

Although "shellfish" is used for saltwater and freshwater invertebrates, such as mollusks, crusta-
ceans, and echinoderms, the term is actually a misnomer because these invertebrates are not fish
at all. Regardless, eating shellfish is a healthy alternative to eating meat because they are low in
saturated fat and high in omega-3 fatty acids. Be careful not to overcook any type of fish (salmon,
sea bass, haddock, etc.), mollusk (clam, mussel, oyster, eye winkles, and scallop), or crustacean
(shrimp, prawn, lobster, crayfish, and crab), or they will become tough and chewy. Carefully follow
the guidelines given for the recipes in this section based on the thickness of the fish or the color
(for shrimp or scallops) to know when they are done.

cooking with the diabetic chef

Since 2005, Chris Smith, a.k.a. the Diabetic Chef, has shown *Diabetic Living*® magazine readers how to cook. Diagnosed with type 1 diabetes at the age of 24, Chris took his experiences as a professional chef and helped educate others on how to cook healthful meals that tasted great. Learn some of his tips in the following menus.

Mixed Greens with Herbed Balsamic Vinaigrette, recipe, page 106

spring family brunch

Living in the Carolinas, we're blessed with mild winters and long springs. That means our family can gather for an outdoor brunch a little earlier than most. Luckily, with my family living close by, getting together happens often. The following brunch menu is pretty typical of what we might serve for our annual Easter gathering.

I grew up on Long Island as one of six kids. Now, having two children of my own, I'm in awe of how my parents raised us. One of our eagerly awaited family rituals was celebrating Easter with brunch at my grandmother Nana's house. Back then, there was no such thing as an SUV. Instead, the mighty station wagon was the driving force in my dad's hands. As soon as we arrived at Nana and Pop's house, we'd begin the procession of kissing and hugging. About this time, the savory smells of the meal would be permeating the house, enticing us as we entered the dining room. The table would be beautifully set, and we kids would "call" who was going to sit next to Nana and Pops. Then we'd run to the basement to look for our Easter baskets, for we all knew that Pops had hidden six full-size baskets stuffed with chocolate bunnies, jelly beans, and a little money to go into our piggy banks.

With the three of my siblings and my parents now living in the Greensboro area, we've revived our annual spring brunch tradition. The only difference is now that I have diabetes, I take a lighter approach to the menu.

My sister Veronica and her husband, Tom, open their backyard to our gathering. Because the size of our family has grown, they've replaced Pop's baskets with small plastic eggs that they stash full of treats and prizes. Veronica and Tom hide more than 130 eggs! From the youngest to the oldest, we have fun discovering small eggs plus one special egg with our name on it.

Soon it's time to end the hunt and line up for the buffet, just like we used to at Nana's. We cherish our time together at these brunches and hope we're passing along the best of our traditions, liberally peppered with the joy and kindness we experienced in our childhoods.

Feta-Stuffed Mini Peppers recipe, page 106

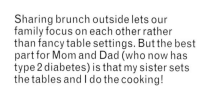

Sharing brunch outside lets our family focus on each other rather than fancy table settings. But the best part for Mom and Dad (who now has type 2 diabetes) is that my sister sets the tables and I do the cooking!

In between bites of grilled salmon or rosemary lamb, we share our memories of those long-ago days.

—Chris Smith, the Diabetic Chef

Rosemary Roast Leg of Lamb with Roasted Fingerling Potatoes
recipes, pages 104 and 105

Wood planks are a great way to add flavor to grilled fish. Choose from different types of woods, such as alder, cedar, or maple. Flavored planks, such as Cajun and lemon-dill, are also available. The planks are used just once. Look for them where barbecue products are sold.

Grilled Salmon with Lemon Thyme

Grilled Salmon with Lemon Thyme

Cedar smoke from grill planks plus lemon give salmon all the flavor it needs.

PER SERVING: 210 cal., 11 g total fat (3 g sat. fat), 69 mg chol., 171 mg sodium, 0 g carbo., 0 g fiber, 26 g pro. Exchanges: 4 very lean meat. Carb choices: 0.

- 2 cedar grill planks (each about 12×6×¾ inches)
- 2 2-pound fresh or frozen salmon fillets (with skin), cut 1 inch thick
- 3 tablespoons olive oil
- 2 teaspoons snipped fresh lemon thyme or ½ teaspoon dried thyme, crushed
- ½ teaspoon salt
- ½ teaspoon ground black pepper
  Fresh lemon thyme sprigs (optional)
- 2 medium lemons, cut into wedges

1. At least 1 hour before grilling, soak planks in enough water to cover, weighing them down to keep them submerged. Thaw salmon, if frozen. Rinse fish; pat dry with paper towels.

2. On each plank, place a fillet, skin side down. Brush oil onto fish. Sprinkle with snipped thyme, salt, and pepper.

3. Place salmon on planks on grill rack directly over low heat. Cover and grill about 20 minutes or until salmon flakes easily when tested with a fork.

4. If desired, garnish with lemon thyme sprigs. Serve with lemon wedges. Makes 14 servings.

Rosemary Roast Leg of Lamb

An herb rub gives tender lamb a robust flavor without adding a lot of calories, fat, or carbohydrates.

PER SERVING: 136 cal., 4 g total fat (1 g sat. fat), 71 mg chol., 218 mg sodium, 0 g carbo., 0 g fiber, 23 g pro. Exchanges: 3 very lean meat, 0.5 fat. Carb choices: 0.

- 1 5- to 7-pound whole lamb leg
- 2 teaspoons snipped fresh rosemary
- 1 teaspoon salt
- 1 teaspoon ground black pepper
- 3 cloves garlic, sliced

1. Preheat oven to 375°F. Trim fat from lamb. Cut small slits in lamb. In a small bowl, combine rosemary, salt,

and pepper; sprinkle evenly onto meat. Rub in with fingers; insert garlic into slits.

2. Place lamb, fat side up, on a rack in a shallow roasting pan. Add 1 cup water to pan. Insert an oven-going meat thermometer into center, making sure bulb of thermometer does not touch bone.

3. Roast until desired doneness, allowing 1½ to 1¾ hours for medium-rare doneness (140°F) or 2 to 2¼ hours for medium (155°F). Cover with foil; let stand for 15 minutes. The temperature of the meat after standing should be 145°F for medium-rare or 160°F for medium. Makes 14 servings.

Mint Pesto

Double the recipe for a crowd. Serve alongside the lamb.

PER TABLESPOON: 68 cal., 7 g total fat (1 g sat. fat), 0 mg chol., 84 mg sodium, 2 g carbo., 0 g fiber, 2 g pro. Exchanges: 1.5 fat. Carb choices: 0.

- 1½ cups loosely packed fresh mint
- 1½ cups loosely packed fresh basil
- ½ cup pine nuts, toasted
- ¼ cup olive oil
- 4 cloves garlic, quartered
- ½ teaspoon salt

1. In a food processor, combine all ingredients. Cover and process until almost smooth. Serve with lamb, salmon, or other meats. Makes 14 (1-tablespoon) servings.

Make-Ahead Directions: Prepare as directed. Cover surface with plastic wrap. Chill up to 24 hours.

Roasted Fingerling Potatoes

Add to the oven with the lamb the last 45 minutes of roasting.

PER SERVING: 93 cal., 2 g total fat (0 g sat. fat), 0 mg chol., 89 mg sodium, 17 g carbo., 2 g fiber, 2 g pro. Exchanges: 1 starch, 0.5 fat. Carb choices: 1.

- 3 pounds fingerling potatoes or round red potatoes
- 2 tablespoons olive oil
- 1 teaspoon paprika
- ½ teaspoon salt
- ¼ to ½ teaspoon ground black pepper

1. Preheat oven to 375°F. Wash potatoes; pat dry. Cut any larger potatoes into 2-inch pieces.

2. Place potatoes in a large roasting pan; drizzle with olive oil. Sprinkle with paprika, salt, and pepper; stir potatoes to coat.

3. Bake, uncovered, about 45 minutes or until potatoes are tender and brown, stirring occasionally. Makes 14 (½-cup) servings.

Mixed Greens with Herbed Balsamic Vinaigrette

Try any herb you like in this vinaigrette.
Pictured on page 102.

PER SERVING: 76 cal., 6 g total fat (1 g sat. fat), 0 mg chol., 86 mg sodium, 5 g carbo., 1 g fiber, 1 g pro. Exchanges: 1 vegetable, 1 fat. Carb choices: 0.

- 1 pound torn mixed baby greens (mesclun) (about 16 cups)
- 1 medium cucumber, halved lengthwise and sliced
- 4 plum tomatoes, sliced
- ¾ cup pitted kalamata or ripe olives
- ¼ cup snipped fresh chives
- 1 recipe Herbed Balsamic Vinaigrette (see recipe, below)

1. In a very large bowl, toss together greens, cucumber, plum tomatoes, olives, and chives. Stir Herbed Balsamic Vinaigrette; pour onto salad. Toss gently to coat. Makes 14 (1-cup) servings.

Herbed Balsamic Vinaigrette: In a food processor or blender, combine ⅓ cup balsamic vinegar, ⅓ cup olive oil, 2 tablespoons fresh oregano, and 2 quartered cloves garlic. Cover and process until mixed. Season to taste with ground black pepper. Makes about ⅔ cup.

Make-Ahead Directions: Prepare vinaigrette; chill for up to 24 hours.

Feta-Stuffed Mini Peppers

Stuff the peppers ahead and pop them into the oven before serving. Pictured on page 102.

PER SERVING: 48 cal., 3 g total fat (2 g sat. fat), 14 mg chol., 186 mg sodium, 2 g carbo., 1 g fiber, 3 g pro. Exchanges: 0.5 medium-fat meat, 0.5 vegetable. Carb choices: 0.

- 28 miniature sweet peppers
- 4 ounces fresh spinach
- 8 ounces feta cheese, crumbled

1. Preheat oven to 375°F. Cut a thin slice from tops or sides of peppers. Scoop out and discard seeds. If desired, reserve tops.

2. For filling, wash spinach; remove stems. Cut spinach leaves into thin strips. In a large bowl, combine spinach and feta cheese.

3. Spoon filling into pepper shells, mounding slightly. In a 3-quart rectangular baking dish, arrange peppers, stuffed sides up. If desired, add pepper tops.

4. Bake peppers, uncovered, for 18 to 20 minutes or until slightly soft. Makes 14 (2-pepper) servings.

Make-Ahead Directions: Prepare peppers as directed through Step 3. Cover and chill for up to 24 hours. Before serving, bake as directed in Step 4.

Citrus Fruit Cups

Tangy lime juice and peel add flavor yet almost no calories.

PER SERVING: 49 cal., 0 g total fat (0 g sat. fat), 0 mg chol., 1 mg sodium, 12 g carbo., 2 g fiber, 1 g pro. Exchanges: 1 fruit. Carb choices: 1.

- 4 medium pink grapefruit
- 3 medium oranges
- 3 medium tangerines
- 2 cups fresh strawberries
- 1 cup fresh blueberries
- 2 kiwifruits, peeled and cut into wedges
- 2 medium limes
- Fresh mint sprigs (optional)

1. Peel and section grapefruit and oranges. Peel tangerines; cut in half lengthwise then slice crosswise. Quarter strawberries.

2. In a large bowl, combine grapefruit, oranges, tangerines, and strawberries. Add blueberries and kiwifruit; toss gently.

3. From limes, finely shred peel to make about 1 tablespoon peel. Squeeze juice to make about ¼ cup juice. Gently stir peel and juice into fruit. Cover and chill.

4. To serve, spoon fruit into dessert cups. If desired, garnish each serving with fresh mint sprigs. Makes 14 (½-cup) servings.

Citrus Fruit Cups

low-country coastal flavors

There's nothing like enjoying the local foods while on vacation. This menu captures some memorable dishes inspired by a getaway. Charleston, part of South Carolina's Low Country, is a favorite destination for my family. As we drive to the coast, we pass farmland and local vegetable stands. When we arrive, the air smells of the sea, and the tall marsh grasses reach for the wide, open sky.

Folks living in the Low Country love comfort foods—dishes that nourish your body and warm your soul. On many menus and dinner tables, you'll find shrimp and grits, greens, fried green tomatoes, and okra.

Traditional recipes, however, often call for fatback, lard, salt, and other ingredients that are unhealthful for us to eat in quantity. After our last vacation, I challenged myself to lighten some of the region's recipes. See how I changed cooking methods (such as frying) and ingredients but kept the delicious tastes. From collard greens and grits to okra and shrimp, this menu just might inspire you to travel to the Low Country yourself.

Baked Tomatoes and Okra
recipe, page 111

> Folks who
> live in the
> Low Country
> love comfort
> foods—dishes
> that nourish
> your body
> and warm
> your soul.
> These
> dishes do
> just that.

—Chef Smith

**Peanut Butter and
Vanilla Custards**
recipe, page 112

This region of the country is famous for its crab and shrimp. My boys are fascinated by these prehistoric-looking gifts from the sea. On our family vacations to Charleston, South Carolina, what we catch in the morning may become dinner that night!

Collard Greens (top),
Cheddar Shrimp and Grits (bottom)

Collard Greens

Rich in vitamins A and C, collard greens are a type of cabbage. Shop for bright green bunches with no brown spots.

PER SERVING: 39 cal., 1 g total fat (0 g sat. fat), 0 mg chol., 137 mg sodium, 6 g carb., 3 g fiber, 2 g pro. Exchanges: 1 vegetable. Carb choices: 0.5.

- 2 pounds fresh collard greens
- 1 teaspoon olive oil
- 1 medium onion, sliced and separated into rings
- 1 14-ounce can reduced-sodium chicken broth
- 1 smoked turkey neck bone or smoked turkey drumstick bone*
- ¼ teaspoon ground black pepper

1. Wash collard greens thoroughly. Cut off stems and discard. Coarsely chop collard greens and set aside. (You should have about 9 cups packed.) In a 4-quart Dutch oven, heat olive oil over medium heat. Add onion; cook about 5 minutes or until tender.

2. Add collard greens, chicken broth, smoked turkey bone, and pepper. Bring to boiling; reduce heat. Cover and simmer about 1 hour or until collard greens are tender. Remove smoked turkey bone and drain off any excess liquid. Serve warm with a slotted spoon. Makes 6 (about ⅓-cup) servings.

Test Kitchen Tip: If using a turkey drumstick, remove meat and reserve for another use; use only the bone for this recipe.

Cheddar Shrimp and Grits

This savory recipe features two Low Country essentials: shrimp and grits.

PER SERVING: 274 cal., 6 g total fat (2 g sat. fat), 152 mg chol., 384 mg sodium, 30 g carb., 2 g fiber, 27 g pro. Exchanges: 2 starch, 3 very lean meat. Carb choices: 2.

- 1¼ pounds fresh or frozen medium shrimp in shells
- 1 14-ounce can reduced-sodium chicken broth
- 1½ cups fat-free milk
- 1 cup regular grits
- 2 teaspoons olive oil
- 1 large onion, thinly sliced into rings
- 2 cloves garlic, minced
- 1 tablespoon snipped fresh parsley
- ½ cup shredded reduced-fat cheddar cheese (2 ounces)
- ¼ cup sliced green onions

1. Thaw shrimp, if frozen. Peel and devein shrimp, leaving tails intact if desired; set aside. In a medium saucepan, combine broth, milk, and grits. Bring to boiling; reduce heat. Cover and simmer for 4 to 5 minutes or until grits are desired consistency, stirring occasionally.

2. In a large skillet, heat olive oil over medium heat. Add onion and garlic; cook and stir about 5 minutes or until onion is tender and lightly browned. Remove onion mixture from skillet and set aside. Add shrimp to hot skillet; cook over medium heat for 2 to 4 minutes or until shrimp are opaque, turning occasionally. Stir in onion mixture and parsley.

3. Divide grits among six bowls; top with shrimp. Sprinkle with cheese and green onions. Makes 6 servings.

Baked Tomatoes and Okra

Tomatoes and okra are a traditional Southern combo. This updated version includes lima beans and is seasoned with lively crushed red pepper. Pictured on page 109.

PER SERVING: 55 cal., 0 g fat, 0 mg chol., 112 mg sodium, 12 g carb., 3 g fiber, 3 g pro. Exchanges: 2 vegetable. Carb choices: 1.

- ½ cup loose-pack frozen lima beans
- 8 ounces fresh okra, washed, stemmed, and cut into ½-inch-thick slices, or 2 cups frozen cut okra, thawed
- 4 medium tomatoes, chopped
- 1 medium onion, sliced and separated into rings
- ½ of a medium yellow or green sweet pepper, seeded and cut into thin strips
- ¼ to ½ teaspoon crushed red pepper
- ¼ teaspoon salt

1. Preheat oven to 350°F. Cook lima beans according to package directions; drain. In a 2-quart casserole, combine lima beans, okra, tomatoes, onion, sweet pepper, crushed red pepper, and salt.

2. Bake, covered, for 45 minutes; stir. Bake, uncovered, for 30 minutes more; stir. Serve with a slotted spoon. Makes 6 (⅔-cup) servings.

Quick Tip

Crab roe, or eggs, traditionally add color to the crab soup, but they are no longer commercially harvested. So you'll need to use a substitute. Try red lumpfish caviar instead; you'll find it in most large supermarkets.

Peanut Butter and Vanilla Custards

Smooth and creamy, these two-tone desserts are made with reduced-fat peanut butter and fat-free half-and-half. Pictured on page 109.

PER SERVING: 171 cal., 6 g total fat (1 g sat. fat), 0 mg chol., 172 mg sodium, 21 g carb., 1 g fiber, 7 g pro. Exchanges: 1.5 other carb., 0.5 high-fat meat. Carb choices: 1.5.

PER SERVING WITH SUGAR SUBSTITUTE: same as above, except 142 cal., 14 g carb. Exchanges: 1 other carb. Carb choices: 1.

- 2 cups fat-free half-and-half
- ¼ cup sugar or sugar substitute* equivalent to ¼ cup sugar
- 1 envelope unflavored gelatin
- ¼ cup reduced-fat creamy peanut butter
- ½ teaspoon vanilla
- 2 tablespoons dry roasted peanuts, chopped

1. In a medium saucepan, combine half-and-half, sugar, and gelatin. Let stand for 5 minutes. Cook and stir over medium heat until gelatin is dissolved. Remove from heat. Add peanut butter and vanilla. Whisk until smooth. Pour into six 6-ounce custard cups. Cover; chill about 3 hours or until set (mixture will separate into layers).

2. To serve, loosen edges and unmold custards onto individual dessert plates. Sprinkle with peanuts. Makes 6 (¾-cup) servings.

*****Sugar Substitutes:** Choose from Splenda Granular or Sweet'N Low bulk or packets. Follow package directions to use product amount equivalent to ¼ cup sugar.

She-Crab Soup

This Carolina favorite is usually made with crab roe. Red caviar, a tasty substitute, is available year-round and gives the soup a rosy hue.

PER SERVING: 160 cal., 3 g total fat (0.5 g sat. fat), 39 mg chol., 579 mg sodium, 19 g carb., 1 g fiber, 9 g pro. Exchanges: 1 starch, 1 very lean meat, 0.5 fat. Carb choices: 1.

- 1 tablespoon olive oil
- 1 cup chopped onion
- ½ cup sliced celery
- 2 cloves garlic, minced
- ⅓ cup dry sherry
- ½ cup brown rice
- 1 recipe Fish Stock (see recipe, below) or 3 cups reduced-sodium chicken broth
- 2 tablespoons crab roe or red caviar
- 2 cups fat-free half-and-half
- 8 ounces fresh or frozen cooked crabmeat, cartilage removed and flaked*
- 1 tablespoon snipped fresh chives

1. In a large saucepan, heat olive oil over medium-high heat; add onion, celery, and garlic. Cook and stir until tender. Add sherry. Bring to boil; reduce heat. Boil gently, uncovered, until liquid is nearly evaporated.

2. Stir in uncooked brown rice. Add Fish Stock and crab roe. Bring to boiling; reduce heat. Cover and simmer about 40 minutes or until rice is very tender. Cool mixture slightly.

3. In a blender, puree rice mixture, half at a time if necessary, until almost smooth. Return to saucepan; stir in half-and-half. Heat through. Stir in crabmeat. Sprinkle individual servings with snipped chives. Makes 8 (¾-cup) servings.

Fish Stock: Place the shells from 1 pound large shrimp in a large saucepan. Add 1 medium carrot, chopped; 1 stalk celery with leaves, chopped; 1 small onion, chopped; 3 sprigs fresh parsley; 1 bay leaf; 3 whole black peppercorns; and ½ teaspoon salt. Add 3½ cups water and 1 tablespoon lemon juice. Bring to boiling; reduce heat. Cover and simmer for 45 minutes. Strain through 100-percent-cotton cheesecloth; discard solids. Store stock in the refrigerator for up to 3 days or in the freezer for up to 6 months. Makes about 3 cups.

*****Test Kitchen Tip:** You can substitute canned lump crabmeat if fresh or frozen is not available.

(10 ways to lighten)

These ideas help make the recipes in this menu lighter.

1. **Fat-free half-and-half** is the rich-tasting secret to the simple yet flavorful custards.
2. **Bake** individual custards for a lovely presentation—and to control portion sizes.
3. **Rice—rather than flour—**is often used to thicken she-crab soup—overcooking the rice makes it easy to blend.
4. **Substitute smoked turkey** for ham hock, bacon, or a hunk of ham often called for in family recipes for greens. If you can't find smoked turkey, use Chris' secret—a tablespoon of peanut butter.
5. **To thin the grits,** add reduced-sodium chicken stock or fat-free milk. Grits should be smooth and silky—not too thick, not too runny.
6. **Concentrate** the flavors of Baked Tomatoes and Okra by cooking down the liquid. The more you reduce it, the more fortified the flavors will be.
7. **Review recipes** to identify high-fat, high-sodium, high-carb, and high-calorie ingredients. Reduce or eliminate those ingredients and find lighter substitutes.
8. **Make sure** the cooking method is healthful. For example, choose baking or oven frying instead of deep-fat frying.
9. **Measure** right-size portions whether the dish is a main course or served on the side.
10. **Balance the menu:** Include steamed or baked nonstarchy vegetables with your meals.

She-Crab Soup

two chefs, one great meal

When I was studying to become a chef at the Culinary Institute of America, I discovered a lifelong mentor and friend—Chef Fritz Sonnenschmidt, culinary dean of students. I'd just been diagnosed with type 1 diabetes, and my doctor recommended that I leave the food industry, knowing how strenuous the life of a chef could be. I was 27 years old and at a loss on how to proceed with my career. That's when I went to see Chef Fritz. As we sat in his office, he listened while I weighed my new health limitations against my love of cooking. He was aware of diabetes and its potential long-term effects. He was also a food expert, having attained the highest culinary status in the world, that of Certified Master Chef. "Christopher," he said, "you have to take diabetic cuisine to the next plateau." At that moment, my culinary path became clear. I began working hard to make diabetic foods more enjoyable for everyone, using fresh ingredients and lighter cooking methods. Over the years, my journey has put me in touch with thousands of people who have diabetes—through cooking programs, television shows, books, and *Diabetic Living*® magazine.

Throughout it all, I've kept in touch with Chef Fritz. During one visit, he shared he'd been diagnosed with type 2 diabetes. We were soon inspiring each other with new ideas about using lighter foods and reinventing classic culinary techniques. We decided to combine our expertise and create a fabulous meal—one that would celebrate dealing successfully with diabetes. That's how, 14 years after our life-changing conversation in his office, Chef Fritz and I reunited in the Better Homes and Gardens® Test Kitchen to prepare a classically inspired Mediterranean menu. We love how the flavors offer naturally healthful alternatives, including fresh ingredients and low-fat cooking methods. Here, we're sharing that meal with you. Invite someone who has inspired you to come over and help prepare our dinner. Fabulous food is never far from creative ideas, lively conversations, and teachers who become great friends.

As we cleaned and cut, cooked and tasted, Chef Fritz and I caught up with each other, pooling our life lessons into our recipes. It was just like being in school again—only much more fun!

"Chef Fritz and I wanted to create a meal that would celebrate dealing successfully with diabetes."

—Chef Smith

Tilapia with Herbed Shiitake Sauce and Caramelized Onion Risotto, recipes page 116

Tilapia with Herbed Shiitake Sauce

When shopping, look for moist, cleanly cut fillets with a fresh, not fishy, aroma. Pictured on page 115.

PER SERVING: 220 cal., 4 g total fat (1 g sat. fat), 75 mg chol., 369 mg sodium, 11 g carb., 1 g fiber, 32 g pro. Exchanges: 0.5 starch, 4 very lean meat, 1 fat. Carb choices: 1.

6 ½- to ¾-inch-thick fresh or frozen skinless tilapia, pollock, or cod fillets (about 2 pounds total)
Nonstick cooking spray
2 teaspoons lemon juice
¼ cup fine dry bread crumbs
¼ teaspoon salt
¼ to ½ teaspoon ground black pepper
1 recipe Herbed Shiitake Sauce (see recipe, below)
Fresh thyme sprigs (optional)
Lemon slices (optional)

1. Thaw fish, if frozen. Preheat oven to 450°F. Lightly coat a shallow baking pan with nonstick cooking spray; set aside.

2. Rinse fish; pat dry with paper towels. Brush fish with lemon juice. Arrange fish fillets, skin sides down, in the prepared baking pan. For coating, in a small bowl, combine bread crumbs, salt, and pepper. Sprinkle the crumb coating evenly onto the top sides of fish. Coat fish generously with spray.

3. Measure the thickness of the fish. Bake fish, crumb sides up, until the flesh flakes easily when tested with a fork. (Allow 4 to 6 minutes per ½-inch thickness of fish.) Do not turn the fish during baking.

4. Serve fish with Herbed Shiitake Sauce. If desired, garnish each serving with thyme sprigs and lemon slices. Makes 6 servings.

Herbed Shiitake Sauce: In a large skillet, heat 2 teaspoons olive oil over medium-high heat. Add 1½ cups sliced shiitake mushrooms and 2 tablespoons finely chopped shallots or sweet onion. Cook, uncovered, about 3 minutes or until mushrooms are tender, stirring occasionally.

Stir in 1 tablespoon all-purpose flour. Stir in ½ cup dry white wine or reduced-sodium chicken broth; cook and stir until thickened and bubbly. Add ¾ cup reduced-sodium chicken broth. Bring to boiling; reduce heat. Simmer, uncovered, for 4 minutes, stirring often.

Stir in 1 tablespoon snipped fresh chives, 1 tablespoon snipped fresh parsley, and 2 teaspoons snipped fresh thyme or ½ teaspoon crushed dried thyme. Heat through. Serve sauce with fish. Makes about 1½ cups sauce.

Quick Tip

When making the risotto, alternately adding the hot stock and rice allows the rice to absorb the liquid yet retain its shape and produce a creamy consistency. Any kind of long grain rice will work, but Italian cooks prefer Arborio rice.

Caramelized Onion Risotto

Browning the onions slowly adds a toasted caramel flavor to the rice. Pictured on page 115.

PER SERVING: 106 cal., 3 g total fat (1 g sat. fat), 4 mg chol., 227 mg sodium, 17 g carb., 0 g fiber, 4 g pro. Exchanges: 1 starch, 0.5 fat. Carb choices: 1.

1 14-ounce can reduced-sodium chicken broth
2 teaspoons olive oil
1 cup chopped onion
2 cloves garlic, minced
¾ cup Arborio rice
⅓ cup grated Parmesan cheese
¼ teaspoon ground white pepper

1. In a medium saucepan, combine chicken broth and 1½ cups *water*; heat over high heat until hot but not boiling. Reduce heat to low and keep warm.

2. Meanwhile, in a large skillet, heat oil over medium heat. Add onion; cook about 10 minutes or until onion is brown and tender. Add garlic; cook and stir for 1 minute.

3. Carefully add ½ cup of the broth mixture to onion mixture, stirring to loosen brown bits in the skillet. Bring to boiling; reduce heat. Simmer, uncovered, about 4 minutes or until the liquid is reduced by half.

4. Add uncooked rice and ½ cup of the broth mixture. Cook and stir for 3 to 4 minutes or until the rice has absorbed the liquid. Continue adding the hot broth mixture, ½ cup at a time, cooking until all of the liquid has been absorbed before adding more, stirring often.

5. When the rice is fully cooked but still slightly firm in the center, remove the skillet from the heat. Stir in the Parmesan cheese and white pepper. Serve warm. Makes 6 (⅓-cup) servings.

Mascarpone-Stuffed Figs with Valencia Orange Glaze

To cut the fat, stuff the figs with light cream cheese instead of rich Italian mascarpone.

PER SERVING: 133 cal., 5 g total fat (2 g sat. fat), 7 mg chol., 35 mg sodium, 22 g carb., 3 g fiber, 3 g pro. Exchanges: 1 fruit, 0.5 carb., 1 fat. Carb choices: 1.5.

PER SERVING WITH SUBSTITUTE: same as above, except 131 cal., 22 g carb.

3   tablespoons mascarpone cheese or reduced-fat cream cheese (Neufchâtel)
1   teaspoon sugar or sugar substitute* equivalent to 1 teaspoon sugar
8   small fresh figs**
3   sheets frozen phyllo dough (14×9-inch rectangles)
    Nonstick cooking spray
3   tablespoons very finely chopped pistachio nuts
1   recipe Valencia Orange Glaze (see recipe, below)

1. Preheat oven to 375°F. For filling, combine cheese, sugar, and 1 teaspoon orange peel (from the glaze below); set aside.

2. Wash figs gently; pat dry. Cut off any stems. Quarter lengthwise, cutting almost to bottoms. If desired, remove any seeds. Using a pastry bag fitted with a large tip or a spoon, fill the fig centers with filling. Gently press each into a teardrop shape.

3. Keep phyllo covered with plastic wrap until needed. On a clean surface, coat a sheet with spray. Sprinkle with 2 teaspoons of the nuts. Repeat with phyllo, spray, and nuts to make a stack of 3 sheets.

4. Cut stack in half lengthwise, then crosswise to make 4 rectangles. Cut each rectangle in half diagonally to make 8 triangles total.

5. For each bundle, place a filled fig on its side about 1½ inches from short edge of triangle. Bring up corners; fold remaining point over fig to enclose. Press edges to seal.

6. Arrange bundles on an ungreased baking sheet. Coat with spray; top with remaining nuts.

7. Bake bundles for 8 to 10 minutes or until phyllo is golden and crisp.

8. To serve, spoon warm Valencia Orange Glaze onto dessert plates. Top with phyllo-wrapped figs and orange wedges. Serve warm. Makes 8 servings.

Valencia Orange Glaze: Cut 2 Valencia or navel oranges into 8 wedges each; set aside. From 2 other oranges, finely shred enough peel to produce 1½ teaspoons peel (use 1 teaspoon in the mascarpone filling). Juice the 2 oranges; measure and add enough orange juice to equal 1 cup juice total.

In a large skillet, heat 1 teaspoon olive oil over medium heat. Add orange wedges; cook about 3 minutes or until brown, turning to brown evenly. Remove wedges; set aside.

In a small saucepan, stir together orange juice, 1 tablespoon honey, 2 teaspoons arrowroot or cornstarch, and remaining ½ teaspoon orange peel. Cook and stir until thickened (do not boil if using arrowroot). (If using cornstarch, cook and stir until thickened and bubbly. Cook and stir for 2 minutes more.) Remove saucepan from heat. Serve with figs. Makes 1 cup glaze.

*Sugar Substitutes: Choose from Splenda Granular or Sweet'N Low bulk or packets. Follow the package directions to use product amount equivalent to 1 teaspoon sugar.

**Test Kitchen Tip: If you can't find fresh figs, use 8 dried figs. In medium saucepan, combine dried figs and enough water to cover. Heat to boiling; reduce heat. Cover and simmer for 5 minutes. Remove from heat; let stand for 15 minutes. Drain and cool. Continue cutting and filling as directed in Step 2.

sweet carolina barbecue

When you're talking good barbecue, everyone has an opinion and that varies by region. Folks living in the Carolinas (my neck of the woods these days) believe nothing's finer than slow-roasted pork.

Since moving to North Carolina, I've tasted as many versions of barbecue as possible. I know I have to take it easy because it's possible to have too much of a good thing—especially when generous cooks are serving up the sides. In the Carolinas, it's not barbecue unless you have some good ol' slaw and baked beans alongside. Both can be good for you, but not if they're laden with high-fat creamy dressing or bacon. So after savoring the flavors, I wanted to re-create them in more healthful ways.

My simple Country Slaw is a great addition to any summer table. You can make it a day ahead to let the flavors develop. For the baked beans, I start with dry beans instead of canned so I can control the sodium and fat. It's a true from-scratch recipe with a few surprises—healthful alternatives to the salty, fatty ham hock that's typically used for flavor.

My style of barbecue pork is not quite the 12-hour process that's traditional in this region. Mine cooks for only 3 or 4 hours. But when it's time to eat, I can't slice it fast enough! Try some of these Carolina-style dishes and savor finger-licking barbecue again.

> In the Carolinas, it's not barbecue unless you have some good ol' slaw and baked beans along-side the meat.
>
> —Chef Smith

Old-Fashioned Peach Cobbler recipe, page 122

Country Slaw recipe, page 121

Carolina Barbecued Pork, recipe, page 122, and **Country Slaw** and **Baked Navy Beans,** recipes, page 121

There's no reason to forgo all the great foods of summer. Take these classic recipes that Chef Chris has modified to fit a diabetic meal plan and serve them at your next summer gathering. Saucy tender pork, classic coleslaw, and cobbler to enjoy for the finale all make summertime even more delicious.

119

(your own style)

You can add flavor to barbecue meats by using different woods, spicy seasoning rubs, and tangy "mopping" sauces.

The wood: To add a smoky flavor, choose hickory, oak, mesquite, apple, or any hardwood from a fruit- or nut-bearing tree. (Don't use a softwood, such as pine, spruce, or fir, because the resin will ruin the meat.) Make sure the wood is seasoned or dry because green wood can be bitter and may affect the flavor of the meat. Use prepackaged, precut wood chunks (about the size of a fist) from a home improvement or hardware store. Soak wood for about 30 minutes so it smolders and smokes rather than burns.

The rub: This blend of dry herbs and spices is rubbed onto the meat for added flavor. Mix and match seasonings as you wish for rubs that range from surprisingly sweet to savory to fire-spitting hot! Use enough to lightly coat the meat, then let it sit at room temperature for 30 minutes or in the refrigerator for up to 24 hours.

The mopping sauce: This thin brush-on usually consists of vinegar, tomato paste, herbs, and spices but can also include beer, wine, broth, and fruit juices. Just keep an eye on the carbs and sodium. Brush the meat with the mopping sauce every hour.

Baked Navy Beans

Start from scratch with dry navy beans to avoid the sodium that's in canned beans. Pictured on page 119.

PER SERVING: 211 cal., 4 g total fat (1 g sat. fat), 0 mg chol., 252 mg sodium, 36 g carb., 10 g fiber, 11 g pro. Exchanges: 2.5 starch, 1 very lean meat. Carb choices: 2.5.

PER SERVING WITH SUBSTITUTE: same as above, except 203 cal., 33 g carb. Exchanges: 2 starch. Carb choices: 2.

- 1 pound dry navy beans
- 8 cups water
- 2 cups chopped onions
- 2 cloves garlic, minced
- 1 tablespoon olive oil
- 2 14-ounce cans (3½ cups) reduced-sodium chicken broth
- 3 cups water
- ¼ cup molasses
- ¼ cup ketchup
- 3 tablespoons peanut butter
- 2 tablespoons packed brown sugar or brown sugar substitute* equivalent to 2 tablespoons brown sugar
- 1 tablespoon yellow mustard
- 1 teaspoon Worcestershire sauce

1. Rinse beans. In a 4-quart Dutch oven, combine beans and the 8 cups water. Cover; let soak in a cool place for 6 to 8 hours or overnight. (Or bring to boiling; reduce heat. Simmer for 2 minutes. Remove from heat. Cover; let stand for 1 hour.) Rinse and drain beans.

2. In the same Dutch oven, cook onions and garlic in hot oil until tender, stirring occasionally.

3. Add the drained navy beans, chicken broth, and the 3 cups water. Bring to boiling; reduce heat. Cover and simmer over low heat for 1 to 1½ hours or until beans are tender, stirring occasionally during cooking. Drain the beans, reserving the cooking liquid.

4. Meanwhile, preheat oven to 300°F. Return drained beans to the Dutch oven. Stir in 2 cups of the reserved cooking liquid, the molasses, ketchup, peanut butter, brown sugar, mustard, and Worcestershire sauce.

5. Bake, covered, about 2½ hours or until desired consistency, stirring the beans occasionally. Makes 12 (½-cup) servings.

*Sugar Substitutes: Choose from Sweet'N Low Brown or Sugar Twin Granulated Brown. Follow the package directions to use the product amount that's equivalent to 2 tablespoons brown sugar.

Country Slaw

A sweet-and-sour dressing and sweet onions lend fantastic flavor to this homey side salad. Pictured on page 119.

PER SERVING: 45 cal., 0 g total fat (0 g sat. fat), 0 mg chol., 159 mg sodium, 10 g carb., 2 g fiber, 2 g pro. Exchanges: 1 vegetable, 0.5 carb. Carb choices: 0.5.

PER SERVING WITH SUBSTITUTE: same as above, except 33 cal., 8 g carb.

- 1 recipe Tomato Vinaigrette (see recipe, below)
- 3 pounds cabbage, cored and cut into small chunks
- 2 medium carrots, peeled and sliced
- 1 medium sweet onion (such as Vidalia, Maui, or Walla Walla), cut into chunks

1. Prepare Tomato Vinaigrette; set aside.

2. Place cabbage, carrots, and onion in a food processor. Working in batches, cover and process vegetables until chopped. Transfer vegetables to a very large bowl.

3. Pour the warm vinaigrette onto chopped vegetables; toss gently to coat. Cover and chill for 2 hours. Makes 16 (about ½-cup) servings.

Tomato Vinaigrette: In a small saucepan, combine ¾ cup cider vinegar, ¼ cup sugar or sugar substitute* equivalent to ¼ cup sugar, ¼ cup ketchup, 1 tablespoon Dijon-style mustard, 1½ teaspoons celery seeds, ½ teaspoon salt, and ¼ teaspoon ground black pepper. Bring to boiling; reduce heat. Simmer, uncovered, for 6 to 8 minutes or until liquid is reduced to ¾ cup. (The aroma from the simmering vinegar is potent! Be careful not to breathe too deeply while liquid is steaming.) Remove from heat; cool for 15 minutes.

*Sugar Substitutes: Choose from Splenda Granular, Equal Spoonful or packets, or Sweet'N Low bulk or packets. Follow the package directions to use the product amount equivalent to ¼ cup sugar. If using Equal Spoonful or packets, stir the sweetener into the vinaigrette after removing the saucepan from the heat.

Make-Ahead Directions: Prepare the slaw as directed, except cover and chill for up to 8 hours.

Carolina Barbecued Pork

Finely chopped pork is traditional in the Lexington area of the Carolinas, while pulled or coarsely chopped pork is more popular on the coast. Pictured on page 119.

PER SERVING: 267 cal., 11 g fat (4 g sat. fat), 113 mg chol., 307 mg sodium, 4 g carb., 0 g fiber, 34 g pro. Exchanges: 5 lean meat. Carb choices: 0.

- **5** or 6 mesquite wood chunks
- **1** 6- to 8-pound boneless pork shoulder roast, rolled and tied
- **1** recipe Sweet 'n' Spicy Rub (see recipe, below)
- **1** recipe Herb Vinegar Basting Sauce (see recipe, below)

1. At least 1 hour before cooking, soak wood chunks in enough water to cover. Drain before using.

2. Sprinkle roast evenly on all sides with Sweet 'n' Spicy Rub; rub in with your fingers. Center roast on spit rod of rotisserie; secure with holding forks.* Test balance, making adjustments as necessary. Arrange medium coals around a drip pan. Add wood chunks to coals. Attach spit, then turn on the motor and cover grill.

3. Let the roast rotate over the drip pan for 3 to 3¼ hours or until an instant-read thermometer inserted in the center of the roast registers 170°F, brushing occasionally with Herb Vinegar Basting Sauce during the last hour of grilling. Add additional coals and wood chunks as needed to maintain temperature and smoke during grilling.

4. Remove the roast from the spit; wrap in foil. Let rest for 15 minutes. Remove foil and string; remove and discard fat. Chop or shred the pork. Makes 16 to 24 servings.

Sweet 'n' Spicy Rub: In a small bowl, stir together 2 tablespoons packed brown sugar, 2 teaspoons chili powder, 1½ teaspoons kosher salt, 1½ teaspoons garlic powder, 1½ teaspoons onion powder, 1½ teaspoons ground cumin, ¾ teaspoon cayenne pepper, and ¾ teaspoon ground black pepper. Makes about ½ cup.

Herb Vinegar Basting Sauce: In a large saucepan, combine 2 cups cider vinegar, 2 tablespoons tomato paste, 1 tablespoon packed brown sugar, 3 minced cloves garlic, 1 teaspoon poultry seasoning, 1 teaspoon crushed red pepper, ½ teaspoon snipped fresh rosemary, and ½ teaspoon snipped fresh thyme. Bring to boiling; reduce heat. Simmer, uncovered, for 5 minutes. Remove from heat; let cool. Strain liquid; discard solids. Makes 1¾ cups.

Quick Tip

When grilling, place big pieces of meat in the center of the grill, with the coals on the sides. Use a meat thermometer to test for doneness—pork should be 160°F. To be sure it's done, check that the meat's texture is fibrous, not fleshy looking.

*Test Kitchen Tip: If you don't have a rotisserie, you can use a covered charcoal grill or a gas grill.

For the charcoal grill, arrange medium coals around a drip pan. Add wood chunks to coals. Test for medium-low heat above the drip pan. Place the roast on the grill rack over the drip pan. Cover and grill roast for 3 to 3¼ hours or until an instant-read thermometer inserted in the center of the roast registers 170°F, brushing occasionally with Herb Vinegar Basting Sauce during the last hour of grilling. Add additional coals and wood chunks as needed to maintain the temperature and smoke during grilling.

For the gas grill, preheat grill. Reduce heat to medium-low. Adjust for indirect cooking. Grill as above, except place roast on a rack in a roasting pan.

Old-Fashioned Peach Cobbler

Taste the peaches to make sure they're ripe and juicy.

PER SERVING: 175 cal., 4 g fat (3 g sat. fat), 11 mg chol., 129 mg sodium, 34 g carb., 4 g fiber, 3 g pro. Exchanges: 1 fruit, 1 carb., 1 fat. Carb choices: 2.

PER SERVING WITH SUBSTITUTE: same as above, except 147 cal., 28 g carb. Exchanges: 0.5 carb.

- **⅓** cup sugar or sugar substitute* equivalent to ⅓ cup sugar
- **2** tablespoons cornstarch
- **½** teaspoon ground cinnamon
- **10** cups sliced, pitted fresh peaches (3½ to 4 pounds) or 10 cups frozen unsweetened peach slices, thawed
- **½** cup water
- **1¼** cups whole wheat flour

Old-Fashioned Peach Cobbler

2 tablespoons sugar or sugar substitute* equivalent to
2 tablespoons sugar
¾ teaspoon baking powder
¼ teaspoon baking soda
¼ teaspoon salt
¼ cup butter
½ cup buttermilk
Vanilla frozen yogurt (optional)

1. Preheat oven to 400°F. For filling, in a very large bowl, stir together the ⅓ cup sugar, the cornstarch, and cinnamon. Add the sliced peaches and toss gently to mix. Gently stir in the water. Spread the peach mixture evenly in a 3-quart rectangular baking dish. Set aside.

2. For the whole wheat biscuit star cutouts, in a medium bowl, stir together whole wheat flour, the 2 tablespoons sugar, the baking powder, baking soda, and salt. Using a pastry blender, cut in butter until mixture resembles coarse crumbs. Make a well in the center of the flour mixture. Add buttermilk all at once. Using a fork, stir just until the flour mixture is moistened. Knead the dough gently to shape into a ball.

3. On a lightly floured surface, roll dough to ½-inch thickness. Using a 2- to 2½-inch star cookie cutter, cut out 12 stars, rerolling as needed. Arrange the dough stars on top of the fruit mixture.

4. Bake, uncovered, for 25 to 30 minutes or until the stars are light brown and the peach mixture is bubbly in the center. Cool on a wire rack for 30 minutes. Serve warm. If desired, serve with frozen yogurt. Makes 12 servings (1 star plus about ⅔ cup peach mixture).

*Sugar Substitutes: Choose from Splenda Granular or Sweet'N Low bulk or packets. Follow the package directions to use the product amounts equivalent to ⅓ cup and 2 tablespoons sugar.

Make-Ahead Directions: Prepare the biscuit star cutouts as directed in Steps 2 and 3. Cover with plastic wrap and chill for up to 4 hours. Continue to assemble the cobbler as directed in Steps 1 and 4.

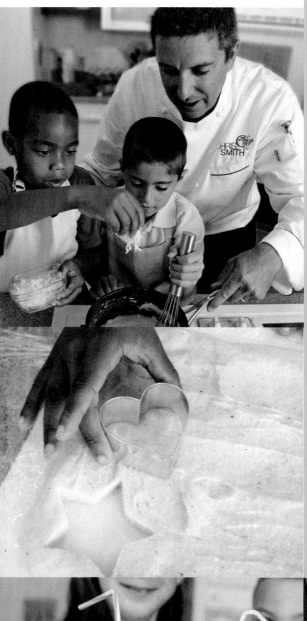

cooking class

As I've learned from my sons, children can have a pretty limited palate. Comfort foods rule, and new items that could broaden young horizons are met with a polite but determined "No, thank you." Unfortunately, top kid picks such as chicken nuggets, pizza, and fries often don't meet nutrition standards. That's why it's important to start kids on the path to healthful eating when they're young to reduce their risk of obesity and diabetes.

The kitchen is the best place to introduce kids to new foods, as I've discovered by teaching children's cooking classes. Start them as young as you like with simple tasks such as picking and washing vegetables.

Making dinner can be a great way for kids to demonstrate their food skills. Imagine your son proudly pouring his homemade ruby-color cooler or your granddaughter showing how she cut out cool polenta shapes. In either case, your young cooks will be more willing to experiment with new flavors and textures, choose more healthful foods, and, as a result, stay healthier as they grow toward and past the teen years. Try our kid-tested and -approved dinner menu with some children you know and taste for yourself.

With each recipe we prepared in class, kids jumped in on the cooking process. The Pomegranate Cooler is a simple mix-and-sip recipe, perfect for little ones to help.

Pomegranate Cooler
recipe, page 126

Start with a bunch of kids; add a pinch of flavor, a few favorite foods, and a dash of fun. What do you have? A lesson that opens a whole new world of healthful cooking and eating.

"It's important to start kids on the path to healthful eating when they're young."

—Chef Smith

125

Chicken Cordon Bleu, Cheese Polenta Cutouts, Pea Pods with **Dipping Sauces,** and **Pomegranate Cooler** recipes begin on page 126

Chicken Cordon Bleu

Cutting pockets in the chicken is more kid friendly than wrapping the pounded meat around the filling.

PER SERVING: 322 cal., 10 g total fat (3 g sat. fat), 114 mg chol., 278 mg sodium, 7 g carbo., 0 g fiber, 47 g pro. Exchanges: 0.5 starch, 6.5 very lean meat, 1 fat. Carb choices: 0.5.

- 6 medium chicken breast halves with bone (3½ to 4 pounds total)
- 2 ounces reduced-sodium cooked boneless ham, finely chopped (about ½ cup)
- ½ cup shredded **Swiss cheese** (2 ounces)
- ¼ cup refrigerated or frozen egg product, thawed, or **1 egg**
- 1 tablespoon water
- ½ cup fine dry bread crumbs
- 2 tablespoons olive oil

1. Preheat oven to 375°F. Line a 15×10×1-inch baking pan with foil; set aside. Remove skin from chicken and discard. Using a small sharp knife, cut a horizontal pocket about 2 inches long and 1 inch deep in the meatier side of each chicken breast half.

2. For stuffing, in a small bowl, combine ham and cheese. Divide stuffing among pockets in chicken breast halves.

3. In a shallow dish, beat egg; stir in water. In another shallow dish, place crumbs. Dip stuffed chicken into egg mixture, then into crumbs, turning to coat. Arrange chicken breast halves, meaty sides up, in the prepared baking pan. Drizzle with olive oil. Bake for 45 to 55 minutes or until chicken is tender and no longer pink (170°F). Makes 6 servings.

Cheese Polenta Cutouts

Make flowers, stars, and hearts.

PER SERVING: 123 cal., 4 g total fat (2 g sat. fat), 11 mg chol., 275 mg sodium, 16 g carbo., 1 g fiber, 6 g pro. Exchanges: 1 starch, 0.5 medium-fat meat. Carb choices: 1.

PER SERVING WITH SPINACH: same as above, except 124 cal., 279 mg sodium, 2 g fiber.

PER SERVING WITH MUSHROOM: same as above, except 146 cal., 6 g total fat (3 g sat. fat), 276 mg sodium, 2 g fiber. Exchanges: 0.5 fat.

- 1 **14-ounce can reduced-sodium chicken broth**
- 1¼ cups cold water
- 1 cup yellow cornmeal
- ½ cup shredded part-skim mozzarella cheese (2 ounces)
- ¼ cup finely shredded **Asiago** or **Parmesan cheese** (1 ounce)
- **Nonstick cooking spray**

1. Line a 13×9×2-inch baking pan with plastic wrap, allowing ends to hang over; set aside. In a medium saucepan, bring broth to boiling. In a small bowl, stir together water and cornmeal; slowly add to boiling broth. Return to boiling, carefully stirring. Reduce heat. Cook about 10 minutes or until very thick, stirring often.

2. Remove from heat. Stir in cheeses. Pour into prepared pan; spread evenly to edges. Cover with plastic wrap; chill for 1 to 24 hours or until firm.

3. Preheat oven to 375°F. Coat a baking sheet with cooking spray; set pan aside. Use plastic wrap to lift polenta from pan. Using 2- to 2½-inch cutters, cut polenta into shapes. (Or using a knife, cut polenta into 2- to 2½-inch squares.)

4. Arrange cutouts on the prepared baking sheet. Bake about 10 minutes or until heated through. Serve warm. Makes 6 servings (four 2-inch or two 2½-inch cutouts each).

Spinach Polenta: Stir 1 cup coarsely chopped fresh spinach into cornmeal mixture after adding cheeses.

Mushroom Polenta: In a medium skillet, cook 1 cup chopped mushrooms in 1 tablespoon hot olive oil until tender. Stir into cornmeal mixture after adding the cheeses.

Pomegranate Cooler

Kids love this fizzy fruit drink—a nutritious option to high-carb sodas. Pictured on page 124.

PER SERVING: 38 cal., 0 g total fat (0 sat. fat), 0 mg chol., 7 mg sodium, 9 g carbo., 0 g fiber, 0 g pro. Exchanges: 0.5 fruit. Carb choices: 0.5.

- 1 cup pomegranate juice (half of a 16-ounce bottle), chilled
- ½ cup chopped fresh pineapple
- 2 cups ice cubes
- 1 cup diet lemon-lime carbonated beverage, chilled

1. In a blender, combine juice and pineapple; cover and blend until smooth. Gradually add ice cubes, blending until slushy.

2. Transfer juice mixture to a pitcher. Slowly pour in the carbonated beverage. Pour into glasses. Makes 5 (6-ounce) servings.

Apple-Apricot Tartlets
Spoon the fruit into Oat Tart Shells.

PER TART: 138 cal., 6 g total fat (4 g sat. fat), 17 mg chol., 118 mg sodium, 18 g carbo., 2 g fiber, 3 g pro. Exchanges: 1 carbo., 1 fat. Carb choices: 1.

1   recipe **Oat Tart Shells** (see recipe, right)
1   medium Granny Smith apple, cored and thinly sliced
2   tablespoons water or apple juice
2   tablespoons low-sugar apricot preserves
4   canned apricot halves, rinsed, drained, and sliced
½   cup fresh or canned pineapple chunks, drained if necessary

1. Prepare Oat Tart Shells; set aside. In a small saucepan, combine apple slices and the water. Bring just to boiling; reduce heat. Cover and simmer for 2 to 3 minutes or just until apple slices are softened. Gently stir in preserves. Stir in apricots and pineapple. Spoon fruit mixture into Oat Tart Shells. Makes 12 tarts.

Oat Tart Shells: Preheat oven to 350°F. In a bowl, stir together $2/3$ cup quick-cooking rolled oats, $1/2$ cup whole wheat flour, and $1/4$ cup all-purpose flour; set aside. In large bowl, combine $1/2$ of an 8-ounce package softened reduced-fat cream cheese (Neufchâtel) and $1/4$ cup softened butter; beat with electric mixer on medium to high speed for 30 seconds. Add $1/4$ cup packed brown sugar,* $1/4$ teaspoon baking soda, $1/4$ teaspoon ground cinnamon, and $1/8$ teaspoon salt; beat until mixed. Beat in as much oat mixture as you can with mixer. Using a wooden spoon, stir in remaining oat mixture. Divide dough among twelve $2 1/2$-inch muffin cups. Press dough onto bottom and about 1 inch up side of each cup. Using a fork, prick dough in several places in each muffin cup. Bake for 10 to 12 minutes or until edges of crusts are light brown. Cool in muffin cups on wire rack for 5 minutes. Remove shells from cups; cool on a wire rack.

*Test Kitchen Tip: We don't recommend using brown sugar substitute for this recipe.

main-dish
salads

Balsamic Chicken over Greens

Including main-dish salads in your meal plans makes good sense. Pack them with colorful veggies and, to keep the fat and sodium low, make your own dressings or vinaigrettes. A well-crafted salad can be as satisfying as any entrée.

Balsamic Chicken over Greens

Basil adds freshness and flavor to this easy salad.

PER SERVING: 150 cal., 2 g total fat (1 g sat. fat), 66 mg chol., 312 mg sodium, 4 g carb., 1 g fiber, 27 g pro. Exchanges: 1.5 vegetable, 3.5 very lean meat. Carb choices: 0.

  4 skinless, boneless chicken breast halves
     (1 to 1¼ pounds total)
  ¾ cup bottled fat-free or reduced-fat balsamic
     vinaigrette salad dressing
  3 cloves garlic, minced
  ¼ teaspoon crushed red pepper
  1 8-ounce package torn mixed greens (8 cups)
  ¼ cup fresh basil leaves

1. Place chicken breast halves in a resealable plastic bag set in a shallow dish.

2. For marinade, combine ½ cup of the vinaigrette, garlic, and pepper; pour onto chicken. Seal bag; turn to coat. Marinate in refrigerator for 1 to 4 hours, turning the bag occasionally.

3. Drain chicken; reserve marinade. Grill on the rack of an uncovered grill directly over medium coals for 12 to 15 minutes or until chicken is no longer pink (170° F), turning once and brushing with marinade halfway through grilling. Discard marinade.

4. Cut each breast across the grain into strips. Arrange greens and basil on four plates; top with chicken strips. Serve with remaining ¼ cup vinaigrette. Makes 4 servings (2 cups greens and 4 ounces chicken each).

Citrus Chicken Salad

Next time you cook chicken breasts,
make extra to save for this salad.

PER SERVING: 304 cal., 8 g total fat (2 g sat. fat), 72 mg chol, 422 mg sodium, 28 g carb., 3 g fiber, 31 g pro. Exchanges: 1 vegetable, 0.5 fruit, 0.5 starch, 0.5 other carb., 4 very lean meat, 1 fat. Carb choices: 2.

- ¼ cup white wine vinegar or cider vinegar
- 2 tablespoons Dijon-style mustard
- ¼ cup snipped fresh oregano or 1 teaspoon dried oregano, crushed
- 4 teaspoons low-calorie orange marmalade
- 4 teaspoons salad oil
- ¼ teaspoon salt
- ¼ teaspoon ground black pepper
- 4 cups fresh baby spinach
- 2 11-ounce cans mandarin orange sections, drained
- 1 cup loose-pack frozen whole kernel corn
- 12 ounces cooked chicken breast, shredded, or two 6-ounce packages refrigerated cooked chicken breast strips*

1. For dressing, in a screw-top jar, combine vinegar, mustard, oregano, marmalade, oil, salt, and pepper; cover and shake well.

2. In a large bowl, place the spinach, orange sections, and corn. Add dressing and chicken to spinach mixture. Toss to coat. Makes 4 (2-cup) servings.

Test Kitchen Tip: If using refrigerated cooked chicken breast strips, omit the ⅛ teaspoon salt from the dressing.

Sesame Chicken Salad

Whole baby corn, colorful radishes, and an aromatic
sesame dressing make this a very special salad.

PER SERVING: 154 cal., 5 g total fat (1 g sat. fat), 44 mg chol., 286 mg sodium, 7 g carb., 2 g fiber, 19 g pro. Exchanges: 1.5 vegetable, 2.5 very lean meat, 0.5 fat. Carb choices: 0.5.

- Nonstick cooking spray
- 4 skinless, boneless chicken breast halves (1 to 1½ pounds total)
- Salt
- Ground black pepper
- 1 10-ounce package torn Italian-style or European-style salad greens
- 1 14- or 15-ounce can whole baby corn, drained and halved crosswise
- ½ cup coarsely shredded carrot
- ¼ cup sliced radishes
- ½ of a large red onion, halved and thinly sliced
- 1 recipe Sesame-Orange Dressing (see recipe, below)
- 1½ teaspoons sesame seeds, toasted*

1. Lightly coat an unheated large nonstick skillet with cooking spray. Preheat over medium heat. Sprinkle chicken lightly with salt and pepper. Place in hot skillet. Cook for 10 to 12 minutes or until no longer pink (170°F), turning once halfway through cooking. Transfer chicken to a cutting board. Cut into bite-size strips; set aside to cool slightly.

2. Divide salad greens among six dinner plates. Arrange chicken, whole baby corn, carrot, radishes, and red onion over greens. Pour dressing over salads. Sprinkle with sesame seeds. Makes 6 servings.

Sesame-Orange Dressing: In a screw-top jar, combine ½ cup orange juice, ¼ cup rice vinegar or white vinegar, 1 tablespoon salad oil, 1 teaspoon toasted sesame oil, ¼ teaspoon salt, and ¼ teaspoon ground black pepper. Cover and shake well. Chill until serving time.

Note: To toast sesame seeds, in a small nonstick skillet, cook and stir sesame seeds over medium heat about 1 minute or just until golden brown. Watch closely so the seeds don't burn. Remove from heat; transfer to a bowl to cool completely.

Grilled Chicken and Wild Rice Salad

Be sure you're using a plain rice mix instead of one with salty seasonings.

PER SERVING: 262 cal., 2 g total fat (0 g sat. fat), 66 mg chol., 982 mg sodium, 29 g carb., 3 g fiber, 31 g pro. Exchanges: 1 vegetable, 1.5 starch, 3.5 very lean meat. Carb choices: 2.

- 1 **6-ounce package long grain and wild rice mix**
- ⅔ **cup bottled fat-free Italian salad dressing**
- 6 **skinless, boneless chicken breast halves (1½ to 1¾ pounds total)**
- 1 **cup loose-pack frozen French-cut green beans**
- 1 **14-ounce can artichoke hearts, drained and quartered**
- 2½ **cups packaged shredded cabbage with carrot (coleslaw mix)**
  Lettuce leaves (optional)

1. Prepare long grain and wild rice mix according to package directions. Transfer to a medium bowl. Cover and chill about 2 hours or until cold.

2. Place 3 tablespoons of the Italian salad dressing in a bowl. Set aside remaining dressing.

3. Place chicken on the rack of an uncovered grill directly over medium coals. Grill for 12 to 15 minutes or until chicken is tender and no longer pink (170°F), turning once and brushing with the 3 tablespoons dressing the last 2 minutes.

4. Meanwhile, rinse frozen green beans with cool water for 30 seconds; drain well. In a large bowl, toss together beans, chilled cooked rice mix, artichoke hearts, and coleslaw mix. Pour the reserved Italian salad dressing over the rice mixture; toss gently to coat.

5. Slice grilled chicken; serve over wild rice mixture. If desired, garnish salad with lettuce leaves. Makes 6 servings (1 cup salad and 1 chicken breast half each).

131

Turkey-Spinach Salad

For the holidays, cut the cranberry sauce into tiny gingerbread man, Santa, or stocking shapes.

NUTRITION FACTS PER SERVING: 120 cal., 1 g total fat (0 g sat. fat), 20 mg chol., 131 mg sodium, 17 g carb., 2 g dietary fiber, 10 g pro. Exchanges: 0.5 other carb., 1 very lean meat, 2 vegetable. Carb choices: 1.

- **1 8-ounce can or ½ of a 16-ounce can jellied cranberry sauce**
- **⅓ cup cider vinegar**
- **2 teaspoons coarsely snipped fresh sage or tarragon or ½ teaspoon dried leaf sage or dried tarragon, crushed**
- **¼ teaspoon salt**
- **⅛ teaspoon ground black pepper**
- **12 cups fresh baby spinach**
- **8 ounces cooked turkey breast, thinly sliced, coarsely chopped, or shredded**
- **1 medium cucumber, halved lengthwise and thinly sliced (about 2 cups)**
- **6 ounces jicama, peeled and cut into thin bite-size strips (about 1½ cups)**
- **6 medium radishes, thinly sliced**
- **½ of a medium red onion, cut into rings**

1. Cut jellied cranberry sauce into ½-inch-thick slices. Using 1- to 1¼-inch cutters, cut 16 designs from the cranberry sauce slices; set aside. Reserve cranberry sauce trimmings.

2. For dressing, place remaining scraps of cranberry sauce in a blender; add vinegar, sage or tarragon, salt, and pepper. Cover and blend until combined. Set aside.

3. In a large bowl, toss together spinach, turkey, cucumber, jicama, radishes, and red onion. Divide spinach mixture among eight serving bowls. Add two of the cranberry cutouts to each serving; drizzle with dressing. Makes 8 servings.

Sweet-and-Sour Chicken Slaw

Spreadable fruit helps keep the dressing for this chicken-studded coleslaw low in calories.

NUTRITION FACTS PER SERVING: 285 cal., 10 g total fat (1 g sat. fat), 72 mg chol., 81 mg sodium, 21 g carb., 3 g fiber, 28 g pro. Exchanges: 1 other carb., 3.5 very lean meat, 1.5 vegetable, 1.5 fat. Carb choices: 1.5.

- **12 ounces cooked chicken breast, shredded or chopped***
- **4 cups packaged shredded cabbage with carrot (coleslaw mix)**
- **1 cup fresh pea pods, trimmed and halved**
- **¼ cup raspberry or strawberry spreadable fruit**
- **2 tablespoons canola oil**
- **4 teaspoons cider vinegar**
- **1 red apple, cored and chopped**

1. In a large bowl, combine chicken, coleslaw mix, and pea pods; set aside. In a small bowl, whisk together spreadable fruit, oil, and cider vinegar; add apple and toss to coat. Add apple mixture to cabbage mixture; toss to coat. Makes 4 (1¾-cup) servings

*Test Kitchen Tip: Use leftover cooked chicken breast, deli-cooked chicken breast, or canned chicken breast, drained.

Make-Ahead Directions: Prepare as directed. Cover and chill for up to 1 hour before serving.

Citrus Turkey Spinach Salad

Pink grapefruit and Orange-Poppy Seed Dressing transform traditional spinach salad into a refreshing meal.

PER SERVING: 251 cal., 10 g total fat (2 g sat. fat), 43 mg chol., 233 mg sodium, 22 g carb., 4 g fiber, 20 g pro. Exchanges: 1 fruit, 2 very lean meat, 1.5 vegetable, 2 fat. Carb choices: 1.5.

8 cups fresh baby spinach or torn fresh spinach
8 ounces cooked turkey, cut up
2 medium pink grapefruit, peeled and sectioned
2 medium oranges, peeled and sectioned
1 recipe Orange-Poppy Seed Dressing (see recipe, right)
2 tablespoons sliced almonds, toasted (optional)

1. In a large bowl, combine spinach, turkey, grapefruit sections, and orange sections.

2. Shake Orange-Poppy Seed Dressing; pour over salad. Toss gently to coat. If desired, sprinkle with almonds. Makes 4 (2-cup) servings.

Orange-Poppy Seed Dressing: In a screw-top jar, combine ¼ cup orange juice, 2 tablespoons olive oil, 1 teaspoon honey, ½ teaspoon poppy seeds, ¼ teaspoon salt, and ¼ teaspoon dry mustard. Cover and shake well. Chill until serving time, up to 24 hours.

Citrus Turkey Spinach Salad

Dilled Tuna
Potato Salad

Grilled Tuna Salad Niçoise

"Niçoise" means that a food is prepared in the cooking style of Nice, a city in France. Traditional ingredients in salad niçoise include anchovies, potatoes, green beans, ripe olives, and tuna.

PER SERVING: 282 cal., 10 g total fat (1 g sat. fat), 51 mg chol., 408 mg sodium, 17 g carb., 4 g fiber, 31 g pro. Exchanges: 0.5 starch, 3.5 very lean meat, 2 vegetable, 1.5 fat. Carb choices: 1.

- 1 pound fresh or frozen tuna steaks, cut 1 inch thick
- 1 recipe **Dijon Sherry Vinaigrette** (see recipe, below)
- 8 ounces tiny new potatoes, quartered
- 6 ounces fresh green beans
- 6 cups **Bibb or Boston lettuce leaves**
- ¾ cup thinly sliced radishes
- ½ cup niçoise olives or ripe olives, pitted
- **Finely chopped red onion (optional)**
- **Cracked black pepper (optional)**

1. Thaw fish, if frozen. Rinse fish; pat dry with paper towels. Brush fish with 1 tablespoon of the Dijon Sherry Vinaigrette. Set aside remaining vinaigrette.

2. Grill fish on the greased rack of an uncovered grill directly over medium heat for 8 to 12 minutes or until fish flakes easily when tested with a fork, gently turning once halfway through grilling.

3. Meanwhile, in a covered medium saucepan, cook potatoes in boiling water for 7 minutes. Add beans; cook about 2 minutes more or until potatoes are tender. Drain; cool slightly.

4. To serve, slice fish. On a platter, arrange fish, potatoes, beans, lettuce leaves, radish slices, and olives. If desired, top with onion and cracked pepper. Stir remaining vinaigrette; serve with salad. Makes 4 servings.

Broiling Directions: Prepare fish as directed in Step 1. Preheat broiler. Arrange on the greased unheated rack of a broiler pan. Broil about 4 inches from heat for 8 to 12 minutes or until fish flakes easily when tested with a fork, turning once halfway through broiling.

Dijon Sherry Vinaigrette: In a small bowl, combine 3 tablespoons sherry vinegar and 2 tablespoons finely chopped shallots. Whisk in 1 tablespoon Dijon-style mustard. Whisking constantly, pour in 2 tablespoons olive oil in a thin, steady stream. Stir in 1 rinsed and mashed anchovy fillet, ⅛ teaspoon salt, and ⅛ teaspoon ground white pepper. Cover and chill.

Dilled Tuna Potato Salad

Light mayonnaise and fat-free yogurt make a slimmer creamy dressing for this spin on the classic.

PER SERVING: 243 cal., 10 g total fat (2 g sat. fat), 96 mg chol., 461 mg sodium, 22 g carb., 5 g fiber, 18 g pro. Exchanges: 1.5 vegetable, 1 starch, 2 very lean meat, 1.5 fat. Carb choices: 1.5.

- 3 medium red potatoes (about 1 pound)
- ½ cup light mayonnaise or salad dressing
- ½ cup plain fat-free yogurt
- 1 tablespoon snipped fresh dill or 1 teaspoon dried dill
- 1 tablespoon fat-free milk
- ½ teaspoon finely shredded lemon peel
- ¼ teaspoon salt
- 1 clove garlic, minced
- 1 cup chopped cucumber
- ¼ cup sliced green onions
- ¼ cup coarsely chopped radishes
- 1 9-ounce can chunk white tuna (water-pack), drained and broken into chunks
- 2 hard-cooked eggs, chopped
- 12 leaves savoy cabbage or Chinese (napa) cabbage

1. Scrub potatoes; cut into ½-inch cubes. In a covered medium saucepan, cook potatoes in a small amount of boiling water for 10 to 12 minutes or just until tender. Drain and cool slightly.

2. Meanwhile, in a large bowl, stir together mayonnaise, yogurt, dill, milk, lemon peel, salt, and garlic. Stir in cucumber, green onions, and radishes. Add cooked potatoes, tuna, and eggs; toss gently to coat. Cover and chill for 4 to 6 hours.

3. To serve, line bowls with cabbage leaves. Gently stir tuna mixture; spoon onto cabbage leaves. Makes 6 (1-cup) servings.

Lemon Shrimp Salad

This tossed salad owes its Louisiana-style flavor
to Cajun seasoning and shrimp.

NUTRITION FACTS PER SERVING: 148 cal., 6 g total fat (1 g sat. fat),
171 mg chol., 310 mg sodium, 5 g carb., 0 g fiber, 19 g pro. Exchanges:
2.5 very lean meat, 1.5 vegetable, 0.5 fat. Carb choices: 0.

1   pound cooked shrimp in shells
¼   cup light mayonnaise dressing or salad dressing
2   tablespoons lemon juice
1   tablespoon water
¼   to ½ teaspoon Cajun seasoning
1   5-ounce package mixed baby salad greens (6 cups)
½   of a small red onion, thinly sliced

1. Peel and devein shrimp, leaving tails intact if
desired. For dressing, in a bowl, stir together mayonnaise
dressing, lemon juice, the water, and Cajun seasoning.

2. In a large bowl, combine shrimp, salad greens, and
red onion. Add dressing; toss gently to coat. Divide
among four serving plates. Makes 4 servings.

(super salads)

Follow a few tips to make your salads the best they can be.

1. Clean and chill ingredients ahead of time. Also chill salad plates and bowls.
2. Add tomatoes to a salad just before tossing to keep them from watering out and diluting the dressing.
3. Mix a tossed salad with its dressing at the last minute to prevent the greens from wilting.
4. Accent salads with red onion or sweet pepper rings, radish roses, pimiento strips, or soynuts.

**Salmon and Spinach Salad
with Flaxseed Vinaigrette**

Salmon and Spinach Salad with Flaxseed Vinaigrette

This hearty bowlful tosses together three health-smart standouts—salmon, spinach, and flaxseeds.

PER SERVING: 239 cal., 15 g total fat (3 g sat. fat), 54 mg chol., 102 mg sodium, 6 g carb., 1 g fiber, 20 g pro. Exchanges: 1 vegetable, 2.5 lean meat, 1.5 fat. Carb choices: 0.5.

12	ounces cooked salmon,* broken into chunks
3	cups fresh baby spinach
1	cup coarsely chopped cucumber
½	cup quartered red onion slices
¼	cup Flaxseed Vinaigrette (see recipe, below)

1. In a large bowl, combine salmon, spinach, cucumber, and red onion. Pour Flaxseed Vinaigrette over salad; toss gently to coat. Makes 4 (1½-cup) servings.

Flaxseed Vinaigrette: Preheat oven to 350°F. In a shallow baking pan, place 1 tablespoon flaxseeds; bake for 10 minutes. Cool. Place toasted flaxseeds in a spice grinder and pulse until ground to a fine powder. In a small bowl, whisk together ground flaxseeds, 3 tablespoons champagne vinegar or white wine vinegar, 2 tablespoons olive oil, 1 tablespoon water, 1 tablespoon finely chopped shallots or green onion, 2 teaspoons Dijon-style mustard, and 1 minced clove garlic. To store, place in a covered container; chill for up to 1 week. Makes about ½ cup.

***Test Kitchen Tip:** To cook the salmon, you'll need a 1-pound fresh or frozen salmon fillet to get 12 ounces after cooking. Thaw salmon, if frozen. Rinse salmon; pat dry with paper towels. To broil the salmon, preheat broiler. Skin salmon; measure thickness of salmon. Place salmon on the unheated rack of a broiler pan. Broil 4 to 5 inches from heat for 4 to 6 minutes per ½-inch thickness of fish or until fish flakes easily when tested with a fork, turning once halfway through broiling.

Salmon Penne Salad
with Raspberry Vinaigrette

Brush some vinaigrette onto the salmon,
then toss the rest with the pasta salad.

PER SERVING: 368 cal., 14 g total fat (2 g sat. fat), 33 mg chol., 42 mg sodium, 41 g carb., 4 g fiber, 18 g pro. Exchanges: 2.5 starch, 1.5 lean meat, 1 vegetable, 1.5 fat. Carb choices: 3.

- **1** 8- to 10-ounce fresh or frozen skinless, boneless salmon fillet or other fish fillet
- **1** recipe Raspberry Vinaigrette (see recipe, right)
- **6** ounces dried penne pasta (about 2 cups)
- **1** cup bias-sliced fresh asparagus spears
- **1** cup fresh red raspberries or sliced fresh strawberries
  Lettuce leaves (optional)
- **2** green onions, sliced

1. Thaw fish, if frozen. Rinse fish; pat dry with paper towels. Measure thickness of the fish. Brush fish with 2 teaspoons of the Raspberry Vinaigrette. Cover and chill remaining vinaigrette until ready to use.

2. Preheat broiler. Place fish on the greased unheated rack of broiler pan; tuck under thin edges. Broil 4 inches from heat for 4 to 6 minutes per ½-inch thickness of fish or until fish flakes easily when tested with a fork, turning once if 1 inch thick.

3. Meanwhile, cook pasta according to package directions, adding asparagus the last 2 minutes of cooking time. Drain; rinse with cold water. Drain again. Return pasta to pan. Add reserved vinaigrette; toss to coat.

4. Flake cooked salmon. Add salmon to pasta; toss gently. Cover and chill until serving time.

5. To serve, add berries to pasta mixture; toss to mix. If desired, serve on four lettuce-lined plates. Top with green onions. Makes 4 (2-cup) servings.

Raspberry Vinaigrette: In a small bowl, whisk together ¼ cup raspberry vinegar, 2 tablespoons olive oil, 1 tablespoon honey mustard, 2 teaspoons sugar, 1 minced clove garlic, and ¼ teaspoon ground black pepper. Cover and chill until serving time.

Make-Ahead Directions: Prepare Raspberry Vinaigrette as directed; cover and chill for up to 24 hours. Make salmon-pasta mixture as directed through Step 4; cover and chill for up to 4 hours. Serve as directed in Step 5.

Crab Cakes with Spring Green Salad

Light mayonnaise and egg white are the low-fat binding for the crab cakes.

PER SERVING: 181 cal., 9 g total fat (1 g sat. fat), 78 mg chol., 426 mg sodium, 8 g carb., 1 g fiber, 18 g pro. Exchanges: 1.5 vegetable, 2 very lean meat, 1.5 fat. Carb choices: 0.5.

- **1 egg white**
- **3 tablespoons light mayonnaise**
- **1 tablespoon Dijon-style mustard**
- **Few drops bottled hot pepper sauce**
- **3 tablespoons finely chopped red or green sweet pepper**
- **2 tablespoons snipped fresh parsley**
- **1 tablespoon sliced green onion**
- **2 teaspoons snipped fresh dill or cilantro or ½ teaspoon dried dill weed**
- **1 pound cooked fresh lump crabmeat or three 6- to 6½-ounce cans lump crabmeat, drained, flaked, and cartilage removed**
- **1¼ cups soft whole wheat or white bread crumbs**
- **1 recipe Lime Dressing (see recipe, right)**
- **8 ounces mixed baby salad greens (8 cups)**
- **1 head Belgian endive, sliced crosswise**
- **1 medium tomato, seeded and chopped**
- **Nonstick cooking spray**
- **Lime wedges (optional)**

1. In a large bowl, whisk together egg white, mayonnaise, mustard, and hot pepper sauce. Stir in sweet pepper, parsley, green onion, and dill. Add crabmeat and ½ cup of the bread crumbs; stir until combined. Using wet hands, shape mixture into six ½-inch-thick patties. Place patties in a 15×10×1-inch baking pan. Cover and chill for 30 minutes.

2. Prepare Lime Dressing; set aside. In a large bowl, combine greens, endive, and tomato. Cover and chill until ready to serve.

3. Preheat oven to 300°F. Place remaining ¾ cup bread crumbs in a shallow dish. Dip crab cakes into bread crumbs, turning to coat both sides. Coat an unheated large nonstick skillet with cooking spray. Preheat over medium heat. Add half of the crab cakes. Cook for 8 to 10 minutes or until golden brown and heated through (160°F), turning once halfway through cooking. Transfer crab cakes to a baking sheet; keep warm in the oven. Repeat with remaining crab cakes.

Quick Tip

Crab, famous for its sweet, succulent meat, is available in myriad convenient-to-use forms. Look for cooked crabmeat that is frozen, pasteurized (which requires refrigeration), or canned. Claw meat, lump meat, and flaked meat are canned crab options.

4. To serve, toss greens mixture with Lime Dressing; divide among six salad plates. Top with warm crab cakes. If desired, garnish with lime wedges. Makes 6 servings (1 crabcake and 1⅓ cups salad each).

Lime Dressing: In a small bowl, whisk together 2 tablespoons olive oil, 2 tablespoons lime juice, 1 minced clove garlic, ⅛ teaspoon salt, and ⅛ teaspoon ground black pepper. Cover and chill.

Curried Crab Salad

It only takes 20 minutes to enhance juicy fresh fruit and crabmeat with a light, curry-seasoned dressing.

PER SERVING: 200 cal., 9 g total fat (2 g sat. fat), 58 mg chol., 361 mg sodium, 17 g carb., 2 g fiber, 14 g pro. Exchanges: 1 vegetable, 1 fruit, 0.5 lean meat, 1 fat. Carb choices: 1.

- **4 cups cut-up fresh fruit (such as pineapple, cantaloupe, honeydew melon, and/or strawberries)**
- **2 6-ounce packages frozen crabmeat, thawed**
- **1¼ cups sliced celery**
- **½ cup light mayonnaise or salad dressing**
- **½ cup plain low-fat yogurt**
- **¼ cup fat-free milk**
- **1 teaspoon curry powder**
- **8 cups torn mixed salad greens**

1. In a very large bowl, combine fresh fruit, crabmeat, and celery; set aside.

2. For dressing, in a small bowl, stir together mayonnaise, yogurt, milk, and curry powder.

3. Divide salad greens among six salad plates. Top with crab salad and dressing. Makes 6 servings (1⅓ cups greens and about ¾ cup crab salad each).

(flavor boosters)

Many dishes rely on fat and sodium for flavoring, but there are other ways to get great taste without compromising a well-managed diet. Acidic flavors from citrus and vinegars stimulate the taste buds while adding few, if any, calories and no fat. Herbs pack a concentrated punch into a recipe without adding fat and with very few calories. When using fresh herbs, snip or mince them and toss them in just before serving.

Crab Cakes with Spring Green Salad

Spicy Shrimp Tabbouleh

For extra flourish, look for cooked shrimp with tails still on.

PER SERVING: 201 cal., 1 g total fat (0 g sat. fat), 111 mg chol., 495 mg sodium, 32 g carb., 6 g fiber, 16 g pro. Exchanges: 0.5 vegetable, 2 starch, 1.5 very lean meat. Carb choices: 2.

1⅓ cups water
⅔ cup bulgur
½ cup bottled fat-free ranch salad dressing
½ teaspoon finely shredded lime peel
2 tablespoons lime juice
¼ teaspoon crushed red pepper
1 cup fresh pea pods, halved crosswise
½ cup chopped radishes or daikon
½ cup snipped fresh cilantro
¼ cup bias-sliced green onions
8 ounces peeled and deveined cooked shrimp, halved lengthwise and frozen

1. In a small saucepan, combine the water and bulgur. Bring to boiling; reduce heat. Cover and simmer about 15 minutes or until most of the water is absorbed and bulgur is tender.

2. Meanwhile, for dressing, in a small bowl, combine ranch dressing, lime peel, lime juice, and red pepper. Cover and chill.

3. Stir pea pods into bulgur; transfer to a large bowl. Stir in radishes, cilantro, green onions, and dressing. Cover and chill for 4 to 24 hours. Stir in shrimp to serve. Makes 4 (1-cup) servings.

Shrimply Delicious Salad

A splash of citrus and a pinch
of pepper sauce give shrimp a kick.

PER SERVING: 331 cal., 13 g total fat (1 g sat. fat), 172 mg chol., 192 mg sodium, 30 g carb., 5 g fiber, 27 g pro. Exchanges: 2.5 vegetable, 1 fruit, 3 very lean meat, 2 fat. Carb choices: 2.

PER SERVING WITH SUBSTITUTE: same as above, except 315 cal., 26 g carb. Carb choices: 1.5.

- 1 pound fresh or frozen peeled, deveined large shrimp (leave tails intact, if desired)
- ¼ cup orange juice
- ¼ cup lime juice
- ½ to 1 teaspoon bottled hot pepper sauce
- ½ teaspoon ground black pepper
- 8 cups torn mixed salad greens
- 2 11-ounce cans mandarin orange sections, drained
- 1½ cups bite-size strips red, green, and/or yellow sweet peppers
- ½ cup thinly sliced red onion
- 1 recipe Sesame-Citrus Vinaigrette (see recipe, below)
- 2 tablespoons sesame seeds, toasted

1. If using wooden skewers, soak in warm water for 30 minutes.

2. Thaw shrimp, if frozen. Rinse shrimp; pat dry with paper towels.

3. In a screw-top jar, combine citrus juices, pepper sauce, and black pepper. Cover and shake to mix.

4. For marinade, place ¼ cup of the juice mixture in a bowl. Reserve remaining juice mixture to use in Sesame-Citrus Vinaigrette. Add shrimp; toss gently to coat. Cover and marinate in the refrigerator for 1 hour.

5. Drain shrimp, discarding marinade. Thread shrimp onto skewers, leaving a ¼-inch space between each shrimp.

6. Grill shrimp on the greased rack of an uncovered grill directly over medium coals for 5 to 8 minutes or until shrimp are pink, turning once halfway through grilling.

7. In a large bowl, combine mixed greens, orange sections, sweet peppers, and red onion. Add Sesame-Citrus Vinaigrette; toss gently to coat. Divide among four plates. Arrange shrimp on top of greens. Sprinkle with sesame seeds. Makes 4 (3-cup) servings.

Sesame-Citrus Vinaigrette: To citrus juice mixture in screw-top jar, add 2 tablespoons canola oil, 4 teaspoons sugar or sugar substitute* equivalent to 4 teaspoons sugar, 2 teaspoons red wine vinegar, and 1 teaspoon toasted sesame oil. Cover; shake well. Makes 1⅓ cups.

Quick Tip

Shrimp do indeed have cholesterol—about 166 mg in a 3-ounce serving. But they also are low in total fat, saturated fat, and calories. So it's OK to satisfy your craving for shrimp every now and then if you are watching your total cholesterol intake from all of the foods you eat.

Make-Ahead Directions: Prepare as directed through Step 5. Cover and chill shrimp and dressing separately for up to 24 hours. Continue as directed in Step 6.

*Sugar Substitute: Try Splenda granular. Follow package directions to measure product amount equivalent to 4 teaspoons sugar.

Shrimply Delicious Salad

**Grilled Salmon Salad
with Oil-Free Vinaigrette**

1 cup steamed asparagus or green beans, cut into
   2-inch pieces and chilled*
½ cup radish slices
¼ cup sliced green onions
   Fresh dill sprigs or tarragon sprigs (optional)

1. Prepare Oil-Free Vinaigrette. Thaw salmon, if frozen. Rinse salmon; pat dry with paper towels. Measure thickness of salmon. Cut salmon into four portions. Sprinkle with pepper.

2. Spray an unheated grill rack with cooking spray. Place salmon, skin sides up, on sprayed grill rack directly over medium coals. Grill for 4 to 6 minutes per ½-inch thickness of fish or until fish flakes easily when tested with a fork, turning once halfway through grilling. Using a wide metal spatula, lift fillets off skin to a platter. (Scrape skin from rack and discard.)

3. In a large bowl, toss together greens, cucumber, asparagus, radishes, and green onions.

4. To serve, divide greens among plates. Top with salmon. Serve with Oil-Free Vinaigrette. If desired, garnish each serving with fresh dill. Makes 4 servings (1½ cups greens mixture and 1 piece salmon each).

Oil-Free Vinaigrette: In a small bowl, stir together 1 tablespoon powdered fruit pectin, 1 teaspoon snipped fresh dill or tarragon or ¼ teaspoon crushed dried dill or tarragon, and ⅛ teaspoon ground black pepper. Stir in ¼ cup water, 2 teaspoons white wine vinegar, and 1 teaspoon honey Dijon-style mustard. Cover; store in the refrigerator for at least 30 minutes or up to 3 days.

*To Steam Vegetables: Place asparagus or beans in a steamer basket in a saucepan. Add water to just below bottom of basket. Bring water to boiling. Add asparagus or beans to basket. Cover; reduce heat. Steam for 3 to 5 minutes for asparagus or 18 to 22 minutes for beans or until vegetables are crisp-tender.

Broiling Directions: Prepare as directed through Step 1. Preheat broiler. Place salmon, skin sides up, on the unheated rack of broiler pan. Broil 4 to 5 inches from heat for 4 to 6 minutes per ½-inch thickness of fish or until fish flakes easily when tested with a fork, turning once halfway through broiling. Continue as directed in Steps 3 and 4.

Grilled Salmon Salad with Oil-Free Vinaigrette

Fruit pectin thickens the dressing without fat.

PER SERVING: 228 cal., 9 g total fat (1 g sat. fat), 78 mg chol., 83 mg sodium, 5 g carb., 2 g fiber, 30 g pro. Exchanges: 1.5 vegetable, 4 lean meat. Carb choices: 0.

1 recipe **Oil-Free Vinaigrette** (see recipe, right)
1¼ pounds fresh or frozen salmon fillet
   Ground black pepper
   Nonstick cooking spray
3 cups torn mixed salad greens
1 cup cucumber slices, halved

Grilled Beef and Avocado Salad with Cilantro-Lime Vinaigrette

For the double-duty marinade/salad dressing, jazz up reduced-calorie dressing with zesty lime peel and juice. Pictured on the cover.

PER SERVING: 199 cal., 10 g total fat (3 g sat. fat), 35 mg chol., 477 mg sodium, 8 g carb., 3 g fiber, 20 g pro. Exchanges: 2.5 very lean meat, 1.5 vegetable, 1.5 fat. Carb choices: 0.5.

- 12 ounces beef flank steak
- ½ cup bottled reduced-calorie clear Italian salad dressing
- ½ teaspoon finely shredded lime peel
- ¼ cup lime juice
- 2 tablespoons snipped fresh cilantro
- ¼ cup chopped onion
- ¼ teaspoon salt
- ¼ teaspoon ground black pepper
- 6 cups torn mixed salad greens
- 2 small yellow and/or red tomatoes, cut into wedges
- 1 small avocado, halved, seeded, peeled, and sliced

1. Score both sides of steak in a diamond pattern by making shallow diagonal cuts at 1-inch intervals. Place in a resealable plastic bag set in a shallow dish.

2. In a screw-top jar, combine salad dressing, lime peel, lime juice, and cilantro. Cover and shake well. Pour half into a small bowl; cover and chill.

3. Add onion to dressing mixture remaining in jar. Cover and shake well; pour over steak in bag. Seal bag; turn to coat steak. Marinate in the refrigerator for 24 hours, turning bag occasionally.

4. Drain beef, discarding marinade. Sprinkle with salt and pepper. Grill steak on rack of an uncovered grill directly over medium heat for 17 to 21 minutes for medium doneness (160°F), turning once.

5. To serve, thinly slice beef across grain. On four plates, arrange greens, tomatoes, beef, and avocado. Add reserved dressing. Makes 4 servings (1¼ cups greens and 3 ounces steak each).

Broiling Directions: Prepare steak as directed. Preheat broiler. On unheated rack of broiler pan, broil 3 to 4 inches from heat for 15 to 18 minutes for medium doneness (160°F), turning once. Serve as directed.

Quick Tip

Making your own dressing isn't as hard as it sounds. Once you do, you'll wonder why you've never made it before. Not only does it taste better than purchased dressings, it is better for you. You control the sodium, sugar, fat, and calories in every bite. Fresh herbs add the finishing touch.

Grilled Summer Vegetable Salad

This side salad is the perfect partner to Balsamic Pork Tenderloin (right), but it goes well with any grilled meat.

PER SERVING: 126 cal., 9 g total fat (1 g sat. fat), 0 mg chol., 55 mg sodium, 11 g carb., 5 g fiber, 2 g pro. Exchanges: 2 vegetable, 1.5 fat. Carb choices: 0.5.

- 1 medium eggplant, cut crosswise into ½-inch slices
- 1 medium onion, cut into ½-inch wedges
- 2 green and/or red sweet peppers, halved, with stems, membranes, and seeds removed
- 6 large cremini mushrooms, stems removed
- 3 roma tomatoes, halved lengthwise
- 3 tablespoons olive oil
- 1 tablespoon cider vinegar
- 1 recipe Herb Vinaigrette (see recipe, right)
  Fresh thyme (optional)

1. In a very large bowl, combine eggplant, onion, sweet peppers, mushrooms, and tomatoes. Add oil and vinegar; toss gently to coat.

2. Place vegetables on the rack of an uncovered grill directly over medium-hot coals. (If grilling with Balsamic Pork Tenderloin, arrange vegetables over coals around outside edge of rack.) Grill for 6 to 7 minutes or until tender, turning once.

3. Cut each pepper half into strips. Arrange vegetables on a platter. Drizzle with Herb Vinaigrette. Serve warm or at room temperature. If desired, garnish with thyme. Makes 6 (1-cup) servings.

Herb Vinaigrette: In a small bowl, whisk together 1 tablespoon olive oil, 2 teaspoons cider vinegar, 1 teaspoon snipped fresh parsley, ¼ teaspoon snipped fresh thyme, ¼ teaspoon snipped fresh rosemary, ⅛ teaspoon salt, and dash ground black pepper. Makes 2 tablespoons.

Balsamic Pork Tenderloin

To thicken the glaze, simmer or reduce balsamic vinegar to give it more body and flavor.

PER SERVING: 126 cal., 4 g total fat (1 g sat. fat), 49 mg chol., 54 mg sodium, 4 g carb., 0 g fiber, 16 g pro. Exchanges: 2.5 very lean meat, 1 fat. Carb choices: 0.

- 1 1-pound pork tenderloin
- ¼ cup balsamic vinegar
- 2 tablespoons olive oil
- 1 tablespoon snipped fresh rosemary
- 2 cloves garlic, minced
- ¾ teaspoon ground black pepper
- ⅛ teaspoon salt
- 1 recipe Balsamic Glaze (see recipe, below)
  Fresh thyme (optional)

1. Place pork in a large resealable plastic bag set in a shallow dish. For marinade, in a small bowl, whisk together balsamic vinegar, oil, rosemary, garlic, pepper, and salt; pour over meat. Seal bag; turn to coat pork. Marinate in the refrigerator for 1 hour, turning the bag occasionally.

2. Remove pork from marinade, discarding marinade. Prepare grill for indirect grilling. Test for medium heat above the drip pan. Place tenderloin on grill rack over drip pan. Cover and grill tenderloin about 40 minutes or until an instant-read thermometer inserted into the center of the meat registers 155°F.

3. Brush tenderloin on all sides with Balsamic Glaze. Grill for 1 minute more. Remove from grill. Cover with foil; let stand for 15 minutes (the meat's temperature will rise 5°F during standing time). If desired, garnish with fresh thyme. Slice to serve. Serve with Grilled Summer Vegetable Salad (left). Makes 6 servings.

Balsamic Glaze: In a small saucepan, bring ½ cup balsamic vinegar to boiling. Reduce heat; simmer, uncovered, for 5 minutes. Makes about ¼ cup.

Balsamic Pork Tenderloin with Grilled Summer Vegetable Salad

(10 great greens)

Becoming familiar with the types of greens available will enable you to enjoy a variety of salads.

1. **Red-tip leaf lettuce** has a tender, sweet, delicate flavor that makes it versatile for many types of green salads.
2. **Leaf lettuce** has a mild, delicate flavor and may be used interchangeably with red-tip leaf lettuce.
3. **Radicchio** is bitter and peppery tasting when eaten alone, but small amounts add a nice accent to other greens.
4. **Spinach** has a mildly hearty flavor and is often used raw in salads.
5. **Swiss chard** has large stems with a delicate flavor similar to celery; leaves have a hearty spinachlike flavor.
6. **Romaine** has large, crisp leaves and a slightly sharp flavor that make this the classic lettuce for Caesar salad.
7. **Curly endive** has a mildly bitter flavor and adds visual interest to salads.
8. **Arugula** has a peppery, pungent flavor that is an ideal contrast when mixed with milder greens.
9. **Mustard greens** have frilly-edge leaves and add a peppery bite to salads, so use torn fresh mustard greens in small amounts.
10. **Dandelion greens** have a slightly bitter flavor with a bite.

(pork perfect)

Pork is a meat you can turn to when you need a meal on the table fast. It's versatile and can be cooked just about any way: grilled, broiled, sautéed, pan broiled, or roasted. Today, the most common cuts of pork produced are 16 percent leaner and have 27 percent less saturated fat than 15 years ago. Also, because of modern feeding practices, trichinosis is no longer a concern. Although trichina is virtually nonexistent in pork today, if it were present, it would be killed at 137°F. That is well below the recommended end cooking temperature for pork, which is 160°F.

Grilled Pork and Pear Salad

Grilled Pork and Pear Salad

Here's a quick dressing trick—stir apple juice concentrate into low-fat mayo and buttermilk.

PER SERVING: 251 cal., 10 g total fat (3 g sat. fat), 50 mg chol., 368 mg sodium, 20 g carb., 4 g fiber, 21 g pro. Exchanges: 1 fruit, 3 very lean meat, 1 vegetable, 1.5 fat. Carb choices: 1.

- 2 **boneless pork loin chops (about 12 ounces total), cut ¾ inch thick**
- 2 **teaspoons olive oil**
- 2 **teaspoons snipped fresh sage or thyme, or 1 teaspoon dried sage or thyme, crushed**
- ¼ **teaspoon salt**
- ¼ **teaspoon ground black pepper**
- 8 **cups torn mixed salad greens**
- 2 **medium pears or apples, thinly sliced**
- 1 **recipe Creamy Apple Dressing (see recipe, below)**
- ¼ **cup broken walnuts, toasted (optional)**

1. Trim fat from chops; brush chops with oil. In a small bowl, stir together sage, salt, and pepper. Sprinkle sage mixture evenly onto all sides of pork chops; rub in with your fingers.

2. Grill chops on the rack of an uncovered grill directly over medium heat for 9 to 11 minutes or until done (160°F) and juices run clear, turning chops once halfway through grilling.

3. To serve, slice chops. On four plates, arrange greens, pear slices, and pork slices. Stir Creamy Apple Dressing; pour over salad. If desired, sprinkle with walnuts. Makes 4 servings (about 2 cups salad and 3 ounces pork each).

Broiling Directions: Preheat broiler. Prepare chops as directed in Step 1. Arrange on the unheated rack of a broiler pan. Broil 3 to 4 inches from the heat for 9 to 11 minutes or until done (160°F) and juices run clear, turning once. Serve as directed.

Creamy Apple Dressing: In a bowl, stir together ½ cup buttermilk; 2 tablespoons low-fat mayonnaise; 1 tablespoon frozen apple juice concentrate or frozen orange juice concentrate, thawed; 1 teaspoon Dijon-style mustard; 1 finely chopped green onion; 1 teaspoon snipped fresh sage or thyme, or ¼ teaspoon dried sage or thyme, crushed; ⅛ teaspoon salt; and ⅛ teaspoon ground black pepper. Cover and chill until serving time, up to 24 hours.

Roast Pork Salad with Ginger-Pineapple Dressing

Roast Pork Salad with Ginger-Pineapple Dressing

If you use fresh pineapple, cut it up in a bowl and save the juice for the dressing.

PER SERVING: 240 cal., 8 g total fat (2 g sat. fat), 60 mg chol., 219 mg sodium, 22 g carb., 3 g fiber, 19 g pro. Exchanges: 1 fruit, 2.5 very lean meat, 1 vegetable, 1.5 fat. Carb choices: 1.5.

- 12 **ounces pork tenderloin**
- ⅛ **teaspoon salt**
- ⅛ **teaspoon ground black pepper**
- 2 **tablespoons honey mustard**
- 6 **cups torn romaine and/or fresh spinach**
- 2 **cups fresh or canned pineapple chunks and/or sliced fresh nectarines or peaches**
  Cracked black pepper (optional)
- 1 **recipe Ginger-Pineapple Dressing (see recipe, below)**

1. Preheat oven to 425°F. Trim fat from pork; sprinkle pork with salt and ground black pepper. Place pork on a rack in a shallow roasting pan. Roast for 20 minutes.

2. Spoon mustard onto pork. Roast for 5 to 10 minutes or until an instant-read thermometer inserted in the thickest part registers 160°F.

3. To serve, thinly slice pork. In four salad bowls or plates, arrange greens, pork, and fruit. If desired, sprinkle salads with cracked black pepper. Stir Ginger-Pineapple Dressing; drizzle over salads. Makes 4 servings (1½ cups greens, 3 ounces pork, and ½ cup fruit each).

Ginger-Pineapple Dressing: In a small bowl, combine ¼ cup low-fat mayonnaise, ¼ cup unsweetened pineapple juice or orange juice, 1 tablespoon honey mustard, and 1 teaspoon grated fresh ginger. Cover; chill until serving time, up to 24 hours.

sensational sandwiches

Spinach Panini

Sandwiches make great meals when you're in a hurry. From classics to panini to burgers, our ideas offer a range of flavors and fillers designed for you. Or think outside the usual bread and choose from our wraps, pockets, and roll-ups.

Spinach Panini

Spinach boosts the nutrition while basil and feta cheese push the flavor over the top.

PER PANINI: 189 cal., 6 g total fat (3 g sat. fat), 17 mg chol., 471 mg sodium, 25 g carb., 5 g fiber, 10 g pro. Exchanges: 1.5 vegetable, 1.5 starch, 0.5 medium-fat meat. Carb choices: 1.5.

Nonstick olive oil cooking spray
8 slices whole wheat bread or 2 whole wheat pita bread rounds, halved crosswise and split horizontally
4 cups fresh baby spinach leaves
8 thin tomato slices (1 medium tomato)
⅛ teaspoon freshly ground black pepper
¼ cup thinly sliced red onion
2 tablespoons shredded fresh basil leaves
½ cup crumbled feta cheese (1 ounce)

1. Lightly coat an unheated panini griddle, covered indoor electric grill, or large nonstick skillet with cooking spray; set aside.

2. Place 4 of the bread slices or 4 pita pieces on a work surface; divide half of the spinach leaves among bread slices or pita pieces. Top spinach with tomato slices. Sprinkle with pepper. Add onion and basil. Top with feta and remaining spinach. Top with bread slices or pita pieces. Press down firmly.

3. Preheat griddle, grill, or skillet over medium heat or heat according to manufacturer's directions. Add sandwiches, in batches if necessary. If using griddle or grill, close lid and grill for 2 to 3 minutes or until bread is toasted. (If using skillet, place a heavy plate on top of sandwiches. Cook for 1 to 2 minutes or until bottoms are toasted. Carefully remove plate, which may be hot. Turn sandwiches and top with the plate. Cook for 1 to 2 minutes more or until bread is toasted.) Makes 4 panini.

Avocado and Cream Cheese on Bagels

Here is a sandwich to count on for a quick at-home or assemble-at-work meatless lunch.

PER SERVING: 222 cal., 8 g total fat (3 g sat. fat), 13 mg chol., 301 mg sodium, 31 g carb., 5 g fiber, 9 g pro. Exchanges: 1 vegetable, 1.5 starch, 1.5 fat. Carb choices: 2.

½ of an 8-ounce tub light cream cheese
1 tablespoon snipped fresh dill or 1 teaspoon dried dill
¼ teaspoon salt
⅛ teaspoon ground black pepper
4 whole wheat bagel halves, toasted
½ of a medium cucumber, sliced
½ of a medium onion, sliced
½ of a medium avocado, halved, seeded, peeled, and sliced
¾ cup bottled roasted red sweet peppers, drained and cut into thin strips
  Fresh dill sprigs (optional)

1. In a bowl, combine cream cheese, snipped or dried dill, salt, and black pepper. Spread onto bagel halves. Top with cucumber slices, onion slices, avocado slices, and red pepper strips. If desired, garnish with fresh dill sprigs. Makes 4 servings.

Veggie Salad in a Pocket

Enjoy leftover Spicy Hummus as a snack with vegetable dippers. Two tablespoons of dip contain 50 calories and 9 grams of carbs.

PER SERVING: 166 cal., 2 g total fat (0 g sat. fat), 0 mg chol., 599 mg sodium, 31 g carb., 6 g fiber, 7 g pro. Exchanges: 0.5 carb. Carb choices: 1.5.

1 cup chopped yellow summer squash and/or zucchini
¾ cup chopped broccoli
2 roma tomatoes, seeded and chopped
8 pitted kalamata or ripe olives, chopped
2 tablespoons snipped fresh flat-leaf or regular parsley
2 tablespoons bottled fat-free Italian salad dressing
2 6- to 7-inch whole wheat pita bread rounds, halved crosswise, or four 6- to 7-inch whole wheat flour tortillas
½ cup Spicy Hummus (see recipe, below)

1. In a medium bowl, combine squash, broccoli, tomatoes, olives, and parsley; toss with salad dressing.

2. Spread insides of pita halves or tortillas each with 2 tablespoons Spicy Hummus.

3. For each sandwich, fill pita half with squash mixture or spoon onto tortilla. Fold or roll tortilla, if using. Makes 4 servings.

Spicy Hummus: In a food processor, combine one 15- to 19-ounce can navy or cannellini beans (white kidney beans), rinsed and drained; ¼ cup bottled fat-free Italian salad dressing; and 1 tablespoon spicy brown mustard. Cover and process until smooth and spreadable. (Or use a potato masher or fork to mash beans. Stir in salad dressing and mustard.) To store, transfer to an airtight storage container. Cover and chill for up to 1 week. Makes 1⅓ cups.

(super sandwiches)

A sandwich can be a humble lunch or a spectacular meal; it's all in how you make it. When you get creative and take advantage of the infinite combinations, a sandwich is something to look forward to. Pita bread, wraps, and breads of all types can take a simple sandwich filling to new heights. But when you experiment with the fillings, the possibilities are endless! A new sandwich to look forward to (like Veggie Salad in a Pocket) can jolt you out of your monotonous noontime rut.

Veggie Salad in a Pocket

Quick Tip

A classic canned tuna sandwich made with mayo is a lunchtime staple. But when you mix the tuna with a lemony dressing and colorful veggies, it becomes a sandwich to celebrate! Top it with a small garnish to elevate a great sandwich to one worth sharing.

Salad Niçoise on Flatbread

Tuna Salad Pockets

1. In a medium bowl, combine tuna, onion, celery, carrot, and capers.

2. Pour Dijon Vinaigrette over tuna mixture; toss gently to coat. Add greens; toss gently to combine. Spoon tuna salad into pita halves. Makes 4 servings.

Dijon Vinaigrette: In a screw-top jar, combine 2 tablespoons olive oil, 2 tablespoons lime juice, 1 tablespoon Dijon-style mustard, and 1 tablespoon champagne vinegar. Cover; shake well to mix.

Salad Niçoise on Flatbread

With this sophisticated sandwich, you can enjoy all the wonderful flavors of the classic salad.

PER SERVING: 210 cal., 5 g total fat (1 g sat. fat), 24 mg chol., 527 mg sodium, 23 g carb., 3 g fiber, 17 g pro. Exchanges: 1.5 starch, 2.5 very lean meat, 1 fat. Carb choices: 1.5.

- 4 ounces fresh green beans, trimmed (if desired) and cut into 1-inch pieces (about 1 cup)
- 1 12-ounce can chunk white or light tuna (water-pack), drained and flaked
- 1 cup halved cherry tomatoes
- ⅓ cup chopped pitted niçoise or kalamata olives
- ¼ cup finely chopped sweet onion (such as Vidalia)
- 2 tablespoons chopped fresh mint
- 1 tablespoon lemon juice
- 2 teaspoons olive oil
- ⅛ teaspoon ground black pepper
- 3 cups packaged mesclun (mixed salad greens)
- 3 Greek pita flatbreads
- 6 short wooden skewers
  Cherry tomatoes, pitted niçoise or kalamata olives, and fresh mint leaves

1. In a covered medium saucepan, cook green beans in boiling water about 4 minutes or until crisp-tender. Drain. Rinse under cold water; drain again.

2. Place green beans in a large bowl. Stir in tuna, the 1 cup cherry tomatoes, the ⅓ cup olives, the onion, and the 2 tablespoons mint. Add lemon juice, oil, and pepper; toss to combine. Stir in mesclun.

3. To serve, cut pita flatbreads in half crosswise. Cut each pita half in half horizontally. Fill each pita half with about ½ cup of the tuna mixture. On each of the wooden skewers, thread a whole cherry tomato, a whole olive, and a mint leaf. Spear each serving with a skewer. Makes 6 servings.

Tuna Salad Pockets

Keep the vinaigrette in the fridge for last-minute sandwiches.

PER SERVING: 272 cal., 10 g total fat (2 g sat. fat), 36 mg chol., 659 mg sodium, 22 g carb., 3 g fiber, 25 g pro. Exchanges: 2 vegetable, 1 starch, 2.5 very lean meat, 2 fat. Carb choices: 1.5.

- 1 12-ounce can solid white tuna (water-pack), drained and broken into chunks
- ¼ cup finely chopped onion
- ¼ cup thinly sliced celery
- ¼ cup shredded carrot
- 1 tablespoon capers, rinsed and drained
- 1 recipe Dijon Vinaigrette (see recipe, above)
- 1½ cups torn mixed salad greens
- 2 large whole wheat pita bread rounds, halved crosswise

Just-Like-Egg Salad Sandwiches

Either sweet or dill pickle relish will taste delicious in this tofu-takeoff on egg salad.

NUTRITION FACTS PER SERVING: 200 cal., 9 g total fat (1 g sat. fat), 5 mg chol., 382 mg sodium, 20 g carb., 3 g fiber, 9 g pro. Exchanges: 1.5 starch, 0.5 medium-fat meat, 1 fat. Carb choices: 1

  8 **ounces extra-firm tub-style tofu (fresh bean curd), drained**
 ½ **cup chopped celery**
 ¼ **cup light mayonnaise or salad dressing**
  2 **tablespoons pickle relish**
  2 **teaspoons yellow mustard**
 12 **party rye or pumpernickel bread slices**
     Fresh dill sprigs (optional)
     Ground black pepper (optional)

1. In a medium bowl, mash tofu with a fork. Stir in celery, mayonnaise dressing, pickle relish, and mustard. Top each slice of the bread with 2 to 3 tablespoons of the tofu mixture. If desired, garnish with fresh dill sprigs and/or sprinkle with black pepper. Makes 4 servings.

Tuna Pita Pockets

Tired of the same old creamy tuna salad? Switch to this delectable vinaigrette version instead.

NUTRITION FACTS PER SERVING: 254 cal., 8 g total fat (1 g sat. fat), 26 mg chol., 463 mg sodium, 20 g carb., 3 g fiber, 25 g pro.
EXCHANGES: 1 starch, 3 very lean meat, 0.5 vegetable, 1.5 fat. Carb choices: 1.

 2 **tablespoons canola oil**
 1 **tablespoon white wine vinegar**
 ⅛ **teaspoon ground black pepper**
 2 **6-ounce cans chunk light tuna (water-pack), drained**
 ¾ **cup quartered grape tomatoes**
 3 **tablespoons sliced green onions**
 2 **large whole wheat pita bread rounds, halved crosswise**
 4 **lettuce leaves**

1. In a medium bowl, stir together oil, vinegar, and pepper. Stir in tuna, grape tomatoes, and green onions. Line pita bread halves with lettuce leaves. Divide mixture among pita bread halves. Makes 4 servings.

(wrap wonders)

We've all done it. We're in a hurry, so we stop by the fast-food takeout window for a burger and fries. Do you know that it would take less time to make a good-for-you sandwich at home? Keep a few healthful foods on hand just for those busy days. Whole wheat tortillas make a wonderful alternative to bread. Fat-free cream cheese is a flavorful spread that pinch-hits for mainstay mayonnaise. Keep a few veggies on hand, too, such as red sweet peppers and leftover steamed asparagus. Tuna or salmon in a pouch both are great choices instead of sliced meat.

Salmon and Asparagus Wraps
Start with hot smoked salmon (not lox-style) and coarsely flake it.

PER WRAP: 160 cal., 3 g total fat (1 g sat. fat), 12 mg chol., 555 mg sodium, 20 g carb., 3 g fiber, 13 g pro. Exchanges: 0.5 vegetable, 1 starch, 1.5 very lean meat, 0.5 fat. Carb choices: 1.

- 12 thin fresh asparagus spears
- ½ of an 8-ounce tub fat-free cream cheese
- 2 teaspoons finely shredded lemon peel
- 2 tablespoons lemon juice
- ⅛ teaspoon cayenne pepper
- 6 ounces smoked salmon, coarsely flaked and skin and bones removed
- ¼ cup snipped fresh basil or 2 teaspoons dried basil, crushed
- 4 6- to 7-inch whole wheat flour tortillas
- ½ of a red sweet pepper, cut into thin bite-size strips

1. Snap off and discard woody bases from asparagus. In a covered large saucepan, cook asparagus in a small amount of boiling lightly salted water for 3 to 5 minutes or until crisp-tender. Drain. Plunge into ice water to cool quickly. Drain again; pat dry with paper towels.

2. In a bowl, stir together cream cheese, lemon peel, lemon juice, and cayenne pepper. Fold in smoked salmon and basil.

3. Spread salmon mixture onto tortillas. For each wrap, arrange 3 of the asparagus spears and half of the sweet pepper strips on salmon mixture. Roll up tortillas. If necessary, secure with toothpicks. Makes 4 wraps.

To Make Ahead: Wrap sandwiches in plastic wrap. Chill overnight or until ready to serve.

Salmon and Asparagus Wraps

**Smoked Salmon
Club Sandwich**

Smoked Salmon Club Sandwich

This version reduces the fat, but it definitely does not reduce flavor—chives and red pepper give it plenty.

PER SERVING : 181 cal., 6 g total fat (3 g sat. fat), 17 mg chol., 501 mg sodium, 23 g carb., 2 g fiber, 10 g pro. Exchanges: 0.5 vegetable, 1.5 starch, 0.5 lean meat, 5 fat. Carb choices: 1.5.

½ of an 8-ounce package reduced-fat cream cheese (Neufchâtel)
1 small carrot, very finely chopped
1 small zucchini, seeded and very finely chopped
1 small red or yellow sweet pepper, seeded and very finely chopped
2 tablespoons snipped fresh chives
 Salt
 Ground cayenne pepper
12 slices sesame sourdough bread
2 tablespoons light dairy sour cream
6 ounces thinly sliced smoked salmon
1½ cups baby spinach leaves
1 large cucumber, thinly bias-sliced

1. For vegetable spread, in a medium bowl, stir together cream cheese, carrot, zucchini, sweet pepper, and chives. Add salt and ground cayenne pepper to taste. If desired, cover and chill for 1 to 24 hours.

2. Spread 4 slices of the bread with dairy sour cream. Arrange salmon on top of sour cream. Add spinach leaves. Spread 4 more slices of the bread with vegetable spread; place on top of sandwich bases, spread sides up. Arrange cucumber slices on spread. Top each sandwich with another slice of bread. Cut sandwiches into quarters. Makes 8 (2-quarter) servings.

Po' Boys

Low-fat coleslaw and baked cornmeal-coated fish give the classic Po' Boy sandwich a delicious, healthful spin.

PER SANDWICH: 345 cal., 13 g total fat (2 g sat. fat), 112 mg chol., 610 mg sodium, 32 g carb., 4 g fiber, 25 g pro. Exchanges: 1 vegetable, 2 starch, 2.5 very lean meat, 1.5 fat. Carb choices: 2.

4 4-ounce fresh or frozen gray sole, flounder, or other thin fish fillets
⅓ cup light mayonnaise or salad dressing
1 tablespoon vinegar
1 tablespoon prepared horseradish
1 teaspoon sugar
3 cups packaged shredded cabbage with carrot (coleslaw mix)
1 stalk celery, finely chopped
3 tablespoons chopped fresh parsley
 Nonstick cooking spray
1 egg, beaten
1 tablespoon fat-free milk
¼ cup yellow cornmeal
¼ cup fine dry bread crumbs
¼ teaspoon salt
¼ teaspoon ground black pepper
2 teaspoons olive oil
4 whole grain rolls

1. Preheat oven to 400°F. Thaw fish, if frozen. In a medium bowl, whisk together mayonnaise, vinegar, horseradish, and sugar. Set aside 2 tablespoons of the mixture. Add coleslaw mix, celery, and parsley to the remaining mayonnaise mixture; stir to coat.

2. Rinse fish; pat dry with paper towels. Measure the thickness of fish fillets. Lightly coat a foil-lined shallow baking pan with cooking spray. In a shallow dish, combine egg and milk. In another shallow dish, combine cornmeal, bread crumbs, salt, and pepper; stir in olive oil until well-mixed. Dip fish into egg mixture, then into cornmeal mixture, turning to coat both sides of fish.

3. Place fish in prepared baking pan. Bake for 4 to 6 minutes per ½-inch thickness of fish or until fish flakes easily when tested with a fork.

4. To assemble sandwiches, cut rolls in half and hollow out some of the insides of the top halves; discard crumbs. Spread the reserved 2 tablespoons mayonnaise mixture on the bottom halves of the rolls. Place fish on top. Cover with coleslaw mixture and the top halves of rolls. Makes 4 sandwiches.

Po' Boys

Open-Face Ratatouille Sandwiches

Open-Face Ratatouille Sandwiches

You can save a bundle of carbs by going topless—with your sandwich, that is. A knife and fork will help in eating these sumptuous veggie-packed stacks.

PER SERVING: 251 cal., 7 g total fat (1 g sat. fat), 0 mg chol., 329 mg sodium, 43 g carb., 8 g fiber, 7 g pro. Exchanges: 2 vegetable, 2 starch, 1 fat. Carb choices: 3.

   Nonstick cooking spray
- **1** small eggplant, cut into 1-inch pieces
- **1** small zucchini or yellow summer squash, cut into ¾-inch slices
- **1** medium red sweet pepper, cut into strips
- **½** of a small red onion, cut into ½-inch wedges
- **1** tablespoon olive oil
- **½** teaspoon herbes de Provence or dried thyme, crushed
- **¼** teaspoon kosher salt
- **⅛** teaspoon ground black pepper
- **2** medium roma tomatoes, each cut lengthwise into 6 wedges

- **8** small or 4 large ½-inch slices whole wheat or white French bread, toasted
- **1** clove garlic, halved
- **2** tablespoons balsamic vinegar
   Fresh thyme sprigs (optional)

1. Preheat oven to 400°F. Coat a large shallow roasting pan with cooking spray. Add eggplant, zucchini, sweet pepper, and red onion to prepared pan. Drizzle with olive oil; sprinkle with herbes de Provence, salt, and black pepper. Toss to coat. Roast vegetables for 30 minutes, tossing once. Add roma tomatoes to roasting pan. Roast for 15 to 20 minutes more or until vegetables are tender and light brown in spots.

2. Meanwhile, rub toasted bread with the cut sides of the garlic clove. Place two small slices or one large slice of the bread on each of four serving plates. Sprinkle balsamic vinegar over vegetables; toss gently to coat. Spoon warm vegetables on top of bread. If desired, garnish with fresh thyme sprigs. Makes 4 servings.

Cheese and Tomato Stack

Fresh summer basil and tomatoes take a cheese sandwich from ordinary to fantastic.

PER SANDWICH: 203 cal., 12 g total fat (4 g sat. fat), 22 mg chol., 531 mg sodium, 16 g carb., 3 g fiber, 10 g pro. Exchanges: 1 starch, 1 medium-fat meat, 0.5 vegetable, 1 fat. Carb choices: 1.

2 **whole wheat English muffins, toasted**
8 **thin red and/or yellow tomato slices**
4 **ounces fresh mozzarella, cut into 4 slices**
4 **teaspoons snipped fresh basil**
4 **teaspoons olive oil**
¼ **teaspoon salt**
¼ **teaspoon cracked black pepper**
4 **grape tomatoes or cherry tomatoes, halved (optional)**

1. For each serving, on one English muffin half, layer a tomato slice, a mozzarella slice, and ½ teaspoon of the basil. Repeat layers. In a small bowl, combine olive oil, salt, and pepper. Drizzle over top. If desired, top with grape tomato halves. Makes 4 open-face sandwiches.

Greek Burgers with Herbed Feta Spread

Oats replace some of the meat in these flavorful burgers, so they're higher in fiber and lower in fat.

PER BURGER: 348 cal., 13 g total fat (5 g sat. fat), 64 mg chol., 585 mg sodium, 31 g carb., 4 g fiber, 27 g pro. Exchanges: 1 vegetable, 1.5 starch, 3 lean meat, 1 fat. Carb choices: 2.

12 ounces 90 percent or higher lean ground beef
½ cup quick-cooking rolled oats
⅓ cup finely chopped red onion
1 egg white
3 tablespoons snipped fresh mint or basil
½ teaspoon garlic salt
1 small red sweet pepper, quartered
1 6-ounce carton plain low-fat or fat-free yogurt
⅓ cup crumbled feta cheese with garlic and herb
2 large whole wheat pita bread rounds, halved
1 cup fresh baby spinach leaves

1. In a medium bowl, combine beef, oats, onion, egg white, 2 tablespoons of the mint, and garlic salt; mix well. Form into four ¾-inch-thick patties.

2. Place patties on the rack of an uncovered grill directly over medium coals. Grill for 12 to 14 minutes or until done (160°F),* turning once. Add pepper quarters to the grill for the last 8 to 10 minutes of grilling or until skins are charred and pepper quarters are tender, turning once.

3. Meanwhile, in a bowl, stir together yogurt and feta cheese. Set aside.

4. If desired, cut grilled pepper quarters into strips, peeling off any loose skin. Serve burgers with pita halves, peppers, feta mixture, and spinach. Top with remaining 1 tablespoon mint. Makes 4 burgers.

*Test Kitchen Tip: The internal color of a burger is not a reliable doneness indicator. A beef patty cooked to 160°F is safe, regardless of color. To measure the doneness of a patty, insert an instant-read thermometer through the side of the patty to a depth of 2 to 3 inches.

Beef and Black Bean Wraps

Whole wheat tortillas and black beans make this sandwich a filling, high-fiber meal with a spicy flavor.

PER WRAP: 267 cal., 10 g total fat (5 g sat. fat), 44 mg chol., 593 mg sodium, 27 g carb., 14 g fiber, 19 g pro. Exchanges: 1.5 starch, 2 medium-fat meat. Carb choices: 2.

8 ounces lean ground beef
1 cup chopped onion
2 cloves garlic, minced
1½ teaspoons ground cumin
1 teaspoon chili powder
½ teaspoon ground coriander
1 15-ounce can black beans, rinsed and drained
1 large tomato, chopped
¼ teaspoon salt
¼ teaspoon ground black pepper
6 8-inch whole wheat flour tortillas
1½ cups shredded lettuce
1 to 1½ cups shredded cheddar or Monterey Jack cheese (4 to 6 ounces)
Purchased salsa (optional)

1. In a large skillet, cook ground beef, onion, and garlic about 5 minutes or until meat is brown. Drain off fat.

2. Stir cumin, chili powder, and coriander into meat mixture in skillet. Cook and stir for 1 minute. Stir in beans, tomato, salt, and pepper. Cover; cook for 5 minutes more, stirring occasionally.

3. To serve, spoon some of the beef mixture down the center of each tortilla. Sprinkle with lettuce and cheese. Roll up. If desired, serve with salsa. Makes 6 wraps.

Greek Burgers with Herbed Feta Spread

Steak Rémoulade Sandwiches

Served in France as an accompaniment, the classic mayonnaise-based sauce called a *rémoulade* brings something new to a steak sandwich.

PER SANDWICH: 416 cal., 15 g total fat (4 g sat. fat), 62 mg chol., 517 mg sodium, 37 g carb., 2 g fiber, 32 g pro. Exchanges: 2.5 starch, 3 lean meat, 0.5 vegetable, 1 fat. Carb choices: 2.5.

- ¼ cup light mayonnaise or salad dressing
- 1½ teaspoons finely minced cornichons or gherkins
- 1 teaspoon drained capers, chopped
- ¼ teaspoon lemon juice
- Black pepper
- 2 8-ounce boneless beef top loin steaks, cut 1 inch thick
- 4 cloves garlic, minced
- 1 large yellow sweet pepper, cut lengthwise into 8 strips
- 4 kaiser or French-style rolls, split and toasted
- 1 cup arugula or fresh spinach leaves

1. For rémoulade, in a small bowl, combine mayonnaise, cornichons, capers, lemon juice, and several dashes black pepper. Cover and chill.

2. Pat steaks dry with a paper towel. Rub garlic over steaks. Sprinkle with additional black pepper.

3. Grill steaks and sweet pepper strips on the rack of an uncovered grill directly over medium heat until meat is desired doneness and sweet pepper strips are crisp-tender, turning once halfway through grilling. Allow 11 to 15 minutes for medium rare (145°F) or 14 to 18 minutes for medium (160°F). Transfer steaks and sweet pepper strips to a cutting board; cut steaks into ¼-inch slices.

4. If desired, grill rolls directly over medium heat about 1 minute or until toasted. Spread rémoulade on cut sides of toasted rolls. Fill rolls with arugula, steak slices, and sweet pepper strips. Add roll tops. Makes 4 servings.

Steak Rémoulade

Beef and Sweet Pepper Tortilla Wraps

If you have more wraps than you need, cut an extra one into small pieces for a midafternoon snack.

PER WRAP: 135 cal., 6 g total fat (3 g sat. fat), 24 mg chol., 186 mg sodium, 10 g carb., 1 g fiber, 8 g pro. Exchanges: 0.5 starch, 1 lean meat, 0.5 fat. Carb choices: 0.5.

- 3 7- or 8-inch flour tortillas
- ½ of an 8-ounce tub light cream cheese with chive and onion or roasted garlic
- 18 to 24 fresh basil leaves
- ½ of a 7-ounce jar roasted red sweet peppers, well-drained and cut into ¼-inch strips
- 4 ounces thinly sliced cooked beef, ham, and/or turkey
- 1 tablespoon low-fat or light mayonnaise or salad dressing

1. Spread each tortilla with one-third of the cream cheese. Cover each with basil leaves, leaving a 1-inch border. Arrange pepper strips on basil leaves. Top with sliced meat. Spread mayonnaise onto meat.

2. Tightly roll up each tortilla into a spiral; cut each wrap in half crosswise. Makes 6 wraps.

Make-Ahead Directions: Wrap each spiral in plastic wrap. Chill for up to 4 hours.

*Test Kitchen Tip:** Because chile peppers contain volatile oils that can burn your skin and eyes, avoid direct contact with them as much as possible. When working with chile peppers, wear plastic or rubber gloves. If your bare hands do touch the peppers, wash your hands and nails well with soap and warm water.

Fast Fajita Roll-Ups

Plan this meal-in-a-bundle for those busy nights when you have little time to cook. It takes just 20 minutes.

PER ROLL-UP: 280 cal., 11 g total fat (5 g sat. fat), 42 mg chol., 425 mg sodium, 19 g carb., 1 g fiber, 25 g pro. Exchanges: 1 starch, 3 lean meat, 0.5 fat. Carb choices: 1.

- 12 ounces beef flank steak or sirloin steak or skinless, boneless chicken breast halves
- 4 8-inch whole wheat, spinach, or flour tortillas
  Nonstick cooking spray
- ⅓ cup finely chopped onion
- ⅓ cup finely chopped green sweet pepper
- ½ cup chopped tomato
- 2 tablespoons bottled fat-free Italian salad dressing
- ½ cup shredded reduced-fat cheddar cheese (2 ounces)
- ¼ cup purchased salsa or bottled taco sauce
- ¼ cup light dairy sour cream (optional)

1. If desired, partially freeze beef for easier slicing. If using beef, trim fat from meat. Cut beef or chicken into bite-size strips.

2. Preheat oven to 350°F. Wrap tortillas tightly in foil. Heat in oven about 10 minutes or until tortillas are heated through.

3. Meanwhile, coat an unheated 12-inch nonstick skillet with cooking spray. Preheat over medium-high heat. Add meat, onion, and sweet pepper to hot skillet. Cook and stir for 2 to 3 minutes or until desired doneness for beef or until chicken is no longer pink. Remove from heat; drain well. Stir in tomato and salad dressing.

4. To serve, fill warm tortillas with meat mixture. Roll up tortillas. Serve with cheese, salsa, and, if desired, sour cream. Makes 4 roll-ups.

Bacon, Lettuce, and Tomato Salsa Wraps

Homemade fresh tomato salsa makes this healthful version of the BLT a cut above the rest.

PER SERVING: 227 cal., 9 g total fat (3 g sat. fat), 30 mg chol., 625 mg sodium, 27 g carb., 2 g fiber, 8 g pro. Exchanges: 1 vegetable, 1.5 starch, 0.5 medium-fat meat, 1.5 fat. Carb choices: 2.

- 2 large ripe tomatoes, seeded and coarsely chopped
- ¼ cup finely chopped red onion
- ¼ cup chopped fresh cilantro
- 1 tablespoon finely chopped fresh jalapeño chile pepper*
- 1 tablespoon lime juice
- ⅛ teaspoon kosher salt
- 8 slices turkey bacon or reduced-sodium turkey bacon
- ¼ cup light mayonnaise or salad dressing
- 4 10-inch vegetable-flavor flour tortillas or flour tortillas
- 2 cups fresh baby spinach

1. For salsa, in a medium bowl, combine tomatoes, red onion, cilantro, and chile pepper. Stir in lime juice and salt. Set aside.

2. Cook bacon according to package directions. Drain well on paper towels; cut bacon into large pieces.

3. To assemble wraps, spread mayonnaise over tortillas; top with spinach. Using a slotted spoon, spoon salsa over spinach. Top with bacon. Roll up tortillas. Cut each tortilla in half. Makes 4 (2-wrap-half) servings.

Roast Beef and
Red Pepper Sandwiches

A combination of Dijon-style mustard, horseradish,
and mayonnaise adds a flavor punch
to this not-so-ordinary roast beef sandwich.

PER SANDWICH: 210 cal., 8 g total fat (3 g sat. fat), 38 mg chol., 312 mg
sodium, 14 g carb., 1 g fiber, 20 g pro. Exchanges: 1 starch, 2.5 lean
meat, 1 fat. Carb choices: 1.

- 1   4-ounce package 8-inch Italian bread shells (2 shells)
  (such as **Boboli** brand)
- 1½   teaspoons light mayonnaise or salad dressing
- 1½   teaspoons **Dijon**-style mustard
- ½   to 1 teaspoon prepared horseradish
- 6   ounces thinly sliced cooked roast beef
- ¼   cup bottled roasted red sweet p[...]
  ¼-inch strips
- 2   ounces thinly sliced Monterey Ja[...] cheese
- 2   cups watercress, tough stems removed

1. Preheat oven to 350°F. Wrap bread shells tightly in
foil. Bake for 10 minutes or until warmed through.

2. In a small bowl, combine mayonnaise, mustard,
and horseradish. Spread one side of each bread shell
with mayonnaise mixture. Top each with roast beef,
sweet pepper strips, cheese, and watercress. Fold bread
in half over filling or roll wrap-style. Slice each in half
crosswise to serve. Makes 4 sandwiches.

Make-Ahead Directions: Wrap sandwiches tightly in
plastic wrap and refrigerate for up to 24 hours.

Tex-Mex Sloppy Joes

Sloppy joes or other types of loose-meat sandwiches are standard fare in many cafes. This recipe gives the popular meal-in-a-bun a twist by using ground chicken or turkey breast instead of ground beef.

PER SANDWICH: 280 cal., 6 g total fat (1 g sat. fat), 44 mg chol., 644 mg sodium, 35 g carb., 4 g fiber, 23 g pro. Exchanges: 1 vegetable, 2 starch, 2 very lean meat, ½ fat. Carb choices: 2.

- 2 teaspoons cooking oil
- 2 medium onions, chopped
- 1 medium green sweet pepper, chopped
- ½ cup fresh or frozen whole kernel corn
- 2 large cloves garlic, minced
- 1 fresh jalapeño chile pepper, seeded (if desired) and finely chopped*
- 1 pound uncooked ground chicken breast or turkey breast
- 1 teaspoon chili powder
- 1 teaspoon ground cumin
- 1 teaspoon dried oregano, crushed
- ¾ cup ketchup
- 4 teaspoons Worcestershire sauce
- 6 whole grain sandwich-style rolls
  Dill pickle slices (optional)

1. In a very large nonstick skillet, heat oil over medium-high heat. Add onions, sweet pepper, corn, garlic, and chile pepper. Cook for 4 to 5 minutes or until onions are tender, stirring occasionally. Stir in chicken or turkey, chili powder, cumin, and oregano. Cook for 5 to 6 minutes more or until chicken or turkey is no longer pink. Stir in ketchup and Worcestershire sauce; heat through.

2. Divide mixture among rolls. If desired, top with pickle slices. Makes 6 sandwiches.

*Test Kitchen Tip: Because chile peppers contain volatile oils that can burn your skin and eyes, avoid direct contact with them as much as possible. When working with chile peppers, wear plastic or rubber gloves. If your bare hands do touch the peppers, wash your hands and nails well with soap and warm water.

Curried Chicken Salad Wraps

You can serve the chicken filling stuffed in tomatoes instead of rolled in tortillas, if you like.

PER WRAP: 246 cal., 5 g total fat (1 g sat. fat), 60 mg chol., 537 mg sodium, 18 g carb., 9 g fiber, 28 g pro. Exchanges: 1 vegetable, 1 starch, 3 very lean meat, 0.5 fat. Carb choices: 1.

- ½ cup fat-free or low-fat mayonnaise or salad dressing
- ½ teaspoon curry powder
- ⅛ teaspoon ground black pepper
- 2 cups chopped cooked chicken breast (about 10 ounces)
- ¼ cup sliced green onions
- 4 7-inch whole wheat flour tortillas
- 4 romaine leaves or 8 fresh spinach leaves
- 1 medium tomato, chopped

1. In a medium bowl, combine mayonnaise, curry powder, and pepper. Stir in chicken and green onions. If desired, cover and chill for 2 to 24 hours.

2. Top tortillas with leaves, chicken mixture, and tomato. Roll up. Makes 4 wraps.

Grilled Chicken Sandwiches

A little lime punches up the flavor in the fat-free dressing.

PER SANDWICH: 259 cal., 2 g total fat (0 g sat. fat), 66 mg chol., 488 mg sodium, 27 g carb., 3 g fiber, 31 g pro. Exchanges: 0.5 vegetable, 1.5 starch, 4 very lean meat. Carb choices: 2.

¼ cup fat-free mayonnaise or salad dressing
½ teaspoon finely shredded lime peel or lemon peel
1 medium zucchini or yellow summer squash, cut lengthwise into ¼-inch slices
3 tablespoons Worcestershire sauce
4 skinless, boneless chicken breast halves (1 to 1¼ pounds total)
4 whole wheat hamburger buns, split and toasted

1. In a small bowl, combine mayonnaise and lime peel. Cover and chill until serving time.

2. Brush zucchini slices with 1 tablespoon of the Worcestershire sauce; set aside. Brush chicken with remaining 2 tablespoons Worcestershire sauce.

3. Place chicken on the rack of an uncovered grill directly over medium coals. Grill chicken for 12 to 15 minutes, adding zucchini the last 6 minutes. Grill until chicken is no longer pink (170°F) and zucchini is tender, turning once.

4. To serve, spread lime dressing onto cut sides of toasted buns. If desired, cut zucchini slices in half crosswise. Place chicken and zucchini slices on bun bottoms; add bun tops. Makes 4 sandwiches.

Grilled Chicken Sandwiches

Turkey Reubens

To lower the calories and fat of a classic reuben use reduced-calorie Thousand Island salad dressing and swap turkey and lightly dressed coleslaw for corned beef and sauerkraut. Use a lower sodium dressing to reduce sodium further.

PER SANDWICH: 379 cal., 11 g total fat (5 g sat. fat), 67 mg chol., 884 mg sodium, 38 g carb., 5 g fiber, 31 g pro. Exchanges: 2 starch, 3 lean meat, 1 vegetable, 0.5 fat . Carb choices: 2.5.

2 cups packaged shredded cabbage with carrot (coleslaw mix)
2 tablespoons bottled reduced-calorie clear Italian salad dressing or white wine vinaigrette salad dressing
2 tablespoons bottled reduced-calorie Thousand Island salad dressing
8 ½-inch-thick slices rye bread
8 ounces sliced, cooked turkey breast
4 slices provolone cheese (4 ounces)
1 medium tomato, sliced
Cucumber spears (optional)

1. In a medium bowl, combine coleslaw mix and Italian salad dressing; set aside.

2. Spread Thousand Island salad dressing on one side of each bread slice. Place four of the bread slices, dressing sides up, on a work surface; top with turkey, cheese, tomato, and coleslaw mixture. Top with remaining bread slices, dressing sides down.

3. Preheat a large skillet over medium heat. Reduce heat to medium-low. Cook sandwiches, half at a time, for 4 to 6 minutes or until the bread is toasted and the cheese is melted, turning once. If desired, serve with cucumber spears. Makes 4 servings.

BBQ Chicken Ranch Wraps

Check the nutrition facts on packages of whole wheat flour tortillas. Then choose the ones that are lowest in carbohydrates and highest in fiber.

NUTRITION FACTS PER SERVING: 279 cal., 7 g total fat (1 g sat. fat), 51 mg chol., 589 mg sodium, 31 g carb., 3 g fiber, 23 g pro. Exchanges: 2 starch, 2 very lean meat, 0.5 vegetable, 1 fat. Carb choices: 2.

- **2** tablespoons bottled reduced-fat ranch salad dressing
- **1** tablespoon light mayonnaise or salad dressing
- **2** cups packaged shredded broccoli (broccoli slaw mix)
- **4** 8-inch whole wheat flour or flour tortillas
- **2** tablespoons bottled barbecue sauce
- **8** ounces cooked chicken breast or turkey breast, shredded

1. In a medium bowl, combine ranch dressing and mayonnaise dressing; stir in shredded broccoli. Spread tortillas with barbecue sauce. Top with chicken. Top with broccoli mixture. Roll up tortillas. Makes 4 servings.

BBQ Chicken Ranch Wraps

Grilled Turkey Burgers with Curry Mustard

Surprise your palate with the flavor of curry and mustard in every bite of these burgers.

PER BURGER: 265 cal., 8 g total fat (2 g sat. fat), 68 mg chol., 428 mg sodium, 26 g carb., 3 g fiber, 20 g pro. Exchanges: 2 starch, 2 lean meat. Carb choices: 2.

½ cup finely shredded carrot
¼ cup thinly sliced green onions
¼ cup soft whole wheat bread crumbs
2 tablespoons milk
¼ teaspoon dried Italian seasoning, crushed
¼ teaspoon garlic salt
  Dash ground black pepper
¾ pound uncooked ground turkey or chicken
4 whole wheat hamburger buns, split and toasted
  Shredded zucchini (optional)
  Sliced tomato (optional)
1 recipe Curry Mustard (see recipe, below) (optional)

1. In a medium bowl, stir together carrot, green onions, bread crumbs, milk, Italian seasoning, garlic salt, and pepper. Add ground turkey or chicken; mix well. Shape meat mixture into four ½-inch-thick patties.

2. Grill burgers on the rack of an uncovered grill directly over medium coals for 14 to 18 minutes or until an instant-read thermometer inserted into the center of burgers registers 160°F,* turning once halfway through grilling. (Or place burgers on unheated rack of a broiler pan. Broil 3 to 4 inches from heat for 12 to 14 minutes or until done, turning once.)

3. To serve, place burgers on buns. If desired, serve burgers with zucchini, tomato, and Curry Mustard. Makes 4 burgers.

Curry Mustard: In a small bowl, stir together ¼ cup Dijon-style mustard and ½ teaspoon curry powder. Makes ¼ cup.

***Test Kitchen Tip:** The internal color of a burger is not a reliable indication of doneness. A turkey patty cooked to 165°F is safe, regardless of color. To check, insert an instant-read thermometer into side to a depth of 2 to 3 inches.

Thai Turkey Burgers

Thai Turkey Burgers

Subbing small buns for big ones and mango slices for cheese lets burgers stay on your A-OK list.

PER BURGER: 213 cal., 4 g total fat (1 g sat. fat), 30 mg chol., 438 mg sodium, 23 g carb., 2 g fiber, 22 g pro. Exchanges: 1 starch, 0.5 fruit, 3 very lean meat. Carb choices: 1.5.

¼ cup refrigerated or frozen egg product, thawed, or 1 egg, beaten
¼ cup fine dry bread crumbs
1 teaspoon Thai seasoning or curry powder
1 pound uncooked ground turkey breast
6 small whole grain buns, split and toasted
¾ cup fresh basil
2 tablespoons bottled peanut sauce
1 medium mango, pitted, peeled, and sliced

1. In a medium bowl, combine egg, bread crumbs, and Thai seasoning. Add turkey; mix well. Shape into six ¾-inch-thick patties.

2. Grill patties on greased rack of an uncovered grill directly over medium heat for 14 to 18 minutes or until done (165°F),* turning once.

3. Top each bun bottom with basil, patty, peanut sauce, mango, and bun top. Makes 6 burgers.

***Test Kitchen Tip:** The internal color of a burger is not a reliable indication of doneness. A turkey patty cooked to 165°F is safe, regardless of color. To check, insert an instant-read thermometer into side to a depth of 2 to 3 inches.

comforting
soups and stews

Vegetable Pasta Soup

Sometimes a bowl of soup is all you need for dinner. These shaped-up, pared-down recipes offer fewer calories but all the flavor to make a meal satisfying. They're perfect when you want something both nourishing and easy.

Vegetable Pasta Soup

Serve this side-dish soup with a sandwich. Or make it a meal of six 1¼-cup servings instead.

PER SERVING: 86 cal., 2 g total fat (1 g sat. fat), 1 mg chol., 227 mg sodium, 14 g carb., 1 g fiber, 4 g pro. Exchanges: 0.5 vegetable, 0.5 starch, 0.5 fat. Carb choices: 1.

- 2 **teaspoons olive oil**
- 6 **cloves garlic, minced**
- 1½ **cups shredded carrots**
- 1 **cup chopped onion**
- 1 **cup thinly sliced celery**
- 1 **32-ounce box reduced-sodium chicken broth**
- 1½ **cups dried ditalini pasta**
- ¼ **cup shaved Parmesan cheese (1 ounce)**
- 2 **tablespoons snipped fresh parsley**

1. In a 5- to 6-quart Dutch oven, heat oil over medium heat. Add garlic; cook and stir for 15 seconds. Add carrots, onion, and celery; cook for 5 to 7 minutes or until tender, stirring occasionally. Add chicken broth and 4 cups *water*; bring to boiling. Add the uncooked pasta; cook for 7 to 8 minutes or until pasta is tender.

2. To serve, top each serving with Parmesan and parsley. Makes 12 (¾-cup) side-dish servings.

Baby Vegetable Minestrone

Baby vegetables are milder in flavor and more tender than their full-size counterparts.

PER SERVING: 77 cal., 2 g total fat (0 g sat. fat), 0 mg chol., 376 mg sodium, 12 g carb., 2 g fiber, 4 g pro. Exchanges: 0.5 starch, 1 vegetable, 0.5 fat. Carb choices: 1.

- 2 teaspoons olive oil
- ½ cup thinly sliced baby fennel
- 1 carrot, halved lengthwise and sliced
- 2 large cloves garlic, minced
- ¼ teaspoon lemon-pepper seasoning
- 2 14-ounce cans reduced-sodium chicken broth or 3½ cups homemade chicken broth
- ½ cup dried ditalini or other small dried pasta
- 6 ounces baby zucchini, halved lengthwise and sliced
- 6 ounces baby yellow squash, halved lengthwise and sliced
- ½ cup sliced green onions
- ¼ cup fresh basil leaves, thinly sliced
- 6 ounces Parmigiano-Reggiano or Romano cheese, cut into 6 very thin wedges (optional)

1. In a very large saucepan, heat oil. Add fennel, carrot, garlic, and lemon pepper; cook and stir over medium heat for 3 to 4 minutes or until carrot is light brown.

2. Carefully stir in broth. Bring to boiling; reduce heat. Simmer, covered, about 8 minutes or until vegetables are just tender.

3. Add pasta. Simmer, covered, for 5 minutes. Add zucchini and squash. Return to boiling; reduce heat. Simmer, covered, for 5 minutes more or until pasta is tender. Stir in green onions and basil.

4. If desired, garnish each serving with a thin wedge of cheese. Makes 6 (1¼-cup) side-dish servings.

Roasted Tomato and Vegetable Soup

For a distinctive flavor, buy canned tomatoes that are "fire-roasted."

PER SERVING: 92 cal., 2 g total fat (0 g sat. fat), 0 mg chol., 641 mg sodium, 16 g carb., 4 g fiber, 6 g pro. Exchanges: 0.5 starch, 1 vegetable, 0.5 very lean meat. Carb choices: 1.

- 1 medium onion, chopped
- 1 stalk celery, sliced
- 1 medium carrot, chopped
- 2 cloves garlic, minced
- 1 tablespoon olive oil
- 3 14-ounce cans reduced-sodium chicken broth
- 2 cups cut-up, peeled, and seeded butternut squash
- 1 14½-ounce can fire-roasted diced tomatoes or diced tomatoes, undrained
- 1 15- to 19-ounce can white kidney beans (cannellini beans), rinsed and drained
- 1 small zucchini, halved lengthwise and sliced
- 1 cup small broccoli and/or cauliflower florets
- 1 tablespoon snipped fresh oregano or 2 teaspoons dried oregano, crushed
- ¼ teaspoon salt
- ¼ teaspoon ground black pepper
- Grated Parmesan cheese (optional)

1. In a 4-quart Dutch oven, cook onion, celery, carrot, and garlic in hot oil over medium heat for 5 minutes or until tender.

2. Stir in chicken broth, squash, and undrained tomatoes. Bring to boiling; reduce heat. Cover and simmer for 20 minutes.

3. Add beans, zucchini, broccoli and/or cauliflower, oregano, salt, and pepper; cook for 5 minutes. If desired, top each serving with grated Parmesan cheese. Makes 8 (about 1⅓-cup) side-dish servings.

Slow-Cooker Directions: Omit the olive oil. In a 3½- to 4-quart slow cooker, combine onion, celery, carrot, garlic, broth, squash, tomatoes, beans, and dried oregano (if using). Cover and cook on low-heat setting for 7 to 8 hours or on high-heat setting for 3½ to 4 hours. If using low-heat setting, turn to high-heat setting. Add zucchini, broccoli and/or cauliflower, fresh oregano (if using), salt, and pepper. Cover; cook about 30 minutes or until tender. Serve as directed.

Quick Tip

Roasting vegetables brings out the natural sugars and concentrates their flavors. Tomatoes that have been roasted add a new flavor dimension to your recipes. Look for canned fire-roasted tomatoes with other tomato products at your supermarket.

Roasted Tomato and Vegetable Soup

Dilled Buttermilk-Pea Soup

Whirl tender peas in the blender to thicken this Scandinavian-style soup without flour.

PER SERVING: 83 cal., 1 g total fat (0 g sat. fat), 1 mg chol., 423 mg sodium, 14 g carb., 4 g fiber, 6 g pro. Exchanges: 1 starch. Carb choices: 1.

- 1 **14-ounce can reduced-sodium chicken broth**
- 2 **cups shelled fresh peas or one 10-ounce package frozen peas**
- 1 **cup torn fresh spinach**
- ¼ **cup chopped onion**
- 1 **tablespoon snipped fresh dill or savory, or ½ teaspoon dried dill or savory, crushed**
- ¼ **teaspoon salt**
- ⅛ **teaspoon ground black pepper**
- ½ **cup buttermilk**
  Fresh dill sprigs (optional)

1. In a medium saucepan, combine broth, peas, spinach, onion, snipped herb, salt, and pepper. Bring to boiling; reduce heat. Cover and simmer for 10 to 15 minutes for fresh peas (or 5 to 6 minutes for frozen peas) or until very tender. Cool slightly.

Dilled Buttermilk-Pea Soup

2. In a blender, blend the pea mixture, half at a time, until smooth. Return pureed mixture to same saucepan. Stir in buttermilk.

3. Heat and stir soup until warm. If desired, garnish each serving with fresh dill sprigs. Makes 4 (¾-cup) side-dish servings.

Make-Ahead Directions: Prepare soup as directed through Step 2; cover and chill for up to 24 hours. Serve as directed in Step 3.

Cheddar Cheesehead Soup

Slow and steady cooking keeps the cheese from curdling.

PER SERVING: 147 cal., 5 g total fat (3 g sat. fat), 16 mg chol., 464 mg sodium, 13 g carb., 0 g fiber, 11 g pro. Exchanges: 1 fat-free milk, 0.5 lean meat, 0.5 fat. Carb choices: 1.

- 1 **stalk celery, sliced**
- 1 **large onion, coarsely chopped**
- 4 **cloves garlic, sliced**
- 1 **tablespoon olive oil**
- 3 **14-ounce cans reduced-sodium chicken broth**
- 2 **12-ounce cans evaporated fat-free milk**
- ½ **cup instant flour or all-purpose flour**
- 2 **cups shredded reduced-fat cheddar cheese (8 ounces)**
- ¼ **teaspoon ground white pepper (optional)**
  Chopped red sweet pepper (optional)

1. In a Dutch oven, cook celery, onion, and garlic in hot oil until tender. Add chicken broth; bring to boiling. Reduce heat; cover and simmer for 25 minutes.

2. Strain the cooked vegetables, reserving broth in pan. Discard vegetables.

3. Stir together milk and flour; stir into broth. Cook and stir until thickened and bubbly.

4. Add cheese; cook and stir over low heat until cheese is melted. If desired, stir in white pepper; garnish each serving with chopped red sweet pepper. Makes 12 (¾-cup) side-dish servings.

Make-Ahead Directions: Prepare as directed through Step 2. Cover; chill for up to 3 days. Continue as directed in Steps 3 and 4.

(cheese, please)

Many favorite cheeses, such as Monterey Jack, cheddar, mozzarella, American, Swiss, and Parmesan, are readily available in lower-fat versions. But some high-flavor cheeses, such as blue cheese, feta, and Asiago, aren't. However, these cheeses have very pungent flavors and a little goes a long way. Just use them sparingly and you can have your cheese and eat it, too.

Cheddar Cheesehead Soup

Versatile (Asian) Vegetable Soup

Versatile Vegetable Soup

Make three different soups with just one recipe.
Choose from two side-dish soups or one main-dish soup.

PER SERVING: 82 cal., 1 g total fat (0 g sat. fat), 0 mg chol., 734 mg sodium,
18 g carb., 4 g fiber, 2 g pro. Exchanges: 0.5 starch, 1.5 vegetable.
Carb choices: 1.

- 2 **leeks, thinly sliced (white parts only)**
- 3 **cloves garlic, minced**
- 1 **teaspoon olive oil**
- 8 **cups water**
- 1 **14½-ounce can stewed tomatoes, undrained**
- 4 **stalks celery, sliced**
- 3 **medium carrots, thinly sliced**
- 1 **medium red apple, cored and coarsely chopped**
- 1 **medium sweet potato, peeled and cut into ½-inch cubes**
- 4 **teaspoons instant vegetable bouillon granules or vegetable bouillon cubes (to make 4 cups broth)**
- 2 **cups shredded cabbage**
- 1 **cup cut-up fresh green beans**
- ¼ **teaspoon salt**
- ¼ **teaspoon ground black pepper**
- ½ **cup snipped fresh parsley**
- 2 **tablespoons lemon juice**

1. In a 4-quart Dutch oven, cook leeks and garlic in hot oil about 3 minutes or until leeks are nearly tender. Carefully add the water, undrained tomatoes, celery, carrots, apple, sweet potato, and bouillon granules. Bring leek mixture to boiling; reduce heat. Cover and simmer for 15 minutes.

2. Add cabbage, beans, salt, and pepper. Return to boiling; reduce heat. Cover; simmer about 10 minutes or until vegetables are tender. Stir in parsley and lemon juice. Makes 10 (1-cup) side-dish servings.

Asian Vegetable Soup: Prepare as directed, except add ½ cup quick-cooking rice and ½ cup water with the cabbage. Substitute rice vinegar for lemon juice. Add 1 cup thinly sliced fresh mushrooms and 2 thinly sliced green onions with the rice vinegar. Heat through. Makes 10 (about 1¼-cup) side-dish servings.

PER SERVING: 111 cal., 1 g total fat (0 g sat. fat), 0 mg chol., 736 mg sodium, 24 g carb., 4 g fiber, 3 g pro. Exchanges: 1 starch, 1.5 vegetable. Carb choices: 1.5.

Tex-Mex Chicken-Vegetable Soup: Prepare as directed, except cook 1 teaspoon ground cumin with leek. Add 1 cup loose-pack frozen whole kernel corn, 1 cup chopped cooked chicken, one drained 4-ounce can chopped green chile peppers, and 3 tablespoons snipped fresh cilantro with lemon juice; heat through. If desired, garnish each serving with lemon wedges and fresh cilantro. Makes 8 (1⅓-cup) main-dish servings.

PER SERVING: 138 cal., 3 g total fat (1 g sat. fat), 16 mg chol., 790 mg sodium, 23 g carb., 5 g fiber, 8 g pro. Exchanges: 1 starch, 0.5 very lean meat, 1.5 vegetable. Carb choices: 1.

Lemon-Leek Vichyssoise

Low-fat buttermilk brings a pleasant tang to this
classic French chilled potato soup.

PER SERVING: 115 cal., 2 g total fat (1 g sat. fat), 2 mg chol.,
329 mg sodium, 19 g carb., 1 g fiber, 5 g pro. Exchanges: 1 starch,
0.5 fat. Carb choices: 1.

- 6 **medium leeks, trimmed and thinly sliced**
- 2 **tablespoons olive oil or cooking oil**
- 3 **pounds potatoes, peeled and sliced**
- 3 **14-ounce cans reduced-sodium chicken broth**
- 2 **teaspoons finely shredded lemon peel**
- ½ **teaspoon salt**
- ½ **teaspoon ground white pepper**
- 1 **quart buttermilk (4 cups)**
- 1 **8-ounce carton fat-free or light dairy sour cream**
- 1 **tablespoon lemon juice**
  Lemon wedges (optional)

1. In a 4- to 5-quart Dutch oven, cook leeks in hot oil until tender. Transfer half to a small container; cover and chill.

2. Add potatoes, broth, lemon peel, salt, and white pepper to leeks in Dutch oven. Bring to boiling; reduce heat. Cover and simmer about 15 minutes or until potatoes are tender. Cool slightly.

3. In a blender or food processor, blend or process potato mixture in small batches until smooth. Transfer to a large container. Stir in buttermilk. Cover and chill until serving time.

4. To serve, ladle soup into small cups or bowls. In a small bowl, combine sour cream and lemon juice; spoon onto soup. Top with chilled leeks. If desired, serve with lemon wedges. Makes 16 (¾-cup) side-dish servings.

Make-Ahead Directions: Prepare soup as directed; cover and chill for up to 48 hours before serving.

Mexican Corn Soup

Serve this chunky, cheesy soup with warm flour tortillas.

PER SERVING: 226 cal., 8 g total fat (4 g sat. fat), 39 mg chol., 471 mg sodium, 23 g carb., 1 g fiber, 17 g pro. Exchanges: 1.5 starch, 1.5 lean meat. Carb choices: 1.5.

- 1 **16-ounce package frozen whole kernel corn, thawed**
- 1 **cup reduced-sodium chicken broth**
- 1 **4-ounce can diced green chile peppers**
- 1 **clove garlic, minced**
- 1 **tablespoon snipped fresh oregano or 1 teaspoon dried oregano, crushed**
- ½ **teaspoon salt**
- ¼ **teaspoon ground black pepper**
- 2 **cups fat-free milk**
- 1 **cup chopped cooked chicken (about 5 ounces)**
- 1 **cup chopped tomatoes**
- 1 **cup shredded Monterey Jack cheese (4 ounces)**
  Snipped fresh parsley (optional)
  Fresh oregano sprigs (optional)

1. In a blender, combine half of the corn and the broth; cover and blend until nearly smooth.

2. In a large saucepan, combine corn puree, remaining corn, chile peppers, garlic, dried oregano (if using), salt, and black pepper. Bring to boiling; reduce heat. Simmer, uncovered, for 10 minutes.

3. Stir in milk, cooked chicken, tomatoes, and snipped oregano (if using); heat through. Remove from heat. Add cheese; stir until melted. If desired, garnish each serving with parsley and oregano sprigs. Makes 6 (1-cup) main-dish servings.

Mexican Corn Soup

Quick Tip

When you're watching your sodium intake, be sure to check the sodium in the broth you use. Here's a comparison of a 1-cup serving of chicken broth:
Low-sodium: 70 mg
Reduced-sodium: 570 mg
Regular: 960 mg
1 bouillon cube: 900 to 1,000 mg

Colorado Lentil Soup

Lentils cook in less time than dry beans and add valuable fiber and no cholesterol.

PER SERVING: 242 cal., 3 g total fat (0 g sat. fat), 0 mg chol., 259 mg sodium, 41 g carb., 16 g fiber, 13 g pro. Exchanges: 1 vegetable, 2.5 starch, 0.5 fat. Carb choices: 3.

- 1 **tablespoon olive oil**
- 1 **large onion, chopped**
- 6 **cloves garlic, minced**
- 6 **cups water**
- 1¼ **cups dry brown lentils**
- 1 **tablespoon fajita seasoning**
- 1 **tablespoon snipped fresh dill or 1½ teaspoons dried dill**
- ¼ **teaspoon salt**
- 6 **ounces round red potatoes, cut into ¾-inch pieces**
- 1 **14½-ounce can no-salt-added diced tomatoes, undrained**
- 1 **6-ounce can no-salt-added tomato paste**
- 2 **tablespoons canned diced green chile peppers**
- 1 **tablespoon snipped fresh parsley**
  Fat-free dairy sour cream (optional)
  Fresh dill sprigs (optional)

1. In a 4-quart Dutch oven, heat olive oil. Add onion and garlic; cook about 4 minutes or until tender.

2. Add the water, dry lentils, fajita seasoning, dried dill (if using), and salt. Bring to boiling; reduce heat. Cover; simmer for 15 minutes. Stir in potatoes. Cook, covered, for 10 to 15 minutes or until tender.

3. Stir in undrained tomatoes, tomato paste, and peppers. Return to boiling; reduce heat. Simmer, uncovered, for 10 minutes.

4. Stir in snipped fresh dill, if using, and parsley. If desired, garnish with sour cream and/or dill sprigs. Makes 6 (1½-cup) main-dish servings.

Sage-White Bean Soup

In the style of country French soups, beans thicken the broth.

PER SERVING: 236 cal., 2 g total fat (0 g sat. fat), 0 mg chol., 630 mg sodium, 40 g carb., 12 g fiber, 15 g pro. Exchanges: 2 starch, 2 very lean meat. Carb choices: 2.

- 1   pound dry **Great Northern** or navy beans
- 1   large onion, chopped
- 1   tablespoon olive oil
- 12 cloves garlic, minced
- 4   14-ounce cans reduced-sodium chicken broth
- 2   tablespoons snipped fresh sage or 2 teaspoons dried sage, crushed
- ½   teaspoon salt
- ½   teaspoon ground black pepper
- 1   recipe **Sage French Bread Toasts** (see recipe, right) (optional)
    Fresh sage leaves (optional)

1. Rinse beans. In a 4-quart Dutch oven, combine beans and 8 cups *water*. Bring to boiling; reduce heat. Simmer, uncovered, for 2 minutes. Remove from heat. Cover; let stand for 1 hour. (Or let uncooked beans soak in water overnight.) Drain and rinse beans; set aside.

2. In the same Dutch oven, cook onion in hot oil over medium heat until tender. Add garlic; cook and stir for 1 minute. Stir in beans and broth. Bring to boiling; reduce heat. Cover; simmer for 1 to 1½ hours or until tender.

3. Stir in the snipped or dried sage, salt, and pepper. If desired, top each serving with Sage French Bread Toasts and sage leaves. Makes 8 (1½-cup) main-dish servings.

Sage French Bread Toasts: Preheat oven to 425°F. Brush a little olive oil onto eight ½-inch-thick slices baguette-style French bread. Rub each slice with a cut garlic clove; sprinkle with snipped fresh or crushed dried sage. Bake for 5 to 7 minutes or until light brown.

Chicken Vegetable Soup

Barley is a tasty addition to this soup. When cooked, pearl barley has a nutty flavor and a slightly chewy texture.

PER SERVING: 249 cal., 5 g total fat (1 g sat. fat), 66 mg chol., 705 mg sodium, 20 g carb., 3 g fiber, 29 g pro. Exchanges: 0.5 vegetable, 1 starch, 3.5 very lean meat, 1 fat. Carb choices: 1.

- 2 pounds skinless, boneless chicken breast halves
- 1 teaspoon poultry seasoning
- 2 tablespoons olive oil
- 1½ cups sliced fresh mushrooms
- 1 cup chopped carrots
- ½ cup chopped onion
- ½ cup chopped green sweet pepper
- 4 cloves garlic, minced
- 2 tablespoons snipped fresh basil or 2 teaspoons dried basil, crushed
- 1 tablespoon snipped fresh parsley or 1 teaspoon dried parsley, crushed
- ¼ teaspoon ground black pepper
- ⅛ teaspoon salt
- 2 tablespoons instant chicken bouillon granules
- 1 pound potatoes, cut into 1-inch pieces
- ½ cup quick-cooking barley

1. Cut chicken into bite-size pieces. In a medium bowl, toss with poultry seasoning; set aside.

2. In a 5- to 6-quart Dutch oven, heat 1 tablespoon of the oil. Add mushrooms, carrots, onion, sweet pepper, garlic, dried basil and parsley (if using), black pepper, and salt; cook for 10 minutes, stirring often. Remove the vegetables.

3. Add remaining 1 tablespoon oil to Dutch oven; heat over medium heat. Add chicken; cook about 5 minutes or until chicken is brown, stirring occasionally.

4. Return vegetables to Dutch oven. Stir in 6 cups *water* and bouillon granules. Bring to boiling; stir in potatoes and barley. Return to boiling; reduce heat. Cover and simmer about 15 minutes or until potatoes are tender. Stir in fresh basil and parsley (if using). Makes 8 (1½-cup) main-dish servings.

Ginger-Chicken Noodle Soup

For a soup that's even quicker, substitute cubed cooked chicken for the chicken thighs and skip the first step.

PER SERVING: 221 cal., 6 g total fat (1 g sat. fat), 72 mg chol., 805 mg sodium, 16 g carb., 2 g fiber, 23 g pro. Exchanges: 1 starch, 3 very lean meat, 1 fat. Carb choices: 1.

- 1 pound skinless, boneless chicken thighs, cut into 1-inch pieces
- 1 tablespoon cooking oil
- 2 medium carrots, cut into thin bite-size sticks
- 3 14-ounce cans reduced-sodium chicken broth
- 1 cup water
- 2 tablespoons rice vinegar
- 1 tablespoon reduced-sodium soy sauce
- 2 to 3 teaspoons grated fresh ginger or ½ to ¾ teaspoon ground ginger
- ¼ teaspoon ground black pepper
- 2 ounces dried rice vermicelli noodles, broken into 2- to 3-inch pieces, or medium noodles
- 1 6-ounce package frozen pea pods, thawed and halved diagonally
  Reduced-sodium soy sauce (optional)

1. In a Dutch oven, cook chicken, half at a time, in hot oil just until brown. Drain off fat.

2. Return chicken to Dutch oven. Add carrots, broth, the water, vinegar, the 1 tablespoon soy sauce, ginger, and pepper. Bring to boiling; reduce heat. Cover and simmer for 20 minutes.

3. Add noodles. Simmer, uncovered, for 8 to 10 minutes or until noodles are tender, adding pea pods the last 1 to 2 minutes. If desired, serve with additional soy sauce. Makes 5 (1½-cup) main-dish servings.

(lovely leftovers)

When a recipe makes a lot, what do you do? Soups, stews, and casseroles are great served for lunch the next day or frozen for a heat-and-serve meal later in the month. To freeze, divide cooked foods into small portions in shallow containers. As a general rule, divide soups and stews into portions that are two to three inches deep and stir them while cooling to speed the release of heat. Arrange containers in a single layer in the freezer until frozen. Stack them after they are completely frozen. Never let perishable foods stand at room temperature too long to cool before they're refrigerated or frozen.

Tuscan Ravioli Stew

Tuscan Ravioli Stew

Broccoli rabe, a leafy green with stalks and broccoli-like buds that is popular in Italy, has a pungent, somewhat bitter flavor. If it is not available, substitute Swiss chard.

PER SERVING: 332 cal., 15 g total fat (4 g sat. fat), 68 mg chol., 548 mg sodium, 36 g carb., 2 g fiber, 14 g pro. Exchanges: 2 starch, 1 vegetable, 1 medium-fat meat, 1.5 fat. Carb choices: 2.5.

- 1 tablespoon olive oil
- 1 large leek, thinly sliced (about ½ cup)
- 3 cloves garlic, minced
- 1 14½-ounce can no-salt added stewed tomatoes, undrained
- 1 14-ounce can beef broth
- ¾ cup water
- ¼ teaspoon crushed red pepper (optional)
- 5 cups coarsely chopped broccoli rabe or **Swiss chard** (about 6 ounces)
- 1 9-ounce package refrigerated chicken-filled or cheese-filled ravioli
- 1 tablespoon snipped fresh rosemary or 1 teaspoon dried rosemary, crushed
  Fresh rosemary sprigs (optional)
- ¼ cup finely shredded **Asiago** cheese (1 ounce)

1. In a large saucepan, heat oil over medium heat. Add leek and garlic; cook about 3 minutes or until tender, stirring occasionally. Stir in undrained tomatoes, beef broth, the water, and, if desired, crushed red pepper; bring to boiling.

2. Stir in broccoli rabe, ravioli, and rosemary. Return to boiling; reduce heat. Cover and simmer for 7 to 8 minutes or until broccoli rabe and ravioli are tender. Ladle into shallow bowls. If desired, garnish with rosemary sprigs. Top individual servings with Asiago cheese. Makes 4 servings.

Quick Tip

Serving soup on a regular basis makes good sense when it comes to eating nutritiously or losing weight. Soups are fairly low in calories and fat (unless it's a cream-base variety) and contain more veggies than meat. And soup fills you up so you'll eat less overall.

Chicken and Rice Soup

What's more comforting than chicken soup? This zesty, Mexican-inspired version.

PER SERVING: 197 cal., 2 g total fat (0 g sat. fat), 33 mg chol., 477 mg sodium, 28 g carb., 2 g fiber, 17 g pro. Exchanges: 0.5 vegetable, 0.5 starch, 2 very lean meat. Carb choices: 2.

- 12 ounces skinless, boneless chicken breast halves
- ⅓ cup chopped onion
- ½ teaspoon salt
- ½ teaspoon ground cumin
- ½ teaspoon dried oregano, crushed
- 1 clove garlic, minced
- ¼ teaspoon ground black pepper
- 1 bay leaf
- 1 14-ounce can reduced-sodium beef broth
- 1 14½-ounce can diced tomatoes, undrained
- 1 cup frozen whole kernel corn
- 1 medium green sweet pepper, seeded and chopped
- ⅔ cup uncooked long grain rice
- ⅓ cup snipped fresh cilantro
- 2 teaspoons chili powder

1. In a Dutch oven, combine 5 cups *water*, chicken, onion, salt, cumin, oregano, garlic, black pepper, and bay leaf. Bring to boiling; reduce heat. Simmer, uncovered, for 10 to 12 minutes or until chicken is no longer pink. Remove chicken and shred into chunks.

2. Stir in broth, undrained tomatoes, corn, sweet pepper, rice, cilantro, and chili powder. Bring to boiling; reduce heat. Simmer, covered, for 25 minutes or until rice is tender. Discard bay leaf. Makes 6 (1⅓-cup) main-dish servings.

Kale, Lentil, and Chicken Soup

Lentils help pack a good amount of fiber into this soothing chicken soup.

PER SERVING: 199 cal., 5 g total fat (1 g sat. fat), 31 mg chol., 833 mg sodium, 20 g carb., 5 g fiber, 18 g pro. Exchanges: 0.5 starch, 2 lean meat, 2.5 vegetable. Carb choices: 1.

- 1 cup chopped onion
- 1 cup coarsely chopped carrots
- 2 cloves garlic, minced
- 1 tablespoon olive oil
- 6 cups reduced-sodium chicken broth
- 1 tablespoon snipped fresh basil or 1 teaspoon dried basil, crushed
- 4 cups coarsely chopped kale (about 8 ounces)
- ½ teaspoon salt
- ⅛ teaspoon ground black pepper
- 1½ cups cubed cooked chicken (about 8 ounces)
- 1 medium tomato, seeded and chopped
- ½ cup dry red lentils*

1. In a large saucepan, cover and cook onion, carrots, and garlic in hot oil over medium-low heat for 5 to 7 minutes or until vegetables are nearly tender, stirring occasionally.

2. Add broth and dried basil (if using) to vegetable mixture. Bring to boiling; reduce heat. Cover and simmer for 10 minutes. Stir in kale, salt, and pepper. Return to boiling; reduce heat. Cover and simmer for 10 minutes.

3. Stir in cooked chicken, tomato, red lentils, and fresh basil (if using). Cover and simmer for 5 to 10 minutes or until kale and lentils are tender. Makes 6 (1⅔-cup) main-dish servings.

*Test Kitchen Tip: If you wish to substitute brown or yellow lentils for the red lentils, you'll need to increase the cooking time. Check the package directions for cooking time and add the lentils in Step 2.

Kale, Lentil, and Chicken Soup

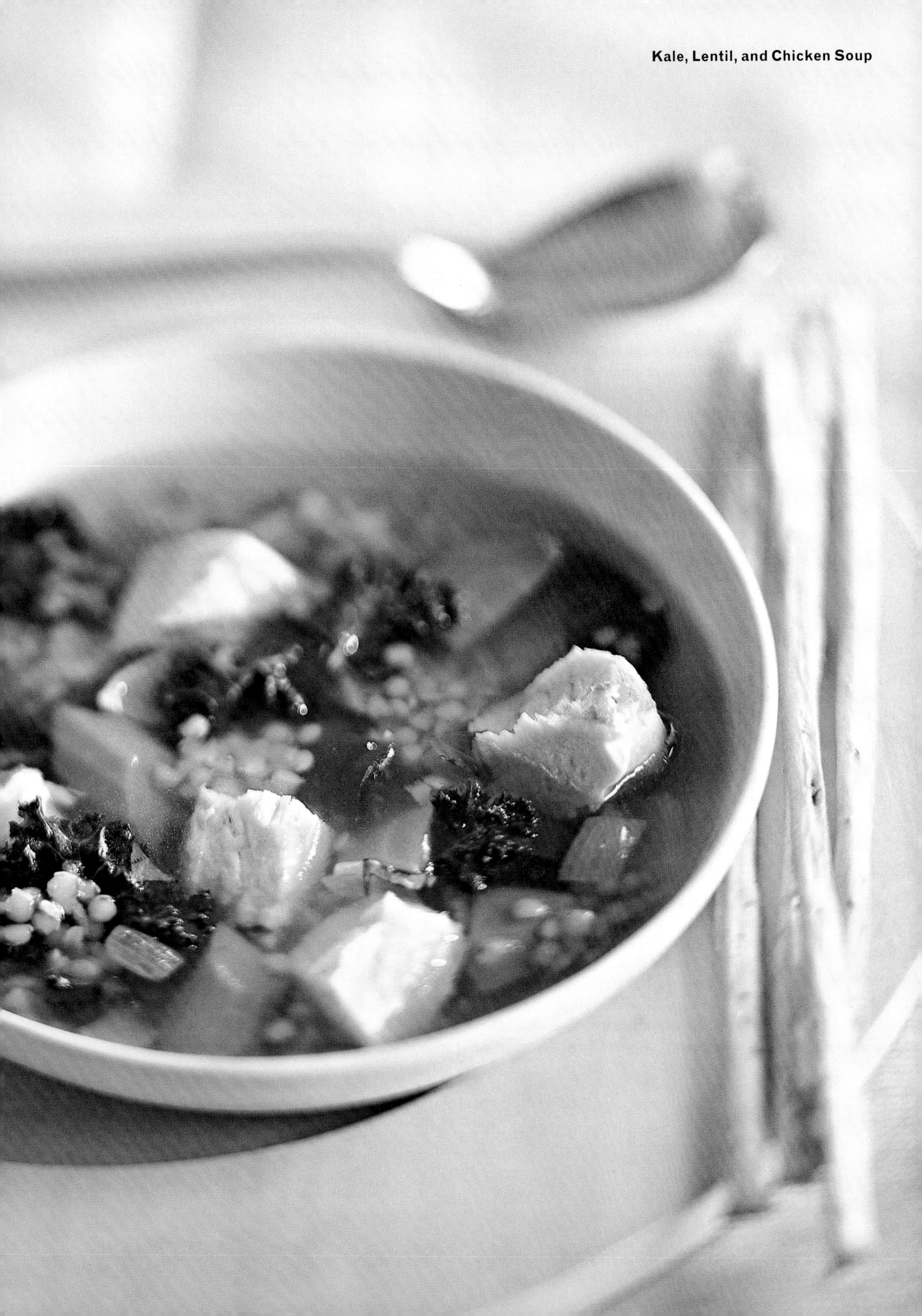

Shrimp and Crab Gumbo
A homemade Cajun spice blend gives
this seafood gumbo its classic kick.

PER SERVING: 263 cal., 5 g total fat (1 g sat. fat), 102 mg chol.,
510 mg sodium, 31 g carb., 4 g fiber, 22 g pro. Exchanges: 1.5 vegetable,
1.5 starch, 2 very lean meat. Carb choices: 2.

  1   **pound fresh or frozen large shrimp in shells**
  ⅓   **cup all-purpose flour**
  2   **tablespoons cooking oil**
  2   **cups chopped onions**
 1½   **cups chopped green and/or red sweet peppers**
  4   **stalks celery, thinly sliced**
  4   **cloves garlic, minced**
  2   **14-ounce cans reduced-sodium beef broth**
  1   **cup water**
  1   **recipe Cajun Spice Mix (see recipe, right)**
  1   **16-ounce package frozen cut okra**
  2   **6-ounce cans crabmeat, drained**
  3   **cups hot cooked long grain rice or brown rice**
      Green onions (optional)
      Bottled hot pepper sauce (optional)

1. Thaw shrimp, if frozen. Peel and devein shrimp,
leaving tails intact if desired. Rinse shrimp; pat dry with
paper towels.

2. In a medium skillet, cook flour over medium heat
about 6 minutes or until brown, stirring often. Transfer
to a medium bowl; set aside.

3. In a 4-quart Dutch oven, heat oil over medium heat.
Add onions, sweet peppers, celery, and garlic; cook and
stir about 5 minutes or until tender.

4. Slowly whisk broth into browned flour. Add broth
mixture, the water, and Cajun Spice Mix to Dutch oven.
Stir in okra. Bring to boiling; reduce heat. Cover and
simmer for 15 minutes.

5. Add shrimp; cook for 2 to 3 minutes or until shrimp
is pink. Gently stir in crabmeat.

6. To serve, spoon gumbo into eight bowls. Top each
serving with rice, a shrimp, and, if desired, a green
onion. If desired, pass hot pepper sauce. Makes 8 main-
dish servings (1¼ cups gumbo and ⅓ cup rice each).

Cajun Spice Mix: In a bowl, combine ½ teaspoon crushed
dried thyme, ¼ teaspoon salt, ¼ teaspoon ground white
pepper, ¼ teaspoon ground black pepper, and ¼ teaspoon
crushed red pepper.

Hot 'n' Spicy Fish Soup
Toast the cumin seeds in a skillet
to really bring out the flavor and aroma.

PER SERVING: 252 cal., 9 g total fat (1 g sat. fat), 54 mg chol.,
389 mg sodium, 5 g carb., 1 g fiber, 36 g pro. Exchanges: 5 very lean
meat, 1 vegetable, 1 fat. Carb choices: 0.

  4   **6-ounce fresh or frozen halibut steaks,**
      cut 1 inch thick
  4   **teaspoons cooking oil**
  ½   **teaspoon cumin seeds**
  1   **medium onion, chopped**
  3   **to 4 teaspoons grated fresh ginger**
  2   **fresh serrano or jalapeño peppers, seeded and finely**
      chopped (see Test Kitchen Tip, page 205)
  4   **small roma tomatoes, chopped**
  1   **teaspoon ground coriander**
  ½   **teaspoon ground turmeric**
      Fresh cilantro leaves (optional)

1. Thaw fish, if frozen. Rinse fish; pat dry. Remove
skin and bones. Cut into 1-inch pieces; set aside.

2. In a medium saucepan, heat oil over medium heat.
Add cumin seeds; cook and stir about 1 minute or until
toasted. Add onion; cook and stir for 4 to 5 minutes or
until tender. Add ginger and peppers; cook and stir for
1 minute. Add tomatoes; cook and stir for 2 to
3 minutes or until soft. Stir in 1½ cups *water*, coriander,
turmeric, and ½ teaspoon *salt*. Bring just to boiling;
reduce heat. Stir in fish.

3. Cover and cook about 5 minutes or just until fish
flakes easily when tested with a fork. If desired, garnish
with cilantro. Makes 4 (1-cup) main-dish servings.

Shrimp and
Crab Gumbo

Creamy Seafood Soup with Basil

Fat-free half-and-half steps in for the usual cream.

PER SERVING: 79 cal., 4 g total fat (1 g sat. fat), 16 mg chol., 456 mg sodium, 7 g carb., 0 g fiber, 3 g pro. Exchanges: 0.5 carb., 0.5 very lean meat, 0.5 fat. Carb choices: 0.5.

2	pounds live mussels in shells or 12 ounces small shrimp in shells*
12	quarts cold water (48 cups)
1	cup salt
1	14-ounce can reduced-sodium chicken broth
1	tablespoon olive oil
1	cup finely chopped leeks**
2	cloves garlic, minced
¼	teaspoon saffron threads or ⅛ teaspoon ground turmeric
¼	teaspoon ground black pepper
1	cup fat-free half-and-half
1	tablespoon finely shredded fresh basil

1. Scrub live mussels under cold running water. Using a sharp knife, cut off the beards between the shells. In a very large bowl, combine 4 quarts (16 cups) of the cold water and ⅓ cup of the salt. Add mussels; soak for 15 minutes. Drain in a colander. Rinse mussels, discarding water. Repeat twice, using fresh salted water. Rinse well. (If using shrimp, omit this step.)

2. In a Dutch oven, combine broth and 1½ cups *water;* bring to boiling. Add mussels; reduce heat. Cover and simmer for 5 to 7 minutes or until shells open. Discard any that do not open. (If using shrimp, cover and simmer in broth mixture for 2 to 3 minutes or until pink.)

3. Strain cooking liquid through a cheesecloth-lined sieve into a large bowl; set aside. Set aside mussels or shrimp until cool enough to handle.

4. In a large saucepan, heat oil over medium heat. Add leeks and garlic; cook and stir for 3 to 5 minutes or until tender. Stir in reserved cooking liquid, saffron, and pepper. Bring to boiling; reduce heat. Simmer gently, uncovered, about 15 minutes or until liquid is reduced to 3 cups total. Stir in half-and-half; heat through.

5. Meanwhile, when mussels are cool enough to handle, remove meat from mussel shells and set aside; discard shells. (Or peel and devein the shrimp; discard shells.)

6. Just before serving, stir the mussels or shrimp into soup; heat through. Sprinkle each serving with basil. Makes 8 (⅔-cup) side-dish servings.

***Note:** If using shrimp, add ⅛ teaspoon salt to soup. Omit the 12 quarts water and 1 cup salt.

****Test Kitchen Tip:** To clean leeks, remove root ends and any heavy dark green portions. Slice lengthwise and submerge in a bowl of cool, clean water. Gently open layers and rinse thoroughly to remove any grit or sand. Repeat washing as needed.

slow cooker favorites

Mushroom-Sauced
Pork Chops

There is nothing better than a hot meal that is ready for the dinner table when you come home from work. Make it possible with your slow cooker. From soups to sandwiches to all-in-one meals, there's a recipe that will satisfy any hungry family at the end of a busy day.

Mushroom-Sauced Pork Chops

Mushroom soup and fresh mushrooms give a double dose of woodsy flavor.

PER SERVING: 314 cal., 12 g total fat (4 g sat. fat), 74 mg chol., 356 mg sodium, 17 g carb., 1 g fiber, 30 g pro. Exchanges: 0.5 vegetable, 1 carb., 4 very lean meat, 2 fat. Carb choices: 1.

- 4 pork loin chops, cut ¾ inch thick (about 2 pounds)
- 1 tablespoon cooking oil
- 1 small onion, thinly sliced
- 2 tablespoons quick-cooking tapioca
- 1 10.75-ounce can reduced-fat and reduced-sodium condensed cream of mushroom soup
- ½ cup apple juice or apple cider
- 1½ teaspoons Worcestershire sauce
- 2 teaspoons snipped fresh thyme or ¾ teaspoon dried thyme, crushed
- ¼ teaspoon garlic powder
- 1½ cups sliced fresh mushrooms
  Fresh thyme sprigs (optional)

1. Trim fat from chops. In a large skillet, heat oil over medium heat. Add chops; cook until brown, turning to brown evenly. Drain off fat.

2. In a 3½- or 4-quart slow cooker,* layer onion and chops. Using a mortar and pestle, crush tapioca. In a medium bowl, combine tapioca, mushroom soup, apple juice, Worcestershire sauce, snipped thyme, and garlic powder; stir in mushrooms. Pour over chops.

3. Cover and cook on low-heat setting for 8 to 9 hours or on high-heat setting for 4 to 4½ hours. Serve sauce over chops. If desired, garnish with thyme. Makes 4 servings.

*Test Kitchen Tip: If using a 5- to 6-quart slow cooker, use 6 pork loin chops. Leave remaining ingredient amounts the same. Prepare as above. Makes 6 servings.

Seeded Pork Roast

A savory blend of seeds creates a crusty calorie-free coating. Apple juice lends a subtle sweetness.

PER SERVING: 220 cal., 9 g total fat (3 g sat. fat), 92 mg chol., 269 mg sodium, 5 g carb., 0 g fiber, 29 g pro. Exchanges: 4 lean meat. Carb choices: 0.5.

- 1 2½- to 3-pound (boneless) pork shoulder roast
- 1 tablespoon reduced-sodium soy sauce
- 2 teaspoons anise seeds, crushed
- 2 teaspoons fennel seeds, crushed
- 2 teaspoons caraway seeds, crushed
- 2 teaspoons dill seeds, crushed
- 2 teaspoons celery seeds, crushed
- ⅔ cup apple juice or apple cider
- ½ cup lower-sodium beef broth
- 1 tablespoon cornstarch

1. Trim fat from meat. If necessary, cut the meat to fit into a 3½- to 5-quart slow cooker. Brush soy sauce onto meat. On a large piece of foil, combine anise seeds, fennel seeds, caraway seeds, dill seeds, and celery seeds. Roll roast in seeds to coat evenly. Place meat in slow cooker. Pour ⅓ cup of the apple juice and the broth around meat.

2. Cover and cook on low-heat setting for 9 to 11 hours or on high-heat setting for 4½ to 5½ hours.

3. Transfer meat to a cutting board, reserving liquid. Slice meat; transfer to a platter. Cover to keep warm.

4. For gravy, strain cooking liquid; skim off fat. Transfer liquid to a small saucepan. In a small bowl, combine remaining ⅓ cup apple juice and cornstarch; stir into liquid in saucepan. Cook and stir over medium heat until thickened and bubbly. Cook and stir for 2 minutes more. Serve over meat. Makes 8 servings.

Spiced Pork Stew

Cinnamon, cumin, and ginger evoke a Moroccan flavor.

PER SERVING: 245 cal., 9 g total fat (3 g sat. fat), 51 mg chol., 530 mg sodium, 22 g carb., 3 g fiber, 17 g pro. Exchanges: 1 starch, 1.5 medium-fat meat, 1.5 vegetable. Carb choices: 1.5.

- 3 **tablespoons all-purpose flour**
- 1 **teaspoon ground cumin**
- 2 **pounds boneless pork shoulder, cut into ¾-inch pieces**
- 1 **medium onion, chopped**
- 2 **tablespoons cooking oil**
- 2 **medium carrots, sliced**
- 2 **medium red potatoes, chopped**
- 1 **medium sweet potato, peeled and chopped**
- 2 **14.5-ounce cans diced tomatoes, undrained**
- ⅓ **cup water**
- 1 **teaspoon salt**
- 1 **teaspoon ground ginger**
- 1 **teaspoon ground cinnamon**
- ½ **teaspoon sugar**
- ½ **teaspoon ground black pepper**
- 2 **cups loose-pack frozen cut green beans**
- 2 **tablespoons snipped fresh cilantro or parsley**
- ½ **cup plain low-fat yogurt (optional)**

1. In a large resealable plastic bag, combine flour and cumin. Add pork pieces to plastic bag; shake to coat. In a 4- to 5-quart Dutch oven, cook meat and onion, half at a time, in hot oil over medium heat until meat is brown. Drain off fat.

2. In a 4- to 5½-quart slow cooker, combine carrots, red potatoes, and sweet potato; top with pork mixture. Combine tomatoes, water, salt, ginger, cinnamon, sugar, and pepper; pour over pork.

3. Cover and cook on low-heat setting for 8 to 10 hours or on high-heat setting for 4 to 5 hours, adding green beans for the last 30 minutes.

4. To serve, top each serving with cilantro and yogurt, if desired. Makes 8 (1¼-cup) servings.

Quick Tip

Freeze leftovers for another day. For the best flavor, freeze soups, stews, and meat dishes with gravy for up to 3 months. Meats with vegetables and pasta can be frozen for up to 1 month. To prevent freezer burn, store the food in freezer containers with tightly fitting lids.

Spiced Pork Stew

Cider Pork Stew

Cider Pork Stew

Apple cider lends a subtle sweetness to this hearty stew.

PER SERVING: 272 cal., 7 g total fat (2 g sat. fat), 73 mg chol., 405 mg sodium, 27 g carb., 3 g fiber, 24 g pro. Exchanges: 1 starch, 0.5 fruit, 3 very lean meat, 0.5 vegetable, 1 fat. Carb choices: 2

- 2 pounds pork shoulder roast
- 3 medium potatoes, cubed (about 2½ cups)
- 3 medium carrots, cut into ½-inch pieces (about 1½ cups)
- 2 medium onions, sliced
- 1 medium apple, cored and coarsely chopped (1 cup)
- ½ cup coarsely chopped celery
- 2 cups apple cider or apple juice
- 3 tablespoons quick-cooking tapioca
- 1 teaspoon salt
- 1 teaspoon caraway seeds
- ¼ teaspoon ground black pepper
- Celery leaves (optional)

1. Trim fat from meat; cut meat into 1-inch cubes. In a 3½- to 5½-quart slow cooker, combine meat, potatoes, carrots, onions, apple, and celery. In a glass measuring cup, stir together apple juice, tapioca, salt, caraway, and pepper; pour over meat and vegetables.

2. Cover and cook on low-heat setting for 10 to 12 hours or high-heat setting for 5 to 6 hours.

3. To serve, spoon into 8 soup bowls. If desired, garnish with celery leaves. Makes 8 (1-cup) servings.

Shredded Pork Sandwiches

To shave a few carbs, skip the bun and top the slow-cooked pork shoulder with broccoli slaw.

PER SANDWICH: 270 cal., 10 g total fat (3 g sat. fat), 55 mg chol., 500 mg sodium, 24 g carb., 2 g fiber, 22 g pro. Exchanges: 1.5 starch, 2.5 lean meat, 0.5 vegetable. Carb choices: 1.5.

- 1½ teaspoons garlic powder
- 1½ teaspoons onion powder
- 1½ teaspoons ground black pepper
- 1 teaspoon celery salt
- 1 3-pound boneless pork shoulder roast
- 2 large onions, cut into thin wedges
- ½ cup water
- 2 cups packaged shredded broccoli (broccoli slaw mix)
- 1 cup light mayonnaise dressing or salad dressing
- 16 whole grain hamburger buns

Shredded Pork Sandwiches

1. In a small bowl, stir together garlic powder, onion powder, pepper, and celery salt. Trim fat from meat. Sprinkle garlic powder mixture evenly onto meat; rub into meat with your fingers. If necessary, cut meat to fit into a 3½- or 4-quart slow cooker.

2. Place onions in slow cooker. Add meat and water. Cover and cook on low-heat setting for 8 to 10 hours or on high-heat setting for 4 to 5 hours.

3. Using a slotted spoon, transfer meat to a cutting board; discard cooking liquid. Using two forks, shred meat. Return meat to slow cooker to keep warm.

4. To serve, in a small bowl, combine broccoli and ¼ cup of the mayonnaise dressing. Spread cut sides of buns with remaining dressing. Spoon meat onto bun bottoms. Top with broccoli mixture and bun tops. Makes 16 sandwiches.

Pork Primavera Sandwiches

A purchased barbecue sauce not only makes these sandwiches a cinch to put together but also gives you the flexibility to choose the flavor profile.

PER SANDWICH: 258 cal., 5 g total fat (1 g sat. fat), 57 mg chol., 418 mg sodium, 28 g carb., 3 g fiber, 24 g pro. Exchanges: 2 starch, 2.5 medium-fat meat. Carb choices: 2.

  2 medium carrots, shredded (about 1 cup)
  1 large red sweet pepper, seeded and coarsely chopped
  1 medium onion, cut into thin wedges
  2 tablespoons quick-cooking tapioca, crushed
  2 to 2½ pounds boneless pork sirloin roast or boneless pork loin roast, trimmed of fat
  ¾ cup bottled reduced-sodium, fat-free barbecue sauce
 10 whole wheat hamburger buns, split and toasted

1. In a 3½- or 4-quart slow cooker, combine carrots, sweet pepper, and onion. Sprinkle with tapioca. Place meat on top of vegetables. Pour barbecue sauce over meat.

2. Cover and cook on low-heat setting for 6 to 7 hours or on high-heat setting for 3 to 3½ hours.

3. Remove meat from slow cooker, reserving juices. Thinly slice meat. Return meat to slow cooker; stir to coat with sauce. Serve meat on buns. Makes 10 sandwiches.

Spicy Pork Sandwiches

These barbecue sandwiches pack a fair amount of heat. Serve with homemade cole slaw for a real Southern treat.

PER SANDWICH: 292 cal., 7 g total fat (2 g sat. fat), 79 mg chol., 402 mg sodium, 23 g carb., 1 g fiber, 31 g pro. Exchanges: 1.5 starch, 3.5 lean meat. Carb choices: 1.5.

  1 2½- to 3-pound pork sirloin roast
  ½ teaspoon garlic powder
  ½ teaspoon ground ginger
  ½ teaspoon dried thyme, crushed
  1 cup chicken broth
  ½ cup vinegar
  ½ teaspoon ground red pepper
  8 to 10 hamburger buns, split and toasted

1. Remove string from roast, if present. Trim fat from roast. If necessary, cut roast to fit into a 3½- to 4-quart slow cooker. In a small bowl, combine garlic powder, ginger, and thyme. Sprinkle garlic powder mixture over roast. Using your fingers, rub mixture into meat. Place roast in cooker. Pour broth over roast.

2. Cover and cook on low-heat setting for 8 to 10 hours or on high-heat setting for 4 to 5 hours.

3. Remove meat from cooker, reserving cooking liquid. Using two forks, shred meat and place in a large bowl. Add 1 cup of the cooking liquid, the vinegar, and ground red pepper to meat in bowl; toss to combine. Serve on buns. Makes 8 to 10 sandwiches.

Barbecued Turkey Thighs

Who needs a grill for barbecue? These saucy turkey thighs hold their form nicely during slow cooking and can hold their own among other grilled turkey dishes.

PER SERVING: 225 cal., 6 g total fat (2 g sat. fat), 100 mg chol., 444 mg sodium, 12 g carb., 1 g fiber, 30 g pro. Exchanges: 1 carb., 4 very lean meat, 1 fat. Carb choices: 1.

½ cup ketchup
2 tablespoons sugar substitute*
1 tablespoon quick-cooking tapioca
1 tablespoon vinegar
1 teaspoon Worcestershire sauce
¼ teaspoon ground cinnamon
¼ teaspoon crushed red pepper
2 to 2½ pounds turkey thighs (about 2 thighs) or meaty chicken pieces (breasts, thighs, and drumsticks), skinned
Hot cooked brown rice or whole wheat pasta (optional)

1. In a 3½- or 4-quart slow cooker, combine ketchup, sugar substitute, tapioca, vinegar, Worcestershire sauce, cinnamon, and red pepper. Place turkey thighs meaty side down on ketchup mixture.

2. Cover and cook on low-heat setting for 10 to 12 hours or high-heat setting for 5 to 6 hours. Transfer turkey to a serving dish. Pour cooking juices into a small bowl; skim off fat. Serve turkey with cooking juices and, if desired, hot cooked rice. Makes 4 to 6 servings.

*Sugar Substitutes: Choose from Splenda Granular, Equal Spoonful or packets, or Sweet'N Low bulk or packets.

Sesame-Ginger Turkey Wraps

Pair these irresistible Asian-inspired slow-cooker wraps with a salad to make a delectable dinner.

PER WRAP: 207 cal., 5 g total fat (1 g sat. fat), 67 mg chol., 422 mg sodium, 20 g carb., 2 g fiber, 20 g pro. Exchanges: 1 vegetable, 1 starch, 2 lean meat. Carb choices: 1.5.

Nonstick cooking spray
3 turkey thighs, skinned (3½ to 4 pounds total)
1 cup bottled sesame-ginger stir-fry sauce
¼ cup water
1 16-ounce package shredded broccoli (broccoli slaw mix)
12 8-inch flour tortillas, warmed*
¾ cup sliced green onions

1. Lightly coat a 3½- or 4-quart slow cooker with cooking spray. Place turkey thighs in slow cooker. In a small bowl, stir together stir-fry sauce and the water. Pour over turkey.

2. Cover and cook on low-heat setting for 6 to 7 hours or on high-heat setting for 3 to 3½ hours.

3. Remove turkey from slow cooker; cool slightly. Remove turkey from bones; discard bones. Using two forks, pull turkey apart into shreds.

4. Meanwhile, place broccoli in the sauce mixture in the slow cooker; stir to coat. Cover and let stand for 5 minutes. Using a slotted spoon, remove broccoli from slow cooker.

5. To assemble, place some of the turkey on each tortilla. Top with broccoli mixture and green onions. Spoon sauce from slow cooker on top of green onions. Roll up. Serve immediately. Makes 12 wraps.

*Test Kitchen Tip: To warm tortillas, wrap them in white microwave-safe paper towels; microwave on 100 percent power (high) for 15 to 30 seconds or until tortillas are softened. (Or preheat oven to 350°F. Wrap tortillas in foil. Heat for 10 to 15 minutes or until warmed.)

Spinach, Chicken, and Wild Rice Soup

Chicken and Shrimp Jambalaya

Removing the skin from a chicken breast half saves about 6 grams of fat and 50 calories per serving.

PER SERVING: 211 cal., 2 g total fat (0 g sat. fat), 88 mg chol., 415 mg sodium, 26 g carb., 4 g fiber, 23 g pro. Exchanges: 1 starch, 1.5 vegetable, 2.5 very lean meat. Carb choices: 2.

- 2 **cups thinly sliced celery**
- 2 **cups chopped onions**
- 1 **14.5-ounce can no-salt-added diced tomatoes**
- 1 **14-ounce can reduced-sodium chicken broth**
- ½ **of a 6-ounce can (⅓ cup) no-salt-added tomato paste**
- 2 **cloves garlic, minced**
- 1 **recipe Homemade Salt-Free Cajun Seasoning (see recipe, below) or salt-free Cajun seasoning**
- ½ **teaspoon salt**
- 1 **pound skinless, boneless chicken breast halves or thighs, cut into ¾-inch pieces**
- 1½ **cups instant brown rice**
- ¾ **cup chopped green, red, and/or yellow sweet pepper**
- 8 **ounces cooked peeled and deveined shrimp, tails intact**
- 2 **tablespoons snipped fresh parsley**
  Celery leaves (optional)

1. In a 3½- or 4-quart slow cooker, stir together celery, onions, undrained tomatoes, broth, tomato paste, garlic, Cajun seasoning, and salt. Stir in chicken.

2. Cover and cook on low-heat setting for 4½ to 5½ hours or on high-heat setting for 2¼ to 2¾ hours.

3. If using low-heat setting, turn to high-heat setting. Stir in uncooked rice and sweet pepper. Cover; cook about 30 minutes more or until most of the liquid is absorbed and rice is tender.

4. Stir in shrimp and parsley. If desired, garnish with celery leaves. Makes 8 (1½-cup) servings.

Homemade Salt-Free Cajun Seasoning: Stir together ¼ teaspoon each ground white pepper, garlic powder, onion powder, paprika, and ground black pepper, and ⅛ to ¼ teaspoon ground red pepper.

Spinach, Chicken, and Wild Rice Soup

If you don't have leftover chicken, stop by the deli and buy a roasted chicken.

PER SERVING: 216 cal., 4 g total fat (1 g sat. fat), 64 mg chol., 397 mg sodium, 19 g carb., 2 g fiber, 26 g pro. Exchanges: 1 starch, 3 very lean meat, 0.5 vegetable, 0.5 fat. Carb choices: 1.

- 3 **cups water**
- 1 **14-ounce can reduced-sodium chicken broth**
- 1 **10.75-ounce can reduced-fat and reduced-sodium condensed cream of chicken soup**
- ⅔ **cup wild rice, rinsed and drained**
- ½ **teaspoon dried thyme, crushed**
- ¼ **teaspoon ground black pepper**
- 3 **cups chopped cooked chicken or turkey (about 1 pound)**
- 2 **cups chopped fresh spinach**

1. In a 3½- or 4-quart slow cooker, combine the water, broth, condensed cream of chicken soup, uncooked wild rice, thyme, and pepper.

2. Cover and cook on low-heat setting for 7 to 8 hours or on high-heat setting for 3½ to 4 hours.

3. To serve, stir in chicken and spinach. Makes 6 (1½-cup) servings.

Chicken, Barley, and Leek Stew

You can freeze this soup in single portions
to heat for a quick lunch.

PER SERVING: 248 cal., 6 g total fat (1 g sat. fat), 63 mg chol., 558 mg sodium, 27 g carb., 6 g fiber, 22 g pro. Exchanges: 0.5 vegetable, 1.5 starch, 2.5 lean meat. Carb choices: 2.

- 1 **pound skinless, boneless chicken thighs, cut into 1-inch pieces**
- 1 **tablespoon olive oil**
- 3 **14-ounce cans reduced-sodium chicken broth**
- ¾ **cups water**
- 1 **cup regular barley (not quick-cooking)**
- 3 **medium leeks, halved lengthwise and sliced**
- 2 **medium carrots, thinly sliced**
- 1½ **teaspoons dried thyme or Italian seasoning, crushed**
- ¼ **teaspoon cracked black pepper**

1. In a large skillet, cook chicken in hot oil until brown. In a 4- to 5-quart slow cooker, combine chicken, broth, water, barley, leeks, carrots, thyme, and pepper.

2. Cover and cook stew on low-heat setting for 4 to 5 hours or on high-heat setting for 2 to 2½ hours or until barley is tender. Makes 6 (1½-cup) servings.

Chicken, Barley, and Leek Stew

Teriyaki and Orange Chicken

This sauce is sweet and full of flavor. Use orange sections or slices to garnish the meal.

PER SERVING: 320 cal., 2 g total fat (0 g sat. fat), 66 mg chol., 432 mg sodium, 41 g carb., 5 g fiber, 32 g pro. Exchanges: 1 vegetable, 1.5 starch, 1 other carb., 3 lean meat. Carb choices: 3.

- **1** 16-ounce package frozen loose-pack broccoli, carrots, and water chestnuts
- **2** tablespoons quick-cooking tapioca
- **1** pound skinless, boneless chicken breast halves or thighs, cut into 1-inch pieces
- **¾** cup reduced-sodium chicken broth
- **3** tablespoons low-sugar orange marmalade
- **2** tablespoons bottled light teriyaki sauce
- **1** teaspoon dry mustard
- **½** teaspoon ground ginger
- **2** cups hot cooked brown rice

1. In a 3½- or 4-quart slow cooker, combine frozen vegetables and tapioca. Add chicken.

2. In a small bowl, combine chicken broth, orange marmalade, teriyaki sauce, dry mustard, and ginger. Pour over mixture in cooker.

3. Cover and cook on low-heat setting for 4 to 5 hours or on high-heat setting for 2 to 2½ hours. Serve with hot cooked rice. Makes 4 servings.

Rosemary Chicken and Artichokes

Start cooking the brown rice first or use microwavable brown rice.

PER SERVING: 168 cal., 4 g total fat (1 g sat. fat), 89 mg chol., 328 mg sodium, 8 g carb., 3 g fiber, 23 g pro. Exchanges: 3 very lean meat, 1.5 vegetable, 0.5 fat. Carb choices: 0.5.

- 1 medium onion, chopped
- 6 cloves garlic, minced
- ⅓ cup reduced-sodium chicken broth
- 1 tablespoon quick-cooking tapioca
- 2 to 3 teaspoons finely shredded lemon peel
- 2 teaspoons snipped fresh rosemary or 1 teaspoon dried rosemary, crushed
- ¾ teaspoon ground black pepper
- 2½ to 3 pounds chicken thighs, skinned
- ½ teaspoon salt
- 1 8- or 9-ounce package frozen artichoke hearts, thawed
- 1 medium red sweet pepper, cut into strips
- Hot cooked brown rice (optional)
- Snipped fresh parsley (optional)
- Fresh rosemary sprigs (optional)

1. In a 3½- to 4-quart slow cooker, combine onion, garlic, broth, tapioca, 1 teaspoon of the lemon peel, the snipped rosemary, and ½ teaspoon of the black pepper. Add chicken. Sprinkle with salt and remaining ¼ teaspoon black pepper.

2. Cover and cook on low-heat setting for 5 to 6 hours or on high-heat setting for 2½ to 3 hours.

3. If using low-heat setting, turn cooker to high heat. Add thawed artichokes and pepper strips. Cover; cook for 30 minutes more.

4. To serve, top with remaining 1 to 2 teaspoons lemon peel. If desired, serve with cooked brown rice, sprinkle with parsley, and garnish with rosemary sprigs. Makes 6 servings.

Italian Chicken and Pasta

For a colorful variation, use spinach or red pepper fettuccine.

PER SERVING: 383 cal., 6 g total fat (2 g sat. fat), 73 mg chol., 392 mg sodium, 52 g carb., 7 g fiber, 28 g pro. Exchanges: 3.5 vegetable, 2 starch, 3 lean meat. Carb choices: 3.5.

- 12 ounces skinless, boneless chicken thighs
- 1 9-ounce package frozen Italian-style green beans
- 1 cup fresh mushrooms, quartered
- 1 small onion, sliced ¼ inch thick
- 1 14.5-ounce can Italian-style stewed tomatoes, undrained
- 1 6-ounce can no-salt-added tomato paste
- 1½ teaspoon dried Italian seasoning, crushed
- 2 cloves garlic, minced
- 6 ounces wide egg noodles, cooked and drained
- 3 tablespoons finely shredded Parmesan cheese (optional)

1. Cut chicken into 1-inch pieces; set aside. In a 3½- or 4-quart slow cooker, place green beans, mushrooms, and onion. Place chicken on vegetables.

2. In a bowl, combine undrained tomatoes, tomato paste, Italian seasoning, and garlic. Pour over chicken.

3. Cover and cook on low-heat setting for 5 to 6 hours or on high-heat setting for 2½ to 3 hours. Serve over hot cooked pasta. Sprinkle with Parmesan cheese, if desired. Makes 4 (1½-cup) servings.

Chicken in Wine Sauce

1. In a 5- or 6-quart slow cooker, place potatoes, carrots, celery, and onion. Place chicken pieces on top of vegetables. Sprinkle with parsley, salt, rosemary, thyme, pepper, and garlic; add broth and wine.

2. Cover and cook on low-heat setting for 8 to 9 hours or on high-heat setting for 4 to 4½ hours. Using a slotted spoon, transfer chicken and vegetables to a serving platter; cover with foil to keep warm.

3. For gravy, skim fat from cooking juices; strain juices. In a large saucepan, melt butter. Stir in flour and cook for 1 minute. Add cooking juices. Cook and stir until thickened and bubbly. Cook and stir 2 minutes more. If desired, sprinkle chicken and vegetables with snipped thyme. Pass gravy with the chicken and vegetables. Makes 6 servings.

Zesty Ginger-Tomato Chicken
Chicken drumsticks or thighs stay moist and tender during the slow cooker's long cooking time.

PER SERVING: 302 cal., 6 g total fat (1 g sat. fat), 81 mg chol., 549 mg sodium, 35 g carb., 4 g fiber, 28 g pro. Exchanges: 1 vegetable, 2 starch, 3 very lean meat, 0.5 fat. Carb choices: 2.5.

- 2½ **to 3 pounds skinless chicken drumsticks and/or thighs**
- 2 **14.5-ounce cans diced tomatoes**
- 2 **tablespoons quick-cooking tapioca**
- 1 **tablespoon grated fresh ginger**
- 1 **tablespoon snipped fresh cilantro or parsley**
- 4 **cloves garlic, minced**
- ½ **teaspoon crushed red pepper**
- ½ **teaspoon salt**
- 3 **cups hot cooked quinoa or brown rice**

1. Place chicken in a 3½- or 4-quart slow cooker. Drain 1 can tomatoes. In a medium bowl, combine drained and undrained tomatoes, the tapioca, ginger, cilantro, garlic, red pepper, and salt. Pour over chicken.

2. Cover and cook on low-heat setting for 6 to 7 hours or on high-heat setting for 3 to 3½ hours.

3. Remove chicken from cooker; skim fat from liquid. Serve with hot cooked quinoa. Makes 6 servings.

Chicken in Wine Sauce
Chicken and hearty vegetables are simmered in a delicate wine-flavored sauce. Choose dark meat chicken—legs, thighs, or drumsticks—for this dish.

PER SERVING: 328 cal., 11 g total fat (5 g sat. fat), 124 mg chol., 544 mg sodium, 24 g carb., 3 g fiber, 29 g pro. Exchanges: 0.5 vegetable, 1.5 starch, 3.5 lean meat. Carb choices: 1.5.

- 4 **medium red-skin potatoes, quartered**
- 4 **medium carrots, cut into ½-inch pieces**
- 2 **stalks celery, cut into 1-inch pieces**
- 1 **small onion, sliced**
- 3 **pounds chicken thighs or drumsticks, skinned**
- 1 **tablespoon snipped fresh parsley**
- ½ **teaspoon salt**
- ½ **teaspoon dried rosemary, crushed**
- ½ **teaspoon dried thyme, crushed**
- ¼ **teaspoon black pepper**
- 1 **clove garlic, minced**
- 1 **cup chicken broth**
- ½ **cup dry white wine**
- 3 **tablespoons butter or margarine**
- 3 **tablespoons all-purpose flour**
- **Snipped fresh thyme (optional)**

(trim and skim)

Slow cooking requires little fat, thanks to low, moist heat. For even lower-fat meals, choose lean cuts of meat and trim away as much visible fat as possible. For poultry, remove the skin before cooking. Brown the meat in a nonstick skillet coated with nonstick cooking spray. Before serving the meal, use a slotted spoon to transfer the meat and vegetables to a serving platter. Pour the cooking liquid into a glass measuring cup and let it stand for a couple of minutes. Once the fat rises to the top, skim off any visible fat with a metal spoon.

Zesty Ginger-Tomato Chicken

(storage safety)

For safety reasons, food should not be left in slow cookers to cool after cooking. Also, don't use slow cookers as storage containers or place them in the refrigerator. To properly store cooked food, remove food from the cooker. (If the food is very hot, transfer it to a large, shallow container to cool.) After it has sufficiently cooled (leave for no longer than 2 hours at room temperature), transfer the food to refrigerator or freezer storage containers. Cover tightly; label and date the containers.

Chicken Gumbo

Chicken Gumbo

Roux ("rue") is generally a mixture of flour and fat that is cooked until very brown and used as a thickener. Here, the flour is browned alone and broth is added to replace the fat.

PER SERVING: 230 cal., 5 g total fat (1 g sat. fat), 48 mg chol., 425 mg sodium, 27 g carb., 3 g fiber, 19 g pro. Exchanges: 0.5 vegetable, 1.5 starch, 2 lean meat. Carb choices: 2.

- ⅓ **cup all-purpose flour**
- 1 **14-ounce can reduced-sodium chicken broth**
- 2 **cups chopped cooked chicken breast or turkey breast (10 ounces)**
- 8 **ounces smoked turkey sausage links, quartered lengthwise and sliced**
- 2 **cups sliced fresh okra or one 10-ounce package frozen cut okra, partially thawed**
- 1 **cup water**
- 1 **cup coarsely chopped onion**
- 1 **cup coarsely chopped red or green sweet pepper**
- ½ **cup sliced celery**
- 4 **cloves garlic, minced**
- 1 **teaspoon dried thyme, crushed**
- ½ **teaspoon ground black pepper**
- ¼ **teaspoon cayenne pepper**
- 3 **cups hot cooked brown rice**

1. For roux, in a heavy medium saucepan, cook flour over medium heat about 6 minutes or until brown, stirring occasionally. Remove from heat; cool slightly. Gradually stir broth into flour. Cook and stir until thickened and bubbly.

2. Pour roux into a 3½- or 4-quart slow cooker. Add chicken, sausage, okra, water, onion, sweet pepper, celery, garlic, thyme, black pepper, and cayenne pepper.

3. Cover and cook on low-heat setting for 6 to 7 hours or high-heat setting for 3 to 3½ hours. Skim off fat. Serve gumbo over cooked brown rice. Makes 8 servings (¾ cup soup plus ⅓ cup rice).

Brown Rice Risotto with Lamb

Curry adds intrigue to this colorful main dish.
Round out the meal with a spinach salad.

PER SERVING: 257 cal., 6 g total fat (2 g sat. fat), 72 mg chol.,
375 mg sodium, 23 g carb., 2 g fiber, 25 g pro. Exchanges: 1 vegetable,
1 starch, 3 very lean meat, 1 fat. Carb choices: 1.5.

1	2- to 2½-pound (boneless) lamb shoulder roast
	Nonstick cooking spray
2½	cups hot-style vegetable juice
1	cup brown rice
1	teaspoon curry powder
¼	teaspoon salt
2	medium carrots, chopped
¾	cup chopped green sweet pepper

1. Trim fat from meat. If necessary, cut meat to fit into a 3½- or 4-quart slow cooker. Coat an unheated large nonstick skillet with cooking spray. Preheat skillet over medium heat. Cook meat in hot skillet until brown, turning to brown evenly. Drain off fat.

2. In the slow cooker, combine vegetable juice, uncooked brown rice, curry powder, and salt. Top with carrots. Place meat on top of carrots.

3. Cover and cook on low-heat setting for 8 to 9 hours or on high-heat setting for 4 to 4½ hours.

4. Add sweet pepper. Cover; let stand for 5 to 10 minutes or until pepper is tender. Makes 8 servings.

Spicy Steak and Beans

Queso fresco (KAY-so FRESK-0) means "fresh cheese" in Spanish. Look for it in Mexican or larger supermarkets.

PER SERVING: 262 cal., 8 g total fat (3 g sat. fat), 45 mg chol., 452 mg sodium, 17 g carb., 4 g fiber, 29 g pro. Exchanges: 1 vegetable, 1 starch, 3.5 very lean meat, 1 fat. Carb choices: 1.

- 1½ pounds beef flank steak
- 1 10-ounce can chopped tomatoes with green chile peppers, undrained
- ½ cup chopped onion
- 2 cloves garlic, minced
- 1 tablespoon snipped fresh oregano or 1 teaspoon dried oregano, crushed
- 1 teaspoon chili powder
- 1 teaspoon ground cumin
- ¼ teaspoon salt
- ¼ teaspoon black pepper
- 2 small green, red, and/or yellow sweet peppers, cut into strips
- 1 15-ounce can pinto beans, rinsed and drained
- Hot cooked brown rice (optional)
- Crumbled queso fresco or feta cheese (optional)

1. Trim fat from meat. Place meat in a 3½- or 4-quart slow cooker. In a bowl, stir together undrained tomatoes, onion, garlic, dried oregano (if using), chili powder, cumin, salt, and black pepper. Pour over meat.

2. Cover and cook on low-heat setting for 7 to 9 hours or on high-heat setting for 3½ to 4½ hours.

3. If using low-heat setting, turn to high-heat setting. Stir in sweet pepper strips and pinto beans. Cover and cook for 30 minutes. Remove meat; cool slightly. Shred or thinly slice meat across the grain. Stir fresh oregano (if using) into bean mixture.

4. If using, spoon rice into soup bowls. Arrange meat on top of rice. Spoon bean mixture over meat. If desired, sprinkle with queso fresco. Makes 6 servings.

Quick Tip

Home-cooked dried beans offer all the nutrients of canned beans without all the sodium. When you have time, cook dried beans and freeze them in 2-cup portions. When a recipe calls for a 15-ounce can of beans, thaw a container of cooked beans to use instead.

Super-Simple Beef Stew

Super-simple is right. It's hard to believe so few ingredients add up to such a satisfying one-dish winner.

PER SERVING: 365 cal., 13 g total fat (0 g sat. fat), 54 mg chol., 830 mg sodium, 32 g carb., 6 g fiber, 31 g pro. Exchanges: 1.5 vegetable, 1.5 starch, 3.5 lean meat, 0.5 fat. Carb choices: 2.

- 12 ounces small red potatoes, quartered (about 2 cups)
- 4 medium carrots, cut into ½-inch pieces
- 1 small red onion, cut into wedges
- 1 pound beef stew meat
- 1 10.75-ounce can condensed cream of mushroom or cream of celery soup
- 1 cup beef broth
- ½ teaspoon dried marjoram or dried thyme, crushed
- 1 9-ounce package frozen cut green beans, thawed

1. In a 3½- or 4-quart slow cooker, place potatoes, carrots, onion, stew meat, soup, beef broth, and marjoram. Stir to combine.

2. Cover and cook on low-heat setting for 8 to 9 hours or on high-heat setting for 4 to 4½ hours.

3. If using low-heat setting, turn to high-heat setting. Stir in thawed green beans. Cover and cook for 10 to 15 minutes more or just until green beans are tender. Makes 4 (1¾-cup) servings.

Super-Simple Beef Stew

(10 slow cooker tips)

Using your slow cooker saves time, but you can do more to make it more efficient and safe.

1. **Check** that your cooker is the right size for the recipe you're making.
2. **Make sure** your cooker is at least half full but no more than two-thirds full so foods cook safely in the given time range.
3. **Look** for do-ahead steps. Can you cook the meat or cut up the vegetables the night before?
4. **Cut vegetables** into suggested sizes. Slower-cooking vegetables may need to be cut into smaller pieces than quicker-cooking vegetables.
5. **Don't add or delete** ingredients that will affect the volume or cooking time.
6. **Don't peek!** Although it's tempting to lift the lid, resist. You'll lose heat and prolong cooking time.
7. **Keep it simple.** Toss a salad with a low-calorie dressing to serve alongside.
8. **To thicken a sauce in your cooker,** remove the meat and vegetables with a slotted spoon from the liner and keep them warm in the oven.
9. **Transfer leftovers** to airtight containers to cool or freeze. Don't reheat them in your cooker.
10. **Add a little water** and dish detergent to the liner when empty. Wash and dry the liner completely.

(ground meat savvy)

Although you might think ground turkey and ground chicken are leaner alternatives to ground beef, beware. Some products contain dark meat and/or skin, which are not as lean as breast meat. When using ground chicken or turkey, look for the leanest meat you can find. If you can't find packages that are specifically labeled as breast meat only, ask the butcher to skin, bone, and grind chicken or turkey breasts for you, or grind the meat yourself using a coarse blade in a food grinder.

Italian Wedding Soup

Italian Wedding Soup

To make even-sized meatballs, pat the meat mixture into a 1-inch-thick square and cut into 12 even portions. Shape and continue as directed.

PER SERVING: 283 cal., 10 g total fat (3 g sat. fat.), 83 mg chol., 515 mg sodium, 26 g carb., 3 g fiber, 21 g pro. Exchanges: 1.5 starch, 2 lean meat, 1 vegetable, 1 fat. Carb choices: 2.

- 1 **large onion**
- 3 **oil-packed dried tomatoes, finely snipped**
- 2 **teaspoons dried Italian seasoning, crushed**
- 1 **pound lean ground beef**
- 1 **egg, slightly beaten**
- ¼ **cup fine dry bread crumbs**
- 2 **teaspoons olive oil**
- 1 **large fennel bulb**
- 2 **14-ounce cans reduced-sodium chicken broth**
- 3½ **cups water**
- 6 **cloves garlic, thinly sliced**
- ½ **teaspoon ground black pepper**
- ¾ **cup dried orzo pasta**
- 5 **cups shredded fresh spinach**

1. Finely chop one-third of the onion; thinly slice remaining onion. In a large bowl, combine chopped onion, dried tomatoes, and 1 teaspoon of the Italian seasoning. Add ground beef, egg, and bread crumbs; mix well. Shape into 12 meatballs.

2. In a large skillet, cook meatballs in hot oil over medium heat until brown, turning occasionally. Carefully drain off fat. Transfer meatballs to a 4½- to 5-quart slow cooker.

3. Meanwhile, cut off and discard upper stalks of fennel. If desired, reserve some fennel leaves for a garnish. Remove any wilted outer layers; cut off a thin slice from fennel base. Cut fennel into thin wedges. Add fennel wedges, broth, garlic, remaining 1 teaspoon Italian seasoning, and the pepper to cooker.

4. Cover and cook on low-heat setting for 8 to 10 hours or on high-heat setting for 4 to 5 hours.

5. If using low-heat setting, turn cooker to high-heat setting. Gently stir orzo into soup. Cover; cook for 15 minutes. Stir in spinach. If desired, garnish soup with reserved fennel leaves. Makes 6 (1⅔-cup) servings.

Fireside Beef Stew

Fireside Beef Stew

The name says it all—a stew to warm you on a wintry night.

PER SERVING: 206 cal., 4 g total fat (1 g sat. fat), 67 mg chol., 440 mg sodium, 15 g carb., 3 g fiber, 27 g pro. Exchanges: 0.5 starch, 2.5 lean meat, 1.5 vegetable. Carb choices: 1.

- 1½ **pounds boneless beef chuck (pot) roast**
- 1 **pound butternut squash**
- 2 **small onions, cut into wedges**
- 1 **14-ounce can lower-sodium beef broth**
- 1 **8-ounce can tomato sauce**
- 2 **tablespoons Worcestershire sauce**
- 2 **cloves garlic, minced**
- 1 **teaspoon dry mustard**
- ¼ **teaspoon ground black pepper**
- ⅛ **teaspoon ground allspice**
- 2 **tablespoons cold water**
- 4 **teaspoons cornstarch**
- 1 **9-ounce package frozen Italian green beans**

1. Trim fat from meat; cut into 1-inch pieces. Peel, seed, and cut squash into 1-inch pieces. In a 3½- to 4½-quart slow cooker, layer meat, squash, and onions. Add broth, tomato sauce, Worcestershire sauce, garlic, mustard, pepper, and allspice.

2. Cover and cook on low-heat setting for 8 to 10 hours or on high-heat setting for 4 to 5 hours.

3. For sauce, in a small bowl, stir together cold water and cornstarch; stir into cooker. Add green beans.

4. Cover and cook on high heat for 15 minutes or until thickened. Makes 6 (1⅓-cup) servings.

Beef Soup with Root Vegetables

This comforting soup is perfect on a cold blustery day.

PER SERVING: 167 cal., 2 g total fat (1 g sat. fat), 37 mg chol., 453 mg sodium, 14 g carb., 2 g fiber, 23 g pro. Exchanges: 1 starch, 2.5 very lean meat, 0.5 vegetable. Carb choices: 1.

1½ **pounds boneless beef round steak**
   Nonstick cooking spray
2 **stalks celery, sliced**
1 **large onion, coarsely chopped**
1 **medium carrot, sliced**
2 **cloves garlic, minced**
2 **medium potatoes, peeled and cut into ¾-inch cubes**
2 **medium turnips, peeled and cut into ¾-inch cubes**
1 **large sweet potato, peeled and cut into ¾-inch cubes**
3 **14-ounce cans reduced-sodium beef broth**
1 **cup water**
2 **tablespoons snipped fresh thyme or 2 teaspoons dried thyme, crushed**
2 **teaspoons Worcestershire sauce**
¼ **teaspoon salt**
¼ **teaspoon black pepper**
1 **bay leaf**

1. Trim fat from steak. Cut steak into ¾-inch cubes. Coat an unheated 4-quart Dutch oven with cooking spray. Preheat over medium-high heat. Cook meat, half at a time, in hot pan until brown.

2. In a 4½- to 6-quart slow cooker, combine celery, onion, carrot, garlic, potatoes, turnips, and sweet potato. Add browned meat. In a medium bowl, combine broth, water, thyme, Worcestershire sauce, salt, pepper, and bay leaf; pour over beef.

3. Cover and cook on low-heat setting for 10 to 12 hours or on high-heat setting for 5 to 6 hours. Before serving, discard bay leaf. Makes 8 (1¼-cup) servings.

Beef and Red Bean Chili

If you usually make chili with ground beef, try chunks of chuck for something different.

PER SERVING: 298 cal., 7 g total fat (2 g sat. fat), 67 mg chol., 455 mg sodium, 26 g carb., 5 g fiber, 30 g pro. Exchanges: 1 starch, 2 vegetable, 3 lean meat, 1 fat. Carb choices: 2.

- 1 cup dry red beans or dry kidney beans
- 1 tablespoon olive oil
- 2 pounds boneless beef chuck pot roast, cut into 1-inch pieces
- 1 cup coarsely chopped onion (1 large)
- 1 15-ounce can no-salt-added tomato sauce
- 1 14.5-ounce can diced tomatoes with mild chiles, undrained
- 1 14-ounce can lower-sodium beef broth
- 1 or 2 chipotle peppers in adobo sauce, finely chopped; plus 2 teaspoons adobo sauce*
- 2 teaspoons dried oregano, crushed
- 1 teaspoon ground cumin
- ¾ cup chopped red sweet pepper (1 medium)
- ¼ cup snipped fresh cilantro

1. Rinse beans. Place beans in a large saucepan or Dutch oven. Add enough water to cover by 2 inches. Bring to boiling; reduce heat. Simmer, uncovered, for 10 minutes. Remove from heat. Cover; let stand for 1 hour.

2. Meanwhile, in a large skillet, cook half of the meat and the onion in hot oil over medium-high heat until meat is brown. Transfer to a 3½- or 4-quart slow cooker. Repeat with remaining meat. Stir tomato sauce, undrained tomatoes, beef broth, chipotle peppers and adobo sauce, oregano, and cumin into mixture in cooker. Drain and rinse the beans; stir into mixture in cooker.

3. Cover and cook on low-heat setting for 10 to 12 hours or on high-heat setting for 5 to 6 hours. Top each serving with red sweet pepper and fresh cilantro. Makes 8 (1-cup) servings.

*Test Kitchen Tip: Because chile peppers contain volatile oils that can burn your skin and eyes, avoid direct contact with them. When working with peppers, wear plastic gloves. If you do touch the peppers, wash your hands and nails well.

Hearty Beef Chili

Beans—choose from black, red, or white— add heart-healthy fiber.

PER SERVING: 206 cal., 4 g total fat (1 g sat. fat), 37 mg chol., 565 mg sodium, 24 g carb., 7 g fiber, 22 g pro. Exchanges: 2 vegetable, 1 starch, 2 very lean meat. Carb choices: 1.5.

- 2 14-ounce cans no-salt-added diced tomatoes, undrained
- 1 10-ounce can chopped tomatoes and green chile peppers, undrained
- 2 cups vegetable juice or tomato juice
- 1 to 2 tablespoons chili powder
- 1 teaspoon ground cumin
- 1 teaspoon dried oregano, crushed
- 3 cloves garlic, minced
- 1½ pounds beef or pork stew meat, cut into 1-inch cubes
- 2 cups chopped onion
- 1½ cups chopped celery
- 1 cup chopped green sweet pepper
- 2 15-ounce cans black beans, kidney beans, and/or garbanzo beans (chickpeas), rinsed and drained
  Toppings (such as shredded reduced-fat cheddar cheese, light dairy sour cream, snipped fresh cilantro, and/or pitted ripe olives) (optional)

1. In a 6-quart slow cooker, combine canned tomatoes, vegetable juice, chili powder, cumin, oregano, and garlic. Stir in meat, onion, celery, and sweet pepper.

2. Cover and cook on low-heat setting for 8 to 10 hours or on high-heat setting for 4 to 5 hours.

3. If using low-heat setting, turn to high-heat setting. Stir in the drained beans. Cover and cook for 15 minutes more. If desired, top each serving with desired toppings. Makes 10 (1½-cup) servings.

Hearty Beef Chili

Sloppy Joes With a Kick

A couple of sassy ingredients—hot-style tomato juice and jalapeño peppers—give these sandwiches a lively twist.

PER SANDWICH: 310 cal., 13 g total fat (5 g sat. fat), 53 mg chol., 522 mg sodium, 27 g carb., 3 g fiber, 21 g pro. Exchanges: 2 starch, 2 lean meat, 2 fat. Carb choices: 2.

1½ pounds lean ground beef
 1 cup chopped onion
 1 clove garlic, minced
 1 6-ounce can vegetable juice
 ½ cup ketchup
 2 tablespoons sugar substitute*
 2 tablespoons chopped, canned jalapeño peppers (optional)
 1 tablespoon prepared mustard
 2 teaspoons chili powder
 1 teaspoon Worcestershire sauce
 8 whole wheat hamburger buns, split and toasted
 Shredded reduced-fat cheddar cheese (optional)

1. In a large skillet, cook ground beef, onion, and garlic until meat is brown and onion is tender. Drain off fat.

2. Meanwhile, in a 3½- or 4-quart slow cooker, combine vegetable juice, ketchup, ½ cup *water*, sugar substitute, jalapeño peppers (if desired), mustard, chili powder, and Worcestershire sauce. Stir in meat mixture.

3. Cover and cook on low-heat setting for 6 to 8 hours or on high-heat setting for 3 to 4 hours. Spoon meat mixture onto bun halves. If desired, sprinkle with cheese. Makes 8 sandwiches.

*Sugar Substitutes: Choose from Splenda Granular, Equal Spoonful or packets, or Sweet'N Low bulk or packets.

Sloppy Joes with a Kick

Beef and Chipotle Burritos

Canned chipotle peppers are smoked jalapeños that lend a smoky flavor to foods.

PER SERVING: 224 cal., 7 g total fat (2 g sat. fat), 54 mg chol., 384 mg sodium, 15 g carb., 9 g fiber, 31 g pro. Exchanges: 0.5 vegetable, 1 starch, 4 lean meat. Carb choices: 1.

1½ pounds boneless beef round steak, cut ¾ inch thick
 1 14.5-ounce can no-salt-added diced tomatoes
 ⅓ cup chopped red onion
 1 to 2 canned chipotle chile peppers in adobo sauce, chopped*
 1 teaspoon dried oregano, crushed
 1 clove garlic, minced
 ¼ teaspoon salt
 ¼ teaspoon ground cumin
 6 6- to 7-inch whole wheat or low-fat flour tortillas, warmed
 ¾ cup shredded reduced-fat cheddar cheese (3 ounces) (optional)
 1 recipe Pico de Gallo Salsa (see recipe, below) (optional)

1. Trim fat from meat. Cut meat into 6 pieces. In a 3½- or 4-quart slow cooker, place meat, undrained tomatoes, onion, chipotle peppers, oregano, garlic, salt, and cumin.

2. Cover and cook on low-heat setting for 8 to 10 hours or on high-heat setting for 4 to 5 hours.

3. Remove meat from slow cooker; reserve cooking liquid. Using two forks, pull meat apart into shreds. Stir enough reserved cooking liquid into meat to moisten.

4. To serve, spoon meat just below centers of tortillas. If desired, top with cheese and Pico de Gallo Salsa. Roll up tortillas. Makes 6 servings.

Pico de Gallo Salsa: In a small bowl, combine 1 cup finely chopped tomatoes, 2 tablespoons finely chopped red onion, 2 tablespoons snipped fresh cilantro, and 1 seeded and finely chopped fresh serrano pepper.* Stir in ½ cup chopped, peeled jicama, and ¼ cup thin strips radishes. Cover and chill salsa for several hours before serving.

*Test Kitchen Tip: Because chile peppers contain volatile oils that can burn your skin and eyes, avoid direct contact with them as much as possible. When working with chile peppers, wear plastic or rubber gloves. If your bare hands do touch the peppers, wash your hands and nails well with soap and warm water.

Quick Tip

To tote slow-cooker foods, wrap the cooker in heavy foil, several layers of newspapers, or a heavy towel. Place the cooker in an insulated container. The food should stay hot for up to 2 hours (do not hold longer than 2 hours). Once you get to your destination, plug it in; turn it on the low-heat setting.

Beef and Chipotle Burritos

Spiced Pot Roast with Root Vegetables

Spiced Pot Roast with Root Vegetables

Garam masala is a blend of ground, dry-roasted spices. The blend varies and can include pepper, cloves, cinnamon, cumin, chiles, fennel, and other spices. Buy garam masala where Indian foods are sold.

PER SERVING: 274 cal., 7 g total fat (2 g sat. fat), 82 mg chol., 381 mg sodium, 18 g carb., 3 g fiber, 32 g pro. Exchanges: 0.5 vegetable, 1 starch, 4 very lean meat, 1 fat. Carb choices: 1.

1	3-pound boneless beef chuck pot roast
3½	teaspoons garam masala
¾	teaspoon salt
1	tablespoon cooking oil
1	cup beef broth
¼	cup dry red wine or beef broth
30	small carrots with tops (about 12 ounces) or 2 cups peeled baby carrots
1	pound round red potatoes, quartered
2	medium parsnips, peeled and cut into ½-inch-thick slices
1	medium rutabaga, peeled and cut into 1-inch pieces
1	red onion, cut into wedges
2	tablespoons cornstarch
2	tablespoons cold water
¼	teaspoon ground black pepper
1	8-ounce carton plain low-fat yogurt

1. Trim fat from roast. For rub, in a bowl, combine 2½ teaspoons of the garam masala and ½ teaspoon of the salt; rub onto meat.

2. In a 4-quart Dutch oven, cook meat in hot oil until brown, turning as needed. Drain off fat.

3. Place meat in a 5- to 6-quart slow cooker. Top with the 1 cup broth, the wine, carrots, potatoes, parsnips, rutabaga, and onion.

4. Cover and cook on low-heat setting for 10 to 12 hours or on high-heat setting for 5 to 6 hours. Transfer meat and vegetables to a serving platter.

5. For gravy, skim and discard fat from cooking liquid; strain liquid. Measure 1½ cups liquid (discard remaining liquid); place in Dutch oven.

6. In a small bowl, stir together cornstarch, cold water, remaining 1 teaspoon garam masala, remaining ½ teaspoon salt, and the pepper; add to Dutch oven. Cook and stir over medium heat until thickened and bubbly. Cook and stir for 2 minutes more. Stir in yogurt; heat through but do not boil. Serve gravy with meat and vegetables. Makes 10 servings.

Cajun Pot Roast with Sweet Peppers

If you're watching sodium intake, read the label on the Cajun seasoning to make sure it's salt-free.

PER SERVING: 174 cal., 5 g total fat (2 g sat. fat), 67 mg chol., 86 mg sodium, 6 g carb., 2 g fiber, 25 g pro. Exchanges: 1 vegetable, 3 very lean meat, 1 fat. Carb choices: 0.5.

- 1 **2- to 2½-pound boneless beef chuck (pot) roast**
- 1 **tablespoon salt-free Cajun seasoning or Homemade Cajun Seasoning (see recipe, page 192)**
- ½ **teaspoon bottled hot pepper sauce**
- ⅛ **teaspoon ground black pepper**
- 1 **14.5-ounce can low-sodium diced tomatoes**
- 1 **medium green sweet pepper, cut into strips**
- 1 **medium red sweet pepper, cut into strips**
- 1 **medium yellow sweet pepper, cut into strips**
  Cracked black pepper (optional)

1. Trim fat from meat. Sprinkle Cajun seasoning evenly onto meat; rub in with your fingers. If necessary, cut meat to fit into a 3½- or 4-quart slow cooker.

2. Place meat in slow cooker. Add pepper sauce and ⅛ teaspoon black pepper. Add undrained tomatoes.

3. Cover and cook on low-heat setting for 8 to 10 hours or on high-heat setting for 4 to 5 hours, adding pepper strips the last 30 minutes of cooking.

4. Transfer meat to a cutting board. Slice meat; transfer to a platter. Drain vegetables, discarding cooking liquid. Serve meat with vegetables. If desired, sprinkle with cracked pepper. Makes 8 servings.

Dilled Pot Roast

This soul-satisfying dish will remind you of stroganoff with its savory dilled yogurt sauce.

PER SERVING: 313 cal., 8 g total fat (2 g sat. fat), 111 mg chol., 185 mg sodium, 22 g carb., 1 g fiber, 35 g pro. Exchanges: 1.5 starch, 4.5 very lean meat, 1 fat. Carb choices: 1.5.

- 1 **2½- to 3-pound boneless beef chuck pot roast**
- 1 **tablespoon cooking oil**
- ½ **cup water**
- 1 **tablespoon snipped fresh dill or 1 teaspoon dried dill**
- ½ **teaspoon ground black pepper**
- ¼ **teaspoon salt**
- ½ **cup plain low-fat yogurt**
- 2 **tablespoons all-purpose flour**
- 4 **cups hot cooked noodles**

1. If necessary, cut roast to fit into a 3½- or 4-quart slow cooker. In a large skillet, brown roast on all sides in hot oil. Transfer roast to slow cooker; add the water. Sprinkle roast with 2 teaspoons of the fresh dill or ¾ teaspoon of the dried dill, pepper, and salt.

2. Cover and cook on low-heat setting for 10 to 12 hours or on high-heat setting for 5 to 6 hours.

3. Transfer roast to a platter, reserving juices; cover and keep warm. Pour juices into a glass measuring cup; skim off fat. Measure 1 cup reserved juices.

4. For sauce, in a small saucepan, stir together yogurt and flour. Stir in the 1 cup reserved cooking juices and remaining 1 teaspoon fresh dill or ¼ teaspoon dried dill. Cook and stir over medium-low heat until thickened and bubbly. Cook and stir for 1 minute more. Serve sauce with meat and noodles. Makes 8 servings.

So-Easy Pepper Steak

Vary the stewed tomatoes each time you make this simple standby—Cajun-, Mexican-, or Italian-style—for a whole new dish.

PER SERVING: 196 cal., 5 g total fat (2 g sat. fat), 54 mg chol., 411 mg sodium, 9 g carb., 1 g fiber, 27 g pro. Exchanges: 1.5 vegetable, 3.5 very lean meat, 1 fat. Carb choices: 0.5.

- 2 **pounds boneless beef round steak, cut ¾ to 1 inch thick**
- ⅛ **teaspoon salt**
- ⅛ **teaspoon ground black pepper**
- 1 **14.5-ounce can Cajun, Mexican, or Italian-style stewed tomatoes**
- ⅓ **cup tomato paste with Italian seasoning**
- ½ **teaspoon bottled hot pepper sauce**
- 1 **16-ounce package frozen pepper stir-fry vegetables (yellow, green, and red peppers with onion)**
- 4 **cups hot cooked whole wheat pasta (optional)**

1. Trim fat from meat. Cut meat into serving-size pieces. Sprinkle with salt and black pepper. Place meat in a 3½- or 4-quart slow cooker.

2. In a medium bowl, combine undrained tomatoes, tomato paste, and hot pepper sauce. Pour tomato mixture over meat in cooker. Top with frozen vegetables.

3. Cover and cook on low-heat setting for 10 to 12 hours or on high-heat setting for 5 to 6 hours. Serve with hot cooked pasta. Makes 8 servings.

Eggplant-Tomato Sauce

Tender chunks of eggplant replace ground beef or sausage in this pasta sauce.

PER SERVING: 231 cal., 2 g total fat (1 g sat. fat), 3 mg chol., 584 mg sodium, 44 g carb., 5 g fiber, 9 g pro. Exchanges: 2 starch, 3 vegetable. Carb choices: 3.

- 1 medium eggplant
- ½ cup chopped onion (1 medium)
- 1 28-ounce can Italian-style tomatoes, undrained and cut up
- 1 6-ounce can Italian-style tomato paste
- 1 4-ounce can sliced mushrooms, drained
- 2 cloves garlic, minced
- ¼ cup dry red wine
- ¼ cup water
- 1½ teaspoons dried oregano, crushed
- ⅓ cup pitted ripe olives, sliced (optional)
- 2 tablespoons snipped fresh parsley
- 4 cups hot cooked penne pasta
- ¼ cup grated or shredded Parmesan cheese

Pasta with Eggplant-Tomato Sauce

1. Peel eggplant, if desired; cut eggplant into 1-inch cubes. In a 3½- to 5½-quart slow cooker, combine eggplant, onion, undrained tomatoes, tomato paste, drained mushrooms, garlic, wine, water, and oregano.

2. Cover and cook on low-heat setting for 7 to 8 hours or on high-heat setting for 3½ to 4 hours. Stir in olives and parsley. If desired, season to taste with salt and ground black pepper. Serve over pasta; sprinkle with Parmesan cheese. Makes 6 servings.

Meatless Burritos

Everyone likes burritos, and this recipe makes enough to serve a crowd. For easy serve-alongs pick up a fruit salad from the deli and a package or two of Mexican-style rice mix.

PER SERVING: 205 cal., 3 g total fat (2 g sat. fat), 7 mg chol., 471 mg sodium, 34 g carb., 6 g fiber, 8 g pro. Exchanges: 0.5 vegetable, 2 starch, 0.5 very lean meat. Carb choices: 2.

- 3 15-ounce cans red kidney and/or black beans, rinsed and drained
- 1 14.5-ounce can diced tomatoes, undrained
- 1½ cups bottled salsa or picante sauce
- 1 11-ounce can whole kernel corn with sweet peppers, drained
- 1 fresh jalapeño chile pepper, seeded and finely chopped (optional)
- 2 teaspoons chili powder
- 2 cloves garlic, minced
- 16 8- to 10-inch flour tortillas, warmed
- 2 cups shredded lettuce
- 1 cup shredded taco cheese or cheddar cheese (4 ounces)
- Sliced green onions and/or dairy sour cream (optional)

1. In a 3½- or 4-quart slow cooker combine beans, undrained tomatoes, salsa, corn, jalapeño pepper (if desired), chili powder, and garlic.

2. Cover and cook on low-heat setting for 6 to 8 hours or on high-heat setting for 3 to 4 hours.

3. To serve, spoon bean mixture just below centers of tortillas. Top with lettuce and cheese. If desired, top with green onions and/or sour cream. Fold bottom edge of each tortilla up and over filling. Fold in opposite sides; roll up from bottom. Makes 16 servings.

Vegetable Stew with Cornmeal Dumplings

Watch the dumplings through the transparent cooker lid as they cook. Resist lifting the lid, which will cause the biscuits to take longer to cook.

PER SERVING: 288 cal., 7 g total fat (2 g sat. fat), 37 mg chol., 442 mg sodium, 45 g carb., 7 g fiber, 12 g prot. Exchanges: 2.5 starch, 2 vegetable, 1 fat. Carb choices: 3.

Vegetable Stew with Cornmeal Dumplings

- 3 cups peeled butternut or acorn squash cut into ½-inch cubes
- 2 cups sliced fresh mushrooms
- 2 14.5-ounce cans diced tomatoes
- 1 15-ounce can great Northern beans, drained
- 1 cup water
- 4 cloves garlic, minced
- 1 teaspoon dried Italian seasoning, crushed
- ¼ teaspoon pepper
- ½ cup all-purpose flour
- ⅓ cup cornmeal
- 2 tablespoons grated Parmesan cheese
- 1 tablespoon snipped fresh parsley
- 1 teaspoon baking powder
- ¼ teaspoon salt
- 1 beaten egg
- 2 tablespoons milk
- 2 tablespoons cooking oil
- 1 9-ounce package frozen Italian green beans or frozen cut green beans
   Paprika

1. In a 3½- or 4-quart slow cooker, combine squash, mushrooms, undrained tomatoes, great Northern beans, water, garlic, Italian seasoning, and pepper.

2. Cover and cook on low-heat setting for 8 to 10 hours or on high-heat setting for 4 to 5 hours.

3. Meanwhile, for dumplings, in a medium bowl, stir together flour, cornmeal, Parmesan cheese, parsley, baking powder, and salt. In a small bowl, combine egg, milk, and oil. Add to the flour mixture; stir with a fork just until combined.

4. If using low-heat setting, turn to high-heat setting. Stir frozen Italian green beans into stew. Drop dumpling mixture by tablespoons on top of stew. Sprinkle dumplings with paprika. Cover and cook for 50 minutes more on high-heat setting, leaving the cover on during the entire cooking time. Makes 6 servings.

Mushroom Goulash

Goulash is typically a meaty dish flavored with paprika and served with noodles. This version does not include meat.

PER SERVING: 251 cal., 5 g total fat (2 g sat. fat), 43 mg chol., 443 mg sodium, 43 g carb., 5 g fiber, 12 g pro. Exchanges: 2 starch, 2 vegetable 1 fat. Carb choices: 3.

- 16 ounces fresh baby portobello mushrooms, sliced
- 1 tablespoon dried minced onion
- 3 cloves garlic, minced
- 1 14-ounce can vegetable broth
- 1 14.5-ounce can no-salt-added diced tomatoes, undrained
- 1 6-ounce can no-salt added tomato paste
- 2 tablespoons paprika
- 1 teaspoon dried oregano, crushed
- 1 teaspoon caraway seeds
- ¼ teaspoon salt
- ¼ teaspoon ground black pepper
- ½ cup light dairy sour cream
- 8 ounces dried egg noodles, cooked and drained

1. In a 3½- to 4-quart slow cooker, combine mushrooms, onion, and garlic. Stir in broth, undrained tomatoes, tomato paste, paprika, oregano, caraway seeds, salt, and pepper.

2. Cover and cook on low-heat setting for 8 to 9 hours or on high-heat setting for 4 to 4/2 hours.

3. Stir sour cream into mushroom mixture before serving. Serve with hot noodles. Makes 6 (scant 1-cup) servings.

simple sides
and salads

Creamy Potato Salad

Often what makes the meal is not the food at the center of the plate but the array of sides. The trick is serving dishes that keep carbs and fat in check. Here, you'll find healthful ideas to round out the meal: whole grain pilaf, veggie and fruit salads, grilled vegetables, and more.

Creamy Potato Salad

This flavorful potato salad will make you feel like you're not missing out on a summer favorite.

PER SERVING: 153 cal., 7 g total fat (2 g sat. fat), 52 mg chol., 261 mg sodium, 18 g carb., 2 g fiber, 6 g pro. Exchanges: 1 starch, 0.5 lean meat, 1 fat. Carb choices: 1.

2½ pounds round white and/or red potatoes
1 cup low-fat or light mayonnaise dressing or salad dressing
1 8-ounce carton light dairy sour cream
2 tablespoons fat-free milk
1 teaspoon seasoned pepper
¼ teaspoon salt
3 hard-cooked eggs, peeled and cut up
¾ cup sliced green onions
½ cup cubed reduced-fat cheddar cheese (2 ounces)
4 slices bacon or turkey bacon, crisp-cooked and crumbled
1 medium avocado

1. In a covered large saucepan, cook potatoes in a large amount of boiling water for 20 to 25 minutes or just until tender. Drain and cool. Cut into bite-size cubes.

2. In a very large storage container or serving bowl, stir together mayonnaise, sour cream, milk, seasoned pepper, and salt. Gently stir in cubed potatoes, hard-cooked eggs, green onions, and cheese. Cover potato mixture and chill for 2 to 24 hours. Cover and chill bacon separately.

3. Before serving, if salad seems dry, stir in 1 to 2 tablespoons additional milk.

4. To serve, seed, peel, and chop avocado; stir into salad. Sprinkle salad with crumbled bacon. Makes 16 servings.

Quick Tip

When you have a side dish—like Blue Cheese-Stuffed Summer Squash—that will wow your dinner companions, a simple meat entrée will suffice. Grill a pork chop, broil a tenderloin steak, or caramelize a piece of fresh salmon in a skillet for a very satisfying meal.

Blue Cheese-Stuffed Summer Squash

Blue Cheese-Stuffed Summer Squash

Piquant blue cheese does contain fat, but it has such big flavor, you only need a little bit.

PER SERVING: 107 cal., 6 g total fat (3 g sat. fat), 15 mg chol., 178 mg sodium, 8 g carb., 1 g fiber, 5 g pro. Exchanges: 0.5 high-fat meat, 1 vegetable, 0.5 fat. Carb choices: 0.5.

Nonstick cooking spray
- 4 medium yellow summer squash and/or zucchini
- ½ of an 8-ounce package reduced-fat cream cheese (Neufchâtel), softened
- ½ cup shredded carrot
- ⅓ cup crumbled blue cheese
- ⅓ cup thinly sliced green onions
- ⅓ cup fine dry bread crumbs
- ¼ cup fat-free or light dairy sour cream
- ⅛ teaspoon ground black pepper
- 2 tablespoons chopped walnuts

1. Preheat oven to 400°F. Coat a 3-quart rectangular baking dish with cooking spray; set aside.

2. Halve the squash lengthwise. Remove seeds with a spoon, leaving a shell about ¼ inch thick. Place squash halves, cut sides down, in prepared baking dish. Bake, uncovered, for 10 minutes. Turn squash halves cut sides up.

3. Meanwhile, for filling, in a medium bowl, stir together cream cheese, carrot, blue cheese, green onions, ¼ cup of the bread crumbs, sour cream, and pepper (the mixture will be stiff).

4. Spoon filling evenly into squash halves. Top with walnuts and remaining bread crumbs. Bake, uncovered, about 10 minutes or until squash is tender and filling is heated through. Makes 8 servings.

Make-Ahead Directions: Prepare as directed through Step 3. Cover and chill for up to 24 hours. Bake as directed in Step 4, except bake about 15 minutes.

Basil and Tomato Pasta Salad

Basil and Tomato Pasta Salad

If you use dried herbs, chill the salad at least two hours so they rehydrate.

PER SERVING: 152 cal., 4 g total fat (1 g sat. fat), 4 mg chol., 161 mg sodium, 23 g carb., 1 g fiber, 6 g pro. Exchanges: 1.5 starch, 0.5 fat. Carb choices: 1.5.

- 1 pound dried gemelli pasta
- 1 pound red and/or yellow tomatoes, chopped
- 1 cup shredded reduced-fat mozzarella cheese (4 ounces)
- ½ cup thinly sliced red onion
- ½ cup quartered pitted kalamata or ripe olives
- ¼ cup thinly sliced fresh basil or 4 teaspoons dried basil, crushed
- 2 tablespoons snipped fresh oregano or 2 teaspoons dried oregano, crushed
- 2 tablespoons capers, rinsed and drained
- 2 cloves garlic, minced
- 2 tablespoons olive oil

1. Cook pasta according to package directions. Drain; rinse under cold water. Drain again.

2. In a large bowl, combine pasta, tomatoes, cheese, onion, olives, basil, oregano, capers, garlic, ¼ teaspoon *salt*, and ⅛ teaspoon ground black *pepper*. Add oil; toss gently to mix. Cover and chill for 2 to 4 hours. Makes 16 (¾-cup) servings.

Tomatoes with Crispy Bread Topping

Tomatoes with Crispy Bread Topping

Thyme supplies a strong, somewhat minty flavor to these roasted tomatoes.

PER SERVING: 75 cal., 4 g total fat (1 g sat. fat), 0 mg chol., 152 mg sodium, 9 g carb., 3 g fiber, 2 g pro. Exchanges: 1.5 vegetable, 1 fat. Carb choices: 0.5.

- 8 roma tomatoes, cored and cut in half lengthwise
- Kosher salt
- Freshly ground black pepper
- ½ cup soft whole wheat bread crumbs
- ¼ cup thinly sliced green onions
- 2 tablespoons chopped fresh thyme
- 1 tablespoon chopped fresh flat-leaf parsley
- 1 tablespoon chopped fresh tarragon
- 1 tablespoon extra virgin olive oil
- 2 cloves garlic, minced

1. Preheat oven to 400°F. Sprinkle the cut sides of the tomatoes with kosher salt and pepper. Arrange tomatoes, cut sides up, in a shallow baking pan. Set aside.

2. In a small bowl, combine bread crumbs, green onions, thyme, parsley, tarragon, olive oil, and garlic.* Sprinkle atop tomato halves. Bake, uncovered, for 15 to 20 minutes or until the tomatoes are heated through and the bread crumbs are browned and crisp. Makes 4 (2-half) servings.

*Test Kitchen Tip: If desired, add 1 tablespoon grated Parmesan cheese to the bread crumb topping.

Mint-Buttered Soybeans

Fresh or frozen soybeans, sometimes labeled as edamame, in pods or shelled can be found at health food stores or in the health food section of the supermarket.

PER SERVING: 139 cal., 7 g total fat (1 g sat. fat), 4 mg chol., 119 mg sodium, 10 g carb., 4 g fiber, 11 g pro. Exchanges: 0.5 starch, 1.5 very lean meat, 1 fat. Carb choices: 0.5.

- 2 teaspoons butter
- 3 cups shelled fresh or frozen sweet soybeans (edamame), thawed
- 3 tablespoons snipped fresh mint
- 1 tablespoon snipped fresh basil
- ¼ teaspoon salt

1. In a medium skillet, melt butter over medium heat. Add soybeans; cook and stir about 5 minutes or until soybeans are tender.

2. Stir mint, snipped basil, and salt into soybeans. Makes 6 (½-cup) servings.

Tex-Mex Black-Eyed Pea Medley

Black-eyed peas are the stars in this spicy combo. Take it to your next potluck or halve the recipe for fewer servings.

PER SERVING: 34 cal., 0 g total fat, 1 mg chol., 223 mg sodium, 6 g carb., 1 g fiber, 2 g pro. Exchanges: 0.5 starch. Carb choices: 0.5.

- 1 cup sliced green onions or finely chopped onion
- ¾ cup finely chopped red or green sweet pepper
- 1 4-ounce can diced green chile peppers, drained
- ½ cup purchased salsa
- ½ cup bottled reduced-calorie Italian salad dressing
- 3 cloves garlic, minced
- ⅛ teaspoon ground black pepper
- Few dashes bottled hot pepper sauce
- 1 15-ounce can black-eyed peas, rinsed and drained*

1. In a large bowl, combine onions, sweet pepper, chile peppers, salsa, salad dressing, garlic, black pepper, and hot pepper sauce. Stir in black-eyed peas. Cover; chill for 3 to 24 hours. Makes 14 (about ¼-cup) servings.

*Test Kitchen Tip: If you prefer, you can substitute ½ of a 16-ounce package frozen black-eyed peas (about 1⅔ cups) for the canned peas. Cook the frozen peas according to package directions. Drain, then rinse in a colander.

(choosing sides)

You choose the entrée for your meals with the utmost care. But if you slather your sides with butter and oil or overcook them, the care you've taken with the main dish is for naught! Vegetables are only as nutritious as your preparation techniques. If you cook a vegetable until it is limp, you've stripped it of its vitamins. Steamed or lightly sautéed veggies that are still a bit firm to the bite are not only tastier but retain their vital nutrients as well. So the next time you serve a vegetable along with your main dish, choose your cooking technique wisely.

Mint-Buttered Soybeans

(10 easy sides)

Looking for a great side? Here are 10 to count on.

1. **Roast** a garlic head until soft. Mash the peeled cloves into cooked mashed potatoes.
2. **Prepare** a purchased brown rice pilaf mix; stir in shredded carrot, sliced mushrooms, and snipped fresh basil.
3. **Stir** a small amount of pesto into mashed potatoes or cooked pasta.
4. **Cut** purchased polenta into ½-inch slices and broil until crispy. Serve sprinkled with Parmesan cheese.
5. **Toss** cut-up zucchini, onion, and red sweet pepper with a little olive oil and grill in a grill wok until tender.
6. **Steam** unseasoned mixed vegetables and toss with snipped fresh oregano and a squeeze of fresh lemon.
7. **Toss** cut-up carrots, onion, and parsnips with a little walnut oil and balsamic vinegar; roast until tender.
8. **Cook** baby carrots in a small amount of chicken broth and sprinkle with curry powder.
9. **Steam** broccoli florets. Drizzle with toasted sesame oil and sprinkle with some sesame seeds.
10. **Roast** small new potatoes with a little olive oil, minced garlic, and snipped fresh rosemary. Add halved cherry tomatoes the last 5 minutes of roasting.

Cheesy Squash Bake

Cheesy Squash Bake

A creamy low-fat cheese sauce dresses up this squash side dish for fewer calories than you'd think.

PER SERVING: 72 cal., 3 g total fat (1 g sat. fat), 7 mg chol., 169 mg sodium, 8 g carb., 1 g fiber, 5 g pro. Exchanges: 1 vegetable, 0.5 medium-fat meat. Carb choices: 0.5.

- 1 **pound yellow summer squash, sliced**
- ½ **cup chopped onion**
- 1 **tablespoon reduced-fat margarine**
- 1 **tablespoon all-purpose flour**
- ½ **cup fat-free milk**
- ½ **cup shredded reduced-fat cheddar cheese (2 ounces)**
- ¼ **teaspoon ground black pepper**
- ⅛ **teaspoon salt**
- **Nonstick cooking spray**
- ½ **cup soft whole wheat bread crumbs, toasted**

1. Preheat oven to 350°F. In a large saucepan, cook squash and onion in a small amount of boiling water for 5 to 10 minutes or until tender; drain and set aside.

2. Meanwhile, in a medium saucepan, melt margarine over medium heat. Stir in flour. Add milk all at once; cook and stir until mixture is thickened and bubbly. Remove from heat. Add shredded cheese, pepper, and salt; stir until cheese is melted. Add the drained squash mixture; toss gently to coat the vegetables.

3. Coat a 1- to 1½-quart baking dish, casserole, or soufflé dish with cooking spray. Spoon the squash mixture into the prepared dish. Sprinkle bread crumbs evenly onto vegetables. Bake about 25 minutes or until the top is golden and the mixture is heated through. Makes 6 (½-cup) servings.

Red Lentil, Quinoa, and Flaxseed Pilaf

Red lentils and quinoa boost the fiber in this side or vegetarian main dish. Look for them with the beans and grains at your supermarket.

PER SIDE-DISH SERVING: 152 cal., 5 g total fat (1 g sat. fat), 0 mg chol., 198 mg sodium, 20 g carb., 4 g fiber, 7 g pro. Exchanges: 1.5 starch, 1 fat. Carb choices: 1.

- ⅓ **cup dry red lentils**
- ⅓ **cup quinoa**
- 1 **tablespoon olive oil**
- ⅓ **cup finely chopped shallots or onion**
- 2 **cloves garlic, minced**

Red Lentil, Quinoa, and Flaxseed Pilaf

- 2 **tablespoons flaxseeds**
- 1 **14-ounce can reduced-sodium chicken broth**
- 1 **large red or green sweet pepper, chopped**
- 1 **teaspoon snipped fresh thyme or ¼ teaspoon dried thyme, crushed**
- **Fresh thyme sprigs (optional)**

1. Rinse and drain lentils and quinoa separately. In a medium saucepan, heat olive oil over medium heat. Add shallots and garlic; cook and stir for 3 minutes.

2. Add quinoa and flaxseeds to shallot mixture in pan; cook and stir about 5 minutes or until the quinoa is light brown.

3. Add lentils and chicken broth to quinoa mixture. Bring to boiling; reduce heat. Cover and simmer for 15 minutes.

4. Stir in sweet pepper and snipped or dried thyme. Cover and cook about 5 minutes more or until quinoa and lentils are tender. Let stand, covered, for 5 minutes. If desired, garnish with thyme sprigs. Makes 5 (½-cup) side-dish or 2 (1¼-cup) main-dish servings

Smoky Gouda-Sauced Broccoli

Everyone will love this side dish, made irresistible with Gouda cheese. Serve it with something simple in flavor, such as a pork roast or grilled pork chops.

PER SERVING: 150 cal., 8 g total fat (5 g sat. fat), 26 mg chol., 319 mg sodium, 14 g carb., 2 g fiber, 8 g pro. Exchanges: 0.5 starch, 0.5 medium-fat meat, 1 vegetable, 1 fat. Carb choices: 1.

1¼ **pounds broccoli, cut into spears**
½ **cup chopped onion (1 medium)**
2 **cloves garlic, minced**
1 **tablespoon butter**
2 **tablespoons all-purpose flour**
¼ **teaspoon salt**
⅛ **teaspoon black pepper**
1½ **cups fat-free milk**
3 **ounces smoked Gouda cheese, shredded (¾cup)**
¾ **cup soft bread crumbs (1 slice)**
2 **teaspoons butter, melted**

1. Place a steamer basket in a large saucepan. Add water to just below the bottom of the steamer basket. Bring water to boiling. Add broccoli to steamer basket. Cover and reduce heat. Steam for 6 to 8 minutes or until just tender.

2. Preheat oven to 425°F. Meanwhile, for sauce, in a medium saucepan, cook and stir the onion and garlic in the 1 tablespoon hot butter until tender. Stir in flour, salt, and pepper. Stir in the milk. Cook and stir until thickened and bubbly. Gradually add cheese, stirring until melted.

3. Transfer broccoli to a 1½-quart au gratin dish or 2-quart square baking dish. Pour sauce over broccoli. Combine bread crumbs and the 2 teaspoons melted butter; sprinkle over sauce. Bake, uncovered, for 15 minutes or until crumbs are lightly browned. Makes 6 servings.

Smoky Gouda-Sauced Broccoli

Root Vegetables with Hazelnuts

Hazelnuts add a satisfying crunch and interesting flavor to this easy dish.

PER SERVING: 77 cal., 4 g total fat (0 g sat. fat), 0 mg chol., 62 mg sodium, 10 g carb., 3 g fiber, 2 g pro. Exchanges: 2 vegetable, 0.5 fat. Carb choices: 0.5.

4 **cups assorted peeled root vegetables (such as parsnips, turnips, and/or rutabaga) cut into 1-inch pieces**
1 **cup baby carrots, peeled (if desired)**
1 **cup pearl onions, peeled**
½ **cup peeled celeriac (celery root) cut into ¾-inch pieces**
⅛ **teaspoon salt**
⅛ **teaspoon ground white pepper**
1 **tablespoon olive oil**
⅓ **cup chopped hazelnuts (filberts), toasted**

1. In a large saucepan, cover and cook root vegetables, carrots, pearl onions, and celeriac in a small amount of boiling water about 5 minutes or until vegetables are nearly tender. Drain.

2. In a large skillet, cook vegetables, salt, and pepper in hot olive oil for 8 to 10 minutes or just until tender, stirring occasionally. To serve, sprinkle with nuts. Makes 10 (¾-cup) servings.

Broccoli with Goat Cheese and Walnuts

Dressed up with tangy buttermilk and a topping of tart chèvre and walnuts, this side dish promises bold flavor.

PER SERVING: 105 cal., 7 g total fat (2 g sat. fat), 4 mg chol., 212 mg sodium, 9 g carb., 3 g fiber, 5 g pro. Exchanges: 1.5 vegetable, 1.5 fat. Carb choices: 0.5.

- 1 pound broccoli, trimmed and cut into 1-inch pieces
- ½ cup buttermilk
- 1 tablespoon chopped fresh flat-leaf parsley
- 1 tablespoon Dijon-style mustard
- 2 teaspoons olive oil
- 1 teaspoon chopped fresh thyme or ½ teaspoon dried thyme, crushed
- 1 teaspoon red wine vinegar
- 1 clove garlic, minced (½ teaspoon minced)
- ¼ teaspoon kosher salt
- ⅛ teaspoon ground nutmeg
- ⅛ teaspoon ground black pepper
- ½ cup thinly sliced red onion
- ¼ cup coarsely chopped walnuts, toasted
- 1 ounce semisoft goat cheese (chèvre) or feta cheese, crumbled

1. In a covered large saucepan, cook broccoli in a small amount of lightly salted boiling water for 6 to 8 minutes or until crisp-tender. Drain and set aside.

2. In a large bowl, whisk together buttermilk, parsley, mustard, olive oil, thyme, red wine vinegar, garlic, kosher salt, nutmeg, and pepper. Add broccoli and red onion; stir gently to coat. Top with walnuts and goat cheese. Makes 6 (³/₄-cup) servings.

Make-Ahead Directions: Prepare as directed, except do not top with nuts and cheese. Cover and chill for up to 4 hours. To serve, top with walnuts and cheese.

Broccoli with Goat Cheese and Walnuts

Garlic-Herb Mushrooms

Serve these mushrooms solo as an appetizer
or as a side, tossed with cooked peas.

PER SERVING: 81 cal., 5 g total fat (1 g sat. fat), 0 mg chol., 118 mg sodium,
5 g carb., 2 g fiber, 5 g pro. Exchanges: 1 vegetable, 1 fat. Carb
choices: 0.5.

3	cloves garlic, minced
3	shallots, peeled and cut into thin wedges
2	tablespoons olive oil or cooking oil
1¼	pounds maitake, shiitake, oyster, or white button mushrooms, broken into clusters or sliced (about 8 cups)
¼	cup snipped fresh mixed herbs such as tarragon, rosemary, basil, oregano, and/or parsley
¼	teaspoon coarse salt or salt
¼	teaspoon cracked black pepper

1. In a large skillet, cook garlic and shallots in hot oil over medium-high heat for 2 minutes. Add maitake mushrooms. Cook, stirring gently occasionally, for 10 to 12 minutes or until tender. (Button and oyster mushrooms take 6 to 8 minutes; shiitake mushrooms take 4 minutes.) Stir in herbs, salt, and pepper. Makes 6 to 8 (½-cup) servings.

Quick Tip

Research suggests that a group of vegetables called cruciferous vegetables contains a phytochemical that helps our bodies break down potential carcinogens. Some examples of cruciferous vegetables include cauliflower, Brussels sprouts, and broccoli.

Braised Brussels Sprouts with Shallots

Cheesy Cauliflower

When oven and stovetop space are at a premium, here's a dish that lightens the load by cooking in a slow cooker.

PER SERVING: 68 cal., 5 g total fat (3 g sat. fat), 16 mg chol, 286 mg sodium, 2 g carb., 1 g fiber, 4 g pro. Exchanges: 1 vegetable, 1 fat. Carb choices: 0.

- 1 large head cauliflower (about 2 ½ pounds), broken into 8 pieces
- ¼ teaspoon salt
- ¼ teaspoon ground black pepper
- ⅔ cup vegetable broth
- ½ of an 8-ounce package reduced-fat cream cheese (Neufchâtel), cubed
- ½ teaspoon dried thyme, crushed
- ½ cup shredded reduced-fat cheddar cheese (2 ounces)

1. Place cauliflower in a 4- to 5-quart slow cooker. Sprinkle with salt and pepper. Add vegetable broth.

2. Cover and cook on low-heat setting for 3 to 4 hours or on high-heat setting for 1½ to 2 hours. Using a slotted spoon, transfer cauliflower to a bowl.

3. For sauce, add cream cheese and thyme to liquid in cooker; whisk until smooth. Spoon sauce over cauliflower. Sprinkle with cheddar cheese. Makes 8 (½-cup) servings.

Braised Brussels Sprouts with Shallots

Sautéed with shallots, these small cabbages are delicious. The key: Don't cook them to the mushy stage; they're done when they're soft.

PER SERVING: 87 cal., 7 g total fat (1 g sat. fat), 0 mg chol., 37 mg sodium, 6 g carb., 2 g fiber, 2 g pro. Exchanges: 1 vegetable, 1.5 fat. Carb choices: 0.5.

- 1 pint fresh Brussels sprouts
- 2 tablespoons olive oil or cooking oil
- 1 shallot, finely chopped
- 1 clove garlic, minced
- 2 tablespoons water
- ¼ teaspoon lemon juice
- ¼ teaspoon fine sea salt
- ¼ teaspoon ground black pepper

1. Trim stems and remove any wilted outer leaves from Brussels sprouts. Wash and cut Brussels sprouts in half lengthwise.

2. Drizzle the oil in a large nonstick skillet and swirl it around until the oil coats the entire surface. Heat over high heat until hot. Reduce heat to medium and add shallot and garlic. Cook and stir until tender.

3. Add Brussels sprouts to skillet; toss to coat with hot oil. Add the water. Reduce heat to medium. Cover and cook for 7 to 8 minutes or until sprouts are soft.

4. Remove saucepan from heat. Sprinkle sprouts with lemon juice, salt, and pepper; toss to coat. Makes 4 (½-cup) servings.

Southern Succotash

Haricots verts are just thin French green beans.

PER SERVING: 72 cal., 1 g total fat (1 g sat. fat), 3 mg chol., 23 mg sodium, 13 g carb., 3 g fiber, 3 g pro. Exchanges: 1 starch. Carb choices: 1.

- **1** **10-ounce package frozen lima beans**
- **2 ½** **cups French green beans (haricots verts) or green beans, trimmed**
- **2** **cups fresh or frozen whole kernel corn**
- **1** **tablespoon butter**
- **½** **to 1 teaspoon cracked black pepper**

1. In a covered large saucepan, cook lima beans in boiling water for 10 minutes. Add green beans; cook for 5 minutes.

2. Add corn to the beans; cook for 5 minutes more. Drain vegetables. Stir in butter and pepper; toss gently to mix. Serve warm. Makes 12 (½-cup) servings.

Southern Succotash

Balsamic Roasted Carrots

A lively blend of brown sugar, molasses, and balsamic vinegar lends a subtle sweetness to make the carrots company special.

PER SERVING: 114 cal., 3 g total fat (2 g sat. fat), 8 mg chol., 179 mg sodium, 21 g carb., 4 g fiber, 2 g pro. Exchanges: 0.5 carb., 2 vegetable, 0.5 fat. Carb choices: 1.5.

- **4** **pounds carrots, bias-cut into 2-inch pieces***
- **4** **ounces shallots (3 large), cut into ½-inch-thick wedges**
- **3** **tablespoons butter**
- **2** **tablespoons packed brown sugar**
- **1** **tablespoon mild-flavor molasses**
- **⅓** **cup balsamic vinegar**
- **½** **teaspoon salt**
- **Fresh herb sprigs (optional)**

1. Preheat oven to 450°F. Place carrots and shallots in a 13×9×2-inch baking pan; set aside.

2. In a large skillet, melt 2 tablespoons of the butter; heat until light brown. Stir in brown sugar, molasses, and balsamic vinegar; bring to boiling, stirring constantly. Boil gently, uncovered, for 2 minutes.

3. Pour balsamic vinegar mixture over carrots and shallots; toss. Roast, uncovered, for 50 to 60 minutes or until carrots are crisp-tender, stirring twice. Stir in remaining 1 tablespoon butter and the salt. Serve warm. If desired, garnish with fresh herb sprigs. Makes 12 (½-cup) servings.

*Note: If carrots are very thick, halve or quarter the thick end pieces after cutting into 2-inch chunks.

Make-Ahead Directions: Prepare as directed. Transfer to a storage container. Cover and refrigerate for up to 24 hours. (Carrots will darken and soften slightly.) Place carrot mixture in a 2-quart microwave-safe casserole. Cover and microwave on 100 percent (high) power for 7 to 8 minutes or until heated through, stirring once.

Braised Parsnips, Squash, and Cranberries

Acorn squash wedges make edible serving bowls.

PER SERVING: 164 cal., 3 g total fat (2 g sat. fat), 0 mg chol., 204 mg sodium, 35 g carb., 6 g fiber, 3 g pro. Exchanges: 2 starch. Carb choices: 2.

- 1 medium acorn squash, halved, seeded, and cut into 8 wedges
- 2 medium parsnips, peeled and cut into ½-inch slices (1¼ cups)
- 1 medium onion, cut into thin wedges
- 2 cloves garlic, minced
- 2 teaspoons olive oil or cooking oil
- ½ of a medium butternut squash, peeled and cut into 1-inch pieces
- ⅓ cup reduced-sodium chicken broth
- 1 teaspoon snipped fresh thyme or ¼ teaspoon dried thyme, crushed
- ¼ teaspoon salt
- ⅛ teaspoon ground black pepper
- ¼ cup dried cranberries
  Fresh thyme sprigs (optional)

1. Preheat oven to 450°F. On a large greased baking sheet, arrange acorn squash wedges, cut sides down. Roast about 20 minutes or until tender, turning once halfway through roasting time.

2. In a large skillet, cook parsnips, onion, and garlic in hot oil over medium heat for 3 minutes, stirring occasionally. Stir in butternut squash, chicken broth, snipped or dried thyme, salt, and pepper. Bring to boiling. Reduce heat; simmer, covered, over medium-low heat about 15 minutes or until vegetables are tender. Stir in cranberries. Cook 1 to 2 minutes more or until most of the liquid has evaporated.

3. Serve parsnip mixture over acorn wedges. If desired, garnish with thyme sprigs. Makes 4 servings.

Savory Pea Pods and Apples

Prep all but the apples ahead of time, then sauté this dish right before serving.

PER SERVING: 62 cal., 2 g total fat (0 g sat. fat), 3 mg chol., 92 mg sodium, 9 g carb., 2 g fiber, 2 g pro. Exchanges: 1.5 vegetable, 0.5 fat. Carb choices: 0.5.

3 slices turkey bacon, cut crosswise into thin strips
2 teaspoons olive oil
3 tart red cooking apples (such as Jonathan), cut into ½-inch-thick slices
2 medium leeks, chopped (⅔ cup)
4 cups fresh pea pods, trimmed
⅛ teaspoon salt
⅛ teaspoon ground black pepper

1. In a 12-inch skillet, cook turkey bacon in hot oil over medium heat for 2 to 3 minutes or just until crisp, stirring occasionally.

2. Add apples and leeks. Cook and stir for 3 to 4 minutes or just until apples are tender.

3. Add pea pods, salt, and pepper. Cover and cook for 2 to 3 minutes or until vegetables are crisp-tender. Makes 10 (½-cup) servings.

Cooked Peas and Celery

This quick-and-easy vegetable medley adds a light, garden-fresh note to any meal.

PER SERVING: 75 cal., 2 g total fat (0 g sat. fat), 0 mg chol., 236 mg sodium, 11 g carb., 3 g fiber, 4 g pro. Exchanges: 1 starch. Carb choices: 1.

- ½ cup coarsely chopped red onion
- 1 tablespoon olive oil
- ½ cup sliced celery
- 2 10-ounce packages frozen peas
- ¼ cup chopped celery leaves (optional)
- ½ teaspoon salt
- ¼ teaspoon ground black pepper

1. In a large skillet, cook red onion in hot oil about 3 minutes or until softened. Stir in celery; cook about 2 minutes more or just until tender. Increase heat to medium-high; add peas. Cover and cook for 5 to 7 minutes more or until peas are heated through. Remove skillet from heat; stir in celery leaves (if desired), salt, and pepper. Makes 8 (½-cup) servings.

Broccoli Rabe with Garlic

Broccoli rabe may also be called broccoli di rape, raab, or rapini. Pictured on page 88.

PER SERVING: 48 cal., 3 g total fat (0 g sat. fat), 0 mg chol., 98 mg sodium, 4 g carb., 3 g fiber, 4 g pro. Exchanges: 1 vegetable, 0.5 fat. Carb choices: 0.

- 3 pounds broccoli rabe or 7 cups broccoli florets
- 2 tablespoons olive oil
- 6 cloves garlic, minced
- ¼ cup reduced-sodium chicken broth
- ½ teaspoon ground black pepper
- ¼ teaspoon salt

1. If using broccoli rabe, remove large leaves and, if necessary, cut stems to 6- to 8-inch-long pieces. In a 6- to 8-quart Dutch oven, cook broccoli, half at a time if necessary, in a large amount of boiling water, allowing 3 minutes for rabe or 6 minutes for florets. Drain well; gently squeeze to remove as much excess moisture as possible.

2. In the Dutch oven, heat oil over medium heat. Add garlic; cook and stir for 30 seconds. Carefully add broccoli (oil will spatter if broccoli is not drained well); cook and stir for 1 minute. Add broth; cook, uncovered, until evaporated, stirring often. Stir in pepper and salt. Serve warm. Makes 12 (½-cup) servings.

Thyme-Roasted Parsn and Carrots

Roasting the carrots and parsnips gives them a slightly nutty flavor. Pictured on page 88.

PER SERVING: 70 cal., 2 g total fat (0 g sat. fat), 0 mg chol., 129 mg sodium, 12 g carb., 3 g fiber, 1 g pro. Exchanges: 1.5 vegetable, 0.5 fat. Carb choices: 1.

- 8 medium carrots, peeled and cut into bite-size pieces (4 cups)
- 2 to 3 medium parsnips, peeled and cut into bite-size pieces (4 cups)
- 2 tablespoons olive oil
- 1 tablespoon snipped fresh thyme or 1 teaspoon dried thyme, crushed
- ½ teaspoon salt
- ½ teaspoon ground black pepper

1. Preheat oven to 375°F. In a shallow roasting pan, combine carrots, parsnips, olive oil, thyme, salt, and pepper; toss to coat. Roast vegetables about 40 minutes or until tender and starting to brown, stirring occasionally. Makes 12 (½-cup) servings.

Ginger-Lime Peas and Carrots

You'll find a million uses for the ginger-lime butter—serve it over any vegetable, with grilled chicken, or drizzle it over fish before or after baking.

PER SERVING: 77 cal., 3 g total fat (0 g sat. fat), 0 mg chol., 53 mg sodium, 11 g carb., 3 g fiber, 2 g pro. Exchanges: 2 vegetable, 0.5 fat. Carb choices: 1.

- 2 cups packaged, peeled baby carrots
- 2 cups sugar snap peas or pea pods
- 4 teaspoons margarine or butter
- 2 medium green onions, sliced
- 1 teaspoon finely shredded lime peel
- 2 tablespoons lime juice
- 1 teaspoon grated fresh ginger

1. In a large saucepan, cook carrots in a small amount of boiling water for 4 minutes. Add snap peas and cook for 2 to 3 minutes more or until vegetables are crisp-tender. Drain in colander.

2. In the same saucepan, melt margarine. Stir in the green onions, lime peel, lime juice, and ginger. Return cooked vegetables to saucepan. Cook and stir over medium-low heat until vegetables are heated through. Makes 6 servings.

Herbed Corn Bread Dressing

Switch to a more healthful fat by using oil instead of butter in your favorite corn bread recipe or mix.

PER SERVING: 226 cal., 8 g total fat (1 g sat. fat), 18 mg chol., 492 mg sodium, 32 g carb., 3 g fiber, 7 g pro. Exchanges: 2 starch, 1.5 fat. Carb choices: 2.

Nonstick cooking spray
- 2 stalks celery, sliced
- ¾ cup chopped onion
- 2 cloves garlic, minced
- 2 tablespoons olive oil or cooking oil
- 4 cups crumbled corn bread
- 3 slices whole wheat bread, dried and crumbled
- ¼ cup snipped fresh parsley
- 1 tablespoon finely snipped fresh sage or 1½ teaspoons dried sage, crushed
- 2 teaspoons finely snipped fresh thyme or 1 teaspoon dried thyme, crushed
- 1 teaspoon finely snipped fresh marjoram or ½ teaspoon dried marjoram, crushed
- ½ teaspoon ground black pepper
- ⅛ teaspoon salt
- ¾ cup refrigerated or frozen egg product, thawed, or 3 eggs, beaten
- ½ to ¾ cup reduced-sodium chicken broth

1. Preheat oven to 375°F. Lightly coat a 2-quart rectangular baking dish with cooking spray; set aside.

2. In a large skillet, cook celery, onion, and garlic in hot oil about 10 minutes or until tender.

3. In a very large bowl, combine corn bread and wheat bread. Add onion mixture, parsley, sage, thyme, marjoram, pepper, and salt; toss gently to mix.

4. Add egg; toss to coat. Add broth for desired moistness. Spoon into dish. Bake, uncovered, about 20 minutes or until hot in center (165°F). Makes 8 (⅔-cup) servings.

Roasted Vegetable Couscous

You can roast the vegetables ahead, if you like. Cover and chill them after roasting, then add to the cooked couscous and heat through.

PER SERVING: 141 cal., 3 g total fat (0 g sat. fat), 0 mg chol., 105 mg sodium, 25 g carb., 3 g fiber, 4 g pro. Exchanges: 1 vegetable, 1 starch, 0.5 fat. Carb choices: 1.5.

Nonstick cooking spray
- 1 Japanese eggplant or 1 small eggplant, halved lengthwise
- 1 small sweet onion (such as Walla Walla or Vidalia), halved
- 1 carrot, halved lengthwise
- 2 sweet pepper halves
- 1 or 2 yellow banana peppers, halved lengthwise and seeded
- ¾ cup quick-cooking couscous
- 1 recipe Balsamic-Mustard Dressing (see below)

1. Preheat oven to 375°F. Coat a shallow baking pan with cooking spray. Place vegetables, cut sides down, in the pan. Roast, uncovered, for 45 to 60 minutes or until tender. Wrap eggplant and peppers in foil; let stand for 20 minutes; peel. Cut vegetables into bite-size pieces.

2. Bring 1 cup water to boiling; stir in couscous. Remove from heat; let stand, covered, for 5 minutes.

3. In a bowl, combine vegetables, couscous, and Balsamic-Mustard Dressing; toss to coat. Makes 6 (⅔-cup) servings.

Balsamic-Mustard Dressing: In a screw-top jar, combine ¼ cup balsamic vinegar, 1 tablespoon salad oil, 1½ teaspoons Dijon-style mustard, ¼ teaspoon Nature's Seasoning blend, and ¼ teaspoon garlic powder. Cover; shake to mix.

228

(10 makeover tips)

Use these 10 strategies to cut fat and calories from your meals:

1. **Add more vegetables and fruit.** Serve a green salad with dinner, for example.
2. **Control portion sizes.** Keep an eye on how much you serve yourself.
3. **Switch to lower-fat dairy** foods. Even a small change from 2 percent to 1 percent will make a difference.
4. **Substitute olive oil** or trans-fat-free margarine for butter.
5. **Use low-calorie sweeteners** instead of sugar.
6. **Drink low-calorie** beverages.
7. **Cook brown rice** instead of white rice.
8. **Never say never.** Allow yourself a dessert or favorite food every now and then so you don't feel deprived.
9. **Choose whole grain** breads and rolls.
10. **Top potatoes** with yogurt instead of sour cream.

Herbed Corn Bread Dressing

(veggie savvy)

Nonstarchy vegetables and legumes include artichokes, asparagus, beans (wax, Italian, and green), beets, broccoli, Brussels sprouts, cabbage, carrots, cauliflower, celery, cucumbers, eggplant, greens, mushrooms, onions, peppers, radishes, spinach, squash, tomatoes (which includes tomato sauce and juice), and zucchini. If you eat less than 1½ cups cooked or 3 cups raw of nonstarchy veggies at a meal, you don't have to count them in your daily meal plan. However, if you eat more than that, count it as a serving of starch.

Starchy vegetables and legumes include beans (baked, black, garbanzo, kidney, lima, pinto, Great Northern, navy or other dried beans), black-eyed or split peas, corn, lentils, mixed vegetables (with corn, peas, or pasta), plantains, sweet and white potatoes, winter squash, and yams. Starchy vegetables have the same amount of carbs as breads and cereals and can be used as the starch portion in the plate method (one-fourth of a 9-inch plate is dedicated to starch). Each portion (typically ½ cup) equals about 15 grams of carbohydrates.

Herbed Tomato Risotto Mix

Keep this mix in case you want a flavorful side dish fast.

PER SERVING OF RISOTTO: 80 cal., 0 g total fat (0 g sat. fat), 0 mg chol., 276 mg sodium, 17 g carb., 2 g fiber, 3 g pro. Exchanges: 1 starch. Carb choices: 1.

3¼ cups Arborio rice (two 12-ounce packages)
¾ cup thin strips dried tomatoes or snipped dried tomatoes (not oil-packed)
3 tablespoons dried minced onion
1 tablespoon dried Italian seasoning, crushed
1 teaspoon dried minced garlic

1. In a medium bowl, combine *uncooked* rice, dried tomatoes, dried minced onion, Italian seasoning, and dried minced garlic. Divide mixture among 8 small resealable plastic bags (about ½ cup mixture per bag). Seal and label. Store at room temperature for up to 3 months. Makes 8 bags dry mix (32 servings).

Herbed Tomato Risotto: In a heavy, medium saucepan, bring 1½ cups reduced-sodium chicken broth to boiling. Add 1 bag Herbed Tomato Risotto Mix. Return to boiling; reduce heat. Cover; simmer for 20 minutes, adding 1 cup desired frozen vegetables the last 5 minutes of cooking. Remove from heat. Let stand, covered, for 5 minutes or until rice is tender. If desired, stir in 2 tablespoons grated Parmesan cheese. Season with ground black pepper. If desired, sprinkle with snipped fresh basil. Makes 4 (½-cup) servings.

Herbed Tomato Risotto

Quick Tip

Arborio is a short grain rice with a higher starch content than long grain or medium grain rices. This starchiness results in a creamier, stickier cooked rice, a much-loved characteristic of Italian risottos. Like other rices, Arborio is a member of the grass family.

Rosemary Roasted Potatoes and Tomatoes

Greek olives and olive oil, which browns and crisps the potatoes, add monunsaturated fat—better for heart health.

PER SERVING: 103 cal., 5 g total fat (1 g sat. fat), 2 mg chol., 208 mg sodium, 11 g carb., 2 g fiber, 3 g pro. Exchanges: 1 starch, 0.5 fat. Carb choices: 1.

Nonstick cooking spray
1 pound tiny new potatoes, scrubbed and quartered (10 to 12)
2 tablespoons olive oil
1 teaspoon snipped fresh rosemary
¼ teaspoon salt
¼ teaspoon ground black pepper
4 plum tomatoes, quartered lengthwise
½ cup pitted kalamata olives, halved
3 cloves garlic, minced
¼ cup shaved Parmesan cheese (1 ounce)

1. Preheat oven to 450°F. Spray a 15×10×1-inch baking pan with nonstick cooking spray; place the potatoes in the pan.

2. In a small bowl, combine oil, rosemary, salt, and pepper; drizzle onto potatoes, tossing to coat. Bake for 20 minutes, stirring once.

3. Add tomato quarters, olives, and garlic; toss gently to coat. Bake for 5 to 10 minutes more or until potatoes are tender and brown on the edges and tomatoes are soft. Serve warm. Sprinkle with Parmesan cheese. Makes 8 (⅔-cup) servings.

~anish Rice
~th Pigeon Peas

~s are known as *gandules* in Hispanic shops.
Pictured on page 80.

PER SERVING: 149 cal., 2 g total fat (0 g sat. fat), 0 mg chol., 307 mg sodium, 28 g carb., 3 g fiber, 5 g pro. Exchanges: 2 starch. Carb choices: 2.

- **2** cloves garlic, minced
- **1** tablespoon snipped fresh cilantro
- **1** teaspoon snipped fresh oregano or ¼ teaspoon dried oregano, crushed
- **1** teaspoon cooking oil
- **1¼** cups reduced-sodium chicken broth
- **1** tablespoon tomato paste
- **1** to 1½ teaspoons adobo sauce from canned chipotle chile peppers in adobo sauce
- **½** cup long grain white rice
- **1** cup canned pigeon peas or black-eyed peas, rinsed and drained

1. In a medium skillet, cook garlic, cilantro, and oregano in hot oil for 30 seconds.

2. Add broth, tomato paste, and adobo sauce; bring to boiling. Add *uncooked* rice; reduce heat. Cover; simmer 15 minutes or until tender, stirring once. Stir in peas; heat through. Makes 4 (about ½-cup) servings.

Spiced Sweet Potato Stuffing

Jamaican jerk spices give flavor to this stuffing.

PER SERVING: 89 cal., 1 g total fat (0 g sat. fat), 0 mg chol., 190 mg sodium, 18 g carb., 2 g fiber, 3 g pro. Exchanges: 1 starch. Carb choices: 1.

- **¾** cup reduced-sodium chicken broth
- **2** cups chopped, peeled sweet potatoes
- **12** slices raisin bread, lightly toasted and cubed (about 12 ounces)
- **2** teaspoons Jamaican jerk seasoning

1. Preheat oven to 325°F. In a medium saucepan, bring broth to boiling. Add sweet potatoes. Return to boiling; reduce heat. Cover and cook for 7 to 10 minutes or just until tender. Do not drain. Stir in raisin bread cubes and jerk seasoning until mixed. Add additional broth, if necessary, to moisten.

2. Spoon stuffing into a 1½-quart casserole. (Or prepare and bake stuffing as directed in Roast Herbed Turkey on page 86.) Cover and bake for 25 to 30 minutes or until heated through. Makes 12 (½-cup) servings.

Zucchini Bread Pudding

Serve this savory bread pudding instead of stuffing for a new twist to your holiday dinner menu.

PER SERVING: 191 cal., 7 g total fat (2 g sat. fat), 7 mg chol., 414 mg sodium, 22 g carb., 2 g fiber, 10 g pro. Exchanges: 1 starch, 1 very lean meat, 0.5 vegetable, 1 fat. Carb choices: 1.5.

- Nonstick cooking spray
- **2** medium zucchini, thinly sliced
- **½** cup fresh or frozen whole kernel corn
- **2** tablespoons olive oil
- **½** cup chopped bottled roasted red sweet peppers
- **1** tablespoon bottled minced garlic (6 cloves)
- **2** tablespoons snipped fresh basil or 2 teaspoons dried basil, crushed
- **1** tablespoon snipped fresh parsley or 1 teaspoon dried parsley flakes, crushed
- **1** tablespoon snipped fresh sage or 1 teaspoon dried sage, crushed
- **5** cups 1-inch sourdough or Italian bread cubes
- **1** cup shredded Italian cheese blend (4 ounces)
- **¼** cup chopped pecans
- **1¼** cups refrigerated or frozen egg product, thawed, or 5 eggs
- **2** cups fat-free milk
- **½** teaspoon salt
- **¼** teaspoon ground black pepper

1. Preheat oven to 350°F. Coat a 2-quart baking dish with nonstick cooking spray; set aside.

2. In a large skillet, cook and stir zucchini and corn in hot oil for 3 minutes. Stir in sweet peppers and garlic; cook and stir about 2 minutes more or until zucchini is tender. Stir in basil, parsley, and sage. Stir in the bread cubes.

3. Place half of the mixture in the prepared dish. Sprinkle with half of the cheese. Repeat the layers. Sprinkle with pecans.

4. In a bowl, beat egg slightly; whisk in milk, salt, and black pepper. Pour over bread mixture.

5. Bake, uncovered, about 35 minutes or until a knife inserted near center comes out clean. Let stand for 10 minutes. Serve warm. Makes 12 (⅔-cup) servings.

Make-Ahead Directions: Prepare as directed through Step 4. Cover and chill for up to 24 hours. Bake as directed in Step 5, except bake about 45 minutes.

Quick Tip

Bread pudding is generally a sweet dessert made with eggs and cream. Savory versions have emerged, also using heavy dairy products. Pare down calories and fat in bread puddings by using milk instead of cream and egg product instead of eggs. Use whole grain breads to add fiber.

Zucchini Bread Pudding

1. In a medium saucepan, cook green beans, covered, in a small amount of boiling lightly salted water about 8 minutes or just until crisp-tender. Drain; rinse with cold water and drain again.

2. In a large bowl, combine beans, cherry tomato halves, and red onion slices. Drizzle with Basil-Tomato Vinaigrette; toss gently to coat. Cover and chill before serving. Makes 6 (about ¾-cup) servings.

Basil-Tomato Vinaigrette: In a screw-top jar, combine ⅓ cup snipped fresh basil, 3 tablespoons red wine vinegar, 2 tablespoons snipped dried tomatoes,* 1 tablespoon olive oil, 2 cloves minced garlic, ¼ teaspoon salt, and ¼ teaspoon ground black pepper. Cover; shake to mix. Chill until ready to use. Makes about ⅔ cup.

*Test Kitchen Tip: To soften dried tomatoes for the vinaigrette, soak them in enough boiling water to cover for 5 minutes; drain well.

Make-Ahead Directions: Prepare Basil-Tomato Vinaigrette as directed. Cover and chill for up to 8 hours. Shake before using.

Thyme-Roasted Asparagus

Bake tender asparagus spears in
a little thyme-laced olive oil.

PER SERVING: 110 cal., 9 g total fat (2 g sat. fat), 5 mg chol., 269 mg sodium, 5 g carb., 2 g fiber, 4 g pro. Exchanges: 1 vegetable, 2 fat. Carb choices: 0.

- **2 tablespoons olive oil**
- **1 teaspoon snipped fresh thyme or ½ teaspoon dried thyme, crushed**
- **¼ teaspoon salt**
- **¼ teaspoon ground black pepper**
- **1 pound fresh asparagus spears, trimmed**
- **½ cup roasted red pepper strips**
- **¼ cup shaved Parmesan cheese (1 ounce)**
- **2 tablespoons snipped fresh parsley**

1. Preheat oven to 400°F. In a small bowl, combine oil, thyme, salt, and black pepper; pour over asparagus. Toss gently to coat.

2. Arrange asparagus spears in a single layer in a 15×10×1-inch baking pan. Bake, uncovered, for 10 to 12 minutes or until tender, turning spears once.

3. Top with pepper strips, Parmesan cheese, and parsley. Makes 4 servings.

Green Bean Salad

Keep some of the homemade vinaigrette
in the refrigerator to perk up tossed green salads.

PER SERVING: 53 cal., 2 g total fat (0 g sat. fat), 0 mg chol., 126 mg sodium, 8 g carb., 3 g fiber, 2 g pro. Exchanges: 1.5 vegetable, 0.5 fat. Carb choices: 0.5.

- **12 ounces fresh green beans, trimmed**
- **8 ounces yellow and/or red cherry tomatoes, halved**
- **½ of a small red onion, thinly sliced**
- **1 recipe Basil-Tomato Vinaigrette (see recipe, right)**

Chipotle Coleslaw

This recipe calls for ground chipotle chile pepper,
which gives the coleslaw a spicy kick.

PER SERVING: 55 cal., 1 g total fat (0 g sat. fat), 1 mg chol., 122 mg sodium, 13 g carb., 2 g fiber, 2 g pro. Exchanges: 2 vegetable. Carb choices: 1.

- **⅓ cup fat-free mayonnaise**
- **1 tablespoon lime juice**
- **2 teaspoons honey**
- **¼ teaspoon ground cumin**
- **⅛ to ¼ teaspoon ground chipotle chili pepper**
- **3 cups shredded green cabbage**
- **¾ cup whole kernel corn, thawed if frozen**
- **¾ cup chopped red sweet pepper**
- **⅓ cup thinly sliced red onion**
- **⅓ cup chopped cilantro**

1. In a small bowl, stir together mayonnaise, lime juice, honey, cumin, and chipotle chile pepper.

2. In a large bowl, combine cabbage, corn, sweet pepper, onion, and cilantro. Pour mayonnaise mixture over cabbage mixture. Toss lightly to coat. Serve coleslaw immediately or cover and chill up to 24 hours. Makes 6 (⅔-cup) servings.

Quick Tip

Eating healthful foods doesn't mean forgoing flavor. Herbs pack a lot of concentrated flavor punch into a recipe without fat and with very few calories. For the best results, toss snipped or minced fresh herbs into the final dish just before serving.

Green Bean Salad

Barley Waldorf Salad

Old-fashioned Waldorf salad gets a makeover with the addition of nutty barley, grapes, and a tangy dressing.

PER SERVING: 145 cal., 5 g total fat (1 g sat. fat), 2 mg chol., 281 mg sodium, 23 g carb., 5 g fiber, 4 g pro. Exchanges: 1.5 starch. 0.5 fat . Carb choices: 1.5.

¾ **cup regular barley, triticale berries, or quinoa**
3¾ **cups water**
¾ **teaspoon salt**
¼ **cup plain lowfat yogurt**
3 **tablespoons light mayonnaise or salad dressing**
¼ **teaspoon finely shredded lemon peel**
1 **tablespoon lemon juice**
¼ **teaspoon sugar**
1½ **cups seedless green and/or red grapes, halved**
1 **medium apple, cored and chopped**
½ **cup chopped celery**
Romaine lettuce leaves (optional)
¼ **cup coarsely chopped walnuts, toasted**
Seedless grapes (optional)
Lemon peel strips (optional)

1. In a 3-quart saucepan, toast barley over medium-low heat for 4 to 5 minutes or until barley is golden, stirring occasionally. Add water and ¼ teaspoon of the salt. Bring to boiling; reduce heat to medium-low. Cover and simmer about 45 minutes for barley or triticale or 15 minutes for quinoa or until tender. Drain. Let stand for 30 minutes to cool.

2. In a large bowl, whisk together yogurt, mayonnaise, shredded lemon peel, lemon juice, sugar, and the remaining ½ teaspoon salt. Stir in cooked barley, 1½ cups grapes, the apple, and celery.

3. To serve, spoon barley mixture onto lettuce leaves, if desired. Sprinkle with walnuts. If desired, garnish with additional grapes and lemon peel strips. Makes 8 (⅔-cup) servings.

Make-ahead directions: Prepare as directed through Step 2. Cover and refrigerate for up to 24 hours. If necessary, stir milk into salad to moisten. Serve as directed in Step 3.

Barley Waldorf Salad

Minted Wild Rice-Barley Salad

Chilling for at least 4 hours gives the salad enough time to soak up all of the wonderful low-fat orange dressing.

PER SERVING: 144 cal., 3 g total fat (0 g sat. fat), 0 mg chol., 105 mg sodium, 27 g carb., 3 g fiber, 4 g pro. Exchanges: 1 starch, 0.5 fruit, 1 vegetable, 0.5 fat . Carb choices: 2.

- 2 cups water
- ½ cup wild rice, rinsed and drained
- ¼ cup regular barley
- 1 cup fresh pea pods, cut into thirds
- ⅓ cup golden raisins
- 3 green onions, sliced
- 1 teaspoon finely shredded orange peel
- ⅓ cup orange juice
- 1 tablespoon olive oil
- ¼ teaspoon salt
- ⅛ teaspoon ground black pepper
- 2 tablespoons snipped fresh mint
- Shredded orange peel (optional)

1. In a large saucepan, bring the water to boiling; stir in uncooked wild rice and barley. Return to boiling; reduce heat. Cover and simmer about 40 minutes or until wild rice and barley are tender. Drain off liquid. Transfer wild rice and barley to a large bowl.

2. Stir in pea pods, golden raisins, green onions, the 1 teaspoon orange peel, the orange juice, oil, salt, and pepper. If desired, cover and chill for up to 6 hours.

3. To serve, stir in mint. If desired, garnish with additional orange peel. Makes 6 (⅔-cup) servings.

Star Fruit Salad

Glossy, golden-yellow star fruit needn't be peeled; simply rinse it thoroughly. Choose smaller fruit for this salad.

PER SERVING: 65 cal., 5 g total fat (1 g sat. fat), 0 mg chol., 6 mg sodium, 5 g carb., 1 g fiber, 1 g pro. Exchanges: 1 vegetable, 1 fat. Carb choices: 0.5.

- ¼ cup raspberry vinegar or red wine vinegar
- 3 tablespoons salad oil
- 1 tablespoon honey
- 1 10-ounce package torn mixed Italian blend salad greens
- 1 small star fruit (carambola), thinly sliced
- ½ small red onion, thinly sliced (⅓ cup)
- Fresh raspberries (optional)

Star Fruit Salad

1. In a screw-top jar, combine raspberry vinegar, oil, and honey. Cover and shake well.

2. In a very large bowl, toss together salad greens, star fruit, and onion. Shake dressing well; pour over salad mixture. Toss salad mixture lightly to coat. If desired, garnish with fresh raspberries. Makes 8 servings.

Wilted Spinach with Olives

(6 valuable veggies)

Vegetables are usually low in calories and carbs, high in fiber, and loaded with vitamins and minerals. Use several for your everyday meals.

1. **Carrots:** Bright orange carrots are loaded with carotenoids, which are good for eye health.
2. **Corn:** Fiber-rich corn contains the carotenoid beta-cryptoxanthin, which seems to protect lungs from cancer.
3. **Eggplant:** This source of potassium offers a fiber benefit, especially when cooked and eaten with the peel. The purple peel contains anthocyanin, an antioxidant that is said to protect from cancer.
4. **Green beans:** The high fiber content of beans, particularly the soluble fiber, can help keep blood glucose levels stable and might lower the risk of heart disease.
5. **Green onions and onions:** Quercetin, an antioxidant, might protect against some cancers. When consumed raw, onions might reduce the risk of diabetes and boost good HDL cholesterol.
6. **Spinach:** This leafy green is a good source of magnesium, a mineral that studies indicate might lower the risk of developing type 2 diabetes.

Kale Salad

Green Pepper Salad with Tangy Cayenne Dressing

If you enjoy fiery foods,
use the ½ teaspoon cayenne pepper.

PER SERVING: 55 cal., 3 g total fat (0 g sat. fat), 1 mg chol., 43 mg sodium, 7 g carb., 1 g fiber, 2 g pro. Exchanges: 1.5 vegetable, 0.5 fat. Carb choices: 0.5.

- **2** medium carrots, cut into thin bite-size strips
- **1** cup thin bite-size strips red, yellow, and/or green sweet pepper
- **½** of a small red onion, cut into strips
- **1** recipe Tangy Cayenne Dressing (see recipe, below)
- **10** cups torn mixed salad greens
- **⅓** cup chopped pecans, toasted

1. In a medium bowl, combine carrots, sweet pepper, and red onion; add Tangy Cayenne Dressing. Toss gently to coat. Serve over mixed greens. Sprinkle with pecans. Makes 12 (1-cup) servings.

Tangy Cayenne Dressing: In a large bowl, combine 1 cup vanilla low-fat yogurt, 2 minced cloves garlic, 1 tablespoon Worcestershire sauce, 1 teaspoon finely shredded lime peel, 1 tablespoon lime juice, and ¼ to ½ teaspoon cayenne pepper. Cover and chill for at least 2 hours.

Wilted Spinach with Olives

This salad might be easy, but the Mediterranean flavors will impress everyone at the table.

PER SERVING: 83 cal., 5 g total fat (2 g sat. fat), 12 mg chol., 392 mg sodium, 6 g carb., 4 g fiber, 5 g pro. Exchanges: 0.5 medium-fat meat, 1 vegetable, 0.5 fat. Carb choices: 0.5.

- Nonstick cooking spray
- **3** tablespoons pitted kalamata olives (about 12)
- **8** cups lightly packed fresh spinach and/or mustard greens, stems removed
- **1** ounce feta cheese, crumbled

1. Coat an unheated large nonstick skillet with nonstick cooking spray. Preheat over medium heat. Add olives. Cook for 3 minutes, stirring often. Remove from skillet; set aside.

2. Increase heat to medium-high. Add spinach; cook 1 to 2 minutes or just until wilted, tossing often.

3. To serve, transfer spinach to a platter. Top with feta cheese and olives. Makes 2 (½-cup) servings.

Kale Salad

Down South, greens cooked with bacon are a soul-food staple.

PER SERVING: 83 cal., 4 g total fat (1 g sat. fat), 0 mg chol., 243 mg sodium, 10 g carb., 3 g fiber, 3 g pro. Exchanges: 2 vegetable, 1 fat. Carb choices: 0.5.

- **3** cups finely chopped fresh kale
- **1** plum tomato, chopped
- **⅓** cup chopped red sweet pepper
- **¼** cup pitted ripe olives, quartered lengthwise
- **3** radishes, thinly sliced and halved
- **2** green onions, sliced
- **2** tablespoons sunflower kernels
- **¼** cup Zesty Lemon Dressing (see recipe, below)

1. In a large salad bowl, combine kale, tomato, sweet pepper, olives, radishes, onions, and sunflower kernels; toss gently. Top with Zesty Lemon Dressing; toss to coat. Makes 4 (1-cup) servings.

Zesty Lemon Dressing: In a screw-top jar, combine 3 tablespoons lemon juice, 3 tablespoons water, 2 tablespoons reduced-sodium soy sauce, 2 teaspoons olive oil, ½ teaspoon onion powder, and ¼ teaspoon garlic powder. Cover and shake well to mix. Chill until ready to serve or for up to 1 week. Makes ½ cup.

Apple Spinach Salad
with Thyme-Dijon Vinaigrette
Pep up any salad with the leftover vinaigrette.

PER SERVING: 93 cal., 6 g total fat (1 g sat. fat), 0 mg chol., 96 mg sodium, 11 g carb., 2 g fiber, 1 g pro. Exchanges: 1 vegetable, 0.5 fruit, 1 fat. Carb choices: 1.

- **4** cups fresh baby spinach
- **1** medium green apple (such as Granny Smith), cored and sliced
- **¼** cup thin red onion wedges
- **2** tablespoons snipped dried tart red cherries
- **¼** cup Thyme-Dijon Vinaigrette (see recipe, right)
- **½** cup crumbled feta cheese or blue cheese (2 ounces) (optional)

1. In a large bowl, toss together spinach, apple, onion, and cherries. Shake Thyme-Dijon Vinaigrette; drizzle onto salad. Toss to coat. If desired, top each serving with cheese. Makes 4 (1-cup) servings.

Thyme-Dijon Vinaigrette: In a screw-top jar, combine ¼ cup olive oil, ¼ cup white or regular balsamic vinegar, 2 teaspoons snipped fresh thyme or ½ teaspoon crushed dried thyme, 1 teaspoon Dijon-style mustard, and ¼ teaspoon salt. Cover and shake well to mix. Chill until ready to serve. Makes ⅔ cup.

Make-Ahead Directions: Prepare the vinaigrette as directed. Cover and chill for up to 1 week.

Quick Tip

Colorful beets brighten any family table for good reason. The beet itself is a good source of folate. Beet greens are high in vitamin A (beta-carotene) and vitamin C and are a good source of riboflavin and magnesium. Look for yellow, white, and striped red and white beets.

Hazelnut, Goat Cheese, and Tomato Salad with Chive Champagne Vinaigrette

If you prefer, use crumbled feta or blue cheese in place of the goat cheese.

PER SERVING: 107 cal., 10 g total fat (2 g sat. fat), 3 mg chol., 75 mg sodium, 3 g carb., 1 g fiber, 3 g pro. Exchanges: 1 vegetable, 2 fat. Carb choices: 0.

- 12 cups torn mixed salad greens (such as spinach, arugula, radicchio, and romaine)
- 2 medium tomatoes, cored and cut into wedges
- 3 ounces soft goat cheese (chèvre), crumbled
- ½ cup hazelnuts, toasted and chopped
- ½ cup Chive Champagne Vinaigrette (see recipe, below)

1. On a platter, arrange mixed greens, tomatoes, goat cheese, and hazelnuts. Drizzle with ½ cup Chive Champagne Vinaigrette. Cover and chill remaining dressing for other salads. Makes 12 (1-cup) servings.

Chive Champagne Vinaigrette: In a food processor, combine 2 finely chopped shallots, ⅓ cup champagne vinegar or white wine vinegar, 1 tablespoon lemon juice, ¼ teaspoon salt, and ¼ teaspoon ground black pepper. Cover and process until smooth. With the processor running, slowly add ½ cup olive oil in a steady stream. Stir in 2 tablespoons snipped fresh chives. Cover and chill. Before serving, let dressing stand at room temperature for 30 minutes. Stir before serving. Makes about 1 cup.

Make-Ahead Directions: Prepare Chive Champagne Vinaigrette as directed. Cover; chill for up to 5 days.

Beet Salad with Goat Cheese and Walnuts

Boost the nutty flavor by toasting the walnuts in the oven until golden.

PER SERVING: 147 cal., 10 g total fat (3 g sat. fat), 7 mg chol., 571 mg sodium, 11 g carb., 3 g fiber, 6 g pro. Exchanges: 0.5 medium-fat meat, 2.5 vegetable, 1.5 fat. Carb choices: 1.

- 2 small cooked beets or one 8¼-ounce can tiny whole beets, chilled
- 1 tablespoon snipped fresh basil or flat-leaf parsley
- ⅛ teaspoon ground black pepper
- 4 tablespoons bottled reduced-fat or fat-free balsamic vinaigrette salad dressing
- 4 cups mixed baby salad greens
- 2 tablespoons coarsely chopped walnuts, toasted
- 1 ounce soft goat cheese (chèvre), crumbled

1. Drain and cut up beets. In a medium bowl, combine cut-up beets, basil, and pepper. Drizzle with 2 tablespoons of the salad dressing; toss to coat.

2. Arrange greens on 2 salad plates; sprinkle with remaining dressing. Top with beet mixture, walnuts, and goat cheese. Makes 2 (1-cup) servings.

Beet Salad with Goat Cheese and Walnuts

(cook a batch of beans)

Canned beans are convenient timesavers in the kitchen. But if you worry about sodium, you might prefer to prepare your own dry beans for recipes. Cook up a batch and follow the directions for freezing them, below. Pull them from the freezer when you need them.

1. Cook a big batch of dried beans according to package directions until just tender.
2. Drain, cool, and place in freezer bags or containers in 1¾-cup portions (1¾ cups cooked beans equals a 15-ounce can of beans). Label; freeze the beans for up to three months.
3. To use, place the beans (thawed or frozen) in a saucepan with ½ cup water for each 1¾ cups of beans. Simmer, covered, over low heat until heated through. Drain and use.

**Black Bean Slaw
with Ginger Dressing**

Black Bean Slaw with Ginger Dressing

This flavorful slaw sings with freshness and color. Take advantage of purchased coleslaw mix to save time.

PER SERVING: 109 cal., 4 g total fat (1 g sat. fat), 0 mg chol, 289 mg sodium, 17 g carb., 5 g fiber, 5 g pro. Exchanges: 1 vegetable, 1 starch, 0.5 fat. Carb choices: 1.

½ of a 15-ounce can black beans, rinsed and drained
3 cups purchased shredded cabbage with carrot (coleslaw mix)
1 medium green apple, cored and chopped (⅔ cup)
½ cup chopped red sweet pepper
2 tablespoons cider vinegar
1 tablespoon reduced-sodium soy sauce
1 tablespoon peanut oil
1 teaspoon grated fresh ginger
1 teaspoon honey
⅛ teaspoon ground black pepper

1. In a large bowl, combine beans, coleslaw, apple, and sweet pepper.

2. For dressing, in a small screw-top jar, combine vinegar, soy sauce, peanut oil, ginger, honey, and black pepper; cover and shake well.

3. Pour dressing onto cabbage mixture; toss mixture to coat. Cover and chill slaw for 1 to 24 hours. Makes 8 (1-cup) servings.

Radish and Garbanzo Bean Salad

Radish and Garbanzo Bean Salad

Winter radishes add crunch and color to your plate.

PER SERVING: 115 cal., 4 g total fat (1 g sat. fat), 0 mg chol., 257 mg sodium, 16 g carb., 4 g fiber, 4 g pro. Exchanges: 0.5 starch, 2 vegetable, 0.5 fat. Carb choices: 1.

- **10** radishes, sliced
- **3** medium tomatoes, chopped
- **½** cup sliced green onions
- **¼** cup chopped red onion
- **1** 15-ounce can garbanzo beans (chickpeas), rinsed and drained
- **1** recipe Salad Vinaigrette (see recipe, below)
- **8** cups torn mixed salad greens
  Cracked black pepper (optional)

1. In a large bowl, combine radishes, tomatoes, green onions, and red onion. Stir in beans.

2. Pour Salad Vinaigrette onto bean mixture; toss gently to coat. Cover and chill for 1 to 24 hours.

3. To serve, toss greens with bean mixture. If desired, top with pepper. Makes 8 (1¾-cup) servings.

Salad Vinaigrette: In a small bowl, whisk 2 tablespoons olive oil, 1 tablespoon white wine vinegar, and 1 teaspoon salad and vegetable seasoning mix.

Fresh Fruit Salad with Creamy Lime Topping

You can serve the lime-kissed cream over any mixed fruit for dessert, a salad, or a breakfast eye-opener.

PER SERVING: 64 cal., 1 g total fat (1 g sat. fat), 3 mg chol., 61 mg sodium, 13 g carb., 2 g fiber, 1 g pro. Exchanges: 1 fruit. Carb choices: 1.

½ cup light dairy sour cream
⅓ cup fat-free or light mayonnaise or salad dressing
1 teaspoon finely shredded lime peel
2 tablespoons powdered sugar
2 tablespoons lime juice
1 tablespoon fat-free milk (optional)
6 cups assorted fresh fruit (such as clementine segments, cut-up mango, raspberries, star fruit slices, pineapple chunks, cut-up kiwifruit, and/or halved strawberries)
Finely shredded lime peel (optional)

1. In a small bowl, stir together sour cream, mayonnaise, the 1 teaspoon lime peel, powdered sugar, and lime juice. If desired, stir in milk to make topping desired consistency.

2. To serve, spoon sour cream mixture onto fruit. If desired, garnish with additional lime peel. Makes 12 (½-cup) servings.

Make-Ahead Directions: Cover and chill sour cream mixture for up to 5 days.

Grapefruit and Avocado Salad

Splash the versatile orange salad dressing onto just about any combination of tossed salad ingredients.

PER SERVING: 106 cal., 7 g total fat (1 g sat. fat), 0 mg chol., 122 mg sodium, 11 g carb., 4 g fiber, 2 g pro. Exchanges: 1 vegetable, 0.5 fruit, 1 fat. Carb choices: 1.

4 cups packaged fresh baby spinach
1 grapefruit, peeled and sectioned
1 small avocado, halved, seeded, peeled, and sliced
1 cup canned sliced beets
1 tablespoon sliced almonds, toasted
1 recipe Orange Vinaigrette (see recipe, below)

1. Top spinach with grapefruit, avocado, beets, and almonds. Drizzle with Orange Vinaigrette. Makes 6 (about 1-cup) servings.

Orange Vinaigrette: In a screw-top jar, combine 1 teaspoon finely shredded orange peel, ⅓ cup orange juice, 2 teaspoons red wine vinegar, 2 teaspoons salad oil, ⅛ teaspoon salt, and a dash ground black pepper. Cover and shake well to mix.

Minty Melon Cups

Midori is a liqueur from Japan that's a vivid green with a flavor reminiscent of honeydew melon.

PER SERVING: 87 cal., 0 g total fat, 0 mg chol., 20 mg sodium, 18 g carb., 1 g fiber, 1 g pro. Exchanges: 1 fruit. Carb choices: 1.

10 cups cut-up melon or melon balls (such as watermelon, honeydew, canary melon, and/or cantaloupe)
½ cup Midori, other melon-flavor liqueur, or low-calorie ginger ale
2 tablespoons snipped fresh mint or 2 teaspoons dried mint, crushed

1. In a very large bowl, combine melon balls, Midori, and mint; toss gently to coat. Makes 10 (1-cup) servings.

Make-Ahead Directions: Cut up and store melon in covered containers in the refrigerator for up to 24 hours. Add liquid before serving.

Quick Tip

Fruit salads such as the one pictured here make a perfect afternoon snack. Keep the Creamy Lime Topping ready in the refrigerator for when you crave something sweet. You can serve it over cut-up fruit or use it as a dipper for strawberries or pineapple chunks.

Fresh Fruit Salad with Creamy Lime Topping

(gelatin know-how)

A few raw foods shouldn't be used in gelatin mixtures because they contain an enzyme that prevents the gelatin from setting up. These include fresh pineapple, kiwifruit, figs, guava, papaya, and gingerroot. After these foods have been cooked or canned, they can be used in gelatin.

Creamy Cranberry Salad

Creamy Cranberry Salad

Rasberries combine with cranberries in this pretty salad.

PER SERVING: 118 cal., 7 g total fat (4 g sat. fat), 22 mg chol., 118 mg sodium, 11 g carb., 1 g fiber, 4 g pro. Exchanges: 1 other carb., 1 fat. Carb choices: 1.

- **1 envelope unflavored gelatin**
- **2 teaspoons sugar**
- **½ cup water**
- **1 cup fresh or frozen raspberries, thawed if needed**
- **½ cup canned whole cranberry sauce**
- **1 8-ounce package reduced-fat cream cheese (Neufchâtel), softened**
- **½ cup low-calorie cranberry juice**
- **¼ cup chopped pecans, toasted (optional)**
- **Sugared cranberries* (optional)**
- **Sugared fresh basil leaves* (optional)**

1. In a small saucepan, stir together the gelatin and sugar. Stir in water. Cook and stir over medium-low heat until gelatin dissolves; set aside.

2. In a large bowl, mash raspberries and cranberry sauce with a potato masher until coarsely mashed. Add cream cheese; beat with an electric mixer on low to medium speed until well combined. Gradually beat in cranberry juice until combined.

3. Stir gelatin mixture and, if desired, pecans into cranberry mixture. Divide mixture among eight 4-ounce stainless steel** gelatin molds or 4-ounce ramekins, or pour mixture into a 1½-quart glass dish. Cover and refrigerate for at least 4 hours or until firm. Unmold onto individual serving plates if using individual molds. If desired, garnish with sugared cranberries and basil. Makes 8 servings.

*Note: To make sugared cranberries and basil leaves, sprinkle berries and leaves with water. Roll in granulated sugar, turning to coat evenly.

**Test Kitchen Tip: It is important to use molds that are not aluminum to avoid a reaction with the acidic gelatin mixture.

Ginger Ale Salad

A double-ginger whammy of crystallized ginger and ginger ale make this refreshing fruit- and nut-studded jello mold a star of the buffet.

PER SERVING: 50 cal., 0 g total fat (0 g sat. fat), 0 mg chol., 63 mg sodium, 11 g carbo., 1 g fiber, 1 g pro. Exchanges: 1.5 other carb. Carb choices: 1.

- **1 0.6-ounce package sugar-free, low-calorie lemon-flavored gelatin**
- **1 cup water**
- **2 cups diet ginger ale**
- **2 cups assorted chopped fruit (such as drained canned pineapple [do not use fresh pineapple]; fresh strawberries; fresh or canned peaches; fresh or canned pears; fresh apple; or fresh grapes)**
- **½ cup chopped celery or toasted nuts**
- **2 tablespoons finely chopped crystallized ginger**

1. In a medium saucepan, combine gelatin and water; heat and stir until gelatin dissolves. Stir in ginger ale. Chill about 30 minutes or until partially set (the consistency of unbeaten egg whites). Fold in fruit, celery, and crystallized ginger.

2. Pour into a 6-cup mold. Cover and chill about 6 hours or until firm. Unmold salad onto a serving plate. Makes 12 servings.

party-perfect appetizers

White Bean and Tomato Bruschetta

Gather with friends at an open house or a casual after-work get-together. You'll be the hit of your party when you offer tantalizing trays of appetizers, such as bruschetta or cheesy stuffed mush-rooms and delightful crackers with a variety of spreads.

White Bean and Tomato Bruschetta

The topper tastes creamy, yet the beans have very little fat.

PER APPETIZER: 75 cal., 2 g total fat (0 g sat. fat), 0 mg chol., 184 mg sodium, 11 g carb., 1 g fiber, 3 g pro. Exchanges: 1 starch. Carb choices: 1.

- 2 tablespoons oil-packed dried tomatoes
- ½ cup snipped fresh watercress or fresh flat-leaf parsley
- 2 tablespoons pine nuts, toasted
- 1 cup canned white kidney beans (cannellini beans), rinsed and drained
- 1 tablespoon fat-free milk
- 2 to 3 teaspoons lemon juice
- 1 teaspoon snipped fresh thyme or ¼ teaspoon dried thyme, crushed
- ¼ teaspoon salt
- ¼ teaspoon ground black pepper
- 2 cloves garlic, cut up
- 12 ½-inch-thick slices baguette-style French bread
  Watercress sprigs (optional)

1. Preheat broiler. Drain the tomatoes, reserving oil; finely snip. In a small bowl, combine tomatoes, 1 teaspoon reserved oil, ½ cup watercress, and nuts; set aside.

2. In a food processor or blender, combine 1 teaspoon reserved oil, the beans, milk, lemon juice, thyme, salt, pepper, and garlic. Cover and process until smooth; set bean mixture aside.

3. On an ungreased baking sheet, arrange bread slices. Broil 4 inches from heat for 1½ to 2 minutes or until lightly toasted, turning once.

4. Spread about 1 tablespoon bean mixture onto each slice, spreading to edges. Broil 4 inches from heat about 1 minute or until bean mixture is warm. Top each with tomato mixture. If desired, garnish with watercress sprigs. Serve warm. Makes 12 appetizers.

Herbed Peppers and Olives

Mix and match olive colors, sizes, and shapes.

PER SERVING: 89 cal., 7 g total fat (1 g sat. fat), 0 mg chol., 355 mg sodium, 6 g carb., 2 g fiber, 0 g pro. Exchanges: 0.5 vegetable, 1.5 fat. Carb choices: 0.5.

- 2 teaspoons olive oil
- 2 cloves garlic, minced
- 2 medium red sweet peppers, seeded and cut into thin strips
- 1 medium banana pepper, seeded and sliced thinly
- 12 ounces assorted unpitted olives (about 2 cups)
- 2 teaspoons snipped fresh oregano or ½ teaspoon dried oregano, crushed

1. In a large skillet, heat oil over medium heat. Add garlic; cook and stir for 30 seconds. Add peppers; cook and stir about 4 minutes or until tender.

2. Add the olives and oregano; cook and stir for 2 minutes or until warm. Serve olive mixture warm. Makes 12 (¼-cup) servings.

Tomato and Basil Chèvre Spread

Soak dried tomatoes in water instead of using the oil-packed kind. Serve spread with crackers.

PER 2 TABLESPOONS: 66 cal., 5 g total fat (3 g sat. fat), 14 mg chol., 125 mg sodium, 2 g carb., 0 g fiber, 4 g pro. Exchanges: 0.5 high-fat meat. Carb choices: 0.

- ⅓ cup dried tomatoes (not oil-packed)
- 4 ounces soft goat cheese (chèvre)
- ½ of an 8-ounce package reduced-fat cream cheese (Neufchâtel), softened
- ¼ cup snipped fresh basil or 2 teaspoons dried basil, crushed
- 3 cloves garlic, minced
- ⅛ teaspoon ground black pepper
- 1 to 2 tablespoons fat-free milk

1. In a bowl, cover tomatoes with boiling water; let stand for 10 minutes. Drain; snip tomatoes.

2. Stir in goat cheese, cream cheese, basil, garlic, and pepper. Stir in enough milk to make a spreading consistency. Cover and chill for 2 to 4 hours. Makes about 1¼ cups spread or 10 (2-tablespoon) servings.

Tomato and Basil Chèvre Spread

Herb-Stuffed Cherry Tomatoes

These tiny bright bite-size gems are a cinch to make. Prepare them up to 2 hours in advance, then cover and refrigerate until serving time. For a colorful variation, use a combination of red, yellow, and orange cherry tomatoes.

PER TOMATO: 40 cal., 3 g total fat (2 g sat. fat), 8 mg chol., 38 mg sodium, 1 g carb., 0 g fiber, 1 g prot. Exchanges: 1 fat. Carb choices: 0.

- 3 dozen cherry tomatoes, 1 to 1½ inches in diameter
- 2 tablespoon purchased pesto
- 1 clove garlic, minced
- 2 tablespoon snipped fresh parsley
- 2 tablespoon snipped fresh chives
- 1 8-ounce package cream cheese
- 4 ounce fresh goat cheese (chèvre) or cream cheese Fresh parsley or fresh dill sprigs (optional)
- 1 tablespoon snipped fresh tarragon or dill

1. Using a sharp knife cut off the top ⅓ of each tomato on the stem end. If desired, set aside the tops for garnish or discard. Hollow out tomatoes; invert on paper towels and set aside to drain.

2. Place pesto, garlic, the 2 tablespoons parsley, and chives in a food processor. Process for 15 seconds; add the cream cheese and chèvre. Process another 30 to 45 seconds or until the filling is smooth.

3. Place the filling in a pastry bag fitted with a star tip and pipe into each cherry tomato. Garnish with fresh parsley or dill sprigs and/or reserved tomato tops. Makes 36 stuffed tomatoes

(top it off)

Whether you call them bruschetta or crostini, toasted slices of French bread make a sturdy base for many spreads and toppers. You can also use toasted pita triangles, thinly sliced party breads, or multigrain crackers for the same types of toppers. And if you're concerned about too many carbohydrates, bias-slice fresh zucchini or cucumber for a colorful and crunchy base.

Herbed Peppers and Olives

Jamaican Jerk Shrimp with Papaya and Pineapple

Wintertime guests will delight in this sunny Carribean-style appetizer. Serve it in a chilled clear-glass bowl on the buffet or in individual portions in chilled martini glasses.

PER SERVING: 107 cal., 2 g total fat (0 g sat. fat), 148 mg chol., 246 mg sodium, 6 g carb., 1 g fiber, 16 g pro. Exchanges: 2 very lean meat, 0.5 fruit. Carb choices: 0.5

2 pounds fresh or frozen peeled, cooked large shrimp (with tails)
1 tablespoon Jamaican jerk seasoning*
1 tablespoon cooking oil
½ of a 24- to 26-ounce jar refrigerated sliced papaya, drained and coarsely chopped (1¼ cups)
1 8-ounce can pineapple tidbits, drained and chopped
¼ cup chopped roasted red sweet peppers
¼ cup sliced green onions
1 teaspoon finely shredded lime peel
2 tablespoons lime juice
2 cloves garlic, minced
   Green onions (optional)

1. Thaw shrimp, if frozen. Place shrimp in a resealable plastic bag. Add jerk seasoning and oil to shrimp. Seal bag; turn to coat shrimp. Chill for 30 minutes.

2. Meanwhile, in a medium bowl, combine papaya, pineapple, sweet peppers, sliced green onions, lime peel, lime juice, and garlic. Cover and chill papaya mixture until serving time.

3. To serve, gently stir together shrimp and fruit mixture. If desired, garnish with whole green onions. Makes 12 (½-cup) servings.

*Test Kitchen Tip: Look for jerk seasoning in the herb and spice section of a large supermarket. To make homemade jerk seasoning, in a small bowl, combine 1½ teaspoons dried thyme, ½ teaspoon ground allspice, ½ teaspoon ground black pepper, ⅛ teaspoon salt, ⅛ teaspoon ground cinnamon, and ⅛ teaspoon cayenne pepper. Store in an airtight container or screw-top jar for several months in a cool dark place.

Shrimp Spring Rolls

Look for fish sauce in Asian markets or
use reduced-sodium soy sauce.

PER ROLL: 65 cal., 0 g total fat (0 g sat. fat), 10 mg chol., 55 mg sodium, 13 g carb., 1 g fiber, 2 g pro. Exchanges: 0.5 starch, 0.5 carb. Carb choices: 1.

- 2 **ounces dried rice vermicelli noodles**
- 24 **medium shrimp, peeled and deveined**
- 2 **cups shredded Chinese cabbage**
- 1 **cup shredded carrots**
- ½ **cup fresh cilantro**
- ½ **cup fresh mint or flat-leaf parsley**
- 24 **8½-inch round rice papers**
- 1 **recipe Rice Vinegar Dipping Sauce (see recipe, below)**

1. In a medium saucepan, cook noodles in lightly salted boiling water for 3 minutes; drain. Rinse under cold water; drain well. Use kitchen shears to snip noodles into small pieces; set aside.

2. In a large saucepan, cook shrimp in lightly salted boiling water for 1 to 2 minutes or until pink; drain. Rinse with cold water; drain again. Halve shrimp lengthwise; set aside.

3. For filling, in a large bowl, stir together cooked vermicelli, shredded cabbage, shredded carrots, cilantro, and mint; set aside.

4. Pour warm water into a shallow dish. Dip rice papers, one at a time, into water; gently shake off excess. Place rice papers between clean, damp, 100-percent-cotton kitchen towels; let stand for 10 minutes.

5. To assemble, brush edges of a rice paper round with a little warm water (keep others covered). Place a well-rounded tablespoon of filling across lower third of softened rice paper. Fold bottom of rice paper over filling; arrange 2 shrimp halves across filling. Fold in paper sides. Tightly roll up paper and filling. Place, seam side down, on a platter. Repeat with remaining rice paper, filling, and shrimp. Cover and chill until ready to serve. Serve with Rice Vinegar Dipping Sauce. Makes 24 spring rolls.

Rice Vinegar Dipping Sauce: In a small saucepan, combine ½ cup water and 2 tablespoons sugar. Bring to boiling over medium heat until sugar is dissolved, stirring occasionally. Remove from heat; stir in 2 tablespoons rice wine vinegar, 1 tablespoon fish sauce or reduced-sodium soy sauce, and 1 tablespoon finely shredded carrot.

Make-Ahead Directions: Prepare as directed through Step 5. Cover with a damp cloth; chill for up to 6 hours. Prepare dipping sauce; cover and chill for up to 24 hours.

Shrimp with Basil

Shrimp with Basil

Fresh basil and balsamic vinegar add flavor
to classic scampi.

PER APPETIZER: 52 cal., 2 g total fat (1 g sat. fat), 53 mg chol., 95 mg sodium, 1 g carb., 0 g fiber, 7 g pro. Exchanges: 1 very lean meat, 0.5 fat. Carb choices: 0.

- 16 **fresh or frozen large shrimp in shells (about 12 ounces)**
- 3 **to 4 cloves garlic, minced**
- 1 **tablespoon butter**
- ¼ **cup snipped fresh basil**
- 1 **tablespoon white balsamic vinegar**
- ⅛ **teaspoon salt**
-    **Fresh watercress or parsley (optional)**

1. Thaw shrimp, if frozen. Rinse shrimp; pat dry with paper towels.

2. Preheat broiler. Use a sharp knife to split each shrimp down the back through shell almost all the way through the meaty portion, leaving tails intact, if desired. Devein shrimp. Loosen shell or remove shrimp from shell. Flatten shrimp with your hand or the flat side of knife blade. On the unheated rack of a broiler pan, arrange shrimp, split sides up, in a single layer.

3. Meanwhile, in a small saucepan, cook garlic in hot butter until tender. Stir in basil, white balsamic vinegar, and salt.

4. Brush shrimp with garlic mixture. Broil 3 to 4 inches from heat for 5 to 8 minutes or just until shrimp are pink. Serve warm. Transfer shrimp to a platter. If desired, garnish with watercress. Makes 8 (2-shrimp) appetizers.

Make-Ahead Directions: Prepare as directed through Step 2. Cover and chill for up to 6 hours. Continue as directed in Steps 3 and 4.

Ginger Shrimp Skewers

These colorful skewers will beautify your party buffet. Ginger, orange, and sesame combine for a zesty Pacific Rim marinade.

PER KABOB: 44 cal., 1 g total fat (0 g sat. fat), 48 mg chol., 58 mg sodium, 2 g carb., 0 g fiber, 7 g pro. Exchanges: 1 very lean meat. Carb choices: 0.

- **16 fresh or frozen large shrimp in shells (about 12 ounces)**
- **1 teaspoon finely shredded orange peel**
- **3 tablespoons orange juice**
- **1 tablespoon white wine vinegar**
- **1 teaspoon toasted sesame oil or olive oil**
- **1 teaspoon grated fresh ginger or ½ teaspoon ground ginger**
- **⅛ teaspoon salt**
- **⅛ teaspoon cayenne pepper**
- **1 clove garlic, minced**
- **16 fresh pea pods**
- **8 canned mandarin orange sections**
- **Reduced-sodium soy sauce (optional)**

1. Thaw shrimp, if frozen. Peel and devein, leaving tails intact (if desired). In a large saucepan, cook shrimp in boiling water for 1 to 3 minutes or until pink; drain. Rinse with cold water; drain. Place in a resealable plastic bag set in a bowl.

2. For marinade, in a small bowl, combine orange peel, orange juice, vinegar, oil, ginger, salt, cayenne pepper, and garlic; pour mixture over shrimp. Seal bag; turn to coat. Marinate in the refrigerator for 1 to 2 hours, turning bag occasionally.

3. Place pea pods in a steamer basket over boiling water. Cover; steam for 2 to 3 minutes or until tender. Rinse with cold water; drain.

4. Drain shrimp, discarding marinade. Wrap a pea pod around each shrimp. On each of eight 6-inch skewers, thread 2 shrimp and 1 orange section. If desired, serve with reduced-sodium soy sauce. Makes 8 kabobs.

Ginger Shrimp Skewers

Caper Shrimp Phyllo Tarts

Miniature phyllo shells and sour cream dip mean these extraordinary tarts are easy and great tasting.

PER TART: 51 cal., 2 g total fat (0 g sat. fat), 32 mg chol., 106 mg sodium, 3 g carb., 0 g fiber, 4 g pro. Exchanges: 1 lean meat. Carb choices: 0.

- **¾ cup dairy sour cream dill dip**
- **½ teaspoon finely shredded lemon peel**
- **1 teaspoon lemon juice**
- **2 2.1-ounce packages baked miniature phyllo dough shells (30 total)**
- **2 tablespoons capers, drained**
- **30 small to medium shrimp (tails intact, if desired), peeled, deveined, and cooked**
- **Fresh dill sprigs (optional)**
- **Finely shredded lemon peel (optional)**

1. In a small bowl, stir together dill dip, the ½ teaspoon lemon peel, and the lemon juice. Fill phyllo shells with dill dip mixture (about 1 teaspoon per shell). Sprinkle with capers. In each shell, place 1 shrimp with tail up. If desired, garnish with dill sprigs and additional finely shredded lemon peel. Makes 30 tarts.

Make-Ahead Directions: Prepare as directed. Cover and chill for up to 2 hours.

Pistachio Salmon Nuggets

A sprinkling of pistachios adds even more heart-healthy benefits.

PER SERVING: 74 cal., 4 g total fat (1 g sat. fat), 24 mg chol., 88 mg sodium, 0 g carb., 0 g fiber, 9 g pro. Exchanges: 1 lean meat, 0.5 fat. Carb choices: 0.

- **1 pound fresh or frozen skinless salmon fillets, about 1 inch thick**
- **2 tablespoons water**
- **2 tablespoons reduced-sodium soy sauce**
- **1 tablespoon grated fresh ginger**
- **2 teaspoons toasted sesame oil or cooking oil**
- **1 tablespoon cooking oil**
- **1 tablespoon finely chopped pistachio nuts**

1. Thaw fish, if frozen. Rinse fish; pat dry with paper towels. Cut fish into 1-inch chunks. Place fish in a resealable plastic bag set in a shallow dish.

2. For marinade, in a small bowl, combine the water, soy sauce, ginger, and the 2 teaspoons sesame oil. Pour marinade onto salmon chunks in bag. Seal bag; turn to coat salmon. Marinate in the refrigerator for 30 minutes, turning bag occasionally.

Quick Tip

The best appetizers are those that need zero time in the kitchen right before or during your party. That means getting a head start. Marinating and stirring up dips are no-brainers, but why not shape meatballs, thread kabobs, or precook vegetables or eggs ahead?

3. Drain salmon, discarding marinade. In a large nonstick skillet, heat the 1 tablespoon cooking oil over medium-high heat. Add half of the salmon chunks to skillet; cook and gently stir for 3 to 5 minutes or until fish flakes easily with a fork. Remove from skillet and place on paper towels. Cook and stir remaining fish; remove and place on paper towels. Transfer to a platter; sprinkle with pistachio nuts. Makes 10 to 12 appetizer servings.

Pistachio Salmon Nuggets

Lamb Meat Balls with Cucumber Raita

Tandoori Chicken Wings

Add a taste of the exotic to your appetizer buffet with this take on a classic Indian chicken dish known for its red color and tantalizing flavor. These spicy wings bake in your oven, not a tandoor, and your guests will love them.

PER SERVING: 119 cal., 4 g total fat (1 g sat. fat), 62 mg chol., 363 mg sodium, 3 g carb., 0 g fiber, 16 g pro. Exchanges: 2 lean meat. Carb choices: 0.

- 5 pounds chicken drumettes* (about 50 drumettes)
- 1 medium onion, cut into wedges
- 1 8-ounce can tomato sauce
- 1 6-ounce carton plain fat-free yogurt
- 1 tablespoon ground coriander
- 4 cloves garlic, coarsely chopped
- 2 teaspoons chopped fresh ginger
- 1½ teaspoons salt
- 1 teaspoon cumin seeds
- 1 teaspoon garam masala
- ½ to 1 teaspoon cayenne pepper (optional)
- ¼ to ½ teaspoon red food coloring
- 2 whole cloves
  Lemon wedges (optional)
  Thin wedges red onion (optional)

1. Place the chicken in a 3-quart rectangular baking dish; set aside.

2. For the tandoori masala, in a blender or food processor, combine onion, tomato sauce, yogurt, coriander, garlic, ginger, salt, cumin seeds, garam masala, cayenne pepper (if desired), red food coloring, and whole cloves. Blend to a very smooth paste. (The color should be deep red.)

3. Pour the tandoori masala over the chicken drumettes; turn chicken drumettes to coat. Cover and marinate in the refrigerator for 4 to 24 hours.

4. Preheat oven to 400°F. Arrange as many of the chicken drumettes on the unheated rack of a broiler pan as will fit in a single layer. Bake for 25 minutes. Turn oven to broil. Broil chicken 4 to 5 inches from the heat for 6 to 8 minutes or until chicken is no longer pink and pieces just start to blacken, turning drumettes once halfway through broiling.

5. Transfer drumettes to a platter. Repeat baking and broiling the remaining chicken. If desired, serve with lemon and red onion wedges. Makes 16 servings (about 3 drumettes each).

*Test Kitchen Tip: If you cannot find chicken drumettes, use 25 chicken wings instead. Cut off and discard tips of chicken wings. Cut wings at joints to form 50 pieces.

Lamb Meat Balls with Cucumber Raita

A cool and creamy cucumber sauce tames the spices.

PER MEATBALL (WITH RAITA): 68 cal., 4 g total fat (2 g sat. fat), 20 mg chol., 154 mg sodium, 2 g carb., 0 g fiber, 6 g pro. Exchanges: 1 lean meat. Carb choices: 0.

- 1 medium onion, finely chopped
- 1¼ teaspoons grated fresh ginger
- 2 or 3 cloves garlic, minced
- 1 teaspoon salt
- 1 teaspoon ground coriander
- 1 teaspoon ground cumin
- ½ teaspoon garam masala
- ¼ to ½ teaspoon cayenne pepper (optional)
- 2 pounds ground lean lamb
- 1 recipe Cucumber Raita (see recipe, below)

1. Preheat oven to 350°F. In a bowl, combine onion, ginger, garlic, salt, coriander, cumin, garam masala, and, if desired, cayenne pepper. Add lamb; mix well. Shape into 32 meatballs; place in a 15×10×1-inch baking pan.

2. Bake about 25 minutes or until cooked through. Drain off fat. Transfer meatballs to a platter. Serve with Cucumber Raita. Makes 32 meatballs.

Cucumber Raita: Peel and shred 1 medium cucumber. Place in a strainer; let stand for 15 minutes. Discard liquid. Place cucumber in a bowl; stir in one 16-ounce carton plain yogurt, 1 teaspoon Roasted Cumin Powder (see below), ¾ teaspoon salt, and, if desired, ¼ teaspoon cayenne pepper. Cover and chill until serving time.

Roasted Cumin Powder: In a small dry skillet in a well-ventilated area, heat 1 tablespoon cumin seeds over medium heat for 5 to 6 minutes or until smoke begins to rise and seeds begin to brown. Remove from skillet. Cool. Grind seeds with a mortar and pestle or a spice grinder.

(stuff it!)

Mushrooms, miniature sweet peppers, cherry tomatoes, and hard-cooked eggs all make great mini cups for flavorful fillings. And mini means bite-size portions, so you can eat more reasonably, too. To help control how much filling you use, fill a pastry bag with a large star tip to pipe the filling into your mini cups. If you don't have a pastry bag, simply spoon the filling into a resealable plastic bag, twist to close, cut off a bottom corner, and squeeze just the right amount of filling into your mini cups. They're not only delicious, they look pretty, too!

Herbed Cheese Mini Peppers
You can substitute sweet pepper wedges
for the mini peppers.

PER APPETIZER: 32 cal., 3 g total fat (2 g sat. fat), 9 mg chol., 46 mg sodium, 1 g carb., 0 g fiber, 1 g pro. Exchanges: 0.5 fat. Carb choices: 0.

- 10 red, yellow, and/or orange miniature sweet peppers (6 to 8 ounces total)
- 1 8-ounce package reduced-fat cream cheese (Neufchâtel), softened
- 2 tablespoons snipped fresh oregano, rosemary, tarragon, or thyme, or ½ to 1 teaspoon dried oregano, rosemary, tarragon, or thyme, crushed
- 1 tablespoon lemon juice
- 1 tablespoon fat-free milk
  Finely shredded lemon peel
  Fresh oregano leaves (optional)

1. Halve sweet peppers lengthwise; discard seeds. Set peppers aside.

2. For filling, in a small bowl, stir together cream cheese, desired herb, lemon juice, and milk. Stir in additional milk, if necessary, to make a piping consistency.

3. Pipe or spoon filling into pepper halves. Top with lemon peel. If desired, garnish with oregano leaves. Makes 20 appetizers.

Make-Ahead Directions: Prepare as directed. Cover and chill for up to 4 hours.

Herbed Cheese
Mini Peppers

Four-Cheese Stuffed Mushrooms

Teaming light ricotta cheese with richer Monterey Jack, Parmesan, and feta keeps the flavor but holds down the fat.

PER MUSHROOM: 42 cal., 3 g total fat (1 g sat. fat), 8 mg chol., 105 mg sodium, 2 g carb., 0 g fiber, 3 g pro. Exchanges: 0.5 medium-fat meat. Carb choices: 0.

24   large fresh mushrooms (1½ to 2 inches in diameter)
1   tablespoon olive oil
8   dried tomatoes (not oil-packed)
1   cup light ricotta cheese
½   cup finely chopped fresh spinach
½   cup shredded Monterey Jack cheese (2 ounces)
3   tablespoons grated Parmesan cheese
1   tablespoon snipped fresh basil or 1 teaspoon dried basil, crushed
2   cloves garlic, minced
¼   teaspoon salt
¼   teaspoon ground black pepper
½   cup crumbled feta cheese (2 ounces)
   Fresh basil leaves (optional)

1. Preheat oven to 350°F. Remove and discard mushroom stems. Brush caps with oil. In a shallow baking pan, arrange caps, stem sides down. Bake for 12 minutes.

2. Meanwhile, in a medium bowl, cover dried tomatoes with boiling water; let stand for 10 minutes.

3. Increase oven temperature to 450°F. Drain mushroom caps and tomatoes, discarding liquid; set mushroom caps aside.

4. For filling, in the same bowl, coarsely snip tomatoes. Stir in ricotta, spinach, Monterey Jack cheese, Parmesan cheese, snipped basil, garlic, salt, and pepper.

5. Turn mushroom caps stem sides up; fill caps with cheese filling. Sprinkle with feta cheese.

6. Bake caps for 8 to 10 minutes or until filling is heated through and light brown. Serve warm. If desired, garnish with basil leaves. Makes 24 mushrooms.

Make-Ahead Directions: Prepare as directed through Step 5. Cover and chill stuffed mushrooms for up to 24 hours. Bake as directed.

Four-Cheese Stuffed Mushrooms

Creamy Fruit Morsels

Use whichever fruit is in season for these colorful fruit bites.

PER MORSEL: 17 cal., 0 g total fat (0 g sat. fat), 1 mg chol., 39 mg sodium, 2 g carb., 0 g fiber, 1 g pro. Exchanges: Free. Carb choices: 0.

- ½ of an 8-ounce package fat-free cream cheese, softened
- ¼ cup low-sugar orange marmalade
- ¼ teaspoon almond extract
- 16 small pieces fresh fruit (such as large strawberries or large dark sweet cherries; small kiwifruits or fresh figs, peeled; and/or halved apricots)

1. In a medium bowl, beat cream cheese with an electric mixer on medium speed until fluffy; beat in orange marmalade and almond extract. If desired, place cream cheese mixture in a pastry bag fitted with a large star tip.

2. If using strawberries, figs, or cherries, slice off a small portion of the stem ends; set aside. If using cherries or apricots, pit them. Pipe or spoon cream cheese mixture on top of fruit. If using strawberries, figs, or cherries, replace stem ends of fruit.

3. Serve immediately or cover and chill for up to 1 hour before serving. Makes 16 morsels.

*Test Kitchen Tip: If necessary, cut small slices from rounded sides of fruit halves so they don't roll on the platter.

Quick Tip

To keep party foods hot, arrange them on baking sheets ahead of time and keep them chilled until needed. Bake and serve one sheet at a time as you need it. You can also set hot appetizers on a warming tray. Or keep hot dips, meatballs, and wings warm in your slow cooker set on low.

Roasted Red Pepper Roll-Ups

Red and green in the filling add splashes of holiday color.

PER SERVING: 74 cal., 3 g total fat (2 g sat. fat), 6 mg chol., 165 mg sodium, 9 g carb., 1 g fiber, 3 g pro. Exchanges: 0.5 starch, 0.5 fat. Carb choices: 0.5.

- ½ of an 8-ounce package reduced-fat cream cheese (Neufchâtel), softened
- 4 ounces soft goat cheese (chèvre)
- 1 tablespoon fat-free milk
- 1 small clove garlic, minced
- ¼ teaspoon ground black pepper
- ½ cup roasted red sweet peppers, drained and finely chopped
- ¼ cup snipped fresh basil
- 8 8-inch whole wheat or plain flour tortillas
- 2 cups packed fresh spinach leaves

1. For filling, in a small mixer bowl, beat cream cheese with an electric mixer on medium speed for 30 seconds. Add goat cheese, milk, garlic, and black pepper; beat until smooth. Stir in sweet peppers and basil.

2. To assemble, divide filling among tortillas, spreading to within ½ inch of edges. Arrange spinach on filling. Roll up tightly. Cover and chill until serving time.

3. To serve, slice roll-ups into 48 (1¼-inch-wide) pieces. Makes 24 (2-slice) servings.

Make-Ahead Directions: Prepare roll-ups as directed through Step 2. Cover; chill for up to 24 hours.

Walnut-Feta Yogurt Dip

Baby carrots, cherry tomatoes, radishes, cucumber or zucchini strips, and sweet pepper strips are all terrific choices for dunking into this Mediterranean-style dip.

PER 2 TABLESPOONS: 68 cal., 4 g total fat (1 g sat. fat), 8 mg chol., 140 mg sodium, 5 g carb., 0 g fiber, 4 g pro. Exchanges: 0.5 milk, 0.5 fat. Carb choices: 0.

- 4 **cups plain low-fat or fat-free yogurt***
- ½ **cup crumbled feta cheese (2 ounces)**
- ⅓ **cup chopped walnuts or pine nuts, toasted**
- 2 **tablespoons snipped dried tomatoes (not oil-packed)**
- 2 **teaspoons snipped fresh oregano or marjoram or**
  1 **teaspoon dried oregano or marjoram, crushed**
- ¼ **teaspoon salt**
- ⅛ **teaspoon ground black pepper**
  Walnut half (optional)

1. For yogurt cheese, line a yogurt strainer, sieve, or small colander with 3 layers of 100-percent-cotton cheesecloth or a clean paper coffee filter. Suspend lined strainer over a bowl. Spoon yogurt into strainer. Cover with plastic wrap. Chill for 24 to 48 hours. Remove from refrigerator. Discard liquid in bowl.

2. Transfer yogurt cheese to a medium bowl. Stir in feta cheese, the nuts, dried tomatoes, oregano, salt, and pepper. Cover and chill for 1 to 24 hours. If desired, garnish with walnut half. Makes 2 cups or 16 (2-tablespoon) servings.

*Test Kitchen Tip: Use yogurt that contains no gums, gelatin, or fillers. These ingredients may prevent the curd and whey from separating to make yogurt cheese.

White Bean and Pine Nut Dip

Serve dip with vegetable dippers or Toasted Pita Chips (see above right).

PER 2 TABLESPOONS: 111 cal., 2 g total fat (0 g sat. fat), 0 mg chol., 197 mg sodium, 20 g carb., 2 g fiber, 5 g pro. Exchanges: 1.5 starch. Carb choices: 1.5.

- ¼ **cup soft whole wheat bread crumbs**
- 2 **tablespoons fat-free milk**
- 1 **15-ounce can white kidney (cannellini) beans or Great Northern beans, rinsed and drained**
- ¼ **cup fat-free dairy sour cream**
- 3 **tablespoons pine nuts, toasted**
- ¼ **teaspoon salt-free garlic-and-herb seasoning blend or other salt-free seasoning blend**

- ⅛ **teaspoon cayenne pepper**
- 2 **teaspoons snipped fresh oregano or basil or**
  ½ **teaspoon dried oregano or basil, crushed**
  Fresh oregano (optional)

1. In a small bowl, combine bread crumbs and milk. Cover and let stand for 5 minutes.

2. Meanwhile, in a blender or food processor, combine beans, sour cream, pine nuts, seasoning blend, and cayenne pepper. Cover and blend or process until nearly smooth. Add bread crumb mixture. Cover and blend or process until smooth. Stir in oregano. Cover and chill for 2 to 24 hours to blend flavors.

3. If desired, garnish with oregano. Makes 1½ cups or 12 (2-tablespoon) servings.

Toasted Pita Chips: Preheat oven to 350°F. Split 4 large pita bread rounds in half horizontally. Using a sharp knife, cut each pita half into 6 wedges. Arrange wedges in a single layer on ungreased baking sheets. Coat pita wedges with nonstick cooking spray. Sprinkle lightly with paprika. Bake for 12 to 15 minutes or until wedges are crisp and golden brown. Makes 48 chips.

Tangy Lemon-Caper Dip

Serve with vegetable dippers or chilled cooled shrimp.

PER 2 TABLESPOONS: 32 cal., 2 g total fat (2 g sat. fat), 8 mg chol., 36 mg sodium, 2 g carb., 0 g fiber, 1 g pro. Exchanges: 0.5 fat. Carb choices: 0.

- 1 **8-ounce carton light dairy sour cream**
- ½ **cup plain low-fat yogurt**
- 1 **tablespoon drained capers, finely chopped**
- 2 **teaspoons snipped fresh dill or thyme or**
  ½ **teaspoon dried dill weed or dried thyme, crushed**
- ½ **teaspoon finely shredded lemon peel**
  Finely shredded lemon peel (optional)
  Snipped fresh dill (optional)

1. In a bowl, stir together sour cream, yogurt, capers, herb, and lemon peel. Cover; chill until serving time.

2. Before serving, stir dip. If desired, garnish with additional lemon peel and fresh dill. Serve with cut-up vegetables. Makes 1½ cups or 12 (2-tablespoon) servings.

Make-Ahead Directions: Prepare dip as directed through Step 1. Cover and chill for up to 24 hours.

(10 ways to lighten)

Lighten your party foods and menus with these tips.

1. **Question** whether you need the salt. Try none and sprinkle it on only if you decide you need it.
2. **Add flavor** with fresh herbs and spices rather than high-sodium bottled condiments.
3. **Halve** the amount of pasta or potatoes in a recipe. You can often substitute nonstarchy vegetables for some of the pasta or potatoes.
4. **Try one crust** instead of two for sweet or savory pies. Or arrange pastry cutouts on top rather than covering the entire surface with a crust.
5. **Switch to low-fat** or fat-free dairy products, such as sour cream, yogurt, milk, and evaporated milk.
6. **Rely** on egg whites or refrig-erated egg substitute instead of using whole eggs.
7. **Opt** for low-sodium or no-salt-added canned items, such as broth and tomato products.
8. **Choose** very lean beef or pork, poultry breast meat without skin, or fish.
9. **Serve** brown rice rather than white rice, whole wheat pasta rather than plain noodles, and whole wheat or corn tortillas rather than flour tortillas.
10. **Use less** cheese overall and opt for reduced-fat cheese varieties.

Walnut-Feta Yogurt Dip (top),
White Bean and Pine
Nut Dip (bottom)

Quick Tip

When you're asked to bring an appetizer to a friend's party, these colorful spirals come to the rescue. Just roll these pinwheels up to a day ahead and carry them to your party in an insulated cooler along with some ice. Dips and spreads can easily ride along, too.

Olive-Pepper Spirals

Olive-Pepper Spirals

The olive-and-caper spread is a takeoff on a classic French condiment, tapenade.

PER SLICE: 68 cal., 4 g total fat (2 g sat. fat), 5 mg chol., 137 mg sodium, 7 g carb., 1 g fiber, 1 g pro. Exchanges: 0.5 starch, 0.5 fat. Carb choices: 0.5.

1 cup pitted ripe or Greek olives, drained
1 tablespoon olive oil or cooking oil
2 teaspoons capers, drained
2 teaspoons lemon juice or lime juice
3 9- to 10-inch whole wheat flour tortillas (any flavor)
½ of an 8-ounce tub cream cheese with chive and onion
  Lettuce leaves
1 cup purchased roasted red sweet peppers, well drained and cut into thin strips
  Fresh flat-leaf parsley sprigs (optional)

1. In a food processor, combine olives, oil, capers, and lemon juice. Cover and process with several on/off turns until olives are very finely chopped.

2. Arrange tortillas on a flat surface. Spread one-third of the cream cheese onto each tortilla; spread one-third of the olive mixture onto each. Place several lettuce leaves on top of olive mixture. Arrange one-third of the pepper strips over lettuce on each tortilla. Roll up tortillas; wrap in plastic wrap. Chill for 1 to 4 hours.

3. To serve, slice each tortilla roll into 7 slices. Arrange spirals on a platter. If desired, garnish with parsley. Makes 21 appetizers.

Turkey-Mango Pinwheels

These turkey-and-tortilla wraps slice into festive bite-size rounds for holiday nibbling.

PER 2-SLICE SERVING: 104 cal., 3 g total fat (2 g sat. fat), 11 mg chol., 242 mg sodium, 13 g carb., 0 g fiber, 6 g pro. Exchanges: 0.5 very lean meat, 1 starch. Carb choices: 1.

6 ounces soft goat cheese (chèvre)
⅓ cup bottled mango chutney
4 9- to 10-inch whole wheat flour tortillas
8 ounces thinly sliced smoked turkey breast
2 cups fresh arugula or fresh spinach leaves
8 refrigerated mango slices, drained and patted dry

1. In a bowl, stir together goat cheese and mango chutney. Spread goat cheese mixture onto tortillas, leaving a 1-inch space along one edge of each tortilla.

2. Arrange turkey slices on goat cheese mixture. Top with arugula. Cut large mango slices in half lengthwise; place on greens opposite the 1-inch space. Roll up tortillas tightly, starting with the mango. Cover and chill for 30 minutes to 4 hours.

3. To serve, cut diagonally into ¾-inch-thick slices. Makes about 32 slices (16 servings).

Vegetable Pita Pizzas

What could be easier than pita bread as a base for pizza? Use any veggie toppers you like for these mini wedges.

PER SERVING: 113 cal., 2 g total fat (1 g sat. fat), 4 mg chol., 291 mg sodium, 20 g carb., 3 g fiber, 5 g pro. Exchanges: 1 starch, 0.5 vegetable, 0.5 fat. Carb choices: 1

2 large whole wheat pita bread rounds
  Nonstick cooking spray
½ cup assorted fresh vegetables (such as small broccoli or cauliflower florets, red sweet pepper strips, sliced fresh mushrooms, and/or chopped carrot)
¼ cup pizza sauce
¼ cup shredded mozzarella cheese (1 ounce)

1. Preheat oven to 400°F. Place pita bread rounds on a baking sheet. Bake for 5 minutes.

2. Meanwhile, coat an unheated small skillet with nonstick cooking spray. Preheat over medium heat. Add vegetables; cook and stir until crisp-tender.

3. Spread pizza sauce onto pita bread rounds; top with vegetables and cheese. Bake for 8 to 10 minutes more or until light brown. Cut each round into 4 wedges. Serve warm. Makes 4 (2-wedge) servings.

Vegetable Pita Pizzas

Rosemary Roasted Nuts

Aromatic rosemary brings a pleasant evergreen flavor to nutty nibble. Fill bags with some for guests to take home.

PER ¼-CUP SERVING: 198 cal., 20 g total fat (2 g sat. fat), 0 mg chol., 102 mg sodium, 4 g carb., 2 g fiber, 5 g pro. Exchanges: 1 high-fat meat, 2 fat. Carb choices: 0.

Nonstick cooking spray
1 egg white
2 teaspoons snipped fresh rosemary or 1 teaspoon dried rosemary, crushed
½ teaspoon salt
½ teaspoon ground black pepper
3 cups walnut pieces, hazelnuts (filberts), and/or whole almonds

1. Preheat oven to 350°F. Line a 13×9×2-inch baking pan with foil; lightly coat foil with nonstick cooking spray. Set aside. In a medium bowl, use a fork to lightly beat egg white until frothy. Add rosemary, salt, and pepper; beat until combined. Add nuts; toss gently to coat.

2. Spread nut mixture in an even layer in the prepared baking pan. Bake for 15 to 20 minutes or until golden, stirring once.

3. Remove foil with nuts from pan; set aside to cool. Break up large pieces. Makes 12 (¼-cup) servings.

Test Kitchen Tip: Store nuts in an airtight container in the freezer for up to 1 month.

Rosemary Roasted Nuts

Mini Spinach Calzones

Reduced-fat cream cheese adds flavor without all the fat.

PER CALZONE: 56 cal., 2 g total fat (1 g sat. fat), 4 mg chol., 125 mg sodium, 8 g carb., 0 g fiber, 2 g pro. Exchanges: 0.5 starch, 0.5 fat. Carb choices: 0.5.

Nonstick cooking spray
½ of a 10-ounce package frozen chopped spinach, thawed and well drained
½ of an 8-ounce package reduced-fat cream cheese (Neufchâtel), softened
3 tablespoons grated Parmesan cheese
2 tablespoons chopped green onions
¼ teaspoon ground black pepper
1 13.8-ounce package refrigerated pizza dough
1 tablespoon egg white
1 tablespoon water

1. Preheat oven to 400°F. Line 2 baking sheets with foil; lightly coat with cooking spray. Set aside.

2. For filling, in a medium bowl, stir together spinach, cream cheese, 2 tablespoons of the Parmesan cheese, green onions, and pepper; set aside.

3. On a lightly floured surface, unroll dough; roll to 15-inch square. Cut into twenty-five 3-inch squares.

4. For each, spoon a slightly rounded teaspoon filling onto each square. In a small bowl, combine egg white and the water; brush onto edges. Lift a corner; stretch over filling to opposite corner, making a triangle. Use a fork to seal edges.

5. On prepared sheet, arrange calzones. Prick tops. Brush with egg white mixture. Sprinkle with the remaining 1 tablespoon Parmesan cheese. Bake for 8 to 10 minutes or until golden. Makes 25 calzones.

Make-Ahead Directions: Prepare the filling; cover and chill in the refrigerator for up to 24 hours.

Feta and Pine Nut Spirals

When you need an appetizer in a hurry, skip the pizza dough and make a dip from the cheesy Mediterranean-style filling, adding a little extra milk. Serve it with precut vegetable dippers from your supermarket's salad bar.

PER SLICE: 87 cal., 4 g total fat (2 g sat. fat), 7 mg chol., 163 mg sodium, 10 g carb., 0 g fiber, 3 g pro. Exchanges: 1 starch. Carb choices: 1.

Nonstick cooking spray

1 **3-ounce package reduced-fat cream cheese (Neufchâtel), softened**

½ **cup crumbled feta cheese with garlic and herb (2 ounces)**

3 **tablespoons toasted pine nuts or chopped toasted almonds**

3 **tablespoons finely chopped pitted, ripe olives**

2 **tablespoons snipped fresh parsley**

1 **tablespoon fat-free milk**

1 **13.8-ounce package refrigerated pizza dough**

Olive oil

Ground black pepper

1. Preheat oven to 375°F. Coat a baking sheet with nonstick cooking spray; set aside. For filling, in a small bowl, stir together cream cheese, feta cheese, nuts, olives, parsley, and milk; set aside.

2. On a lightly floured surface, roll pizza dough into a 14×10-inch rectangle. Cut dough in half crosswise to form two 10×7-inch rectangles. Spread half of the filling onto each dough rectangle to within 1 inch of edges. Starting from a long side, roll up each rectangle into a spiral. Seal seams and ends. Place spirals, seam sides down, on prepared baking sheet. Brush surfaces of spirals with oil; sprinkle with pepper.

3. Bake for 18 to 20 minutes or until golden. Cool on baking sheet on a wire rack for 5 minutes. Using a serrated knife, cut spirals into 1-inch-thick slices. Serve warm. Makes 20 slices.

good-for-you
snacks

**Citrus Salsa with
Baked Chips**

Healthful, homemade snacks help to keep your blood glucose levels in check. It's easy to make your own nibbles and dips to have on hand at home. At work, stash some quick-prep energy bars in your desk to avoid trips to the vending machine for high-fat chips or salt-laden pretzels.

Citrus Salsa with Baked Chips
Oranges and grapefruit meet tomatoes.
PER SERVING: 44 cal., 0 g total fat, 0 mg chol., 80 mg sodium, 10 g carb., 2 g fiber, 1 g pro. Exchanges: 0.5 starch. Carb choices: 0.5.

4   corn tortillas
Nonstick cooking spray
½   cup chopped grapefruit segments*
½   cup chopped orange segments*
½   cup chopped tomato
½   cup chopped cucumber
2   tablespoons chopped green onion
2   tablespoons snipped fresh cilantro
¼   teaspoon salt
¼   teaspoon crushed red pepper

1. Preheat oven to 400°F. For chips, lightly coat one side of each tortilla with cooking spray. Cut tortillas into 8 wedges. Arrange on an ungreased baking sheet. Bake for 8 to 10 minutes or until light brown and crisp. Cool.

2. For salsa, in a small bowl, stir together grapefruit segments, orange segments, tomato, cucumber, green onion, cilantro, salt, and red pepper. Makes 8 servings (¼ cup salsa and 4 chips each).

Make-Ahead Directions: Prepare chips as directed in Step 1. Place in an airtight container; cover and store at room temperature for up to 3 days. Prepare salsa as directed in Step 2. Spoon into an airtight container; cover and store in refrigerator for up to 4 hours.

*Test Kitchen Tip: You can substitute other varieties of citrus fruits (such as clementines, blood oranges, cara cara oranges, kumquats, and/or tangerines) for the grapefruit and/or oranges.

Quick Tip

Purchased chips and snack foods are generally high in both fat and calories. Making your own snacks keeps your health goals in check. Because you make them yourself, you have control over what is added. Your prep time is worth the health benefits.

Chutney-Topped Cheese Rounds

Light semisoft cheese helps keep these low in carbs, fat, and calories.

PER SERVING: 68 cal., 3 g total fat (2 g sat. fat), 15 mg chol., 160 mg sodium, 5 g carb., 1 g fiber, 6 g pro. Exchanges: 1 lean meat. Carb choices: 0.

½ cup finely chopped fresh peach or frozen unsweetened peach slices, thawed
1 tablespoon finely chopped dried cherries
1 teaspoon lemon juice
⅛ teaspoon ground cinnamon
4 0.75-ounce rounds light semisoft cheese

1. For chutney, in a bowl, combine peach, cherries, lemon juice, and cinnamon. Toss gently to combine.

2. To serve, split each cheese round in half horizontally. Spoon peach mixture onto the half-rounds. If desired, arrange half-rounds in a circle on a microwave-safe plate; microwave on 100 percent power (high) for 20 to 35 seconds or just until cheese is softened. Makes 4 (2-half-round) servings.

Make-Ahead Directions: Prepare as in Step 1. Cover and chill for up to 6 hours. Continue as in Step 2.

Crispy Parmesan Chips

These light-as-air chips are great on their own or used as dippers (see pages 274 to 276 for dip recipes).

PER 10 CHIPS: 103 cal., 4 g total fat (1 g sat. fat), 4 mg chol., 168 mg sodium, 14 g carb., 0 g fiber, 3 g pro. Exchanges: 1 starch, 0.5 fat. Carb choices: 1.

30 wonton wrappers
    Nonstick cooking spray
2 tablespoons olive oil
1 clove garlic, minced
½ teaspoon dried basil, crushed
¼ cup grated **Parmesan cheese** or **Romano cheese**

1. Preheat oven to 350°F. Using a sharp knife, cut wonton wrappers diagonally in half to form 60 triangles. Coat a baking sheet with cooking spray. Arrange a third of the triangles in a single layer on baking sheet.

2. Stir together oil, garlic, and basil. Lightly brush wonton triangles with some of the oil mixture; sprinkle with cheese. Bake about 8 minutes or until golden. Cool completely. Repeat with remaining wonton triangles, oil mixture, and cheese. Makes 60 chips.

Chutney-Topped Cheese Rounds

Crispy Parmesan Chips

(snack sense)

Snacking is important to any balanced diet. It helps your body go with the flow during the day and keeps your energy expenditure on an even keel, with fewer peaks and valleys. When you take the edge off of your appetite, you tend to eat less during mealtimes. Some of the best snacks to enjoy are those high in protein. Yogurt fits that role well. Keep some frozen fruit (such as strawberries or tart cherries) in the freezer and plain nonfat yogurt in the fridge. Thaw some fruit in the microwave, add some yogurt, and sweeten with your favorite sweetener. Toss in a few walnuts for crunch. Yum!

Peanut-Stuffed
Belgian Endive

Basil-Garlic Tomatoes

Basil-Garlic Tomatoes

Try another herb such as oregano or thyme in these tiny red treats.

PER SERVING: 31 cal., 1 g total fat (1 g sat. fat), 4 mg chol., 27 mg sodium, 4 g carb., 1 g fiber, 2 g pro. Exchanges: 0.5 vegetable. Carb choices: 0.

- 2 **tablespoons light dairy sour cream**
- 2 **tablespoons snipped fresh basil**
- 1 **tablespoon light cream cheese**
- 1 **clove garlic, minced**
- 16 **cherry tomatoes, halved**

1. In a small bowl, combine sour cream, basil, cream cheese, and garlic. Stir until mixed. Place in a resealable plastic bag; seal. Cut a small hole in one corner. Pipe onto cut sides of tomato halves. Makes 4 (8-tomato-half) servings.

Make-Ahead Directions: Prepare as in Step 1. Cover; chill for up to 24 hours. Continue as in Step 2.

Peanut-Stuffed Belgian Endive

Coleslaw takes on a new dimension when tossed with hoisin sauce.

PER SERVING: 100 cal., 6 g total fat (1 g sat. fat), 0 mg chol., 158 mg sodium, 9 g carb., 2 g fiber, 4 g pro. Exchanges: 0.5 high-fat meat, 1 vegetable, 0.5 fat. Carb choices: 0.5.

- 2 **tablespoons bottled hoisin sauce**
- 2 **teaspoons creamy peanut butter**
- 1 **teaspoon water**
- ½ **teaspoon cider vinegar**
- ⅛ **teaspoon crushed red pepper (optional)**
- 2 **cups packaged shredded cabbage with carrot (coleslaw mix)**
- ¼ **cup unsalted peanuts, chopped**
- 16 **green or red Belgian endive leaves or 4 butterhead (Bibb or Boston) lettuce leaves**

1. In a small bowl, whisk together hoisin sauce, peanut butter, the water, vinegar, and, if desired, red pepper. Add coleslaw mix and nuts; toss to coat.

2. Spoon mixture into endive leaves or divide among lettuce leaves; roll up lettuce leaves, if using. Makes 4 servings (4 filled endive leaves or 1 lettuce wrap each).

Spinach-Turkey Roll-Ups

It's a wrap, but turkey instead of a tortilla keeps the carbs low.

PER SERVING: 40 cal., 1 g total fat (1 g sat. fat), 9 mg chol., 220 mg sodium, 2 g carb., 0 g fiber, 5 g pro. Exchanges: 1 very lean meat. Carb choices: 0.

- 2 **teaspoons honey mustard**
  Dash ground nutmeg
- 8 **thin slices oven-roasted turkey breast (3 ounces)**
- 1 **cup fresh baby spinach leaves or fresh basil leaves**
- ½ **of a medium red or green sweet pepper, seeded and cut into thin strips**
- 4 **sticks mozzarella string cheese, cut lengthwise into quarters**

1. In a small bowl, stir together honey mustard and nutmeg. Carefully spread mustard mixture evenly onto turkey slices.

2. Divide spinach evenly and place on turkey slices, allowing leaves to extend beyond the turkey. Top with pepper strips and cheese.

3. Starting at an edge of a turkey slice with cheese, roll up each turkey slice. If desired, cut each roll-up in half. Makes 8 servings.

Make-Ahead Directions: Prepare turkey roll-ups as directed. Wrap each roll-up in plastic wrap. Chill roll-ups for up to 4 hours.

1. For dip, in a small storage container, stir together sour cream, powdered sugar, lime peel, and lime juice; cover and chill until serving time.

2. Wash strawberries, but do not remove stems or caps. Drain strawberries on paper towels. Transfer strawberries to a storage container; cover and chill until serving time.

3. Serve berries with dip. Makes 8 servings (2 tablespoons dip and ½ cup strawberries each).

Pesto and Tomato Bruschetta
Arugula adds a twist to the traditional Italian pine nut pesto.

PER SERVING: 92 cal., 5 g total fat (1 g sat. fat), 3 mg chol., 217 mg sodium, 9 g carb., 1 g fiber, 4 g pro. Exchanges: 0.5 starch, 1 fat. Carb choices: 0.5.

- 1 recipe **Pine Nut Pesto** (see recipe, below)
- 24 ½-inch-thick slices baguette-style French bread, toasted, or whole grain crackers
- 1 ounce Parmesan or Romano cheese, shaved
- 1 cup red and/or yellow cherry tomatoes, halved or quartered, or 2 plum tomatoes, sliced
  Fresh basil sprigs (optional)
  Pine nuts, chopped walnuts, or chopped almonds, toasted (optional)

1. Spread Pine Nut Pesto onto baguette slices. Top with shaved Parmesan and tomatoes. If desired, top with basil and nuts. Makes 12 (2-slice) servings.

Pine Nut Pesto: In a small food processor, combine 1 cup firmly packed fresh basil; 1 cup torn fresh arugula or spinach; ¼ cup grated Parmesan or Romano cheese; ¼ cup toasted pine nuts, chopped walnuts, or chopped almonds; 1 quartered clove garlic; 1 tablespoon olive oil; 1 tablespoon white balsamic vinegar; and ¼ teaspoon salt. Cover and process with several on-off turns until a paste forms, stopping several times to scrape the side. Process in enough water, adding 1 tablespoon at a time, until pesto reaches the consistency of soft butter.

Make-Ahead Directions: Toast bread slices and prepare Pine Nut Pesto as directed. Cover and chill for up to 24 hours. Serve as directed in Step 1.

Hold-That-Lime Strawberries

Hold-That-Lime Strawberries
Four ingredients are all you need for this delicious dip.

PER SERVING: 58 cal., 0 g total fat, 2 mg chol., 36 mg sodium, 12 g carb., 2 g fiber, 1 g pro. Exchanges: 1 fruit. Carb choices: 1.

- 1 8-ounce carton fat-free dairy sour cream or light dairy sour cream
- 2 tablespoons powdered sugar
- 2 teaspoons finely shredded lime peel
- 1 tablespoon lime juice
- 4 cups fresh strawberries

Quick Tip

Traditional pesto is delicious but can be high in fat and calories. When your basil is in abundance, why not make your own pesto? It will put any purchased pesto to shame. Keep it covered in the refrigerator for up to one week. Use it in omelets, on bread, or tossed with pasta.

Pesto and Tomato Bruschetta

White Bean Hummus

The chipotle pepper in adobo sauce lends a touch of heat and a smoky accent to this velvety dip.

PER SERVING: 57 cal., 1 g total fat (0 g sat. fat), 2 mg chol., 166 mg sodium, 9 g carb., 2 g fiber, 3 g pro. Exchanges: 0.5 vegetable, 0.5 starch. Carb choices: 0.5.

- 1 15-ounce can navy beans, rinsed and drained
- ¼ cup light dairy sour cream
- 2 tablespoons light mayonnaise
- 1 tablespoon fat-free milk
- ½ of a canned chipotle chile pepper in adobo sauce (optional)
- ¼ teaspoon ground cumin
- 1 clove garlic, chopped
- Snipped fresh chives (optional)
- Sliced cucumber

1. In a food processor,* combine beans, sour cream, mayonnaise, milk, chipotle pepper (if desired), cumin, and garlic. Cover and process until smooth, scraping side of container as needed.

2. Transfer hummus to a serving bowl. If desired, sprinkle with chives. Serve with cucumber slices. Makes 12 servings (2 tablespoons hummus and 4 or 5 cucumber slices each).

*Test Kitchen Tip: For a chunkier hummus, place beans in a medium bowl and mash with potato masher or fork until nearly smooth. Stir in remaining ingredients.

Roasted Red Pepper Dip

Roasted Red Pepper Dip

This creamy dip is perfect with celery sticks.

PER 2 TABLESPOONS DIP: 23 cal., 0 g total fat, 0 mg chol., 72 mg sodium, 4 g carb., 0 g fiber, 1 g pro. Exchanges: free. Carb choices: 0.

1 8-ounce carton fat-free dairy sour cream or light dairy sour cream
¼ cup chopped bottled roasted red sweet peppers
2 tablespoons sliced green onion
1 tablespoon snipped fresh basil or ½ teaspoon dried basil, crushed
1 clove garlic, minced
¼ teaspoon salt

1. In a small bowl, stir together sour cream, roasted red peppers, green onion, basil, garlic, and salt. Cover and chill for 4 to 24 hours to allow flavors to blend.

2. Stir dip before serving. Serve with assorted vegetable dippers, baked tortilla chips, and/or baked pita chips. Makes about 1¼ cups.

Creamy Peanut Dip

Use regular peanut butter because the reduced-fat kind has more carbs.

PER SERVING: 82 cal., 4 g total fat (1 g sat. fat), 0 mg chol., 42 mg sodium, 10 g carb., 2 g fiber, 2 g pro. Exchanges: 1 fat, 0.5 other carb. Carb choices: 0.5.

2 tablespoons creamy peanut butter
1 tablespoon fat-free milk
⅓ cup frozen fat-free whipped dessert topping, thawed
Red and/or green pear or apple wedges*

1. In a small bowl, whisk together peanut butter and milk until combined. Gently fold in whipped dessert topping, leaving some streaks of whipped topping. Serve with fruit wedges. Makes 4 servings (2 tablespoons dip and 2 pear wedges each).

*Test Kitchen Tip: To prevent cut fruit from browning, toss with a little orange or lemon juice.

(10 great snacks)

To avoid getting too hungry between meals, always carry a healthy, portable snack with you.

1. **Pair** plain yogurt with blueberries for a treat that has a similar texture to ice cream.
2. **Combine** a banana with almond butter. The combo keeps you satisfied for a longer time than either on its own because of the fiber in the banana and the protein and fat in the almond butter.
3. **Turn to** hummus with pita bread. Add some veggies to make a sandwich.
4. **Snack on** salsa and baked tortilla chips. Purchase the baked varieties to lower fat, and be sure to look for those that list zero trans fats on their nutrition labels.
5. **Nosh on** light microwave popcorn for its high fiber and B vitamin content.
6. **Top** low-fat chocolate pudding with low-fat granola.
7. **Stir** chopped peaches (packed in juice) into low-fat cottage cheese and sprinkle with sliced almonds.
8. **Stir together** some canned salmon, reduced-fat mayonnaise, and Cajun seasoning. Serve with whole grain crackers.
9. **Spread** apple slices with sunflower-seed butter.
10. **Spoon** some apple butter on a rice cake.

Lemon Avocado Dip

Use light sour cream; it's lower in carbs than fat-free sour cream.

PER SERVING: 72 cal., 5 g total fat (1 g sat. fat), 5 mg chol., 49 mg sodium, 7 g carb., 3 g fiber, 2 g pro. Exchanges: 1 vegetable, 1 fat. Carb choices: 0.5.

- 1 ripe avocado, halved, seeded, and peeled
- 1 tablespoon lemon juice or lime juice
- ½ cup light dairy sour cream
- 1 clove garlic, minced
- ⅛ teaspoon salt
  Lemon wedge (optional)
- 4 medium red, yellow, and/or green sweet peppers, seeded and cut into strips

1. In a bowl, mash avocado with lemon juice. Stir in sour cream, garlic, and salt. If desired, garnish with lemon wedge. Serve with pepper strips. Makes 8 servings (2 tablespoons dip and ½ pepper each).

Make-Ahead Directions: Prepare as directed. Cover surface of dip with plastic wrap; chill for up to 4 hours.

Herbed Soy Snacks

Each serving of these roasted soybeans is rich in protein, polyunsaturated fats, and phytoestrogens. Enjoy these soynuts alone or mix with popcorn or other party mixes.

PER SERVING: 75 cal., 3 g total fat (1 g sat. fat), 0 mg chol., 17 mg sodium, 4 g carb., 3 g fiber, 7 g pro. Exchanges: 0.5 starch, 0.5 medium-fat meat. Carb choices: 0.

Herbed Soy Snacks

8	ounces dry roasted soybeans (2 cups)
1½	teaspoons dried thyme, crushed
¼	teaspoon garlic salt
⅛ to ¼	teaspoon cayenne pepper

1. Preheat oven to 350°F. In a 15×10×1-inch baking pan, spread soybeans in an even layer. In a small bowl, combine thyme, garlic salt, and cayenne pepper. Sprinkle soybeans with thyme mixture. Bake for 5 minutes or just until heated through, shaking pan once. Cool completely. Store up to 1 week at room temperature in an airtight container. Makes 16 (2-tablespoon) servings.

Sweet Chili Soy Snacks: Prepare Herbed Soy Snacks as directed, except increase garlic salt to ½ teaspoon and combine with 2 teaspoons brown sugar and 1½ teaspoons chili powder; sprinkle over soybeans before baking. Omit thyme and cayenne pepper.

Sesame-Ginger Soy Snacks: Prepare Herbed Soy Snacks as directed, except combine 2 teaspoons toasted sesame oil, ¾ teaspoon ground ginger, and ½ teaspoon onion salt; sprinkle over soybeans before baking. Omit thyme, garlic salt, and cayenne pepper.

Indian-Spiced Soy Snacks: Prepare Herbed Soy Snacks as directed, except combine ½ teaspoon garam masala and ¼ teaspoon salt with cayenne pepper; sprinkle over soybeans before baking. Omit thyme and garlic salt.

Asian Trail Mix

Just four ingredients add up to a satisfying snack.

PER SERVING: 102 cal., 3 g total fat (1 sat. fat), 0 mg chol., 78 mg sodium, 17 g carb., 1 g fiber, 2 g pro. Exchanges: 1 starch, 0.5 fat. Carb choices: 1.

4	cups assorted Asian rice crackers
¾	cup dried apricots, halved lengthwise
¾	cup lightly salted cashews
¼	cup crystallized ginger pieces and/or golden raisins

1. In a medium bowl, stir together all ingredients. Serve immediately. Makes 16 (⅓-cup) servings.

Fruit and Peanut Snack Mix

This snack has a little of everything—the sweetness of the colorful dried fruit, the zest of the cheese-flavored crackers, and the satisfying crunch of peanuts.

PER SERVING: 212 cal., 8 g total fat (2 g sat. fat), 5 mg chol., 139 mg sodium, 34 g carb., 3 g fiber, 5 g pro. Exchanges: 1 fruit, 1.5 starch, 1 fat. Carb choices: 2.

1	6-ounce package plain, pretzel, and/or cheddar cheese-flavored bite-size fish-shape crackers (1½ cups)
1	6-ounce package dried cranberries (1½ cups)
1	7-ounce package dried pears, snipped (1⅓ cups)
1	cup cocktail peanuts

1. In a medium bowl, stir together all ingredients. Serve immediately. Makes about 12 (½-cup) servings.

Cherry-Almond Snack Mix

Herbed Mixed Nuts

This mix is good to have on hand when
you need a snack to tide you over until mealtime.

PER SERVING: 199 cal., 16 g total fat (2 g sat. fat), 3 mg chol., 81 mg sodium, 8 g carb., 4 g fiber, 9 g pro. Exchanges: 0.5 starch, 1 high-fat meat, 1.5 fat. Carb choices: 0.5.

1 tablespoon butter, melted
1 tablespoon Worcestershire sauce
2 teaspoons dried basil and/or oregano, crushed
½ teaspoon garlic salt
3 cups walnuts, soy nuts, and/or almonds
2 tablespoons grated Parmesan cheese

1. Preheat oven to 325°F. In a bowl, combine melted butter, Worcestershire sauce, herb, and garlic salt. Add nuts; stir to coat.

2. Line a 15×10×1-inch baking pan with foil; spread nuts in pan. Top with Parmesan; stir to coat. Bake for 15 minutes, stirring twice. Cool. Cover tightly; store up to 1 week. Makes 12 (¼-cup) servings.

Cherry-Almond Snack Mix

Almonds star in this handy snack or breakfast cereal.

PER SERVING: 82 cal., 3 g total fat (1 g sat. fat), 3 mg chol., 58 mg sodium, 12 g carb., 1 g fiber, 2 g pro. Exchanges: 1 carb., 0.5 fat. Carb choices: 1.

4 cups sweetened oat square cereal
½ cup sliced almonds
2 tablespoons butter, melted
½ teaspoon apple pie spice
  Dash salt
1 cup dried cherries and/or golden raisins

1. Preheat oven to 300°F. In a 15×10×1-inch baking pan, combine cereal and almonds. In a small bowl, stir together melted butter, apple pie spice, and salt. Drizzle butter mixture onto cereal mixture; toss to coat cereal and almonds evenly.

2. Bake about 20 minutes or until almonds are toasted, stirring once during baking. Cool snack mix in pan on a wire rack for 20 minutes.

3. Stir in cherries. Cool mixture completely. Cover tightly; store up to 1 week. Makes 20 (¼-cup) servings.

Chili Mixed Nuts

This will squelch your hungries, but be sure to watch your serving size. Nuts pack in calories that can add up fast.

PER SERVING: 232 cal., 21 g total fat (3 g sat. fat), 0 mg chol., 269 mg sodium, 8 g carb., 3 g fiber, 6 g pro. Exchanges: 0.5 starch, 1 high-fat meat, 2 fat. Carb choices: 0.5.

3 cups mixed nuts or peanuts
1 tablespoon olive oil
2 teaspoons chili powder
½ teaspoon garlic powder
½ teaspoon ground cumin
¼ teaspoon cayenne pepper
1¼ teaspoons celery salt
¼ teaspoon ground cinnamon

1. Preheat oven to 325°F. In a bowl, combine nuts and oil; stir to coat. In another bowl, stir together chili powder, garlic powder, cumin, cayenne pepper, celery salt, and cinnamon; sprinkle on nut mixture. Toss to coat.

2. Spread nuts in a 15×10×1-inch baking pan. Bake for 15 minutes, stirring twice. Cool. Cover tightly; store up to 2 weeks. Makes 12 (¼-cup) servings.

(nutty note)

Nuts are plucky little packets of nutrition power. True, a lot of calories are packed into each bite, but most of those calories come from heart-healthy monounsaturated fats that keep cholesterol in check. Besides providing energy, nuts contain important trace minerals, such as calcium, zinc, and the antioxidant mineral selenium. One of the best sources of vitamin E, nuts also are rich in folate and other B vitamins. Because of their high calorie content, limit your intake to only a few.

Spiced Popcorn

Spiced Popcorn

Zip up a bowl of popcorn with a few well-chosen spices.

PER SERVING: 31 cal., 0 g total fat, 0 mg chol., 50 mg sodium, 6 g carb., 1 g fiber, 1 g pro. Exchanges: 0.5 starch. Carb choices: 0.5.

½ teaspoon ground cumin
½ teaspoon chili powder
¼ to ½ teaspoon salt
 Dash cayenne pepper
 Dash ground cinnamon
12 cups air-popped popcorn
 Nonstick cooking spray

1. In a small bowl, stir together cumin, chili powder, salt, cayenne pepper, and cinnamon; set aside.

2. Remove uncooked kernels from popped corn. Spread popcorn in a large shallow baking pan. Lightly coat popcorn with cooking spray. Sprinkle cumin mixture evenly over popcorn; toss gently to coat. Makes 12 (1-cup) servings.

Indian-Spiced Popcorn: Prepare Spiced Popcorn as directed, except substitute ½ teaspoon curry powder, ½ teaspoon garam masala, ¼ teaspoon ground turmeric, and ¼ teaspoon ground black pepper for the cumin, chili powder, cayenne pepper, and cinnamon.

Quick Tip

If you thought energy bars were recent concoctions created for athletes, think again. Legend has it that medieval Italian crusaders toted a version called *panforte*—bread of strength—to sustain them on long journeys. Make your own for the best you can get.

Make-Your-Own Energy Bars

Modern-day crusaders on a quest for fitness can make their own fruit-and-nut bars for optimal health.

PER BAR: 126 cal., 3 g total fat (0 g sat. fat), 9 mg chol., 30 mg sodium, 24 g carb., 1 g fiber, 2 g pro. Exchanges: 1 fruit, 0.5 starch, 0.5 fat. Carb choices: 1.5.

    Nonstick cooking spray
 1 cup quick-cooking rolled oats
½ cup all-purpose flour
½ cup wheat-and-barley nugget cereal
    (such as Grape Nuts cereal)
½ to 1 teaspoon ground ginger
 1 egg, beaten
⅓ cup unsweetened applesauce
 3 tablespoons packed brown sugar
 3 tablespoons honey
 2 tablespoons cooking oil
 2 7-ounce packages mixed dried fruit bits
¼ cup shelled sunflower seeds
¼ cup chopped walnuts

1. Preheat oven to 325°F. Line an 8×8×2-inch baking pan with foil. Coat foil with cooking spray. Set pan aside.

2. In a large bowl, combine oats, flour, cereal, and ginger. Add egg, applesauce, brown sugar, honey, and oil; mix well. Stir in fruit bits, sunflower seeds, and walnuts. Press mixture evenly into prepared pan.

3. Bake for 30 to 35 minutes or until lightly browned around the edges. Cool on a wire rack. Lift edges of foil to remove bars from pan; cut. Makes 24 bars.

Pick-Me-Up Energy Bars

Dates and whole wheat flour provide a combination of fast carb energy along with slower carb energy to help pick you up and keep you energized.

PER BAR: 89 cal., 1 g total fat (0 g sat. fat), 0 mg chol., 36 mg sodium, 20 g carb., 2 g fiber, 2 g pro. Exchanges: 1 fruit, 0.5 starch. Carb choices: 1.

    Nonstick cooking spray
 3 tablespoons honey
¼ cup orange juice
 2 tablespoons lemon juice
24 pitted whole dates, snipped
2½ cups whole wheat flour
½ teaspoon baking soda
¼ teaspoon baking powder
¼ cup unsweetened applesauce
 3 tablespoons pure maple syrup
 2 egg whites
 1 tablespoon canola or cooking oil

1. Preheat oven to 350°F. Line a 13×9×2-inch baking pan with foil. Lightly coat foil with cooking spray; set aside. In a small bowl, combine honey, orange juice, and lemon juice. Stir in the dates; set aside.

2. In a large mixing bowl, combine the flour, soda, and baking powder. In a second bowl, combine applesauce, syrup, egg whites, and oil. Add applesauce mixture to flour mixture. Beat with an electric mixer until just combined (mixture will be crumbly). Stir in date mixture. Spoon batter in the prepared baking pan; press evenly into pan with fingers or the back of the spoon.

3. Bake for 12 to 15 minutes or until a toothpick inserted near the center comes out clean. Cool on a wire rack. Lift edges of foil to remove bars from pan; cut. Makes 24 bars.

Test Kitchen Tip: To store, wrap and freeze individual bars. Thaw before eating.

Apricot Iced Tea

You'll need a gallon-size heatproof pitcher to brew the tea, or divide it between two 2-quart pitchers.

PER SERVING: 55 cal., 0 g total fat, 0 mg chol., 3 mg sodium, 14 g carb., 1 g fiber, 0 g pro. Exchanges: 1 fruit. Carb choices: 1.

- 16 black tea bags
- 12 cups boiling water
- 1 cup loosely packed fresh mint
- 6 12-ounce cans apricot nectar
- 2 teaspoons vanilla
- Ice cubes
- Fresh apricot wedges (optional)
- Fresh mint sprigs (optional)

1. In a 1-gallon heatproof pitcher, combine tea bags, boiling water, and the 1 cup mint leaves. Let steep for 5 minutes.

2. Remove and discard tea bags and mint. Cover tea; let stand for 1 hour.

3. Stir apricot nectar and vanilla into tea; cover and chill up to 48 hours.

4. To serve, fill tall glasses with ice cubes. Add tea. If desired, garnish with apricot wedges and/or mint sprigs. Makes 21 (8-ounce) servings.

Chocolate-Banana Sipper

Ginger-Pineapple Spritzer

You'll enjoy this ginger-spiked fruit drink—a nutritious alternative to high-calorie sodas.

PER SERVING: 93 cal., 0 g total fat (0 g sat. fat), 0 mg chol., 2 mg sodium, 23 g carb., 0 g fiber, 1 g prot. Exchanges: 1.5 fruit. Carb choices: 1.5.

- 4 cups unsweetened pineapple juice
- 1 tablespoon chopped crystallized ginger
- Ice cubes
- 2 cups carbonated water, chilled
- Skewered fresh pineapple chunks (optional)

1. In a pitcher, combine pineapple juice and ginger. Cover and chill for at least 2 hours or up to 24 hours. Strain mixture, discarding ginger.

2. For each serving, pour pineapple juice into a tall glass over ice, filling each glass about three-fourths full. Add enough carbonated water to each glass to fill. If desired, garnish with skewered fresh pineapple. Makes 6 (8-ounce) servings.

Chocolate-Banana Sipper

This midafternoon snack drink is simply superb. Halve the ingredients for a 2-serving sipper.

PER SERVING: 122 cal., 1 g total fat (0 g sat. fat), 2 mg chol., 65 mg sodium, 23 g carb., 1 g fiber, 5 g pro. Exchanges: 1 carb., 0.5 milk. Carb choices: 1.5.

- 2 cups fat-free milk
- 1 medium banana, sliced and frozen*
- 2 to 3 tablespoons unsweetened cocoa powder
- 2 tablespoons honey
- 1 teaspoon vanilla

1. In a blender, combine milk, banana, cocoa powder, honey, and vanilla. Cover and blend until smooth and frothy. Makes 4 (1-cup) servings.

*Test Kitchen Tip: Peel and slice banana. Place banana slices in a single layer on a baking sheet lined with plastic wrap. Freeze at least 1 hour or until firm.

fresh-baked
breads

**Chocolate-Cherry
Banana Bread**

The tantalizing aroma of bread baking is a temptation that's hard to resist, especially when the breads have homey touches. With these multigrain and fruit specialties, you don't have to pass on the bread basket, because you benefit so much from the fiber and the vitamins.

Chocolate-Cherry Banana Bread

Miniature chocolate pieces scatter throughout this quick bread, making a little chocolate seem like a lot.

PER SLICE: 119 cal., 2 g total fat (0 g sat. fat), 0 mg chol., 61 mg sodium, 23 g carb., 1 g fiber, 2 g pro. Exchanges: 0.5 starch, 1 carb., 0.5 fat. Carb choices: 1.5.

PER SLICE WITH SUBSTITUTE: same as above, except 108 cal., 19 g carb. Exchanges: 0.5 carb. Carb choices: 1.

Nonstick cooking spray
1½ cups all-purpose flour
⅔ cup sugar or sugar substitute blend* equivalent to ⅔ cup sugar
2 teaspoons baking powder
¼ teaspoon baking soda
¼ cup refrigerated or frozen egg product, thawed, or 1 egg
¼ cup fat-free dairy sour cream
¼ cup fat-free milk
2 teaspoons cooking oil
1 teaspoon vanilla
⅔ cup mashed banana (about 2 medium bananas)
8 maraschino cherries, drained and chopped
¼ cup chopped walnuts
2 tablespoons miniature semisweet chocolate pieces

1. Preheat oven to 350°F. Lightly coat the bottom of a 9×5×3-inch loaf pan with cooking spray; set aside.

2. In a bowl, stir together flour, sugar, baking powder, and baking soda. Make a well in center; set aside.

3. In a medium bowl, beat egg; stir in sour cream, milk, oil, and vanilla. Stir in banana; add to flour mixture. Stir just until moistened (batter should be lumpy). Fold in cherries, walnuts, and chocolate pieces.

4. Spoon batter into prepared pan. Bake for 35 to 40 minutes or until a toothpick inserted near the center comes out clean. Cool in pan on a rack for 10 minutes. Remove from pan. Cool on rack. Makes 1 loaf (16 slices).

*Sugar Substitutes: Choose from Splenda Sugar Blend for Baking or Equal Sugar Lite. Follow the package directions to use the amount equivalent to ⅔ cup sugar.

Orange-Date Pumpkin Bread

Serve this bread with reduced-fat cream cheese flavored with a little grated orange peel stirred in.

PER SLICE: 129 cal., 4 g total fat (1 g sat. fat), 0 mg chol., 87 mg sodium, 22 g carb., 2 g fiber, 3 g pro. Exchanges: 0.5 starch, 1 carb., 0.5 fat. Carb choices: 1.5.

PER SLICE WITH SUBSTITUTE: same as above, except 120 cal., 20 g carb. Carb choices: 1.

Nonstick cooking spray

- 2 **cups all-purpose flour**
- 1⅓ **cups whole wheat flour**
- 2 **teaspoons baking powder**
- 1 **teaspoon ground nutmeg**
- ½ **teaspoon salt**
- ½ **teaspoon baking soda**
- 1 **cup refrigerated or frozen egg product, thawed, or 4 eggs**
- 1 **15-ounce can pumpkin**
- ¾ **cup sugar or sugar substitute blend* equivalent to ¾ cup sugar**
- ½ **cup honey**
- ⅓ **cup cooking oil**
- 1 **teaspoon finely shredded orange peel**
- ⅓ **cup orange juice**
- ½ **cup chopped walnuts or pecans**
- ½ **cup snipped pitted dates or raisins**

1. Preheat oven to 350°F. Coat the bottom and ½ inch up the sides of two 8×4×2-inch loaf pans with cooking spray; set aside.

2. In a large bowl, stir together all-purpose flour, whole wheat flour, baking powder, nutmeg, salt, and baking soda; set aside.

3. In a medium bowl, beat egg slightly; stir in pumpkin, sugar, honey, oil, orange peel, and orange juice.

4. Using a wooden spoon, stir pumpkin mixture into flour mixture just until combined. Stir in nuts and dates. Divide mixture between the prepared pans.

5. Bake about 50 minutes or until a wooden toothpick inserted near centers comes out clean.

6. Cool in pans on wire racks for 10 minutes. Remove from pans. Cool completely on wire racks. Makes 2 loaves (32 slices).

*Sugar Substitutes: Choose from Splenda Sugar Blend for Baking or Equal Sugar Lite. Follow the package directions to use the product amount equivalent ¾ cup sugar.

Date-Nut Bread

Be sure to purchase pitted whole dates rather than chopped dates, which are coated with sugar.

PER SLICE: 120 cal., 3 g total fat (1 g sat. fat), 13 mg chol., 172 mg sodium, 22 g carb., 3 g fiber, 3 g pro. Exchanges: 1 starch, 0.5 fruit. Carb choices: 1.5.

- 1 **8-ounce package pitted whole dates, snipped**
- 1 **cup all-purpose flour**
- 1 **cup whole wheat flour**
- 1 **teaspoon baking soda**
- 1 **teaspoon baking powder**
- 1 **egg or ¼ cup refrigerated or frozen egg product, thawed**
- 1 **teaspoon vanilla**
- ½ **cup sliced almonds, toasted and coarsely chopped**

1. In a medium bowl pour 1½ cups boiling water over dates. Let stand about 20 minutes or until dates are softened and mixture has cooled slightly.

2. Preheat oven to 350°F. Lightly grease bottom and 1/2 inch up sides of an 8×4×2-inch loaf pan; set aside. In a large bowl, stir together flours, baking soda, baking powder, and ½ teaspoon *salt*. In a small bowl, beat together egg and vanilla with a fork; stir into cooled date mixture. Add date mixture and almonds to flour mixture; stir until mixed. Spoon batter into pan, spreading evenly.

3. Bake for 50 to 55 minutes or until a toothpick inserted near the center comes out clean. Cool in pan on a wire rack for 10 minutes. Remove from pan. Cool completely on wire rack. Wrap in plastic wrap; store overnight before slicing. Makes 1 loaf (16 slices).

Spiced Fan Biscuits

These company-special biscuits taste so rich,
they need no spread.

PER BISCUIT: 121 cal., 4 g total fat (1 g sat. fat), 0 mg chol., 190 mg sodium,
18 g carb., 1 g fiber, 3 g pro. Exchanges: 1 starch, 1 fat. Carb choices: 1.

   Nonstick cooking spray
 2 cups all-purpose flour
 4 teaspoons baking powder
 ½ teaspoon cream of tartar
 ¼ teaspoon salt
 ¼ cup shortening
 ¾ cup fat-free milk
 2 tablespoons sugar
 1 teaspoon ground cinnamon

1. Preheat oven to 450°F. Coat twelve 2½-inch muffin cups with nonstick cooking spray; set aside.

2. In a large bowl, stir together flour, baking powder, cream of tartar, and salt. Using a pastry blender, cut in shortening until mixture resembles coarse crumbs. Make a well in center; add milk. Stir just until the dough clings together.

3. Turn out dough onto a lightly floured surface. Knead by folding and gently pressing dough for 10 to 12 strokes or until dough is nearly smooth. Divide dough in half. Roll one half into a 12×10-inch rectangle.

4. In a small bowl, combine sugar and cinnamon. Sprinkle half of the sugar mixture onto rectangle.

5. Cut rectangle into five 12×2-inch strips. Stack strips; cut into six 2-inch-square stacks. Place each stack, cut side down, in a prepared muffin cup. Repeat with remaining dough and sugar mixture.

6. Bake for 10 to 12 minutes or until golden. Serve warm. Makes 12 biscuits.

Cranberry-Walnut Whole Wheat Rolls

Serve these crown-shaped rolls, studded with fruit and nuts, for dinner or breakfast.

PER ROLL: 119 cal., 3 g total fat (1 g sat. fat), 6 mg chol., 127 mg sodium, 19 g carb., 1 g fiber, 3 g pro. Exchanges: 1 starch, 0.5 fat. Carb choices: 1.

2¾ to 3¼ cups all-purpose flour
  1 package active dry yeast
  1 cup fat-free milk
  ¼ cup butter, margarine, or shortening
  2 tablespoons sugar
  1 teaspoon salt
  ½ cup refrigerated or frozen egg product, thawed, or
    2 eggs
1¼ cups whole wheat flour
  ⅔ cup snipped dried cranberries
  ⅓ cup toasted and finely chopped walnuts or pecans
  2 teaspoons finely shredded orange peel
    Nonstick cooking spray

1. In a large mixing bowl, stir together 2 cups of the all-purpose flour and the yeast; set aside.

2. In a medium saucepan, heat and stir milk, butter, sugar, and salt just until warm (120°F to 130°F) and butter is almost melted.

3. Add warm mixture and egg to flour mixture. Beat with an electric mixer on medium for 30 seconds, scraping bowl. Beat on high for 3 minutes. Stir in whole wheat flour, cranberries, nuts, orange peel, and as much of the remaining all-purpose flour as you can.

4. Turn out onto a lightly floured surface. Knead in enough remaining all-purpose flour to make a moderately stiff dough that is smooth and elastic (6 to 8 minutes total). Shape into a ball. Place in a greased bowl; turn once to grease surface. Cover; let rise in a warm place until double in size (about 1 hour).

5. Punch dough down. Turn out onto a lightly floured surface. Divide dough in half. Cover; let rest for 10 minutes. Lightly coat twenty-four 2½-inch muffin cups with cooking spray; set aside.

6. To shape, divide each dough portion into 36 pieces. Shape each piece into a ball, pulling edges under to make smooth tops. Place 3 dough balls into each prepared muffin cup, smooth sides up. Cover and let rise in a warm place until nearly double in size (about 30 minutes).

7. Preheat oven to 375°F. Bake for 12 to 15 minutes or until golden. Remove rolls from muffin cups. Serve warm, or cool on wire racks. Makes 24 rolls.

Make-Ahead Directions: Prepare the dough as directed though Step 4, except do not let rise. Cover with greased plastic wrap; chill overnight or up to 24 hours. Let dough stand at room temperature for 30 minutes. Continue shaping as directed in Steps 5 through 7 (the rising in Step 6 may need an additional 10 to 15 minutes). You can also bake and freeze the rolls ahead of time and just reheat before serving.

Lefse

Serve half-rounds of this tender Norwegian flatbread.

PER SERVING: 95 cal., 3 g total fat (1 g sat. fat), 4 mg chol., 28 mg sodium, 14 g carb., 0 g fiber, 2 g pro. Exchanges: 1 starch, 0.5 fat. Carb choices: 1.
PER SERVING WITH SUBSTITUTE: same as above, except 90 cal., 13 g carb.

- 2 **cups all-purpose flour**
- 2 **tablespoons sugar or sugar substitute* equivalent to 2 tablespoons sugar**
- ⅛ **teaspoon salt**
- ½ **cup fat-free milk**
- ¼ **cup water**
- 3 **tablespoons shortening or canola oil****
- 2 **tablespoons butter, melted**
- 3 **tablespoons sugar**
- ¼ **teaspoon ground cinnamon**

1. In a large bowl, stir together flour, the 2 tablespoons sugar, and salt. In a small saucepan, heat and stir milk, the water, and shortening until warm (105°F to 115°F) and shortening (if using) is nearly melted. Pour onto flour mixture; stir until combined. Form into a ball. Cover dough with a wet, warm kitchen towel to keep slightly warm and moist while cooking lefse.

2. Pinch off about 3 tablespoons of the dough; shape into a ball. Dust ball lightly with flour; place on a well-floured surface. Using a well-floured rolling pin, roll out dough ball into a circle about 8 inches in diameter (dough will be very thin). If necessary, lightly flour the top of the dough to prevent it from sticking to the rolling pin.

Quick Tip

Do you like the idea of using whole wheat flour but prefer the flavor of white flour? Why not give white whole wheat flour a try? It has a lighter flavor than whole wheat, has a finer grind, and can be used in most recipes as a 100 percent substitution for white flour.

Using a lefse stick or large spatula, loosen the dough from the surface often, carefully pushing the stick between the dough and surface.

3. Heat an ungreased large flat griddle or large skillet over medium heat. (Or preheat a lefse grill.) Drape dough round over lefse stick or rolling pin and transfer it to the hot griddle. Cook lefse about 2 minutes or until light brown, turning about halfway through cooking (the top surface will be bubbly). Reduce heat, if necessary, to prevent overbrowning. (If the edges of lefse rounds begin to dry or curl, shorten cooking time. If the lefse rounds remain light in color, slightly increase cooking temperature.)

4. Place cooked lefse on a large kitchen towel. Cover with another towel. Repeat rolling and cooking remaining dough. Stack cooked lefse rounds; cover with kitchen towels to prevent drying.

5. To serve, brush one side of each lefse round very lightly with melted butter. In a small bowl, combine 3 tablespoons sugar and the cinnamon; sprinkle onto each lefse round. Roll up lefse rounds; cut in half. Makes 9 rounds (18 servings).

*Sugar Substitutes: Choose from Splenda granular, Equal Spoonful or packets, or Sweet'N Low bulk or packets. Follow package directions to use product amount equivalent to 2 tablespoons sugar.

**Test Kitchen Tip: If using canola oil, the dough will be quite sticky. Roll it out on a well-floured surface and use a floured rolling pin.

Make-Ahead Directions: Place stacked lefse in an airtight container; cover. Store in the refrigerator for up to 1 week or freeze for up to 3 months. Before serving, rinse each lefse lightly with warm water and place between kitchen towels; let stand for at least 15 minutes. When lefse rounds are soft, serve as directed in Step 5.

Wild Rice and Oat Bran Bread

Wild rice with its nutty flavor and chewy texture speckles this wholesome loaf.

PER SLICE: 120 cal., 2 g total fat (1 g sat. fat), 4 mg chol., 128 mg sodium, 22 g carb., 2 g fiber, 4 g pro. Exchanges: 1.5 starch. Carb choices: 1.5.

- 1¼ to 1¾ **cups bread flour**
- 1 **package active dry yeast**
- 1 **cup fat-free milk**
- 2 **tablespoons honey**
- 2 **tablespoons butter or shortening**
- ¾ **teaspoon salt**
- 1 **cup whole wheat flour**
- ¾ **cup cooked wild rice,* drained and cooled**
- ⅓ **cup oat bran**
- **Nonstick cooking spray**

1. In a large mixer bowl, stir together 1 cup of the bread flour and the yeast; set aside. In a medium saucepan, heat and stir milk, honey, butter, and salt just until warm (120°F to 130°F) and butter is almost melted. Add milk mixture to the flour mixture. Beat with an electric mixer on low speed for 30 seconds, scraping bowl constantly. Beat on high speed for 3 minutes. Using a wooden spoon, stir in whole wheat flour, wild rice, oat bran, and as much of remaining bread flour as you can.

2. Turn out dough onto a lightly floured surface. Knead in enough of the remaining bread flour to make a moderately stiff dough that is smooth and elastic (6 to 8 minutes total). Shape dough into a ball. Place in a lightly greased bowl; turn once to grease the surface. Cover and let rise in a warm place until double in size (1 to 1¼ hours).

3. Punch dough down. Turn out onto a lightly floured surface. Cover and let rest for 10 minutes. Coat an 8×4×2-inch loaf pan with cooking spray; set aside.

4. Shape dough into a loaf by patting or rolling. To shape by patting, gently pat and pinch dough into a loaf shape, tucking edges beneath. To shape by rolling, on a lightly floured surface, roll dough into a 12×8-inch rectangle. Roll up, starting from a short side. Seal seams with fingertips as you roll.

5. Place shaped dough in prepared pan. Cover; let rise in a warm place until nearly double in size (30 to 45 minutes). Preheat oven to 375°F.

6. Bake for 35 to 40 minutes or until bread sounds hollow when tapped. If necessary, cover loosely with foil the last 10 minutes to prevent overbrowning. Remove from pan. Cool on a wire rack. Makes 1 loaf (16 slices).

Bread Machine Directions: Add the ingredients to a 1½-pound loaf bread machine according to the manufacturer's directions, except use 1¾ cups all-purpose flour and 1¼ teaspoons active dry yeast or bread machine yeast. If available, select the whole grain cycle or the basic white bread cycle. During the kneading cycle, check dough and, if necessary, add more bread flour or milk, 1 teaspoon at a time, to make a dough that forms a smooth ball. Remove hot bread from machine as soon as it is done. Cool on a wire rack.

*Test Kitchen Tip: For ¾ cup cooked wild rice, bring ¾ cup water and ¼ cup uncooked wild rice to boiling; reduce heat. Cover and simmer about 40 minutes or until wild rice is tender. Drain well.

Wild Rice and Oat Bran Bread

Four-Grain Bread

(10 whole grains)

Search out these grains for a new way to enjoy baked goods.

1. **Amaranth:** These tiny yellow to dark seeds cultivated by the Aztecs can be cooked or ground into flour.
2. **Brown rice:** Unpolished brown rice kernels may be ground into flour.
3. **Buckwheat:** You can buy buckwheat in the form of flour to make pancakes.
4. **Corn:** Use ground dried yellow or white cornmeal for baking corn bread, tamale pie, or cornmeal mush.
5. **Flax:** These small reddish brown seeds may be ground into flaxseed meal and used like flour. The seeds contain soluble fiber, which can help regulate blood glucose and lower blood cholesterol.
6. **Millet:** The oldest of cultivated grains, tiny unpolished whole millet kernels can be cooked whole or ground into millet flour.
7. **Quinoa:** These tiny South American seeds can be ground into flour.
8. **Rye:** Dark rye contains more bran than light rye and, therefore, more fiber.
9. **Wheat:** This grain is commonly ground into flour.
10. **Wild rice:** Not a true rice, this grain can be ground into flour.

Granary Bread

Millet lends a nutty, mildly sweet flavor to this bread. It contains high amounts of fiber, B vitamins, iron, and some vitamin E. Millet is thought to be one of the first cereal grains used for food.

PER SLICE: 125 cal., 1 g total fat (0 g sat. fat), 1 mg chol., 116 mg sodium, 24 g carb., 2 g fiber, 5 g pro. Exchanges: 1.5 starch. Carb choices: 1.5.

¼ cup bulgur
2 tablespoons millet
1¾ to 2¼ cups bread flour
1 tablespoon gluten flour (optional)
1 package active dry yeast
2 tablespoons molasses or honey
2 teaspoons butter or shortening
¾ teaspoon salt
1 cup whole wheat flour
¼ cup rolled oats
2 tablespoons toasted wheat germ
Nonstick cooking spray

1. In a bowl, combine bulgur and millet. Add 1 cup *boiling water*. Let stand for 5 minutes; drain well.

2. In a large mixer bowl, stir together 1 cup of the bread flour, gluten flour (if using), and yeast; set aside.

3. In a saucepan, heat and stir 1¼ cups *water*, molasses, butter, and salt until warm (120°F to 130°F) and butter is almost melted. Add to flour mixture. Beat with an electric mixer on low for 30 seconds, scraping sides. Beat on high speed for 3 minutes. Stir in bulgur mixture, whole wheat flour, oats, wheat germ, and as much remaining bread flour as you can.

4. Turn out onto a lightly floured surface. Knead in enough of the remaining bread flour to make a moderately stiff dough that is smooth and elastic (6 to 8 minutes total). Shape into a ball. Place in a lightly greased bowl; turn once. Cover and let rise in a warm place until double in size (1 to 1¼ hours).

5. Punch dough down. Turn out onto a lightly floured surface. Cover; let rest for 10 minutes. Coat an 8×4×2-inch loaf pan with cooking spray; set aside.

6. Shape dough into a loaf; place loaf in prepared pan. Cover; let rise in a warm place until nearly double in size (about 30 minutes). Preheat oven to 375°F.

7. Bake for 35 to 40 minutes or until bread sounds hollow. Cover bread loosely with foil for the last 10 minutes to avoid overbrowning. Remove from pan. Cool on a wire rack. Makes 1 loaf (16 slices).

Four-Grain Bread

The fiber-rich four include oats, barley, whole wheat, and cornmeal. Freeze some loaves to bring out for company.

PER SLICE: 118 cal., 2 g total fat (0 g sat. fat), 0 mg chol., 183 mg sodium, 21 g carb., 2 g fiber, 4 g pro. Exchanges: 1.5 starch. Carb choices: 1.5.

⅓ cup quick-cooking rolled oats
⅓ cup quick-cooking barley
1¾ to 2¼ cups bread flour
½ cup whole wheat flour
1 package active dry yeast
1¼ cups warm water (120°F to 130°F)
2 tablespoons sugar
2 tablespoons cooking oil
⅓ cup cornmeal
Nonstick cooking spray

1. Preheat oven to 375°F. Spread oats and barley in a shallow baking pan. Bake about 10 minutes or until light brown, stirring occasionally. Cool. Transfer mixture to blender. Cover; blend until ground. Set aside.

2. In a large mixer bowl, stir together 1 cup of the bread flour, the whole wheat flour, and yeast. Add warm water, sugar, oil, and 1¼ teaspoons *salt*. Beat with an electric mixer on low speed for 30 seconds, scraping bowl constantly. Beat on high speed for 3 minutes. Using a wooden spoon, stir in cornmeal, oat mixture, and as much of the remaining bread flour as you can.

3. Turn out dough onto a lightly floured surface. Knead in enough of remaining bread flour to make a moderately stiff dough that is smooth and elastic (6 to 8 minutes total). Shape into a ball. Place in a lightly greased bowl; turn once to grease the surface. Cover; let rise in a warm place until double in size (1 to 1¼ hours).

4. Punch dough down. Turn out onto a lightly floured surface. Cover; let rest for 10 minutes. Coat an 8×4×2-inch loaf pan with cooking spray; set aside. Shape dough into a loaf. Place in prepared pan. Cover; let rise in a warm place until nearly double (about 30 minutes).

5. Preheat oven to 375°F. Bake 40 minutes or until top is golden and bread sounds hollow when tapped. Remove from baking pan. Cool on a wire rack. Makes 1 loaf (16 slices).

Hearty Oat and
Grain Bread

Hearty Oat and Grain Bread

Toasted and served with spreadable fruit or low-calorie preserves, this bread makes a simple breakfast special.

PER SLICE: 115 cal., 2 g total fat (0 g sat. fat), 0 mg chol., 124 mg sodium, 21 g carb., 3 g fiber, 4 g pro. Exchanges: 1.5 starch. Carb choices: 1.5.

⅓ cup cracked wheat
2 tablespoons cooking oil
2 tablespoons molasses
1 package active dry yeast
1 cup rolled oats
¼ cup nonfat dry milk powder
¼ cup oat bran or toasted wheat germ
1 teaspoon salt
1½ cups whole wheat flour
1½ to 2 cups all-purpose flour
1 tablespoon rolled oats
  Nonstick cooking spray

1. In a small saucepan, bring 2 cups *water* to boiling; add cracked wheat. Reduce heat; cover and simmer for 5 minutes. Remove from heat; transfer to a large bowl.

Stir in oil and molasses. Cool to lukewarm (105°F to 115°F). Add yeast; stir until dissolved. Add the 1 cup rolled oats, milk powder, oat bran, and salt.

2. Using a wooden spoon, stir in whole wheat flour; stir in as much of the all-purpose flour as you can. Turn out dough onto a lightly floured surface. Knead in enough of the remaining all-purpose flour to make a moderately stiff dough that is smooth and elastic (6 to 8 minutes total). Shape into a ball. Place in a lightly greased bowl; turn once to grease the surface. Cover and let rise in a warm place until double in size (about 1 hour).

3. Punch dough down. Cover; let rest for 10 minutes. Coat a baking sheet with cooking spray. Shape dough into an 8-inch round loaf; place on sheet. Cover; let rise in a warm place until nearly double (30 to 45 minutes).

4. Preheat oven to 375°F. Make 3 diagonal shallow slits across the top of the loaf. Brush lightly with *water*; sprinkle with the 1 tablespoon rolled oats.

5. Bake for 30 to 35 minutes or until loaf sounds hollow when tapped. Cool on rack. Makes 1 loaf (20 slices).

Seven-Grain Bread

This healthful loaf is full of robust wheat flavor—with a touch of honey for sweetness—and plenty of good-for-you grains, too.

PER SLICE: 111 cal., 2 g total fat (0 g sat. fat), 13 mg chol., 151 mg sodium, 20 g carb., 2 g fiber, 4 g pro. Exchanges: 1.5 starch. Carb choices: 1.5.

- ¾ to 1¼ cups all-purpose flour
- ½ cup seven-grain cereal
- 1 package active dry yeast
- ⅔ cup water
- ⅓ cup unsweetened applesauce
- 2 tablespoons honey
- 1 teaspoon salt
- 1 egg or ¼ cup refrigerated or frozen egg product, thawed
- 1¾ cups whole wheat flour
- ⅓ cup shelled sunflower kernels
  Nonstick cooking spray

1. In a large mixing bowl, stir together ¾ cup of the all-purpose flour, the cereal, and yeast; set aside.

2. In a medium saucepan, combine the water, applesauce, honey, and salt; heat and stir just until warm (120°F to 130°F). Add applesauce mixture and egg to flour mixture. Beat with an electric mixer on low to medium speed for 30 seconds, scraping side of bowl constantly. Beat on high speed for 3 minutes. Using a wooden spoon, stir in the whole wheat flour, sunflower kernels, and as much of the remaining all-purpose flour as you can.

3. Turn out dough onto a lightly floured surface. Knead in enough of the remaining all-purpose flour to make a moderately stiff dough that is smooth and elastic (6 to 8 minutes total). Shape dough into a ball. Place in a lightly greased bowl; turn once to grease surface of dough. Cover; let rise in a warm place until double in size (1 to 1½ hours).

4. Punch dough down. Turn out onto a lightly floured surface; cover and let rest for 10 minutes. Coat an 8×4×2-inch loaf pan with cooking spray; set aside.

5. Shape dough into loaf. Place in prepared pan. Cover and let rise in a warm place until nearly double (30 to 45 minutes).

6. Preheat oven to 375°F. Bake for 40 to 45 minutes or until bread sounds hollow when lightly tapped. (If necessary, cover loosely with foil for the last 10 minutes of baking to prevent overbrowning.) Immediately remove bread from pan. Cool on a wire rack. Makes 1 loaf (16 slices).

Maple Oatmeal Bread

Taste two favorite morning flavors: coffee and maple syrup.

PER SLICE: 149 cal., 3 g total fat (2 g sat. fat), 21 mg chol., 196 mg sodium, 26 g carb., 1 g fiber, 4 g pro. Exchanges: 1.5 starch, 0.5 other carb. Carb choices: 2.

- 5¾ to 6¼ cups all-purpose flour
- 2 packages active dry yeast
- 1½ cups prepared coffee
- 1 cup quick-cooking rolled oats
- ¾ cup maple syrup
- ⅓ cup butter
- 2 teaspoons salt
- 2 eggs or ½ cup refrigerated or frozen egg product, thawed
  Nonstick cooking spray

1. In a very large mixing bowl combine 2 cups of the flour and the yeast. In a medium saucepan heat the coffee, rolled oats, maple syrup, butter, and salt just until warm (120° to 130°F) and butter is almost melted. Add to flour mixture along with eggs. Beat with an electric mixer on low to medium speed for 30 seconds, scraping sides of bowl constantly. Beat on high speed for 3 minutes. Using a wooden spoon, stir in as much of the remaining flour as you can.

2. Turn dough out onto a lightly floured surface. Knead in enough remaining flour to make a moderately soft dough that is smooth and elastic (3 to 5 minutes total). Shape dough into a ball. Place in a lightly greased bowl, turning once to grease surface of dough. Cover; let rise in a warm place until double in size (about 1 hour).

3. Punch dough down. Turn dough out onto a lightly floured surface. Divide dough in half. Cover; let rest for 10 minutes. Coat two 9×5×3-inch loaf pans with cooking spray; set aside.

4. Shape dough into 2 loaves by patting or rolling. To shape by patting, gently pat and pinch, tucking edges underneath. To shape by rolling, on a lightly floured surface, roll each dough half into a 12×8-inch rectangle. Roll up each rectangle, starting from a short side. Seal seams with your fingertips. Place shaped dough in prepared pans. Cover and let bread rise in a warm place until nearly double in size (30 to 45 minutes).

5. Preheat oven to 375°F. Bake about 30 minutes or until bread sounds hollow when lightly tapped (if necessary, cover loosely with foil the last 10 to 15 minutes of baking to prevent overbrowning). Immediately remove bread from pan. Cool on rack. Makes 2 loaves (28 slices).

Parmesan Corn Bread

This crunchy, flavorful corn bread makes the perfect go-with for a holiday soup supper.

PER SLICE: 150 cal., 5 g total fat (1 g sat. fat), 3 mg chol., 241 mg sodium, 22 g carb., 2 g fiber, 5 g pro. Exchanges: 1.5 starch, 0.5 fat. Carb choices: 1.5.

¼ cup bulgur
1 cup coarsely ground or regular yellow cornmeal
1 cup all-purpose flour
½ cup grated Parmesan cheese
2 tablespoons sugar
1 tablespoon baking powder
½ teaspoon salt
½ cup refrigerated or frozen egg product, thawed, or 2 eggs
1 cup fat-free milk
⅓ cup sliced green onions
3 tablespoons olive oil or cooking oil
2 tablespoons snipped fresh basil or 2 teaspoons dried basil, crushed
   Olive oil or cooking oil (optional)
   Coarsely ground or regular yellow cornmeal (optional)

1. Preheat oven to 375°F. In a small bowl, pour 1 cup *boiling water* over bulgur; let stand for 5 minutes. Generously grease and flour a 1½-quart soufflé dish or 9×5×3-inch loaf pan. Set aside.

2. In a large bowl, stir together cornmeal, flour, Parmesan cheese, sugar, baking powder, and salt. Make a well in the center.

3. In a medium bowl, beat egg slightly; stir in milk, green onions, 2 tablespoons of the oil, and basil. Drain bulgur; stir into egg mixture. Add bulgur mixture all at once to flour mixture; stir just until moistened (the batter should be lumpy).

4. Pour batter into prepared dish or pan. Bake until a wooden toothpick inserted near center comes out clean, allowing 45 to 50 minutes for the soufflé dish or 40 to 45 minutes for the loaf pan. If necessary, cover loosely with foil for the last 10 to 15 minutes of baking to prevent overbrowning.

5. Cool on a wire rack for 10 minutes. Remove from dish. Serve warm. If desired, brush with oil; sprinkle with cornmeal. Makes 1 loaf (12 slices).

Harvest Breadsticks

Top these hearty potato breadsticks with one or a combination of the various seeds and spices listed.

PER BREADSTICK: 87 cal., 1 g total fat (0 g sat. fat), 2 mg chol., 131 mg sodium, 17 g carb., 1 g fiber, 3 g pro. Exchanges: 1 starch. Carb choices: 1.

- **2 small potatoes, peeled and cubed (1⅓ cups)**
- **1 cup buttermilk**
- **2 tablespoons sugar**
- **2 tablespoons butter or margarine**
- **6 to 6 ½ cups all-purpose flour**
- **2 packages active dry yeast**
- **1 egg white**
- **Desired toppings such as sesame seeds, fennel seeds, dill seeds, cumin seeds, red curry powder, chili powder, and/ or crushed red peppercorns (optional)**

1. In a small saucepan, bring 1¼ cups water and potatoes to boiling. Simmer, covered, about 15 minutes or until potatoes are very tender; do not drain. Mash potatoes in water. Measure potato mixture. If necessary, add additional water to make 1⅔ cups mixture total. Return potato mixture to pan. Add buttermilk, sugar, butter, and 2 teaspoons *salt*. Heat or cool as necessary until warm (120°F to 130°F), stirring constantly.

2. In a large mixing bowl, combine 2 cups of the flour and the yeast. Add the potato mixture. Beat with an electric mixer on low to medium speed for 30 seconds, scraping the side of the bowl constantly. Beat on high speed 3 minutes. Using a wooden spoon, stir in as much of the remaining flour as you can.

3. Turn dough out onto a lightly floured surface. Knead in enough of the remaining flour to make a moderately stiff dough (6 to 8 minutes). Shape dough into a ball. Place in a lightly greased bowl, turning once to grease dough. Cover; let rise in warm place until double in size (30 to 45 minutes).

4. Punch dough down. Turn dough out onto a lightly floured surface; divide dough in half. Cover and let rest 10 minutes. Roll 1 portion to a 15×8-inch rectangle. Cut into twenty 8×¾-inch pieces. Stretch and roll each piece to form a 15-inch-long stick. Place ¾ to 1 inch apart on lightly greased baking sheets. Repeat with remaining dough.

5. Cover; let breadsticks rise 20 minutes. Preheat oven to 375°F. Stir together egg white and 1 tablespoon water; brush onto breadsticks. If desired, sprinkle with toppings. Bake for 15 minutes or until light brown. Transfer to a wire rack. Serve warm or at room temperature. Makes 40 breadsticks.

Quick Tip

"Whole grain" simply refers to grain kernels that have the bran and germ intact. Because these components contain much of the grain's fiber and nutrients, foods made with whole grains are more nutritious than those made with refined flours or other cereal products.

Harvest Breadsticks

Swiss Cheese Almond Flatbread

This cheesy flatbread is robust enough
to stand alone as an appetizer, but you also can
team it with a bowl of soup for a light meal.

PER SLICE: 97 cal., 3 g total fat (1 g sat. fat), 3 mg chol., 138 mg sodium,
14 g carb., 1 g fiber, 3 g pro. Exchanges: 1 starch, 0.5 fat. Carb choices: 1.

3 ½ to 4 cups all-purpose flour
1 package active dry yeast
1 teaspoon salt
1 ¼ cups warm water (120°F to 130°F)
2 tablespoons olive oil
⅔ cup finely shredded Swiss cheese
⅓ cup sliced almonds
½ teaspoon cracked black pepper
½ teaspoon coarse sea salt

1. In a large mixer bowl, stir together 1¼ cups of the flour, the yeast, and the 1 teaspoon salt. Add the warm water and 1 tablespoon of the olive oil. Beat with an electric mixer on low to medium speed for 30 seconds, scraping side of bowl. Beat on high speed for 3 minutes. Using a wooden spoon, stir in as much of the remaining flour as you can.

2. Turn out dough onto a lightly floured surface. Knead in enough of the remaining flour to make a stiff dough that is smooth and elastic (8 to 10 minutes total). Shape dough into a ball. Place in a lightly greased bowl; turn once to grease surface of dough. Cover; let rise in a warm place until double in size (about 1 hour).

3. Punch dough down. Turn out onto a lightly floured surface. Divide in half. Lightly oil 2 baking sheets. Shape each half of the dough into a ball. Place on prepared baking sheets. Cover and let rest for 10 minutes. Flatten each ball into a circle about 9 inches in diameter. Using your fingers, press ½-inch-deep indentations about 2 inches apart into the surface. Brush with the remaining 1 tablespoon olive oil. Sprinkle with cheese, almonds, pepper, and coarse salt. Cover; let rise in a warm place until nearly double in size (about 20 minutes).

4. Preheat oven to 375°F. Bake flatbread for 25 to 30 minutes or until golden brown. Remove from baking sheets; cool on wire racks. Makes 2 rounds (24 slices).

Flaxseed and Rye Breadsticks

Flaxseeds contain both soluble and insoluble fiber.
Soluble fiber helps regulate blood glucose levels.

PER BREADSTICK: 134 cal., 4 g total fat (0 g sat. fat), 0 mg chol.,
185 mg sodium, 21 g carb., 3 g fiber, 4 g pro. Exchanges: 1.5 starch,
0.5 fat. Carb choices: 1.5.

⅓ cup flaxseeds
2 ¼ to 2 ¾ cups all-purpose flour
1 cup rye flour
1 package active dry yeast
1 ½ cups warm water (120°F to 130°F)
2 tablespoons olive oil
1 tablespoon honey
1 ¼ teaspoons salt
    Nonstick cooking spray
2 tablespoons flaxseeds

1. Heat a large skillet over medium-low heat. Add the ⅓ cup flaxseeds; cook and stir for 5 to 7 minutes or until seeds pop; cool. In a blender, cover and blend until ground (you should have about ½ cup).

2. In a large mixer bowl, stir together 1 cup of the all-purpose flour, the rye flour, and yeast. Add warm water, oil, honey, and salt. Beat with an electric mixer on low speed for 30 seconds, scraping bowl constantly. Beat on high speed for 3 minutes. Using a wooden spoon, stir in the ground flaxseeds and as much of the remaining all-purpose flour as you can.

3. Turn out dough onto a lightly floured surface. Knead in enough of the remaining all-purpose flour to make a moderately stiff dough that is smooth and elastic (6 to 8 minutes total). Shape into a ball. Place in a lightly greased bowl; turn to grease the surface. Cover; let rise until nearly double in size (about 1 hour).

4. Punch dough down. Turn out onto a lightly floured surface. Cover; let rest for 10 minutes. Coat 2 baking sheets with cooking spray; set aside.

5. Roll dough into a 16×8-inch rectangle. Brush generously with water. Sprinkle with 2 tablespoons flaxseeds. Gently pat flaxseeds into dough. Cut dough crosswise into 1-inch-wide strips.

6. Place strips 1 inch apart on prepared baking sheets, twisting breadsticks 2 to 3 times, if desired. Cover; let rise in a warm place until nearly double in size (about 30 minutes).

7. Preheat oven to 425°F. Bake breadsticks for 12 to 15 minutes or until golden. Remove from baking sheets. Cool on wire racks. Makes 16 breadsticks.

Flaxseed and Rye Breadsticks

Orange-Rye Spirals

(why rye?)

If you've never used rye in baking, here's your chance. Rye is a cereal grain with a distinctive, robust flavor. Rye flour often is used in baking bread, but you can also serve cracked rye as a cooked breakfast cereal and in pilafs. Cooked rye berries are suitable for using in casseroles, soups, and stuffings. Store all forms of rye in an airtight container in a cool, dry place for up to 1 month. Rye flour and cracked rye keep for up to 3 months in the refrigerator or freezer. Keep rye berries for up to 5 months in the refrigerator or freezer.

Orange-Rye Spirals

Orange and caraway make these yeast rolls a memorable addition to a special holiday brunch.

PER ROLL: 164 cal., 4 g total fat (1 g sat. fat), 0 mg chol., 390 mg sodium, 29 g carb., 2 g fiber, 4 g pro. Exchanges: 1 starch, 1 carb., 0.5 fat. Carb choices: 2.

2¾ to 3¼ cups all-purpose flour
 1 package active dry yeast
 1 cup water
 ¼ cup sugar
 ¼ cup cooking oil
 ¾ teaspoon salt
 2 egg whites
1¼ cups rye flour
 ¼ cup finely chopped candied orange peel
 1 teaspoon caraway seeds, crushed
   Nonstick cooking spray
 ¼ cup low-sugar orange marmalade or orange marmalade, melted

1. In a large mixer bowl, stir together 2 cups all-purpose flour and yeast. In a medium saucepan, heat and stir water, sugar, oil, and salt just until warm (120°F to 130°F). Add water mixture and egg whites to flour mixture. Beat with an electric mixer on low to medium speed for 30 seconds, scraping side of bowl occasionally. Beat on high speed for 3 minutes. Using a wooden spoon, stir in rye flour, orange peel, caraway seeds, and as much of the remaining all-purpose flour as you can.

2. Turn out dough onto a lightly floured surface. Knead in enough of the remaining all-purpose flour to make a moderately stiff dough that is smooth and elastic (6 to 8 minutes total). Shape dough into a ball. Place in a lightly greased bowl; turn once. Cover; let rise in a warm place until double in size (about 1 to 1½ hours).

3. Punch dough down. Turn out dough onto a lightly floured surface. Divide dough in half. Cover; let rest for 10 minutes. Coat 2 baking sheets with cooking spray.

4. Divide each half of the dough into 8 pieces. On a lightly floured surface, roll each piece into a 12-inch-long rope. Form each rope into an "S" shape, coiling each end snugly. Place rolls on prepared baking sheets. Cover and let rise in a warm place until nearly double in size (about 30 minutes).

5. Preheat oven to 375°F. Bake about 14 minutes or until golden brown. Transfer to a wire rack. Cool slightly. Brush rolls with orange marmalade while warm. Serve warm. Makes 16 rolls.

Potato Parker House Rolls

Serve these rolls with butter, honey butter, or preserves.

PER ROLL: 77 cal., 3 g total fat (2 g sat. fat), 13 mg chol., 94 mg sodium, 11 g carb., 0 g fiber, 2 g pro. Exchanges: 1 starch. Carb choices: 1.

 1 potato (about 5 ounces), peeled and cut into chunks
3½ to 4 cups all-purpose flour
 1 package active dry yeast
 ¾ cup fat-free milk
 6 tablespoons butter or margarine
 3 tablespoons sugar
 1 egg or ¼ cup refrigerated egg product, thawed
   Melted butter
   Nonstick cooking spray

1. In a covered saucepan, cook potato in a small amount of boiling salted water for 10 to 12 minutes or until tender; drain. Mash potato with a potato masher or beat with an electric mixer on medium speed until smooth. Measure ½ cup mashed potato; cool to room temperature. Discard remaining mashed potato.

2. In a large bowl, combine 2 cups of the flour and yeast. In a saucepan, heat and stir the ¾ cup milk, the 6 tablespoons butter, ½ cup *water*, sugar, and 1 teaspoon *salt* just until warm (120°F to 130°F). Add milk mixture to flour mixture along with egg and mashed potato. Beat with an electric mixer on low speed for 30 seconds, scraping side of bowl. Beat on high for 3 minutes. Using a wooden spoon, stir in as much remaining flour as you can.

3. Transfer dough to a lightly floured surface. Knead in enough remaining flour to make a moderately stiff dough that is smooth and elastic (6 to 8 minutes total). Shape dough into a ball. Place in a lightly greased bowl, turning once to grease surface. Cover; let dough rise in a warm place until double in size (1 to 1½ hours).

4. Punch dough down; divide in half. Cover; let rest for 10 minutes. Coat baking sheets with cooking spray; set aside. On a lightly floured surface, roll each dough half to ⅜-inch thickness. Using a floured 2½- to 2¾-inch round cutter, cut out circles. Gather scraps; set aside. Lightly brush circles with butter. With the handle of a wooden spoon, firmly press an off-center crease in each circle. Fold each circle along crease. Press folded edge firmly. Place rolls 2 to 3 inches apart on prepared sheets.

5. Gather scraps; lightly knead. Roll, cut, and shape as above. Brush rolls with *milk*. Cover with plastic wrap; let rise until almost double in size (30 minutes). Preheat oven to 375°F. Bake for 12 to 15 minutes or until golden. Transfer to a rack; cool. Serve warm. Makes 36 rolls.

best-loved cookies

Raspberry-Fig Linzer Cookies

Gather your children, grandchildren, or kids at heart in the kitchen for a snowy afternoon of baking cookies that everyone can enjoy. Our Test Kitchen has come up with ways to make cookies that taste great and that you can enjoy, too.

Raspberry-Fig Linzer Cookies

These pretty cookies showcase a crimson raspberry and fig filling in the "window" of the top cookie.

PER 2-INCH COOKIE: 65 cal., 2 g total fat (1 g sat. fat), 2 mg chol., 27 mg sodium, 11 g carb., 0 g fiber, 1 g pro. Exchanges: 1 carb., 0.5 fat. Carb choices: 1.

PER COOKIE WITH SUBSTITUTE: same as above, except 62 cal., 10 g carb. Exchanges: 0.5 carb. Carb choices: 0.5.

2 tablespoons butter, softened
¼ cup granulated sugar or sugar-substitute blend* equivalent to ¼ cup sugar
½ teaspoon baking powder
2 tablespoons cooking oil
¼ cup refrigerated egg product or 1 egg
½ teaspoon vanilla
2 cups sifted cake flour
3 tablespoons yellow or white cornmeal
1 recipe Raspberry-Fig Filling (see recipe, page 302)
Powdered sugar

1. In a mixing bowl, beat butter, sugar, baking powder, and ⅛ teaspoon *salt* with a mixer on medium speed until combined. Beat in oil, egg, and vanilla until combined. Beat in as much flour as you can. Stir in remaining flour and cornmeal. Halve dough. Wrap; chill for 2 hours.

2. Preheat oven to 375°F. On a lightly floured surface, roll each dough portion to ⅛-inch thickness. Using a 1½- to 2-inch cookie cutter, cut into desired shapes. Using a ¾- to 1-inch cutter, cut out centers of half of the cutouts. Arrange shapes 1 inch apart on ungreased cookie sheets. Bake about 5 minutes or just until edges are firm. Transfer to a wire rack; cool.

3. Spread Raspberry-Fig Filling onto each whole cookie. Sprinkle remaining cookies with powdered sugar; place on top of filled cookies. Makes about 26 (2-inch) or 46 (1½-inch) sandwich cookies.

Sugar Substitutes: Choose from Splenda Sugar Blend for Baking or Equal Sugar Lite. Follow package directions for product amount equal to ¼ cup sugar.

Raspberry-Fig Filling

Use this filling for the Linzer cookies.
Fresh or frozen raspberries work equally well.

- ⅓ cup orange juice
- ⅓ cup fresh or frozen red raspberries
- 3 tablespoons finely snipped dried figs
- 1 recipe Raspberry-Fig Linzer Cookies (see recipe, page 301)

1. In a small saucepan, combine orange juice, raspberries, and figs. Bring to boiling; reduce heat.

2. Simmer, uncovered, for 5 to 7 minutes or until mixture is thickened, stirring frequently. Remove from heat. Transfer mixture to a blender or food processor. Cover and blend or process until nearly smooth. Cool completely. Use in Raspberry-Fig Linzer Cookies. Makes about ½ cup.

Sugar Cookie Cutouts

Decorating cookies with Cream Cheese Frosting with reduced-fat cream cheese and butter flavoring in place of butter helps keep fat in check.

PER COOKIE (NOT DECORATED): 48 cal., 2 g total fat (1 g sat. fat), 3 mg chol., 26 mg sodium, 6 g carb., 0 g fiber, 1 g pro. Exchanges: 0.5 carb., 0.5 fat. Carb choices: 0.5.

PER COOKIE WITH SUBSTITUTE: same as above, except 44 cal., 5 g carb. Carb choices: 0.

- ¼ cup butter, softened
- ½ cup sugar or sugar-substitute blend* equivalent to ½ cup sugar
- 1 teaspoon baking powder
- ¼ teaspoon salt
- ¼ cup cooking oil
- ¼ cup refrigerated or frozen egg product, thawed, or 1 egg
- 1 teaspoon vanilla
- 2½ cups sifted cake flour
- 1 recipe Cream Cheese Frosting (see recipe, right) (optional)

1. In a large mixing bowl, beat butter with an electric mixer on medium speed for 30 seconds. Beat in sugar, baking powder, and salt. Add oil, egg, and vanilla; beat until combined. Beat in as much of the flour as you can. Stir in any remaining flour. Divide dough in half. Cover; chill for 1 to 2 hours or until easy to handle.

2. Preheat oven to 375°F. On a lightly floured surface, roll dough, half at a time, to ⅛-inch thickness. Using a 2½-inch cookie cutter, cut into desired shapes. Place cutouts 1 inch apart on ungreased cookie sheets. Reroll scraps as needed.

3. Bake for 6 to 8 minutes or until edges are firm and just starting to brown. Transfer to a wire rack; cool. If desired, frost with Cream Cheese Frosting and decorate. Makes about 48 cookies.

*Sugar Substitutes: Choose from Splenda Sugar Blend for Baking or Equal Sugar Lite. Follow package directions to use product amount equivalent to ½ cup sugar.

Cream Cheese Frosting

If you like, thin this frosting with fat-free milk to make it a drizzling consistency and add food coloring for tints. Use it for Sugar Cookie Cutouts, left.

PER TEASPOON: 28 cal., 0 g total fat (0 g sat. fat), 1 mg chol., 8 mg sodium, 6 g carb., 0 g fiber, 0 g pro. Exchanges: 0.5 carb. Carb choices: 0.5.

- ½ of an 8-ounce package reduced-fat cream cheese (Neufchâtel), softened
- 1 teaspoon vanilla
- ½ teaspoon butter flavoring (optional)
- 3 to 3½ cups powdered sugar*
- Food coloring (optional)

1. In a large mixing bowl, beat cream cheese, vanilla, and butter flavoring (if using) with electric mixer on medium speed until very smooth. Gradually beat in enough powdered sugar to make a frosting of spreading or piping consistency. If desired, tint frosting with food coloring. Makes about 1¼ cups (sixty 1-teaspoon servings).

Chocolate Cream Cheese Frosting: Beat in 2 tablespoons unsweetened cocoa powder with vanilla. Reduce powdered sugar to 2½ to 3 cups.

Mint Cream Cheese Frosting: Add ¼ teaspoon mint extract with vanilla.

Coffee Cream Cheese Frosting: Add 2 teaspoons instant coffee crystals with the vanilla.

*Sugar Substitutes: We don't recommend using a sugar substitute for this recipe.

Sugar Cookie Cutouts

Soft Snickerdoodles

Soft Snickerdoodles

This cookie classic is updated with whole wheat flour, dried fruit, and peanuts. Kids might like it even more!

PER COOKIE: 96 cal., 5 g total fat (2 g sat. fat), 9 mg chol., 68 mg sodium, 13 g carb., 1 g fiber, 2 g pro. Exchanges: 1 carb., 1 fat. Carb choices: 1. PER COOKIE WITH SUBSTITUTE: same as above, except 89 cal., 10 g carb. Exchanges: 0.5 carb., 1 fat. Carb choices: 0.5.

1½ cups sugar or sugar substitute baking blend* equivalent to 1½ cups sugar
3 teaspoons ground cinnamon
1 cup butter, softened
¾ cup refrigerated or frozen egg product, thawed, or 3 eggs
2 teaspoons vanilla
2 cups all-purpose flour
¾ cup whole wheat flour
2 teaspoons cream of tartar
1 teaspoon baking soda
¼ teaspoon salt
1 cup chopped peanuts
1 cup dried currants
1 6-ounce package dried cranberries (1 cup)

1. Preheat oven to 400°F. In a small bowl, combine 2 tablespoons of the sugar or substitute and 1 teaspoon of the cinnamon; set aside.

2. In a large mixing bowl, combine butter and the remaining sugar or substitute; beat with an electric mixer on medium speed until combined. Add egg and vanilla; beat until combined.

3. In a medium bowl, stir together flours, cream of tartar, baking soda, the remaining 2 teaspoons cinnamon, and salt. Add to beaten mixture; beat until mixed. Stir in peanuts, currants, and cranberries.

4. Drop dough by rounded teaspoons 2 inches apart onto ungreased cookie sheets. Sprinkle with cinnamon-sugar mixture.

5. Bake for 7 to 8 minutes or until light brown. Transfer to wire racks; cool. Makes about 60 cookies.

*Sugar Substitutes: Choose from Splenda Sugar Blend for Baking or Equal Sugar Lite. Follow package directions to use the product amount equivalent to 1½ cups sugar.

Almond Fudge Rounds (back) and Mint Fudge Rounds (front)

Almond Fudge Rounds
You'll love both versions of this fancy cookie.

PER ALMOND FUDGE ROUND: 73 cal., 3 g total fat (1 g sat. fat), 5 mg chol., 46 mg sodium, 10 g carb., 0 g fiber, 2 g pro. Exchanges: 0.5 carb., 0.5 fat. Carb choices: 0.5.

PER ALMOND FUDGE ROUND WITH SUBSTITUTE: same as above, except 66 cal., 44 mg sodium, 8 g carb.

- ⅓ cup butter, softened
- ¾ cup packed brown sugar or brown sugar-substitute blend* equivalent to ¾ cup brown sugar
- 1 teaspoon instant espresso coffee powder
- ¾ teaspoon baking soda
- 2 egg whites
- ⅓ cup plain low-fat yogurt
- ½ teaspoon almond extract
- ⅔ cup unsweetened cocoa powder
- 1½ cups all-purpose flour or white whole wheat flour
- 1 ounce white baking chocolate squares (with cocoa butter)
- ¼ teaspoon shortening
- 36 to 40 whole almonds, toasted

1. In a large mixing bowl, beat butter with an electric mixer on medium to high speed for 30 seconds. Add brown sugar, espresso powder, and baking soda; beat until combined, scraping bowl occasionally. Add egg whites, yogurt, and almond extract; beat until combined. Beat in cocoa powder. Beat in as much of the flour as you can with the mixer. Using a wooden spoon, stir in any remaining flour. If necessary, cover and chill dough for 1 to 2 hours or until easy to handle.

2. Preheat oven to 350°F. Shape dough into 1-inch balls. Place 2 inches apart on ungreased cookie sheets. Bake for 6 to 8 minutes or just until edges are firm.

3. Using the back of a small round measuring spoon, immediately make an indentation in the center of each warm cookie. Transfer cookies to a wire rack; cool.

4. In a small saucepan, heat and stir white baking chocolate and shortening over low heat until melted and smooth. Dip each almond halfway into chocolate mixture. Place an almond into the indentation in each cookie. Let stand until chocolate is set. Makes about 36 cookies.

*Sugar Substitutes: Use Splenda Brown Sugar Blend to substitute for brown sugar. Follow package directions to use the amount equivalent to ¾ cup brown sugar.

Mint Fudge Rounds: Prepare as directed, except substitute mint extract for almond extract; omit almonds and indentations. After placing dough balls on cookie sheets, use the bottom of a glass lightly coated with nonstick spray to slightly flatten. Bake as directed. Drizzle with melted chocolate. If desired, garnish each cookie with a fresh mint leaf.

Apricot-Ginger Pinwheels

Prepare these swirls one day, then bake them the next.

PER COOKIE: 63 cal., 3 g total fat (1 g sat. fat), 5 mg chol., 36 mg sodium, 9 g carb., 1 g fiber, 1 g pro. Exchanges: 0.5 carb., 0.5 fat. Carb choices: 0.5.

PER COOKIE WITH SUBSTITUTE: same as above, except 57 cal., 35 mg sodium, 8 g carb.

¾ cup dried apricot halves, finely snipped

1 tablespoon granulated sugar or sugar substitute* equivalent to 1 tablespoon sugar

¾ teaspoon ground ginger

⅓ cup butter, softened

⅓ cup packed brown sugar or brown sugar-substitute blend* equivalent to ⅓ cup brown sugar

¼ teaspoon baking soda

⅛ teaspoon salt

1 egg white

2 tablespoons fat-free milk

½ teaspoon vanilla

1 cup whole wheat flour

½ cup all-purpose flour

⅓ cup finely chopped pistachio nuts

Nonstick cooking spray

1. For filling, in a small saucepan, combine apricots, ¼ cup *water*, granulated sugar, and ¼ teaspoon of the ginger. Bring to boiling; reduce heat. Cook and stir for 1 minute. Cover; cool completely.

2. In a large mixing bowl, beat butter with an electric mixer on medium to high speed for 30 seconds. Add brown sugar, the remaining ½ teaspoon ginger, the baking soda, and salt; beat until combined, scraping bowl occasionally. Beat in egg white, milk, and vanilla until combined. Beat in as much of the whole wheat flour and all-purpose flour as you can with the mixer. Using a wooden spoon, stir in remaining flours.

3. Roll dough between 2 pieces of waxed paper or parchment paper into a 12×10-inch rectangle. Remove top sheet of paper. Spread apricot filling onto dough, leaving a ½-inch border around edges. Starting at a long side, roll up dough. Pinch edges of dough to seal.

4. Spread nuts on a large piece of waxed paper or parchment paper. Roll dough pinwheel in the nuts to evenly coat the outside, pressing nuts in gently so they stick to the dough. Wrap dough in waxed paper or plastic wrap. Chill for 2 hours.

5. Preheat oven to 375°F. Coat a cookie sheet with nonstick cooking spray. Cut dough pinwheel into ¼-inch-thick slices. Place slices 1 inch apart on prepared cookie sheet. Bake for 8 to 10 minutes or until edges are light brown. Transfer cookies to a wire rack; cool. Makes about 32 cookies.

*Sugar Substitutes: For the granulated sugar substitute, choose from Splenda granular, Equal Spoonful or packets, or Sweet'N Low bulk or packets. For the brown sugar substitute, use Splenda Brown Sugar Blend. Follow package directions to use product amounts equivalent to 1 tablespoon granulated sugar and ⅓ cup brown sugar.

Make-Ahead Directions: Prepare pinwheel logs as directed through Step 4. Wrap tightly and chill for up to 24 hours before slicing and baking as directed.

Oatmeal Cookies

Reduced-fat peanut butter gives this classic any-day cookie lots of flavor but just a little fat.

PER COOKIE: 76 cal., 4 g total fat (2 g sat. fat), 7 mg chol., 69 mg sodium, 9 g carb., 1 g fiber, 2 g pro. Exchanges: 0.5 carb., 0.5 fat. Carb choices: 0.5.

½ cup butter, softened

½ cup reduced-fat peanut butter

⅓ cup granulated sugar*

⅓ cup packed brown sugar*

½ teaspoon baking soda

2 egg whites

½ teaspoon vanilla

1 cup all-purpose flour

1 cup quick-cooking rolled oats

1. Preheat oven to 375°F. In a large mixing bowl, combine butter and peanut butter. Beat with an electric mixer on medium to high speed about 30 seconds or until combined.

2. Add granulated sugar, brown sugar, and baking soda. Beat until combined, scraping bowl occasionally. Beat in egg whites and vanilla until combined. Beat in as much of the flour as you can with the mixer. Using a wooden spoon, stir in any remaining flour. Stir in oats.

3. Drop dough by rounded teaspoons 2 inches apart on ungreased cookie sheets. Bake for 7 to 8 minutes or until edges are golden brown. Cool on cookie sheet for 1 minute. Transfer cookies to a wire rack; cool. Makes about 40 cookies.

*Sugar Substitutes: We don't recommend using a sugar substitute for this recipe.

Apricot-Ginger Pinwheels

(cookie strategies)

Use these tips to make home-baked cookies more healthful.

1. **Reduce saturated fat** by using canola oil in place of some of the butter.

2. **Choose a sugar substitute** that's appropriate for baking. Because sugar tenderizes, browns, and crisps cookies, a sugar-substitute blend works better than a plain substitute.

3. **Switch to cake flour** to make cookies more tender.

4. **Substitute reduced-fat cream cheese** for some of the butter in cookies and frostings.

5. **Incorporate whole grains** to increase cookies' fiber content. Fiber helps stabilize blood glucose.

6. **Use cocoa powder** instead of melted chocolate. This reduces the fat content and lets you use less flour, which lowers the carb count.

7. **Make your own fillings** so you can lower the level of sugar or use a sugar substitute.

8. **Opt for dried fruits** instead of candied fruits.

9. **Include a moderate amount** of healthful nuts, especially walnuts, almonds, and pecans.

10. **Try citrus peel,** extracts, and spices for flavor.

Cranberry-Hazelnut Tarts

(pearl of a fruit)

The holidays just wouldn't be the holidays without cranberries, and with good reason. Research has shown that compounds in cranberries play a role in controlling diabetes, promoting dental health, and preventing heart disease and cancer. In particular, cranberries contain anthocyanins, antioxidants that prevent the damage from free radicals that occurs in diabetes. So go ahead and savor this nugget of nutrition in your holiday baking and include cranberry juice in your daily meal plan.

Cranberry-Hazelnut Tarts

A cinnamon-spiced shell cradles cranberries and nuts for a bite-size gem on a cookie tray.

PER TART: 83 cal., 4 g total fat (2 g sat. fat), 9 mg chol., 60 mg sodium, 11 g carb., 1 g fiber, 1 g pro. Exchanges: 0.5 carb., 1 fat. Carb choices: 1.

²⁄₃ cup quick-cooking rolled oats
½ cup whole wheat flour
¼ cup all-purpose flour
½ of an 8-ounce package reduced-fat cream cheese (Neufchâtel), softened
¼ cup butter, softened
¼ cup packed brown sugar *
¼ teaspoon baking soda
¼ teaspoon ground cinnamon
⅛ teaspoon salt
¼ cup hazelnuts, toasted** and chopped
1 recipe Cranberry-Hazelnut Filling (see below)

1. Preheat oven to 350°F. For dough, in a small bowl, combine oats, whole wheat flour, and all-purpose flour.

2. In a large mixing bowl, beat cream cheese and butter with an electric mixer on medium to high speed for 30 seconds. Add the ¼ cup brown sugar, baking soda, ¼ teaspoon cinnamon, and salt; beat until combined. Beat in as much of the oat mixture as you can with the mixer. Using a wooden spoon, stir in remaining oat mixture.

3. Divide dough evenly among twenty-four 1¾-inch muffin cups. Press onto bottom and up sides of cups.

4. Spoon Cranberry-Hazelnut Filling evenly into dough-lined cups. Sprinkle with 2 tablespoons of the hazelnuts. Bake for 15 to 20 minutes or until edges of crusts are golden. Cool in cups for 5 minutes. Remove tarts from cups; cool on a wire rack. Makes 24 tarts.

Cranberry-Hazelnut Filling: In a small saucepan, combine ⅓ cup brown sugar, 2 teaspoons cornstarch, and ½ teaspoon ground cinnamon. Add 1¼ cups fresh cranberries and ²⁄₃ cup water. Cook and stir over medium heat until thickened and bubbly. Stir in 2 tablespoons of the hazelnuts.

***Sugar Substitutes:** We don't recommend using brown sugar substitute for this recipe.

****Test Kitchen Tip:** To toast hazelnuts, preheat oven to 350°F. Place nuts in a shallow baking pan. Bake about 10 minutes or until toasted, stirring once or twice so nuts don't burn. Place warm nuts on a clean kitchen towel. Rub nuts with towel to remove the loose skins.

Lemon Gingersnaps

You can also top the mousse with mandarin orange sections or fresh raspberries instead of the kumquats.

PER COOKIE: 42 cal., 1 g total fat (0 g sat. fat), 0 mg chol., 72 mg sodium, 8 g carb., 1 g fiber, 1 g pro. Exchanges: 0.5 carb. Carb choices: 0.5.

½ of a 4-serving-size package sugar-free lemon-flavored gelatin (1¼ teaspoons)
⅓ cup boiling water
¼ cup cold water
½ of an 8-ounce package fat-free cream cheese, softened
½ cup frozen fat-free whipped dessert topping, thawed
30 purchased small gingersnaps
Sliced fresh kumquats and/or orange peel strips

1. Line a 7½×3½×2-inch loaf pan with plastic wrap; set aside. Place gelatin in a small bowl; add the boiling water and stir to dissolve. Stir in the cold water.

2. In a medium mixing bowl, beat cream cheese with an electric mixer on medium speed until fluffy; gradually beat in gelatin mixture on low speed until combined. Fold in whipped dessert topping. Pour into prepared pan. Cover and chill for 4 to 24 hours or until set.

3. Using the plastic wrap, lift mousse out of pan. Cut in half lengthwise; then cut crosswise into ¼-inch-thick slices. If desired, cut into shapes using small cookie cutters or hors d'oeuvres cutters.

4. To serve, place one slice of the mousse on top of each gingersnap. Top with kumquat slices and/or orange peel strips. (Assemble only as many as you need at one time.) Makes 30 cookies.

Lemon Gingersnaps

All-Star Peanut Butter Cookies.

Three ingredients? The kids can make these!

PER COOKIE: 66 cal., 4 g total fat (1 g sat. fat), 6 mg chol., 35 mg sodium, 7 g carb., 0 g fiber, 2 g pro. Exchanges: 0.5 carb., 0.5 fat. Carb choices: 0.5.

- 1 cup sugar*
- 1 cup peanut butter
- 1 egg or ¼ cup refrigerated or frozen egg product, thawed
  Sugar*

1. Preheat oven to 375°F. Grease cookie sheets; set aside. In a medium bowl, stir together the 1 cup sugar, the peanut butter, and egg until mixed.

2. Using your hands, roll peanut butter mixture into 1-inch balls; arrange 2 inches apart on prepared cookie sheets. Lightly grease a drinking glass; dip into sugar. Using glass, flatten each ball slightly. Lightly grease a small star-shape cookie cutter; dip into sugar. Press a star indentation into the center of each cookie.

3. Bake about 9 minutes or until edges are set and bottoms are light brown. Makes 36 cookies.

***Sugar Substitutes:** We don't recommend using a sugar substitute for this recipe.

Brownie Cookies

Give yourself a present—a delightful chocolate treat.

PER COOKIE: 73 cal., 2 g total fat (1 g sat. fat), 6 mg chol., 38 mg sodium, 12 g carb., 0 g fiber, 1 g pro. Exchanges: 1 carb., Carb choices: 1.

- 1 cup all-purpose flour
- ¼ teaspoon baking soda
- ¼ cup butter
- ⅔ cup granulated sugar*
- ⅓ cup unsweetened cocoa powder
- ¼ cup packed brown sugar*
- ¼ cup buttermilk or sour milk**
- 1 teaspoon vanilla
  Nonstick cooking spray
- 1 tablespoon sifted powdered sugar

1. In a small bowl, stir together flour and baking soda; set aside. In a medium saucepan, melt butter; remove from heat. Stir in granulated sugar, cocoa powder, and brown sugar. Stir in buttermilk and vanilla. Stir in flour mixture just until combined. Cover and chill dough for 1 hour (dough will be stiff).

2. Preheat oven to 350°F. Lightly coat cookie sheets with nonstick cooking spray. Drop chilled dough by rounded teaspoons onto cookie sheet.

3. Bake for 8 to 10 minutes or until edges are set. Cool on sheet for 1 minute. Transfer to a wire rack; cool. Sprinkle with powdered sugar. Makes 24 cookies.

***Sugar Substitutes:** We don't recommend using a sugar substitute for this recipe.

****Test Kitchen Tip:** To make ¼ cup sour milk, place ¾ teaspoon lemon juice or vinegar in a glass measuring cup. Add enough milk to make ¼ cup total liquid; stir. Let mixture stand for 5 minutes before using.

Mocha Meringue Stars

These delicate drops look like holiday decorations.

PER COOKIE: 32 cal., 1 g total fat (0 g sat. fat), 0 mg chol., 7 mg sodium, 5 g carb., 0 g fiber, 1 g pro. Exchanges: 0.5 starch. Carb choices: 0.5.

- ⅓ cup sifted powdered sugar
- 2 tablespoons unsweetened cocoa powder
- 1 tablespoon cornstarch
- 1 teaspoon instant espresso coffee powder or 2 teaspoons instant coffee powder
- 3 egg whites
- ½ teaspoon vanilla
- ¼ cup granulated sugar*
- ⅓ cup semisweet chocolate pieces
- 1 teaspoon shortening

1. Preheat oven to 250°F. Line a cookie sheet with parchment paper or foil; set aside. In a small bowl, stir together powdered sugar, cocoa powder, cornstarch, and espresso powder; set mixture aside.

2. In a mixing bowl, beat egg whites and vanilla with an electric mixer on high speed until foamy. Add granulated sugar, 1 tablespoon at a time, beating until stiff peaks form. Gradually fold in cocoa mixture.

3. Transfer the mixture to a pastry bag fitted with a large star tip. Pipe twenty-four 2-inch stars onto prepared cookie sheet. (Or drop by rounded teaspoons onto prepared cookie sheet.)

4. Bake for 1 hour. Cool on cookie sheet on wire rack. When cool, carefully remove from parchment paper.

5. In a small saucepan, combine chocolate pieces and shortening. Cook and stir over low heat until melted. Drizzle chocolate over cookies. Makes 24 cookies.

***Sugar Substitutes:** We don't recommend using a sugar substitute for this recipe.

Lemon Cardamom Meringue Cookies

To store, place these airy cookies in an airtight container for 3 days at room temperature or freeze for up to 3 months.

PER COOKIE: 9 cal., 0 g total fat (0 g sat. fat), 0 mg chol., 6 mg sodium, 2 g carb., 0 g fiber, 0 g pro. Exchanges: free. Carb choices: 0.

- 3 **egg whites**
- ¼ **cup sugar***
- 1 **tablespoon cornstarch**
- ⅛ **teaspoon ground cardamom**
- ½ **teaspoon vanilla**
- ¼ **teaspoon cream of tartar**
- 1 **teaspoon finely shredded lemon, lime, or orange peel**

1. Let egg whites stand at room temperature for 30 minutes. Line a very large cookie sheet (or two smaller cookie sheets) with parchment paper or foil. In a bowl, stir together sugar, cornstarch, and cardamom.

2. Preheat oven to 300°F. In a medium mixing bowl, combine egg whites, vanilla, and cream of tartar. Beat with an electric mixer on high speed until soft peaks form (tips curl). Gradually add the sugar mixture, 1 tablespoon at a time, beating on high speed until stiff peaks form (tips stand straight). Fold in citrus peel.

3. Spoon mixture into a pastry bag fitted with an extra-large star tip. Pipe mixture into 30 swirls on prepared cookie sheet(s), making each about 2 inches in diameter and 1½ inches tall, leaving a 1½-inch space between swirls. (Or spoon mixture into a resealable plastic bag. Snip off one corner. Pipe into 30 mounds.)

4. Bake for 20 minutes (if using 2 cookie sheets, bake at the same time on separate oven racks). Turn off oven. Let cookies dry in oven, with door closed, for 30 minutes. Remove from oven and gently peel off the parchment paper or foil. Makes 30 cookies.

***Sugar Substitutes:** We don't recommend using a sugar substitute for this recipe.

Lemon Cardamom Meringue Cookies

Vanilla Biscotti

Celebrate with a cup of coffee and these crunchy cookies.

PER COOKIE: 63 cal., 2 g total fat (1 g sat. fat), 19 mg chol., 61 mg sodium, 9 g carb., 0 g fiber, 1 g pro. Exchanges: 0.5 carb., 0.5 fat. Carb choices: 0.5.

- 3 **cups all-purpose flour**
- 1 **tablespoon baking powder**
- ¼ **teaspoon salt**
- 3 **eggs**
- ¾ **cup sugar***
- ½ **cup butter, melted and cooled**
- 2 **teaspoons vanilla**
  Nonstick cooking spray

1. Preheat oven to 325°F. Coat a cookie sheet with nonstick cooking spray; set aside. In a bowl, combine flour, baking powder, and salt; set aside. In a mixing bowl, beat eggs with an electric mixer on high for 1 minute. Gradually beat in sugar, beating on high for 1 minute. Add butter and vanilla; beat on low speed until combined. Beat in as much of flour mixture as you can with mixer. Using a wooden spoon, stir in remaining flour mixture.

2. Divide dough into thirds. On a lightly floured surface, roll each third into a 14-inch-long roll. Arrange rolls 2½ inches apart on a prepared cookie sheet; flatten rolls slightly to 1½-inch widths. Bake about 25 minutes or until firm and light brown. Cool on cookie sheet for 15 minutes.

3. Preheat oven to 350°F. On a large cutting board, use a serrated knife to cut rolls diagonally into ½-inch-thick slices. Arrange, cut sides down, on cookie sheet. Bake for 10 minutes. Turn slices; bake about 10 minutes more or until crisp. Cool on cookie sheet. Makes 48.

*Sugar Substitutes: We don't recommend using a sugar substitute for this recipe.

312

Coffee 'n' Cream Biscotti

Take time to relax and enjoy a flavorful reward.

PER COOKIE: 89 cal., 3 g total fat (2 g sat. fat), 5 mg chol., 51 mg sodium, 14 g carb., 0 g fiber, 2 g pro. Exchanges: 1 carb., 0.5 fat. Carb choices: 1.

¼ cup butter, softened
¼ of an 8-ounce package reduced-fat cream cheese (Neufchâtel), softened
⅔ cup sugar*
1 tablespoon baking powder
¾ cup refrigerated or frozen egg product, thawed, or 3 eggs
1 teaspoon vanilla
2½ cups all-purpose flour
2 tablespoons unsweetened cocoa powder
2 tablespoons instant espresso coffee powder
2 tablespoons all-purpose flour
½ cup semisweet chocolate pieces and/or white baking pieces

1. Preheat oven to 375°F. In a large mixing bowl, beat butter and cream cheese with an electric mixer on medium to high speed 30 seconds. Add sugar and baking powder; beat until combined, scraping bowl occasionally. Add egg and vanilla; beat until combined. Beat in as much of the 2½ cups flour as you can. Using a wooden spoon, stir in any remaining flour.

2. Divide dough in half; transfer one portion to a medium bowl. In a small bowl, combine cocoa powder and espresso powder; add to dough in bowl. Knead until combined. Add the 2 tablespoons flour to the remaining portion of dough; knead until combined.

3. Divide each dough portion in half. Shape each portion into a rope about 12 inches long. Twist together a chocolate rope and a plain rope. Gently roll twisted ropes together to form a 14-inch-long rope. Pat to make a log about 2 inches wide. Repeat with the remaining two ropes to make 2 logs. Place logs about 4 inches apart on an ungreased large baking sheet.

4. Bake about 18 minutes or until light brown. Cool on cookie sheet for 1 hour.

5. Preheat oven to 325°F. Transfer baked logs to a cutting board. Bias-slice logs into ½-inch-thick slices. Place slices on the same cookie sheet. Bake in the 325°F oven for 8 minutes. Turn slices; bake for 8 to 10 minutes more or until crisp and light brown. Transfer cookies to a wire rack; cool.

6. For a chocolate drizzle, in a small saucepan, heat semisweet chocolate pieces over low heat until melted. (If using both semisweet chocolate and white baking pieces, melt in separate saucepans.) Cool slightly. Drizzle semisweet and/or white chocolate onto cooled biscotti. Let cookies stand until chocolate is set. Makes about 32 cookies.

*Sugar Substitutes: We don't recommend using a sugar substitute for this recipe.

Tarragon Biscotti

Tarragon's light licorice flavor adds spark to these cookies.

PER COOKIE: 113 cal., 6 g total fat (2 g sat. fat), 8 mg chol., 66 mg sodium, 14 g carb., 1 g fiber, 2 g pro. Exchanges: 1 carb., 1 fat. Carb choices: 1.

Nonstick cooking spray
3¼ cups all-purpose flour
2 teaspoons baking powder
½ cup butter, softened
⅔ cup sugar*
¼ cup snipped fresh tarragon
1 tablespoon finely shredded lemon peel
¼ teaspoon salt
¾ cup refrigerated or frozen egg product, thawed, or 3 eggs
1 cup chopped walnuts

1. Preheat oven to 375°F. Coat a cookie sheet with nonstick cooking spray; set aside. In a small bowl, stir together flour and baking powder; set aside.

2. In a large mixing bowl, beat butter with an electric mixer on medium to high speed for 30 seconds. Add sugar, tarragon, peel, and salt; beat until combined.

3. Beat in egg until combined. Beat in as much of the flour mixture as you can with the mixer. Using a spoon, stir in any remaining flour mixture and the walnuts.

4. Divide the dough in half. Shape each half into an 11-inch loaf. On prepared cookie sheet, place the loaves about 5 inches apart. Flatten each loaf slightly until each is 2 inches wide.

5. Bake for 20 to 25 minutes or until tops are light brown. Cool loaves on cookie sheet on wire rack about 1 hour or until completely cool.

6. Preheat oven to 325°F. Transfer loaves to a cutting board. Cut each crosswise diagonally into ¾-inch-thick slices. Arrange on ungreased cookie sheets. Bake in the 325°F oven for 10 minutes. Turn over slices; bake for 10 to 12 minutes more or until crisp. Remove from cookie sheets; cool on wire racks. Makes 32 cookies.

*Sugar Substitutes: We don't recommend using a sugar substitute for this recipe.

delightful desserts

Honey-Apricot Frozen Yogurt (back), page 316
Very Berry Sorbet (middle), page 315
Strawberry Sherbert (front), page 316

Having diabetes can take the fun out of enjoying sweets. But you don't have to forgo desserts altogether. Just choose wisely. Reach for these good-for-you treats the next time you want to celebrate. We've lightened them all—just for you.

Very Berry Sorbet

If fresh berries aren't in season, use purchased frozen blueberries and raspberries instead.

PER SERVING: 67 cal., 0 g total fat, 0 mg chol., 7 mg sodium, 16 g carb., 3 g fiber, 1 g pro. Exchanges: 0.5 carb., 0.5 fruit. Carb choices: 1.

2 cups fresh blueberries, frozen*
2 cups fresh raspberries, frozen*
½ cup cold water
¼ cup frozen pineapple-orange-banana juice concentrate or citrus beverage concentrate
Fresh blueberries and/or raspberries (optional)

1. In a large bowl, combine frozen berries, the water, and frozen concentrate. Place half of the mixture in a food processor. Cover and process until almost smooth. Repeat with remaining mixture. Serve immediately with additional blueberries and/or raspberries, if desired. Makes 6 (½-cup) servings.

Make-Ahead Directions: Prepare as directed. Transfer mixture to a 1½-quart freezer container. Cover and freeze about 4 hours or until firm. Use within 2 days.

*Test Kitchen Tip: To freeze, place berries in a single layer on a pan; place in the freezer. Transfer frozen berries to a freezer container; seal, label, and store for up to 12 months.

Quick Tip:

Aspartame, one of the most popular sugar substitutes, isn't stable when heated and can't be used for cooking and baking, but acesulfame K is stable when heated. For all sugar alternatives, read the labels to be sure you'll get the sweet rewards you seek—with success.

Strawberry Sherbet

This luscious strawberry delight is made from packaged frozen strawberries. Be sure to use strawberries packed in light syrup. Pictured on page 314.

PER SERVING: 68 cal., 0 g total fat, 1 mg chol., 33 mg sodium, 14 g carb., 0 g fiber, 2 g pro. Exchanges: 1 carb. Carb choices: 1.

- ¼ cup sugar
- 4 teaspoons cornstarch
- 1 teaspoon finely shredded lemon peel
- 1 12-ounce can evaporated fat-free milk
- 1½ teaspoons vanilla
- 2 10-ounce packages frozen strawberries in light syrup, thawed
- 1 tablespoon lemon juice
  Fresh strawberries, halved (optional)

1. In a small saucepan, stir together sugar, cornstarch, and lemon peel. Stir in milk. Cook and stir until thickened and bubbly. Cook and stir for 2 minutes more. Stir in vanilla. Cover; chill about 1 hour or until cold.

2. In a food processor, combine strawberries in light syrup and lemon juice. Cover; process until smooth.

3. Stir strawberry mixture into chilled milk mixture. Pour into a 1½- to 2-quart ice cream freezer. Freeze according to manufacturer directions. Pack the mixture into a freezer container. Cover and freeze about 3 hours or until firm. If desired, serve with fresh strawberries. Makes 12 (½-cup) servings.

Honey-Apricot Frozen Yogurt

To save even more carbs, choose a yogurt that's made with a sugar substitute. Pictured on page 314.

PER SERVING: 93 cal., 1 g total fat (1 g sat. fat), 4 mg chol., 50 mg sodium, 18 g carb., 1 g fiber, 4 g pro. Exchanges: 0.5 other carb., 0.5 milk. Carb choices: 1.

- 3 cups pitted and finely chopped fresh apricots* or nectarines
- 4 cups vanilla low-fat yogurt
- 2 tablespoons honey
  Sliced fresh apricots and/or nectarines (optional)

1. In a large food processor, combine half of the chopped apricots, the yogurt, and honey. Cover; process until smooth. (Process in two batches, if necessary.)

2. Pour the apricot mixture into a 2-quart freezer container. Stir in remaining chopped apricots. Cover and freeze about 4 hours or until firm.

3. Chill the mixer bowl for a heavy stand electric mixer. Spoon frozen mixture into chilled bowl. Beat with the mixer on medium speed until slightly fluffy, starting slowly and gradually increasing the speed. Return to freezer container. Cover and freeze about 6 hours or until firm.

4. Let frozen yogurt stand at room temperature for 20 minutes before serving. If desired, serve with sliced apricots. Makes 12 (½-cup) servings.

*Test Kitchen Tip: If you can't find fresh apricots, drain and use three 15-ounce cans unpeeled apricot halves in light syrup.

Mango Mousse

This light, impressive dessert is one you can turn to when you are entertaining or for a special meal.

PER SERVING: 97 cal., 2 g total fat (2 g sat. fat), 0 mg chol., 12 mg sodium, 17 g carb., 0 g fiber, 3 g pro. Exchanges: 1 carb., 0.5 fat. Carb choices: 1.

- 2 cups mango nectar
- 1 envelope unflavored gelatin
- 2 teaspoons lime juice
- 5 drops yellow food coloring (optional)
- 1 drop red food coloring (optional)
- ½ of an 8-ounce container frozen light whipped dessert topping, thawed
- 1 ripe mango, seeded, peeled, and cut into thin strips
  Fresh mint leaves (optional)

1. In a medium saucepan, stir together mango nectar and unflavored gelatin. Cook and stir over low heat until gelatin is dissolved. Remove from heat.

2. Stir in lime juice and, if using, food coloring. Cover and chill about 2 hours or until mixture mounds when lifted with a spoon, stirring occasionally.

3. Gently whisk whipped topping into mango mixture until smooth. Spoon into eight dessert dishes or parfait glasses. Cover; chill about 2 hours or until set.

4. Arrange mango strips on top of mango mixture. If desired, garnish each serving with a mint leaf. Makes 8 servings ($\frac{1}{3}$ cup mousse and fruit each).

Mango Mousse

Rocky Road Parfaits

Rocky Road Parfaits

Sugar-free pudding and light whipped dessert topping trim and slim these chocolaty treats.

PER SERVING: 162 cal., 6 g total fat (2 g sat. fat), 2 mg chol., 386 mg sodium, 21 g carb., 1 g fiber, 7 g pro. Exchanges: 0.5 fat-free milk, 1 carb., 1 fat. Carb choices: 1.5.

1 **4-serving-size package sugar-free instant chocolate or chocolate fudge pudding mix**
2 **cups fat-free milk**
½ **cup frozen light whipped dessert topping, thawed**
¼ **cup unsalted peanuts, coarsely chopped**
¼ **cup tiny marshmallows**
 Chocolate curls (optional)

1. Prepare pudding mix according to package directions using the fat-free milk. Remove ¾ cup of the pudding and place in a small bowl; fold in whipped topping until combined.

2. Divide the remaining plain chocolate pudding among four 6-ounce glasses or dessert dishes. Top with chocolate-dessert topping mixture. Let stand for 5 to 10 minutes or until set.

3. Just before serving, sprinkle each parfait with peanuts and marshmallows. If desired, garnish with chocolate curls. Makes 4 servings.

Make-Ahead Directions: Prepare as directed through Step 2. Cover and chill parfaits for up to 24 hours. Serve as directed in Step 3.

Black Forest Trifle

If fresh dark cherries aren't available, don't worry. Frozen cherries will also work in this dessert.

PER SERVING: 102 cal., 1 g total fat (1 g sat. fat), 1 mg chol., 110 mg sodium, 22 g carb., 1 g fiber, 3 g pro. Exchanges: 1.5 carb. Carb choices: 1.5.

1 **8-ounce package no-sugar-added low-fat chocolate cake mix**
1 **4-serving-size package sugar-free instant chocolate pudding mix**
2 **cups fat-free milk**
1 **pound fresh dark sweet cherries, pitted, or one 16-ounce package frozen unsweetened pitted dark sweet cherries, thawed and well-drained**
2 **cups frozen fat-free whipped dessert topping, thawed**
 Unsweetened cocoa powder (optional)

Black Forest Trifle

1. Prepare cake mix according to package directions in a 13×9×2-inch baking pan. Cool in pan on a wire rack for 10 minutes; remove from pan. Cut into 1-inch pieces.

2. Meanwhile, prepare pudding mix according to package directions using the 2 cups fat-free milk. Cover; chill about 30 minutes or until set.

3. In a 3-quart trifle bowl or glass bowl, layer half of the cake cubes, half of the cherries, half of the chocolate pudding, and half of the whipped topping. Repeat the layers. If desired, sprinkle with cocoa powder. Makes 16 (⅔-cup) servings.

Make-Ahead Directions: Prepare trifle as directed. Cover and chill for up to 4 hours.

Kona Trifle Cups

Kona, Hawaii's prized coffee, is featured in this dessert. But any strong-brewed coffee will do.

PER SERVING: 141 cal., 6 g total fat (3 g sat. fat), 56 mg chol., 87 mg sodium, 17 g carb., 0 g fiber, 4 g pro. Exchanges: 1 carb., 1.5 fat. Carb choices: 1.

PER SERVING WITH SUBSTITUTE: same as above, except 106 cal., 8 g carb. Exchanges: 0.5 carb. Carb choices: 0.5.

½ of a 3-ounce package ladyfingers (12 halves), cubed
¼ cup strong-brewed **Kona** or other coffee
¼ of an 8-ounce package reduced-fat cream cheese (**N**eufchâtel), softened
⅓ cup light dairy sour cream
3 tablespoons sugar or sugar substitute* equivalent to 3 tablespoons sugar
1 teaspoon vanilla
2 to 3 teaspoons fat-free milk

1. Divide ladyfinger cubes among four 4- to 6-ounce dessert dishes or custard cups. Drizzle ladyfinger cubes with coffee. Set aside.

2. In a small bowl, stir together cream cheese, sour cream, sugar, and vanilla. Beat with a wire whisk until smooth. Stir in enough of the milk to make desired consistency. Spoon cream cheese mixture onto ladyfinger cubes. Cover and chill for 1 hour. Makes 4 servings.

*Sugar Substitutes: Choose from Equal Spoonful or packets or Sweet'N Low bulk or packets. Follow package directions to use product amount equivalent to 3 tablespoons sugar.

Summer Berry Panna Cotta

This luscious dessert will enchant everyone with its beauty and seemingly rich flavor.

PER SERVING: 115 cal., 0 g total fat, 0 mg chol., 62 mg sodium, 22 g carb., 4 g fiber, 2 g pro. Exchanges: 0.5 fruit , 1 carb. Carb choices: 1.

2 tablespoons water
1 ¼ teaspoons unflavored gelatin
1 ½ cups fat-free half-and-half
2 tablespoons sugar or sugar substitute* equivalent to 2 tablespoons sugar
1 teaspoon finely shredded lemon peel
1 teaspoon vanilla
1 tablespoon raspberry liqueur or sugar-free raspberry preserves
1 tablespoon orange liqueur or orange juice

Summer Berry Panna Cotta

4 cups fresh berries (such as raspberries, sliced strawberries, blueberries, and/or blackberries)
Fresh mint sprigs (optional)

1. In a medium bowl, for panna cotta, combine the water and gelatin; let stand about 5 minutes or until softened (mixture will be very thick).

2. In a small saucepan, combine half-and-half, 1 tablespoon of the sugar, and lemon peel. Cook and stir over medium heat just until bubbling. Remove from heat; stir into gelatin mixture until gelatin is dissolved. Stir in vanilla. Cover and chill for 3 to 6 hours or until soft set.

3. Meanwhile, in a large bowl, stir together remaining 1 tablespoon sugar, raspberry liqueur, and orange liqueur. Gently fold in berries.

4. Whisk gelatin mixture until smooth. Spoon about 3 tablespoons panna cotta into each glass. Divide the berry mixture among six dessert glasses or dishes. If desired, garnish with mint. Makes 6 servings (about ¼ cup panna cotta and ⅔ cup fruit each).

*Sugar Substitutes: Choose from Splenda granular or Sweet'N Low bulk or packets. Follow package directions to use product amounts equivalent to the sugar.

No-Bake Chocolate Swirl Cheesecake

Low-fat cream cheese and sour cream keep this lovely cheesecake light and luscious.

PER SERVING: 184 cal., 11 g total fat (7 g sat. fat), 29 mg chol., 232 mg sodium, 15 g carb., 1 g fiber, 7 g pro. Exchanges: 1 carb., 2 fat. Carb choices: 1.

PER SERVING WITH SUBSTITUTE: same as above, except 168 cal., 11 g carb.

½ cup crushed graham crackers
2 tablespoons butter, melted
1 envelope unflavored gelatin
¾ cup fat-free milk
2 8-ounce packages reduced-fat cream cheese (Neufchâtel), softened
1 8-ounce package fat-free cream cheese, softened
1 8-ounce carton fat-free dairy sour cream
⅓ cup sugar or sugar substitute* equivalent to ⅓ cup sugar
2 teaspoons vanilla
4 ounces semisweet chocolate, melted and cooled
Chocolate curls (optional)

1. For crust, in a bowl, combine cracker crumbs and butter until moistened. Press onto the bottom of an 8-inch springform pan (may not cover completely). Cover and chill.

2. For filling, in a saucepan, sprinkle gelatin into milk; let stand for 5 minutes. Stir over low heat until gelatin is dissolved. Remove from heat; cool for 15 minutes.

3. In a bowl, beat cream cheeses until smooth. Beat in sour cream, sugar, and vanilla; slowly beat in gelatin mixture. Divide in half. Stir chocolate into one portion.

4. Spoon half of the chocolate filling onto chilled crust; spread evenly. Carefully spoon half of the white filling onto chocolate in small mounds. Using a narrow spatula or knife, swirl chocolate and white fillings. Top with remaining chocolate and white fillings, spreading each evenly. Swirl again. Cover and chill for 6 to 24 hours.

5. To serve, loosen cheesecake from pan; remove pan side. If desired, top with chocolate curls. Makes 16 servings.

*Sugar Substitutes: Choose from Splenda granular, Equal Spoonful or packets, or Sweet'N Low bulk or packets. Follow package directions to use product amount equivalent to ⅓ cup sugar.

No-Bake Chocolate Swirl Cheesecake

Mini Cranberry Phyllo Tarts

Short on time? Substitute a 2.1-ounce package baked miniature phyllo dough shells (15) for the phyllo tart shells. Prepare as directed, starting with Step 6.

PER TART: 29 cal., 0 g total fat (0 g sat. fat), 0 mg chol., 17 mg sodium, 6 g carb., 0 g fiber, 0 g pro. Exchanges: 0.5 carb. Carb choices: 0.5.

Nonstick cooking spray
4 **sheets frozen phyllo dough (14×9-inch rectangles), thawed**
¾ **cup fresh cranberries**
½ **cup water**
1 **tablespoon sugar**
⅓ **cup canned whole cranberry sauce**
⅓ **cup lemon fat-free yogurt**
3 **tablespoons frozen light whipped dessert topping, thawed**
Fresh mint leaves (optional)

1. Preheat oven to 350°F. Coat twelve 1¾-inch muffin cups with nonstick cooking spray; set aside.

2. Unfold phyllo dough. Remove one sheet of the phyllo dough; lightly coat phyllo sheet with nonstick cooking spray. Working quickly, top with the remaining phyllo sheets, coating each sheet with nonstick cooking spray.

3. Cut phyllo stack lengthwise into three 3-inch-wide strips. Cut each strip crosswise into five 2¾×3-inch rectangles, making 15 rectangles total.

4. For tart shells, press each phyllo rectangle into a prepared muffin cup, pleating edges as needed to fit. Bake about 8 minutes or until golden.

5. Cool phyllo tart shells in muffin cups on a wire rack for 5 minutes. Carefully remove tart shells from muffin cups; cool on a wire rack.

6. Meanwhile, for topping, in a small saucepan, combine cranberries, the water, and sugar. Cook and stir over medium heat until boiling. Reduce heat; simmer, uncovered, for 1 minute.

7. Remove from heat. Cool cranberries for 15 minutes. Drain and discard the cooking liquid. Place cranberries in a small bowl; cover and chill for 4 hours.

8. For filling, in a small bowl, stir cranberry sauce to break up. In another small bowl, fold together yogurt and whipped dessert topping.

9. Just before serving, place 1 teaspoon of the cranberry sauce filling into each phyllo tart shell. Divide yogurt mixture among tarts. Top each tart with about 3 chilled cooked cranberries. If desired, garnish with fresh mint leaves. Makes 15 tarts.

Make-Ahead Directions: Prepare phyllo tart shells as directed through Step 5. Place phyllo shells in a single layer in an airtight container; store at room temperature for up to 2 days. Prepare the cranberry topping as directed in Steps 6 and 7; cover and chill for up to 2 days. Continue as directed in Steps 8 and 9.

Devil's Food Ice Cream Pie

Add the chocolate syrup after freezing the pie—otherwise, the chocolate flavor won't be as strong.

PER SERVING: 192 cal., 6 g total fat (3 g sat. fat), 16 mg chol., 132 mg sodium, 34 g carb., 1 g fiber, 5 g pro. Exchanges: 2.5 carb., 0.5 Fat. Carb choices: 2.5.

1 **6¾-oz. box low-fat devil's food cookie cakes (12 cookies)**
¼ **cup reduced-fat peanut butter**
¼ **cup hot water**
1 **cup sliced bananas**
4 **cups no-sugar-added light vanilla ice cream, softened**
2 **tablespoons chocolate-flavored syrup**

1. Coarsely chop cookie cakes. Place cookie pieces in the bottom of an 8-inch springform pan.

2. In a small bowl, whisk together peanut butter and the hot water until smooth. Drizzle evenly over cookies.

3. Top with banana slices and carefully spoon ice cream evenly over all. Spread ice cream on top until smooth. Cover with plastic wrap and place in freezer until firm, about 8 hours.

4. Let stand at room temperature for 15 minutes before serving. Remove the sides of the pan; drizzle chocolate syrup over all. Makes 10 servings.

(ode to pumpkin)

The humble pumpkin deserves some respect. Not only is pumpkin delicious in pies, muffins, breads, and soups, but it is also a nutritional powerhouse. For starters, pumpkin is packed with beta-carotene, a potent antioxidant. It's also a terrific source of fiber. A half cup of canned pumpkin contains 5 grams of fiber. Yet it has only about 40 calories and 0.5 gram of fat, while providing small amounts of vitamins and minerals. So go ahead. Try one—or all three—of our pumpkin desserts.

Light and Luscious Pumpkin Pie

Everyone will give thanks for this streamlined pie—just as satisfying as the original.

PER SERVING: 195 cal., 8 g total fat (1 g sat. fat), 1 mg chol., 108 mg sodium, 28 g carb., 2 g fiber, 5 g pro. Exchanges: 0.5 starch, 1.5 carb., 1 fat. Carb choices: 2.
PER SERVING WITH SUBSTITUTE: same as above, except 171 cal., 22 g carb. Exchanges: 1 carb. Carb choices: 1.5.

- 1 recipe **Oil Pastry** (see recipe, right)
- ½ cup refrigerated or frozen egg product, thawed, or 2 eggs
- 1 15-ounce can pumpkin
- ⅓ cup sugar or sugar substitute* equivalent to ⅓ cup sugar
- 2 tablespoons honey
- 1 teaspoon ground cinnamon
- 1 teaspoon vanilla
- ¼ teaspoon ground ginger
- ¼ teaspoon ground nutmeg
- ¾ cup evaporated fat-free milk
  Frozen fat-free whipped dessert topping, thawed (optional)

Light and Luscious Pumpkin Pie

1. Preheat oven to 450°F. On a well-floured surface, flatten Oil Pastry. Roll dough from center to edge into a round about 12 inches in diameter.

2. Wrap pastry around rolling pin; unroll into a 9-inch pie plate. Ease pastry into plate, being careful not to stretch. Trim to ½ inch beyond edge of pie plate. Fold under extra pastry. Flute or crimp edge as desired. Do not prick shell. Line pastry with a double thickness of heavy foil. Bake for 8 minutes. Remove foil. Bake for 5 minutes more. Cool on a wire rack.

3. Set oven temperature to 375°F. In a bowl, beat egg; stir in pumpkin, sugar, honey, cinnamon, vanilla, ginger, and nutmeg. Beat just until combined. Slowly stir in milk. Pour into pastry shell. To prevent overbrowning, cover edge of pie with foil.

4. Bake for 40 to 45 minutes or until filling appears set (edges of filling may crack slightly). Cool on a wire rack for 1 hour. Cover and chill for at least 2 hours. If desired, serve with dessert topping. Makes 10 servings.

Oil Pastry: In a medium bowl, stir together 1⅓ cups all-purpose flour and ¼ teaspoon salt. Add ⅓ cup cooking oil and 3 tablespoons fat-free milk all at once to flour mixture. Stir lightly with a fork. Form into a ball.

***Sugar Substitutes:** Choose from Splenda granular or Sweet'N Low bulk or packets. Follow the package directions to use the product amount equivalent to ⅓ cup sugar.

Raisin-Pumpkin Tart

If you like, make this two-layer tart more elegant
with fat-free whipped dessert topping.

PER SERVING: 229 cal., 13 g total fat (4 g sat. fat), 49 mg chol., 151 mg
sodium, 23 g carb., 1 g fiber, 6 g pro. Exchanges: 0.5 starch, 1 carb.,
0.5 medium-fat meat, 2 fat. Carb choices: 1.5.

PER SERVING WITH SUBSTITUTE: same as above, except 214 cal.,
19 g carb. Exchanges: 0.5 carb. Carb choices: 1.

1 recipe **Oil Pastry** (see recipe, page 323)
1 **8-ounce package reduced-fat cream cheese
   (Neufchâtel), softened**

1 **egg yolk**
1 **tablespoon honey**
¼ **cup sliced almonds, toasted and finely chopped**
¼ **cup golden raisins, snipped**
1 **cup canned pumpkin**
1 **5-ounce can (⅔ cup) evaporated fat-free milk**
¼ **cup sugar or sugar substitute* equivalent to
   ¼ cup sugar**
1 **egg**
1 **egg white**
2 **teaspoons pumpkin pie spice**
2 **tablespoons sliced almonds, toasted (optional)**

Since most desserts contain carbohydrates, you can substitute a serving of dessert for other carbohydrate-rich foods in your meal plan. Ask your dietitian for advice on the best way to include sweets in your meal plan during special times of the year.

1. Preheat oven to 450°F. Prepare Oil Pastry. On a well-floured surface, slightly flatten dough. Roll pastry from center to edge into a 12-inch round.

2. To transfer, wrap pastry around rolling pin. Unroll pastry into a 10-inch tart pan with a removable bottom. Ease pastry into pan, being careful not to stretch pastry. Press edge of pastry against edge of pan. Trim edges. Do not prick shell. Line pastry with a double thickness of heavy foil. Bake for 8 minutes. Remove foil. Bake for 4 to 5 minutes more or until golden.

3. Meanwhile, for cream cheese layer, in a medium mixing bowl, combine cream cheese, egg yolk, and honey; beat with an electric mixer on low to medium speed until combined. Stir in chopped almonds and raisins; set mixture aside.

4. For pumpkin layer, in another medium bowl, stir together pumpkin, evaporated milk, sugar, whole egg, egg white, and pumpkin pie spice; set aside.

5. Reduce oven temperature to 375°F. Carefully spoon cream cheese filling into hot baked pastry; spread evenly. Pour pumpkin mixture over cream cheese layer; spread evenly.

6. Bake for 30 to 35 minutes or until set. Cool on a wire rack for 1 hour. Cover and chill for at least 2 hours.

7. To serve, remove side of pan; using a large spatula, carefully lift tart from pan bottom and slide onto a platter. If desired, garnish with sliced almonds. Makes 12 servings.

*Sugar Substitutes: Choose from Splenda granular, Equal Spoonful or packets, or Sweet'N Low bulk or packets. Follow the package directions to use the product amount equivalent to ¼ cup sugar.

No-Bake Pumpkin Swirl Cheesecake

A narrow, thin-bladed spatula or a table knife works best for swirling the batter.

PER SERVING: 179 cal., 7 g total fat (4 g sat. fat), 23 mg chol., 331 mg sodium, 19 g carb., 1 g fiber, 9 g pro. Exchanges: 1 carb., 1.5 fat. Carb choices: 1.

PER SERVING WITH SUGAR SUBSTITUTE: same as above, except 149 cal., 10 g carb.

- ¾ cup finely crushed graham crackers
- 2 tablespoons butter, melted
- 1 8-ounce package reduced-fat cream cheese (Neufchâtel)
- ½ cup sugar or sugar substitute* equivalent to ½ cup sugar
- ½ cup fat-free milk
- 2 teaspoons vanilla
- ½ teaspoon finely shredded orange peel
- 2 8-ounce packages fat-free cream cheese
- 1 15-ounce can pumpkin
- 1 teaspoon pumpkin pie spice
- 1 envelope unflavored gelatin
- ¼ cup orange juice

1. For crust, in a bowl, combine graham cracker crumbs and melted butter; stir until crumbs are moistened. Press onto bottom of an 8-inch springform pan. Cover; chill.

2. For white filling, in a food processor, combine the reduced-fat cream cheese, ¼ cup of the sugar, ¼ cup of the milk, the vanilla, and peel. Cover; process until smooth. Transfer to a bowl; set aside.

3. For pumpkin filling, in a food processor, combine the fat-free cream cheese, pumpkin, remaining ¼ cup sugar, remaining ¼ cup milk, and the pumpkin pie spice. Cover; process until smooth.

4. In a small saucepan, sprinkle gelatin over juice; let stand for 5 minutes. Cook and stir over low heat until gelatin is dissolved. Stir 1 tablespoon gelatin mixture into white filling; stir remaining gelatin into pumpkin filling.

5. Pour pumpkin filling into crust. Carefully pour white filling onto pumpkin filling. Use a knife to swirl pumpkin and white mixtures. Cover and chill overnight. To serve, loosen cheesecake from side of pan; remove side of pan. Cut into wedges. Makes 12 servings.

*Sugar Substitutes: Choose from Splenda Granular, Equal Spoonful or packets, or Sweet'N Low bulk or packets. Follow package directions to use the product amount equivalent to ½ cup sugar.

Berry Pie with Creamy Filling

Yogurt cheese, which is used in the pie filling, takes 24 hours to make. Keep that in mind when you are planning to make this gorgeous pie.

PER SERVING: 160 cal., 4 g total fat (2 g sat. fat), 10 mg chol., 87 mg sodium, 27 g carb., 3 g fiber, 5 g pro. Exchanges: 1 fruit, 1 carb., 0.5 fat. Carb choices: 2.

- **1   16-ounce carton plain fat-free or low-fat yogurt***
- **2   tablespoons powdered sugar**
- **½   teaspoon vanilla**
- **¾   cup low-calorie cranberry-raspberry drink**
- **1   tablespoon cornstarch**
- **1   recipe Zwieback Crust (see recipe, below)**
- **6   cups fresh raspberries, blackberries, blueberries, and/or halved strawberries**
- **Fresh mint and/or Lemon Cream (see recipe, below) (optional)**

1. For yogurt cheese, set a sieve over a large bowl; line with three layers of 100-percent-cotton cheesecloth. Spoon in yogurt. Cover with plastic wrap and chill for 24 hours. Discard the liquid from the yogurt cheese. In a medium bowl, combine yogurt cheese, powdered sugar, and vanilla. Cover and chill until ready to use.

2. For glaze, in a saucepan, stir together fruit drink and cornstarch. Cook and stir over medium heat until thickened and bubbly; cook and stir for 2 minutes more. Transfer to a bowl. Cover surface with plastic wrap; let stand at room temperature for 1 to 2 hours or until cool.

3. Spread yogurt cheese mixture into Zwieback Crust. In a large bowl, gently toss berries and cooled glaze. Spoon onto yogurt mixture. Cover; chill for 3 to 6 hours. If desired, garnish with mint and/or serve with Lemon Cream. Makes 10 servings.

*Test Kitchen Tip: For yogurt cheese, choose a yogurt that contains no gums, gelatin, or fillers because they may prevent the whey from separating from the curd.

Zwieback Crust: Preheat oven to 350°F. Coat a 9-inch pie plate with nonstick cooking spray. In a medium bowl, combine 1⅓ cups finely crushed zwieback (about 17 slices) and 2 tablespoons packed brown sugar. Add 1 slightly beaten egg white and 2 tablespoons melted butter; stir until mixed. Press evenly onto bottom and up side of pie plate. Bake for 10 to 12 minutes or until edge is brown. Cool on a wire rack.

Lemon Cream: In a bowl, combine 1½ cups thawed light whipped dessert topping and ¾ teaspoon finely shredded lemon peel.

Glazed Tropical Fruit Pie

You can use peaches or nectarines instead of the mango.

PER SERVING: 185 cal., 7 g total fat (4 g sat. fat), 16 mg chol., 104 mg sodium, 29 g carb., 2 g fiber, 2 g pro. Exchanges: 1 fruit, 1 carb., 1.5 fat. Carb choices: 2.

- **1   cup pineapple-orange juice**
- **1   tablespoon cornstarch**
- **2   cups 1-inch pieces seeded, peeled mango**
- **2   cups 1-inch pieces seeded, peeled papaya**
- **1½ cups half-slices peeled kiwifruit**
- **1   recipe Graham Cracker Pie Shell (see recipe, below) or 1 purchased 9-inch graham cracker crumb pie shell***
- **Frozen light whipped dessert topping, thawed (optional)**

1. In a small saucepan, combine juice and cornstarch; cook and stir until thickened and bubbly. Cook and stir for 2 minutes more. Transfer to a large bowl. Cover surface with plastic wrap; cool for 30 minutes.

2. Divide juice mixture among three small bowls. In each bowl, fold one fruit into juice mixture. Spoon fruit into pie shell, arranging as desired. Cover and chill for 3 to 4 hours. If desired, serve with dessert topping. Makes 10 servings.

Graham Cracker Pie Shell: Preheat oven to 375°F. In a small saucepan, melt ⅓ cup butter. Stir in ¼ cup sugar. Add 1¼ cups finely crushed graham crackers; mix well. Press evenly onto bottom and up side of a 9-inch pie plate. Bake for 4 to 5 minutes or until edge is light brown. Cool on a wire rack.

*Test Kitchen Tip: To more easily cut the pie using the purchased graham cracker pie shell, preheat oven to 375°F. Brush the pie shell with a slightly beaten egg white; bake for 5 minutes. Cool on a wire rack before filling.

(10 keys to success)

To keep your diabetes in check, follow these guidelines.

1. **Follow** a meal plan—it takes away the guesswork.
2. **Measure** and weigh foods— estimate when eating out or on special occasions.
3. **Limit** starches and balance meals with nonstarchy vegetables.
4. **Eat** vegetables and fruits daily—three to four servings of each.
5. **Enjoy** almost anything, but watch your portion sizes (especially with desserts!).
6. **Avoid** munching throughout the day.
7. **Bake,** broil, or grill foods— avoid fried foods.
8. **Cut down** on desserts overall—but have a small serving on special occasions.
9. **Split** a meal when eating out and order an extra side salad instead of fries.
10. **Keep** food, exercise, and blood glucose records.

Berry Pie with
Creamy Filling

Incredible Apple Tart

(ending on a sweet note)

When preparing desserts, experiment using the minimum amount of sweetener possible to get the desired results and the flavor you like. Make the sweetness of sugar work harder by magnifying it with vanilla or spices, such as cinnamon and cloves. And you don't always have to use bar chocolate either. When a recipe calls for unsweetened chocolate and when it is feasible, substitute unsweetened cocoa powder, a lower-fat alternative to bar chocolate. For each ounce of bar chocolate, stir together 3 tablespoons of cocoa powder and 1 tablespoon water.

Incredible Apple Tart

Jonathan, Rome Beauty, or Winesap apples
are great choices for this tart.

PER SERVING: 153 cal., 9 g total fat (5 g sat. fat), 21 mg chol., 149 mg
sodium, 15 g carb., 2 g fiber, 4 g pro. Exchanges: 1 carb., 1.5 fat. Carb
choices: 1.

- 1 recipe Pecan Tart Crust (see recipe, below)
- Nonstick cooking spray
- ½ of an 8-ounce package reduced-fat cream cheese (Neufchâtel)
- ⅓ cup light dairy sour cream
- 1 egg white
- 4 tablespoons low-sugar orange marmalade
- ¼ teaspoon ground cardamom
- 2 medium red cooking apples, cored and very thinly sliced*

1. Preheat oven to 375°F. Pat Pecan Tart Crust dough evenly onto the bottom and up the sides of a lightly greased 9-inch tart pan with a removable bottom. Line pastry with a double thickness of foil that has been coated with cooking spray. Bake pastry for 4 minutes. Remove foil. Bake for 3 minutes more. Cool completely on a wire rack.

2. Meanwhile, in a medium bowl, combine cream cheese, sour cream, egg white, 2 tablespoons of the orange marmalade, and cardamom; beat with electric mixer until smooth. Spread cream cheese mixture onto cooled crust.

3. Arrange apple slices in two concentric rings on top of the cream cheese mixture in tart pan, overlapping slices slightly. Cover top of tart with foil.

4. Bake for 35 minutes. Uncover and bake for 10 to 15 minutes more or until crust is golden and apples are just tender.

5. Place remaining 2 tablespoons orange marmalade in a small microwave-safe bowl. Cover; microwave on 50 percent power (medium) for 10 seconds. Stir; microwave about 10 seconds more or until melted. Brush onto apples. Serve tart slightly warm or cool. Makes 12 servings.

Pecan Tart Crust: In a small bowl, combine ⅔ cup quick-cooking rolled oats, ½ cup white whole wheat flour or whole wheat flour, and ¼ cup toasted ground pecans. In a large bowl, combine half of an 8-ounce package reduced-fat cream cheese (Neufchâtel) and 2 tablespoons softened butter; beat with an electric mixer on medium to high speed for 30 seconds. Add 2 tablespoons packed brown sugar, 1 teaspoon finely shredded orange peel, ¼ teaspoon baking soda, and ⅛ teaspoon salt; beat until mixed. Beat in as much of the oat mixture as you can with the mixer. Using a wooden spoon, stir in any remaining oat mixture. If necessary, cover and chill for 30 to 60 minutes or until the dough is easy to handle.

*Test Kitchen Tip: If you have a mandoline, use it to slice the apples about ⅛ inch thick.

Easy Blueberry Tarts

The addition of cayenne pepper is optional but will give
these tarts a hint of spice and distinct Mexican flair.

PER SERVING: 131 cal., 1 g total fat (0 g sat. fat), 0 mg chol., 93 mg sodium,
29 g carb., 3 g fiber, 2 g pro. Exchanges: 1 carb., 1 fruit. Carb
choices: 2.

- Nonstick cooking spray
- 3 tablespoons sugar
- 1 teaspoon cornstarch
- ⅛ teaspoon cayenne pepper (optional)
- ¼ cup water
- 1 cup fresh blueberries
- 1 cup fresh raspberries
- ¼ teaspoon ground cinnamon
- 4 sheets frozen phyllo dough (9×14-inch rectangles), thawed

1. Preheat oven to 375°F. Lightly coat four 4×2×½-inch rectangular tart pans that have removable bottoms with cooking spray; set aside. In a small saucepan, stir together 2 tablespoons of the sugar, cornstarch, and, if desired, cayenne pepper. Stir in the water and half of the blueberries. Cook and stir over medium heat until mixture is thickened and bubbly. Fold in remaining blueberries and the raspberries; set aside.

2. In a small bowl, stir together remaining 1 tablespoon sugar and cinnamon. Place one sheet of phyllo on cutting board. Lightly coat with cooking spray; sprinkle with about 1 teaspoon sugar mixture. Repeat layering with remaining phyllo and sugar mixture, ending with cooking spray. With a sharp knife, cut phyllo stack in half lengthwise and crosswise, forming four rectangles. Ease rectangles into prepared tart pans.

3. Bake for 8 minutes or until phyllo is golden brown. Cool slightly; remove shells from pans. Spoon filling into shells just before serving. Serve warm or cool. Makes 4 servings.

Orange-Cranberry Cake

Cranberries add a merry accent and tangy flavor in addition to powerful antioxidants to this cake.

PER SERVING: 187 cal., 4 g total fat (2 g sat. fat), 44 mg chol., 122 mg sodium, 34 g carb., 1 g fiber, 4 g pro. Exchanges: 1 starch, 1.5 carb., 0.5 fat. Carb choices: 2.

PER SERVING WITH SUBSTITUTE: same as above, except 165 cal., 26 g carb. Exchanges: 1 starch, 1 carb. Carb choices: 2.

> **Nonstick cooking spray**
> 2 cups all-purpose flour
> 1¼ teaspoons baking powder
> ½ teaspoon baking soda
> 3 tablespoons butter, softened
> 1 cup granulated sugar or sugar substitute baking blend* equivalent to 1 cup sugar
> 2 eggs
> ⅔ cup plain fat-free yogurt
> 2 cups fresh cranberries, chopped
> 1 teaspoon finely shredded orange peel
> **Sifted powdered sugar (optional)**

1. Preheat oven to 350°F. Coat a 10-inch fluted tube pan with nonstick cooking spray; set aside. In a medium bowl, stir together flour, baking powder, and baking soda; set aside.

2. In a large mixing bowl, beat butter with an electric mixer on medium speed for 30 seconds. Add granulated sugar; beat until fluffy. Add eggs, 1 at a time, beating well after each addition. Alternately add flour mixture and yogurt to egg mixture, beating after each addition just until combined. Fold in cranberries and peel.

3. Spoon batter into prepared pan; spread evenly. Bake about 40 minutes or until a toothpick inserted near the center comes out clean.

4. Cool in pan on a wire rack for 10 minutes. Remove from pan. Cool completely on a wire rack. If desired, sprinkle with powdered sugar. Makes 12 servings.

*Sugar Substitutes: If using a substitute, add ¼ cup water to yogurt before adding to egg mixture. Choose from Splenda Sugar Blend for Baking or Equal Sugar Lite. Follow the package directions to use the product amount equivalent to 1 cup sugar.

Apple Cake with Hot Coconut-Brown Sugar Topping

Leave on the apple peels for added fiber, nutrients, and, of course, ease. Young guests will love this cake.

PER SERVING: 186 cal., 9 g total fat (4 g sat. fat), 19 mg chol., 112 mg sodium, 26 g carb., 2 g fiber, 2 g pro. Exchanges: 1.5 carb., 2 fat. Carb choices: 2.

PER SERVING SUBSTITUTE: same as above, except 164 cal., 19 g carb. Exchanges: 1 carb. Carb choices: 1.

> **Nonstick cooking spray**
> ¾ cup granulated sugar or sugar substitute blend* equivalent to ¾ cup granulated sugar
> ½ cup vanilla fat-free yogurt
> ¼ cup cooking oil
> 1 egg or ¼ cup refrigerated or frozen egg product, thawed
> 1½ teaspoons ground cinnamon
> 1 teaspoon vanilla
> ½ teaspoon baking powder
> ¼ teaspoon salt
> ¼ teaspoon baking soda
> ¼ teaspoon ground ginger
> ¼ teaspoon ground nutmeg
> 1¼ cups all-purpose flour
> 1 pound green cooking apples (such as **Granny Smith** or **Crispin**), cored and coarsely chopped (3 cups)
> 1 cup flaked coconut
> 3 tablespoons butter
> 3 tablespoons packed brown sugar or brown sugar substitute* equivalent to 3 tablespoons brown sugar
> 2 tablespoons fat-free milk

Orange-Cranberry Cake

1. Preheat oven to 325°F. Line two 8×4×2-inch loaf pans with foil; lightly coat foil with nonstick cooking spray. Set aside.

2. In a large bowl, stir together granulated sugar, yogurt, oil, egg, 1 teaspoon of the cinnamon, the vanilla, baking powder, salt, baking soda, ginger, and nutmeg. Stir in flour just until combined. Fold in apples (the batter will be thick and chunky).

3. Spoon batter into prepared pans; spread evenly. Bake about 45 minutes or until a toothpick inserted near centers comes out clean and tops are brown.

4. Meanwhile, for topping, in a small saucepan, combine coconut, butter, brown sugar, milk, and remaining ½ teaspoon cinnamon. Cook and stir over low heat until the butter is melted.

5. Preheat the broiler. Gently spread topping evenly onto cakes. Broil 4 inches from heat for 2 to 3 minutes or until topping is bubbly and light brown.

6. Cool cakes in pans on wire racks for 45 minutes. Use foil to lift cakes from pans; remove foil. Serve warm or cool. Makes 2 cakes (16 servings total).

*Sugar Substitutes: For cake, choose from Splenda Sugar Blend for Baking or Equal Sugar Lite. Follow the package directions to use the product amount that's equivalent to ¾ cup granulated sugar. For topping, choose from Sweet'N Low Brown or Sugar Twin Granulated Brown. Follow the package directions to use product amount equivalent to 3 tablespoons brown sugar.

Make-Ahead Directions: Prepare as directed; cool. Wrap and store in the refrigerator for up to 3 days.

Walnut Berry-Cherry Crisp

The golden crisp topper boasts walnuts, flaxseeds, and oats.

PER SERVING: 171 cal., 9 g total fat (1 g sat. fat), 0 mg chol., 3 mg sodium, 23 g carb., 3 g fiber, 3 g pro. Exchanges: 0.5 fruit, 0.5 starch, 0.5 carb., 1.5 fat. Carb choices: 1.5.

PER SERVING WITH SUBSTITUTE: 158 cal., 20 g carb. Carb choices: 1.

- 2   **cups fresh or frozen blueberries**
- 2   **cups frozen unsweetened pitted tart red cherries**
- 4   **tablespoons all-purpose flour**
- 1   **tablespoon honey**
- 2   **tablespoons flaxseeds, toasted***
- ½   **cup rolled oats**
- ⅓   **cup chopped walnuts**
- 2   **tablespoons packed brown sugar or brown sugar substitute** equivalent to 2 tablespoons brown sugar
- 2   **tablespoons canola oil**

1.   Thaw fruit, if frozen (do not drain). Preheat oven to 375°F. In a medium bowl, combine blueberries, cherries, 2 tablespoons of the flour, and the honey. Divide blueberry mixture among eight 6-ounce ramekins or custard cups, or spoon blueberry mixture into a 1½-quart casserole.

2.   Place toasted flaxseeds in a spice grinder and pulse until ground to a fine powder. In a medium bowl, stir together ground flaxseeds, oats, walnuts, the remaining 2 tablespoons flour, brown sugar, and oil. Sprinkle onto fruit mixture.

3.   Bake for 15 to 20 minutes for ramekins or custard cups or 25 to 30 minutes for casserole or until topping is golden and fruit mixture is bubbly around edges. Serve warm. Makes 8 (about ½-cup) servings.

*Test Kitchen Tip: To toast flaxseeds, place in a small dry skillet over medium heat. Cook and stir until the seeds are fragrant and begin to pop.

**Sugar Substitutes: Choose from Sweet'N Low Brown or Sugar Twin Granulated Brown. Follow package directions to use product amount equivalent to 2 tablespoons brown sugar.

Raspberry-Peach Crisp

A crunchy oat topping adds a little extra fiber and toasted flavor.

PER SERVING: 159 cal., 4 g total fat (2 g sat. fat), 8 mg chol., 23 mg sodium, 31 g carb., 4 g fiber, 3 g pro. Exchanges: 1 fruit, 0.5 carb., 0.5 starch, 0.5 fat. Carb choices: 2.

PER SERVING WITH SUBSTITUTES: same as above, except 137 cal., 25 g carb. Carb choices: 1.5.

- 4   **cups sliced fresh peaches or frozen unsweetened peach slices, thawed**
- 2   **tablespoons granulated sugar or sugar substitute* equivalent to 2 tablespoons granulated sugar**
- 1   **tablespoon quick-cooking tapioca**
- 2   **tablespoons sugar-free red raspberry preserves**
- ⅔   **cup quick-cooking rolled oats**
- 2   **tablespoons whole wheat flour**
- 2   **tablespoons packed brown sugar or brown sugar substitute* equivalent to 2 tablespoons brown sugar**
- ½   **teaspoon ground cinnamon**
- 2   **tablespoons butter**
     Vanilla low-fat frozen yogurt (optional)

1.   Preheat oven to 375°F. For fruit filling, thaw fruit, if frozen; do not drain. In a large bowl, combine peach slices, granulated sugar, tapioca, and raspberry preserves. Place fruit mixture in a 2-quart square baking dish.

Walnut Berry-Cherry Crisp

Raspberry-Peach Crisp

2. For topping, in a medium bowl, stir together oats, whole wheat flour, brown sugar, and cinnamon. Using a pastry blender, cut in the butter until crumbly. Sprinkle topping onto fruit in dish.

3. Bake for 45 to 50 minutes or until the fruit filling is bubbly. Cool on a wire rack; serve warm. If desired, serve with frozen yogurt. Makes 8 (½-cup) servings.

*Sugar Substitutes: Choose from Splenda granular or Sweet'N Low bulk or packets for the granulated sugar. Choose from Sweet'N Low Brown, Sugar Twin Granulated Brown, or Splenda Brown Sugar Blend for the brown sugar. Follow package directions to use equivalent product amounts.

Tiramisu

Tiramisu

Fool your guests with this lighter knockoff of the creamy classic Italian coffee-flavored dessert.

PER SERVING: 186 cal., 8 g total fat (5 g sat. fat), 67 mg chol., 182 mg sodium, 22 g carb., 0 g fiber, 5 g pro. Exchanges: 1.5 carb., 1.5 fat. Carb choices: 1.5.

- 2 8-ounce cartons fat-free dairy sour cream or light dairy sour cream
- 2 8-ounce packages reduced-fat cream cheese (Neufchâtel), softened
- ⅔ cup sugar
- ¼ cup fat-free milk
- ½ teaspoon vanilla
- ½ cup strong coffee
- 2 tablespoons coffee liqueur or strong coffee
- 2 3-ounce packages ladyfingers, split
- 2 tablespoons sifted unsweetened cocoa powder
- Unsweetened cocoa powder (optional)
- White and/or dark chocolate curls (optional)

1. In a large mixing bowl, combine sour cream, cream cheese, sugar, milk, and vanilla. Beat with an electric mixer on high speed until smooth.

2. In a small bowl, combine the ½ cup coffee and the coffee liqueur.

3. In a 2-quart rectangular dish, layer 1 package of the ladyfingers, cut sides up. Brush with half of the coffee mixture. Spread with half of the cream cheese mixture. Repeat with remaining ladyfingers, coffee mixture, and cream cheese mixture. Sprinkle with the 2 tablespoons cocoa powder. Cover and chill for 4 to 24 hours.

4. To serve, cut dessert into squares; arrange on a platter. If desired, sprinkle with additional unsweetened cocoa powder and garnish with white and/or dark chocolate curls. Makes 15 servings.

Cherry-Chocolate Bread Pudding

Whole grain bread adds heartiness to our upscale version of a humble dessert.

PER SERVING: 147 cal., 4 g total fat (2 g sat. fat), 1 mg chol., 152 mg sodium, 25 g carb., 3 g fiber, 7 g pro. Exchanges: 1.5 carb., 0.5 fat. Carb choices: 1.5.

- Nonstick cooking spray
- 2 cups firm-textured whole grain bread cubes (about 3 ounces)
- 3 tablespoons snipped dried tart red cherries
- 1 tablespoon toasted wheat germ
- ⅔ cup fat-free milk
- ¼ cup semisweet chocolate pieces
- ⅓ cup refrigerated or frozen egg product, thawed
- 1 teaspoon finely shredded orange peel
- ½ teaspoon vanilla
- Frozen light whipped dessert topping, thawed (optional)
- Unsweetened cocoa powder (optional)

1. Preheat oven to 350°F. Coat four 6-ounce individual soufflé dishes or custard cups with nonstick cooking spray. Divide bread cubes, cherries, and wheat germ among prepared dishes.

2. In a small saucepan, combine milk and chocolate. Cook and stir over low heat until the chocolate is melted; remove from heat. If necessary, beat smooth with a wire whisk.

3. In a small bowl, gradually stir chocolate mixture into egg. Stir in orange peel and vanilla. Pour mixture over bread cubes in dishes. Use the back of a spoon to press lightly to moisten bread.

4. Bake for 15 to 20 minutes or until tops appear firm and a knife inserted near centers comes out clean.

5. Serve warm. If desired, top with dessert topping and cocoa powder. Makes 4 servings.

Make-Ahead Directions: Prepare as directed through Step 3. Cover and chill for up to 2 hours. Preheat oven to 350°F. Continue as directed in Steps 4 and 5.

Cherry-Chocolate Bread Pudding

Cinnamon Raisin
Apple Indian Pudding

Serve this colonial favorite for dessert or breakfast.

PER SERVING: 128 cal., 1 g total fat, (0 g sat. fat), 37 mg chol., 148 mg sodium, 26 g carb., 2 g fiber, 5 g pro. Exchanges: 0.5 carb., 1 fruit, 0.5 fat-free milk. Carb choices: 2.

PER SERVING WITH SUBSTITUTE: same as above, except 110 cal., 21 g carb. Exchanges: 0 carb. Carb choices: 1.5.

    Nonstick cooking spray
  2 cups fat-free milk
  ⅓ **cup yellow cornmeal**
  2 tablespoons packed brown sugar or brown sugar substitute* equivalent to 2 tablespoons brown sugar
  ½ **teaspoon ground cinnamon**
  ¼ **teaspoon salt**
  1 egg
  2 medium cooking apples (such as Jonathan or Rome Beauty), cored and chopped
  ¼ **cup raisins**

1. Preheat oven to 350°F. Coat six 6-ounce custard cups with cooking spray; place in a shallow baking pan. Set aside.

2. In a medium saucepan, heat 1½ cups of the milk just until boiling. In a small bowl, combine cornmeal and remaining ½ cup milk; whisk into hot milk. Cook and stir until boiling. Reduce heat. Cook and stir for 5 to 7 minutes or until thick. Remove from heat. Stir in brown sugar, cinnamon, and salt.

3. In a large bowl, beat egg; slowly stir in hot mixture. Stir in apples and raisins. Divide apple mixture among prepared cups. Bake about 30 minutes or until a knife inserted in centers comes out clean. Cool slightly. Serve warm. Makes 6 servings.

*Sugar Substitutes: Choose from Sweet'N Low Brown or Sugar Twin Granulated Brown. Follow the package directions to use the product amount equivalent to 2 tablespoons sugar.

Creamy Lime Mousse

This dessert offers a light touch to a big holiday meal.

PER SERVING: 112 cal., 9 g total fat (2 g sat. fat), 0 mg chol., 106 mg sodium, 4 g carb., 0 g fiber, 3 g pro. Exchanges: 1.5 fat, 0.5 medium-fat meat. Carb choices: 0.

  1 4-serving-size package sugar-free lime-flavored gelatin
  1 cup boiling water
  ½ **teaspoon finely shredded lime peel**
  2 tablespoons lime juice
  ¾ **cup Tofu Sour Cream (see below) or one 8-ounce carton light dairy sour cream**
  1⅓ **cups frozen light whipped dessert topping, thawed**
    Lime peel curls or lime slices (optional)

1. In a large bowl, combine gelatin and water; stir about 2 minutes or until gelatin is dissolved. Stir in lime peel and juice. Cool for 10 to 15 minutes or until cool but not set. Whisk in Tofu Sour Cream. Gently whisk in 1 cup dessert topping. Pour into six 6- to 8-ounce glasses.

2. Cover and chill for 2 to 24 hours or until set. Garnish each with a tablespoon of topping and, if desired, lime peel or slices. Makes 6 (about ½-cup) servings.

Tofu Sour Cream: In a blender, combine half of a 12.3-ounce package extra-firm silken-style tofu (fresh bean curd), patted dry with paper towels; 3 tablespoons cooking oil; 4 teaspoons lemon juice; ¼ teaspoon honey; and ⅛ teaspoon salt. Cover and blend on high speed until smooth and creamy, stopping to push mixture into blades as needed. Makes about ¾ cup.

(sugar swap)

Based on our Test Kitchen results, we make the following recommendations for using sugar substitutes:

1. **In baking, replace no more than half of the sugar** with a sugar substitute.
2. **Check baked foods 5 to 10 minutes earlier** because they may cook faster.
3. **Use a sugar substitute blend** for cakes and cookies.
4. **When food will be cooked for more than 30 minutes,** avoid using aspartame (Equal), which breaks down with prolonged heat.
5. **If using aspartame** (Equal), add it to hot mixtures after cooking.
6. **For yeast breads,** leave some sugar as food for the yeast.
7. **Baked products made with sweeteners may dry out faster;** wrap them tightly with plastic wrap.
8. **Refrigerate jams and jellies when sugar is not acting as a preservative** and expect a softer set.
9. **Weigh whether the savings in calories and carbohydrates** is worth the expense in dollars.
10. **Decide if flavor is more important** and whether you can splurge on the real thing.

Creamy Lime Mousse

Brown Rice Pudding

Add this treat to your dessert buffet.

PER SERVING: 129 cal., 1 g total fat (0 g sat. fat), 2 mg chol., 126 mg sodium, 26 g carb., 1 g fiber, 6 g pro. Exchanges: 0.5 fat-free milk, 0.5 carb., 1 starch. Carb choices: 2.

PER SERVING WITH SUBSTITUTE: same as above, except 106 cal., 20 g carb. Exchanges: 0 carb. Carb choices: 1.

Nonstick cooking spray
4 cups fat-free milk
¾ cup regular brown rice
¼ cup sugar or sugar substitute* equivalent to ¼ cup sugar
¼ teaspoon salt
Ground cinnamon
½ cup chopped almonds, toasted (optional)

1. Preheat oven to 350°F. Lightly coat a 2-quart baking dish with nonstick cooking spray. In the prepared dish, combine milk, *uncooked* rice, sugar, and salt.

2. Cover and bake about 2 hours or until rice is very tender, stirring occasionally (the liquid will not be completely absorbed). Let stand, covered, for 30 minutes (mixture will thicken while standing). Serve warm. Sprinkle each serving with cinnamon and, if desired, almonds. Makes 8 (about ⅓-cup) servings.

Brown Rice Pudding

*Sugar Substitutes: Choose from Splenda granular or Sweet'N Low bulk or packets. Follow package directions to use product amount equivalent to ¼ cup sugar.

Make-Ahead Directions: Prepare pudding as directed, except cover and chill for up to 24 hours before serving. If necessary, to thin, stir in 2 to 4 tablespoons fat-free milk.

Cranberry Poached Pears

When company's coming, serve these delicate double-cranberry pears as an elegant finale to dinner.

PER SERVING: 103 cal., 1 g total fat (0 g sat. fat), 2 mg chol., 36 mg sodium, 24 g carb., 3 g fiber, 2 g pro. Exchanges: 1.5 fruit. Carb choices: 1.5.

2½ cups reduced-calorie cranberry juice
3 small pears, halved, peeled, and cored
1 vanilla bean,* halved lengthwise
2 3-inch-long cinnamon sticks
¼ teaspoon freshly ground black pepper
½ cup fresh cranberries
1 6-ounce carton plain low-fat yogurt
2 teaspoons honey

1. In a medium saucepan, bring cranberry juice to a simmer. Add pears, split vanilla bean, stick cinnamon, and pepper. Return to a simmer; cover and cook for 10 minutes. Remove from heat. Add cranberries. Let stand, covered, for 1 hour, turning pears once.

2. Remove vanilla bean and scrape seeds into a small bowl; stir in yogurt and honey.

3. Divide cooking liquid among six individual dessert dishes. Add a pear half to each. Top with yogurt mixture. Makes 6 servings.

*Test Kitchen Tip: Instead of using a vanilla bean, you can add 1 teaspoon vanilla to the cooking liquid before letting the mixture stand and stir ½ teaspoon vanilla into the yogurt mixture.

Make-Ahead Directions: Prepare as directed through Step 2. Place pears and the cooking liquid in an airtight container. Place yogurt mixture in another airtight container. Cover and chill for up to 24 hours. Serve as directed in Step 3.

Lemon Soufflé Dessert

If you use sugar substitute, expect a browner top.

PER SERVING: 190 cal., 5 g total fat (3 g sat. fat), 111 mg chol., 92 mg sodium, 29 g carb., 0 g fiber, 7 g pro. Exchanges: 2 carb., 0.5 medium-fat meat, 0.5 fat. Carb choices: 2.

PER SERVING WITH SUBSTITUTE: same as above, except 156 cal., 20 g carb. Exchanges: 1.5 carb. Carb choices: 1.

Nonstick cooking spray
- 6 **tablespoons granulated sugar or sugar-substitute blend* equivalent to 6 tablespoons sugar**
- ¼ **cup all-purpose flour**
- 2 **teaspoons finely shredded lemon peel**
- ¼ **cup lemon juice**
- 1 **tablespoon butter, melted**
- 2 **egg yolks**
- 1 **cup fat-free milk**
- 3 **egg whites**
  Sifted powdered sugar

1. Preheat oven to 350°F. Spray a 1-quart soufflé dish with nonstick cooking spray. In a large bowl, combine 2 tablespoons sugar and flour; whisk in peel, juice, and butter until smooth. In a small bowl, whisk together yolks and milk; whisk into lemon mixture. Set aside.

2. In a mixing bowl, beat egg whites with an electric mixer on medium speed until soft peaks form (tips curl). Slowly add 4 tablespoons of the granulated sugar, beating on high speed until stiff peaks form (tips stand straight). Fold a small amount of whites into lemon mixture. Fold in the remaining egg whites (batter will be thin).

3. Pour batter into soufflé dish; place in a pan. Place on oven rack; pour boiling water into pan around dish to a depth of 1 inch. Bake, uncovered, about 40 minutes or until the top springs back when lightly touched. Cool for 5 minutes on a rack. Top with powdered sugar. Serve warm. Makes 4 servings.

*Sugar Substitutes: Choose from Splenda Sugar Blend for Baking. Follow directions to use product amount equivalent to 6 tablespoons sugar.

Mocha Cream Puffs

(the sweet truth)

A healthful meal plan for people with diabetes can include some sugar. That's a good thing because sugar plays an important role in baking. Besides adding sweetness, sugar adds shape and structure and contributes to browning and tenderness in baked foods such as cakes. Another good thing: Some of our recipes allow for sugar substitutes and blends that retain sweetness and save on calories. For more on sugar and substitutes, see "Low-Calorie Sweeteners," page 385, and "How Sweet It Is," page 386.

Mocha Cream Puffs

These light-as-air puffs can be made, covered, and stored at room temperature for up to 24 hours before filling. The filling can be prepared and chilled up to 2 hours ahead.

PER PUFF: 63 cal., 3 g total fat (2 g sat. fat), 37 mg chol., 42 mg sodium, 6 g carb., 0 g fiber, 2 g pro. Exchanges: 0.5 carb., 0.5 fat. Carb choices: 0.5.

Nonstick cooking spray
¾ cup water
3 tablespoons butter
1 teaspoon instant coffee crystals
⅛ teaspoon salt
¾ cup all-purpose flour
3 eggs
1 recipe Mocha Filling (see recipe, below)

1. Preheat oven to 400°F. Coat a very large baking sheet with cooking spray; set aside.

2. In a saucepan, combine water, butter, coffee crystals, and salt. Bring to boiling. Add flour all at once, stirring vigorously. Cook and stir until a ball forms that doesn't separate. Cool for 5 minutes.

3. Add eggs, 1 at a time, beating with a wooden spoon after each addition until smooth. Drop into 20 small mounds onto prepared baking sheet. Bake about 25 minutes or until brown. Cool on a wire rack. Split puffs; remove soft dough from insides.

4. Using a pastry bag fitted with a star tip or a spoon, pipe or spoon Mocha Filling into cream puff bottoms. Add cream puff tops. Makes 20 puffs.

Mocha Filling: In a medium bowl, combine ½ cup low-fat vanilla yogurt, 2 tablespoons unsweetened cocoa powder, and 1 teaspoon instant coffee crystals. Fold in half of an 8-ounce container light whipped dessert topping, thawed. Cover and chill filling up to 2 hours.

Apple-Mango Crisp

Fresh mango is often available, but if you can't find it, look for the refrigerated variety in a jar in the produce section.

PER SERVING: 164 cal., 6 g total fat (2 g sat. fat), 8 mg chol., 2 mg sodium, 28 g carb., 3 g fiber, 3 g pro. Exchanges: 0.5 starch, 0.5 carb., 1 fruit, 1 fat. Carb choices: 2.

PER SERVING WITH SUBSTITUTE: same as above, except 138 cal., 21 g carb. Exchanges: 0 carb. Carb choices: 1.5.

Nonstick cooking spray
¾ cup all-purpose flour
¾ cup rolled oats
½ cup toasted wheat germ
½ cup packed brown sugar or brown sugar
   substitute* equivalent to ½ cup brown sugar
1½ teaspoons ground cinnamon
¼ cup butter, melted
4 green cooking apples (such as Granny Smith)
2 red cooking apples (such as Gala, Rome Beauty, or Fuji), cored and chopped
3 tablespoons lime juice
2 medium mangoes, pitted, peeled, and chopped
⅓ cup chopped pecans
   Frozen light whipped dessert topping, thawed (optional)

1. Preheat oven to 375°F. Coat two 1½- or 2-quart baking dishes or a 3-quart rectangular baking dish with nonstick cooking spray.

2. For topping, in a medium bowl, stir together ½ cup of the flour, the oats, wheat germ, brown sugar, and cinnamon. Stir in butter; set aside.

3. Place apples in a very large bowl. Stir in lime juice. Stir in remaining ¼ cup flour. Fold in mangoes.

4. Place apple-mango mixture in prepared baking dish(es). Top with oat topping. Bake, uncovered, for 30 minutes. Sprinkle with pecans; bake for 10 to 15 minutes more or until apples are tender.

5. Cool slightly. Serve warm. If desired, top with dessert topping. Makes 16 (¾-cup) servings.

***Sugar Substitutes:** Choose from Sweet'N Low Brown or Sugar Twin Granulated Brown. Follow the package directions to use amount equivalent to ½ cup brown sugar.

Apple-Mango Crisp

Double Chocolate Brownies

Applesauce-Oatmeal Cake

Serve this hearty cake as a dessert or a snack.

PER SERVING: 157 cal., 4 g total fat (2 g sat. fat), 9 mg chol., 121 mg sodium, 28 g carb., 2 g fiber, 3 g pro. Exchanges: 2 carb., 0.5 fat. Carb choices: 2.

Nonstick cooking spray
1 cup all-purpose flour
1 cup whole wheat pastry flour
⅔ cup quick-cooking rolled oats
2 teaspoons baking powder
1½ teaspoons ground cinnamon
½ teaspoon baking soda
¼ teaspoon salt
¼ teaspoon ground nutmeg
⅔ cup packed brown sugar
⅓ cup butter, softened
¼ cup refrigerated or frozen egg product, thawed, or 1 egg
2 teaspoons vanilla
1¾ cups unsweetened applesauce
¾ cup mixed dried fruit bits or raisins
½ cup quick-cooking rolled oats
3 tablespoons toasted wheat germ
2 tablespoons packed brown sugar
Fresh raspberries (optional)

1. Preheat oven to 350°F. Lightly coat a 13×9×2-inch baking pan with nonstick cooking spray; set aside.

2. In a medium bowl, use a fork to stir together all-purpose flour, whole wheat pastry flour, the ⅔ cup oats, baking powder, cinnamon, baking soda, salt, and nutmeg. Set the flour mixture aside.

3. In a large bowl, combine the ⅔ cup brown sugar and the butter. Beat with an electric mixer on medium speed until mixed. Beat in egg and vanilla. Alternately add flour mixture and applesauce to beaten mixture, beating after each addition just until combined. Stir in fruit bits. Spread batter into the prepared pan.

4. For topping, in a small bowl, combine the ½ cup oats, the wheat germ, and the 2 tablespoons brown sugar. Sprinkle mixture onto batter; press lightly into batter.

5. Bake for 25 to 30 minutes or until a toothpick inserted near center comes out clean. Cool in pan on a wire rack. Cut into squares to serve. If desired, top each square with raspberries. Makes 20 servings.

Double Chocolate Brownies

Semisweet chocolate and cocoa powder give twice the flavor with half the fat.

PER BROWNIE: 113 cal., 4 g total fat (2 g sat. fat), 8 mg chol., 37 mg sodium, 17 g carb., 0 g fiber, 1 g pro. Exchanges: 1 carb., 1 fat. Carb choices: 1.

Nonstick cooking spray
¼ cup butter or margarine
⅔ cup granulated sugar
½ cup cold water
1 teaspoon vanilla
1 cup all-purpose flour
¼ cup unsweetened cocoa powder
1 teaspoon baking powder
¼ cup miniature semisweet chocolate pieces
Sifted powdered sugar (optional)

1. Preheat oven to 350°F. Lightly coat the bottom of a 9×9×2-inch baking pan with cooking spray, being careful not to coat sides of pan.

2. In a medium saucepan, melt butter; remove from heat. Stir in granulated sugar, the water, and vanilla. Add flour, cocoa powder, and baking powder; stir until combined. Stir in chocolate pieces.

3. Pour batter into prepared pan. Bake for 15 to 18 minutes or until a toothpick inserted near the center comes out clean. Cool in pan on a wire rack.

4. Before serving, if desired, sprinkle with powdered sugar. Cut into 16 bars. Makes 16 brownies.

Applesauce-Oatmeal Cake

Nutty Carrot Cake Bars

A small amount of oil (which has no saturated fat, unlike butter) is what makes these bars moist.

PER BAR: 121 cal., 7 g total fat (2 g sat. fat), 5 mg chol., 64 mg sodium, 12 g carb., 1 g fiber, 3 g pro. Exchanges: 1 carb., 1 fat. Carb choices: 1.
PER BAR WITH SUBSTITUTE: same as above, except 102 cal., 7 g carb. Exchanges: 0.5 carb. Carb choices: 0.5.

Nutty Carrot Cake Bars

Nonstick cooking spray
- ¾ cup all-purpose flour
- ½ cup sugar or sugar substitute* equivalent to ½ cup sugar
- ¼ cup whole wheat flour
- 1½ teaspoons pumpkin pie spice
- 1 teaspoon baking powder
- ⅛ teaspoon salt
- 1 cup finely shredded carrots
- ¾ cup chopped walnuts or pecans, toasted
- ⅓ cup refrigerated or frozen egg product, thawed, or 3 egg whites, lightly beaten
- ¼ cup cooking oil
- ¼ cup fat-free milk
- 1 recipe Fluffy Cream Cheese Frosting (see recipe, below)

1. Preheat oven to 350°F. Line a 9×9×2-inch baking pan with foil, extending over edges. Lightly coat foil with cooking spray. Set aside.

2. In a medium bowl, combine all-purpose flour, sugar, whole wheat flour, pumpkin pie spice, baking powder, and salt. Add carrots, ½ cup of the nuts, eggs, oil, and milk. Stir just until combined. Spread evenly in pan.

3. Bake for 15 to 18 minutes or until a toothpick inserted near center comes out clean. Cool bars in pan on a wire rack.

4. Using the edges of the foil, lift uncut bars out of pan. Spread top evenly with Fluffy Cream Cheese Frosting. Sprinkle with remaining ¼ cup nuts. Cut into bars. Store, covered, in the refrigerator for up to 3 days. Makes 20 bars.

Fluffy Cream Cheese Frosting: Thaw ½ cup frozen light whipped dessert topping. In a medium bowl, beat half of an 8-ounce package softened reduced-fat cream cheese (Neufchâtel) with an electric mixer on medium speed until smooth. Beat in ¼ cup vanilla low-fat yogurt until smooth. Fold in thawed whipped topping.

***Sugar Substitute:** Use Sweet'N Low bulk or packets. Follow package directions to use product amount equivalent to ½ cup sugar.

Peanut-Apple Crunch Balls

Wetting your hands makes the peanut mixture easier to shape for these no-bake cereal treats.

PER BALL: 94 cal., 6 g total fat (2 g sat. fat), 1 mg chol., 76 mg sodium, 9 g carb., 1 g fiber, 2 g pro. Exchanges: 0.5 carb., 1 fat. Carb choices: 0.5.

- ⅓ cup chunky peanut butter
- ¼ cup 68 percent vegetable oil spread
- 2 tablespoons honey
- 1 cup rice and wheat cereal flakes, crushed slightly
- 1 cup bran flakes, crushed slightly
- ⅓ cup finely snipped dried apples
- 2 tablespoons finely chopped peanuts
- ⅛ teaspoon apple pie spice
- 2 ounces white baking chocolate (with cocoa butter), chopped
- ¼ teaspoon shortening

1. In a medium saucepan, combine peanut butter, vegetable oil spread, and honey. Cook over low heat just until melted and nearly smooth, whisking constantly. Stir in rice and wheat cereal flakes, bran flakes, apples, peanuts, and apple pie spice until mixed.

2. Divide cereal mixture into 18 portions. Using slightly wet hands, shape the cereal mixture into balls. Let stand on a waxed-paper-lined baking sheet about 15 minutes or until firm.

3. In a small saucepan, combine white chocolate and shortening. Cook over low heat until melted, stirring constantly. Drizzle balls with melted white chocolate. Let stand about 15 minutes or until white chocolate is set (if necessary, chill balls until white chocolate is firm). Makes 18 balls.

(fruit is fine)

All fruit—raw, cooked, canned, frozen, dried, or juiced—contains fruit sugar, or fructose. However, raw fruit has a higher fiber content, which has been associated with a lower rise in blood glucose. For example, a small apple and ½ cup of apple juice both contain 15 grams of carbohydrates. The apple offers 3 grams of dietary fiber, while the juice contains none. Raw fruits can also be more satisfying, but remember to watch portion sizes—a bigger fruit equals more sugar.

Carrot-Pumpkin Bars

These pumpkin bars are simple ending to a big meal.

PER BAR: 117 cal., 7 g total fat (1 g sat. fat), 0 mg chol., 89 mg sodium, 12 g carb., 1 g fiber, 2 g pro. Exchanges: 0.5 starch, 0.5 carb., 1 fat. Carb choices: 1.

Carrot-Pumpkin Bars

Nonstick cooking spray
- 1 ¼ cups all-purpose flour
- 1 teaspoon baking powder
- ½ teaspoon ground allspice
- ¼ teaspoon baking soda
- ¼ teaspoon salt
- ½ cup refrigerated or frozen egg product, thawed, or 2 eggs, slightly beaten
- ½ cup sugar or sugar substitute-sugar blend equivalent to ½ cup sugar*
- ¾ cup canned pumpkin
- ⅓ cup cooking oil
- 1 teaspoon finely shredded lime peel
- 2 tablespoons lime juice
- ½ cup finely shredded carrot
- ⅓ cup chopped macadamia nuts or almonds
- **Powdered sugar (optional)**

1. Preheat oven to 350°F. Coat a 9×9×2-inch baking pan with cooking spray; set aside.

2. Combine flour, baking powder, allspice, baking soda, and salt. In a medium bowl, beat eggs slightly; stir in sugar. Stir in pumpkin, oil, lime peel, and lime juice. Stir in carrot and nuts.

3. Add pumpkin mixture all at once to flour mixture, stirring until combined. Spoon batter into prepared pan, spreading evenly.

4. Bake for 25 to 30 minutes or until a toothpick inserted near center comes out clean. Cool in pan on a wire rack. If desired, sift powdered sugar over top. Makes 16 bars.

***Sugar Substitutes:** Choose from Splenda Sugar Blend for Baking or Equal Sugar Lite. Follow package directions to use product amount equivalent to ½ cup sugar.

from our kitchen to yours

Mixed Garden Greens Salad
recipe, page 351

Knowing someone else has had similar experiences to yours and hearing how they cope with diabetes is comforting. Just knowing you're not alone helps. Inspiring, real, and uplifting, the stories in the following pages offer a message of courage and hope.

**Garden Chicken
with Cheddar Sauce**
recipe, page 351

recipe, page 351

(rosalie misco)

blooming good health

Rosalie Misco knew for years that she needed to stave off diabetes because it ran in her family. "I'd had pre-diabetes for a while, so I'd known it would come. My two grandmothers had it and one of my brothers has it," Rosalie, of Appleton, Wisconsin, says. "I was always interested in nutrition and exercise, so I managed to keep diabetes at bay for about 10 years," she says. But it finally caught up to her in 1994. Soon after learning she had type 2 diabetes, Rosalie discovered a surprising but effective therapy—gardening. "I spend hours in the garden every day. I just love being out there," says Rosalie. "And with all the raking, weeding, digging, mulching, planting, and picking, I burn a lot of calories and don't even feel it."

Rosalie was diagnosed with diabetes about the same time she and her husband, Bill, retired. They sold her silk floral business, moved to a new house on sunnier land, and began planting flowers, vegetables, and herbs. As Rosalie's garden grew, so did her knowledge about managing diabetes. Rosalie learned that the vegetables and herbs she was planting were the very foods she and Bill, who also has type 2 diabetes, should eat.

She uses her vegetables in salads, side dishes, and soups. Rosalie also has a food dehydrator to dry hot peppers for her low-sodium seasoning mixes and celery for her dry soup mixes. "I don't like to eat processed foods because they're often high in sugar and sodium, and that's not good for us. My whole philosophy is to cook wholesome foods the way they come from the ground," Rosalie says.

Gardening has become a favorite activity for Bill and Rosalie. Because both of them have diabetes, cooking is easy. "We both have to watch what we eat," Rosalie says. From morning to evening, Rosalie and Bill enjoy the fruits and vegetables of their garden, focusing on natural foods and moderate portions. Bill has lost weight and Rosalie feels better. "Bill was just eating the natural foods I was cooking and he lost about 19 pounds without going hungry at all," says Rosalie. "I can honestly say that in the 10 years since being diagnosed, I've never had a day where I felt bad from diabetes," she says. "I feel very energized and good about my health."

Rosalie's grandchildren enjoy working in the garden with their grandmother and eating her nutritious meals. "My grandkids love my chocolate chip cookies. They don't realize how healthful they are."

I feel very energized
and good about my health.

Rosalie Misco, Appleton, Wisconsin

Pepper and Four-Bean Salad
recipe, page 352

**Herbed Salmon Loaf
with Creamed Peas**

Herbed Salmon Loaf with Creamed Peas

With this loaf, you benefit from the omega-3s in the salmon and the fiber in both the barley and the peas.

PER SERVING: 276 cal., 7 g total fat (1 g sat. fat), 109 mg chol., 734 mg sodium, 17 g carb., 3 g fiber, 36 g pro. Exchanges: 1 starch, 4.5 very lean meat, 1 fat. Carb choices: 1.

¾ cup water
⅓ cup quick-cooking barley
2 14- to 15-ounce cans salmon, drained
1 stalk celery, finely chopped
1 small onion, finely chopped
¼ cup fine dry bread crumbs
2 tablespoons snipped fresh parsley or 2 teaspoons dried parsley flakes
2 tablespoons lemon juice
1 tablespoon snipped fresh dill or 1 teaspoon dried dill
¼ teaspoon ground black pepper
4 egg whites, ½ cup refrigerated or frozen egg product, thawed, or 2 eggs, slightly beaten
Nonstick cooking spray
1 recipe Creamed Peas (see recipe, right)
Fresh dill sprigs (optional)

1. In a small saucepan, combine water and barley. Bring to boiling; reduce heat. Cover; simmer for 10 to 12 minutes or until barley is tender. Drain, if necessary.

2. Preheat oven to 350°F. Remove skin and bones from salmon; flake. In a large bowl, combine salmon, celery, onion, bread crumbs, parsley, lemon juice, snipped or dried dill, and pepper. Stir in barley. Stir in egg whites.

3. Lightly coat an 8×4×2-inch loaf pan with cooking spray. Press salmon mixture into pan.

4. Bake about 1 hour or until an instant-read thermometer inserted into the center reaches 160°F. Cover and let stand for 10 minutes.

5. To serve, carefully invert pan to remove loaf. Invert loaf onto a platter. Cut into 12 slices. Serve warm with Creamed Peas. If desired, garnish with fresh dill sprigs. Makes 6 (2-slice) servings.

Creamed Peas: In a covered small saucepan, cook ½ cup shelled fresh peas in boiling water for 10 to 12 minutes or until tender. (Or use thawed frozen peas.) Drain. In a small saucepan, stir together 1 cup fat-free milk, 2½ teaspoons cornstarch, ¼ teaspoon salt, and dash ground black pepper. Cook and stir until thickened and bubbly. Cook and stir for 2 minutes more. Stir in peas and ⅛ teaspoon finely shredded lemon peel. Heat through. Makes about 1 cup.

Mixed Garden Greens Salad

If you don't grow a variety of greens like Rosalie does, you can use your favorite salad mix. Pictured on page 346.

PER SERVING: 99 cal., 7 g total fat (2 sat. fat), 4 mg chol., 72 mg sodium, 7 g carb., 2 g fiber, 2 g pro. Exchanges: 1.5 vegetable, 1.5 fat. Carb choices: 0.5.

- 2 cups torn romaine
- 2 cups fresh spinach
- 1½ cups torn curly endive
- 1½ cups arugula
- 2 small red, green, and/or yellow sweet peppers, cut into thin strips
- 1 small red onion, thinly sliced
- 1 cup red or yellow grape, pear, or cherry tomatoes, halved
- 1 medium carrot
- ¼ cup finely shredded cheddar cheese
- ½ cup **Low-Calorie French Salad Dressing** (see recipe, below) or ½ cup bottled reduced-calorie French salad dressing

1. In a large bowl, combine romaine, spinach, curly endive, arugula, sweet peppers, red onion, and tomatoes. Using a vegetable peeler, slice carrot lenthwise into long, thin ribbons. Top salad with carrot ribbons and cheddar cheese. Serve with Low-Calorie French Salad Dressing. Makes 8 (about 1-cup) servings.

Low-Calorie French Salad Dressing: In a blender, combine ¼ cup low-sodium tomato juice or vegetable juice, 3 tablespoons vinegar, 1 tablespoon honey, 1 teaspoon paprika, 1 minced garlic clove, 1 teaspoon Worcestershire sauce, ¼ teaspoon ground black pepper, and ⅛ teaspoon salt. With the blender running, slowly add ⅓ cup olive oil through the hole in the lid; continue blending until mixture reaches desired consistency. Cover and chill for up to 1 week. Makes about ¾ cup.

Quick Tip

Rosalie plants a variety of herbs to use in all of her favorite recipes because of the way they flavor foods. Most importantly, herbs don't add fat, sodium, or a lot of calories. Basil, sage, dill, chives, and thyme are great herbs to have on hand. Add them to soups, salads, and dressings.

Garden Chicken with Cheddar Sauce

Wisconsin cheese tastes perfect in the silky sauce. Pictured on page 348.

PER SERVING: 253 cal., 6 g total fat (3 g sat. fat), 82 mg chol., 260 mg sodium, 14 g carb., 3 g fiber, 35 g pro. Exchanges: 1.5 vegetable, 0.5 starch, 4 very lean meat, 0.5 high-fat meat. Carb choices: 1.

- 4 small skinless, boneless chicken breast halves (about 1 pound total)
- 2 cups broccoli florets, cut into 1-inch pieces
- 1½ cups cauliflower florets, cut into 1-inch pieces
- 2 large carrots, cut into ¼-inch-thick slices
- 1 recipe **Cheddar Sauce** (see recipe, below)

1. In a microwave-safe 2-quart rectangular baking dish, arrange chicken in a single layer; cover with plastic wrap, turning back one corner. Microwave on 100 percent power (high) for 6 to 9 minutes or until chicken is no longer pink (170°F), rearranging once. Transfer chicken to a platter, reserving juices in baking dish. Cover to keep warm.

2. Add broccoli, cauliflower, and carrots to juices in baking dish. Cover with vented plastic wrap. Microwave on 100 percent power (high) for 4 to 6 minutes or until crisp-tender. Drain. Meanwhile, prepare Cheddar Sauce; spoon over vegetables and chicken. Makes 4 servings.

Cheddar Sauce: In a small saucepan, stir together 1¼ cups fat-free milk, 1 tablespoon cornstarch, 1 teaspoon snipped fresh marjoram or thyme or ¼ teaspoon crushed dried marjoram or thyme, 1 teaspoon prepared horseradish, and 1 teaspoon Dijon-style mustard. Cook and stir until thickened and bubbly. Reduce heat. Add ½ cup shredded cheddar or American cheese; cook and stir until melted.

Barley-Vegetable Chicken Soup

Pepper and Four-Bean Salad

Rosalie uses more vinegar and less oil in her tarragon vinaigrette to keep the fat low. Pictured on page 349.

PER SERVING: 117 cal., 4 g total fat (0 g sat. fat), 0 mg chol., 146 mg sodium, 17 g carb., 5 g fiber, 5 g pro. Exchanges: 1.5 vegetable, 0.5 starch, 1 fat. Carb choices: 1.

PER SERVING WITH SUBSTITUTE: same as above, except 114 cal., 16 g carb.

- **4 cups trimmed 1½-inch pieces fresh green and/or wax beans or one 16-ounce package frozen cut green beans**
- **1 15- to 16-ounce can kidney beans, rinsed and drained**
- **1 15- to 16-ounce can garbanzo beans (chickpeas), rinsed and drained**
- **3 medium green, red, and/or yellow sweet peppers, cut into thin strips**
- **1 small red or white onion, thinly sliced and separated into rings**
- **½ cup vinegar**
- **¼ cup olive oil**
- **1 tablespoon sugar or sugar substitute* equivalent to 1 tablespoon sugar**
- **2 teaspoons snipped fresh tarragon or thyme or ½ teaspoon dried tarragon or thyme, crushed**
- **½ teaspoon ground black pepper**
- **Lettuce leaves (optional)**

1. In a covered large saucepan, cook fresh green beans in a small amount of boiling water for 8 to 10 minutes or just until tender. (If using frozen beans, cook according to package directions, except omit the salt.) Drain beans into a colander, then submerge beans in ice water to cool quickly. Drain beans again. In a large bowl, combine green beans, kidney beans, garbanzo beans, sweet peppers, and onion.

2. For marinade, in a medium bowl, whisk together vinegar, olive oil, sugar, tarragon, and black pepper until combined. Pour marinade over bean mixture. Toss mixture gently to coat. Cover and chill for 4 hours, stirring occasionally.

3. To serve, line a serving bowl with lettuce leaves, if desired. Using a slotted spoon, spoon bean salad into the bowl. Makes 14 (about ⅔-cup) servings.

*Sugar Substitutes: Choose from Splenda Granular, Equal Spoonful or packets, or Sweet'N Low bulk or packets. Follow package directions to use product amount that's equivalent to 1 tablespoon sugar.

Barley-Vegetable Chicken Soup

Rosalie simmers her garden gems in a soup, then freezes the chunky soup in serving-size portions to savor on cold Wisconsin winter days.

PER SERVING: 137 cal., 1 g total fat (0 g sat. fat), 33 mg chol., 631 mg sodium, 14 g carb., 3 g fiber, 18 g pro. Exchanges: 1 vegetable, 0.5 starch, 2 very lean meat. Carb choices: 1.

- **8 cups reduced-sodium chicken broth**
- **½ cup regular barley**
- **4 skinless, boneless chicken breast halves (1 to 1¼ pounds total), cut into ¾-inch cubes**
- **3 stalks celery, sliced**
- **3 medium carrots, sliced**
- **1 medium onion, chopped**
- **¼ cup snipped fresh parsley or 2 tablespoons dried parsley**
- **1 tablespoon snipped fresh sage or rosemary or 1 teaspoon dried sage or rosemary, crushed**
- **¼ teaspoon ground black pepper**
- **1 cup chopped green, yellow, and/or red sweet pepper**

1. In a 4-quart Dutch oven, bring the chicken broth to boiling. Add uncooked barley; return to boiling. Reduce heat. Cover and simmer for 30 minutes.

2. Add chicken pieces, celery, carrots, onion, dried parsley (if using), dried sage or rosemary (if using), and black pepper to the barley-broth mixture. Return soup to boiling; reduce heat. Cover; simmer for 10 minutes.

3. Add chopped sweet pepper to the soup; cover and simmer about 5 minutes more or until chicken is no longer pink and vegetables are tender. Stir in fresh parsley (if using) and fresh sage or rosemary (if using). Serve warm. Makes 8 (1½-cup) main-dish servings.

(rosie's top tips)

Rosalie has thought of health-ful food ideas while cooking at home and baking for her shop. Try them in your own kitchen.

1. **Thicken sauces** and soups with barley flour instead of all-purpose flour.

2. **Use old-fashioned oats** in piecrusts, granolas, fruit crisps, and cookies. To save time, Rosalie cooks a large batch of steel-cut oats, then chills the porridge to reheat over the next few days.

3. **Flaxseeds** help to lower bad (LDL) cholesterol, but use ground seeds to get the health benefit. Rosalie grinds hers in a coffee grinder and stores them in the freezer to keep them fresh.

4. **Cook chicken breasts** in the microwave oven, in poaching liquid, or on the grill instead of frying them in a skillet with added fat.

5. **Cook fresh vegetables** with a little water in the microwave oven to retain vitamins. Frozen vegetables may not need any water.

6. **Add fresh herbs** for flavor without extra calories. If you're unsure about how to pair an herb with a food, try a little and taste to see if you like it.

7. **Use a sugar substitute** blend such as Splenda Sugar Blend for Baking or Equal Sugar Lite in place of sugar when baking moist items such as muffins and zucchini bread.

now we're cooking

Every time Priscilla (Pinky) Fernandez attended her diabetes class, she felt guilty. "Here we were getting all these great new recipes and I wasn't changing a thing. I wasn't even opening my book," she admits. Week after week, Pinky looked around at her classmates, all newly diagnosed or trying to bring diabetes under control. She began to realize that they, like her, were struggling with the changes they needed to make. "I knew I should change the way I was eating. My husband and I were going out to dinner all the time, so I was being tempted by all the wrong things," Pinky says. "What's really sad is that I love to cook! I wondered why they weren't showing our class how to plan a perfect diabetic meal. I wanted some hands-on practice, so I decided to offer my home and see if anyone else wanted to cook together."

The next week at the last class, Pinky announced: "We have all these great recipes and need to learn to cook a whole new way. Who would like to form a diabetic cooking club to meet at my house?" Although only one person raised her hand, a group eventually was formed. They called themselves DDD for Diabetic Dining by Design.

When the group members first gathered at Pinky's house to lay the ground rules, they realized they had a unique opportunity not only to eat more healthfully but to learn about foods from different cultures and to try unfamiliar ingredients. Each person takes a turn at picking out a menu, shopping, and preparing food ahead of time. Members can make recipes from nondiabetic cookbooks but must modify recipes to diabetic standards. Everyone except the cook helps with cleaning up.

Pinky keeps a binder of the group's menus so members can copy recipes they'd like to make at home. Unlike her diabetes class binder that stayed shut from week to week, the group binder is a frequent reference. "This group is like family to me now," Pinky says. "And our binder is the family cookbook."

> " Wanting hands-on practice, I offered my home to see if anyone else wanted to form a cooking club. "
>
> —Pinky Fernandez

Colorados (Red Bean Soup)
recipe, page 357

Cuban-Style Swordfish
recipe, page 356

Priscilla (Pinky) Fernandez (above right) cooks with other club members in her home. Although she is Mexican American, her cooking style reflects her husband's Cuban roots—fish, beans, and herbs.

Grilled Vegetable-Lamb Skewers
recipe, page 357

Chicken-Tofu Stir-Fry

onion and sweet pepper; cook and stir for 2 minutes. Stir in bok choy and/or bean sprouts.

3. Add undrained chicken mixture; heat through. Serve with hot cooked rice. Makes 6 (1 cup stir-fry plus ½ cup rice) servings.

Cuban-Style Swordfish

With grilling and broiling options, this fish-and-salsa medley makes a great meal any time of year. Pictured on page 355.

PER SERVING: 190 cal., 8 g total fat (2 g sat. fat), 43 mg chol., 254 mg sodium, 6 g carb., 3 g fiber, 24 g pro. Exchanges: 1 vegetable, 3 very lean meat, 1.5 fat. Carb choices: 0.5.

- 1 **pound fresh or frozen swordfish steaks, cut 1 inch thick**
- 1 **large clove garlic, halved**
- 2 **tablespoons lime juice**
- ½ **teaspoon ground cumin**
- ¼ **teaspoon ground black pepper**
- ⅛ **teaspoon salt**
- **Nonstick cooking spray**
- 1 **recipe Fresh Tomato Salsa (see recipe, below)**

1. Thaw fish, if frozen. Rinse fish; pat dry with paper towels. Cut fish into 4 serving-size pieces. Rub fish on both sides with garlic. Place fish in a shallow glass dish; drizzle with lime juice. Cover; marinate in the refrigerator for 30 minutes, turning once. Drain fish. In a bowl, combine cumin, black pepper, and salt; sprinkle onto fish.

2. Coat a cold grill rack with cooking spray. Grill fish on rack of an uncovered grill directly over medium heat for 8 to 12 minutes or until fish flakes easily when tested with a fork, turning once halfway through grilling. Serve swordfish with Fresh Tomato Salsa. Makes 4 servings.

Fresh Tomato Salsa: In a medium bowl, combine 1 cup chopped red and/or yellow tomato; ¼ cup chopped tomatillo; ¼ cup chopped avocado; 2 tablespoons snipped fresh cilantro; 1 medium fresh jalapeño pepper, seeded and finely chopped (see tip, page 205); 1 minced clove garlic; 1 tablespoon lime juice; ⅛ teaspoon salt; and ⅛ teaspoon ground black pepper. Serve immediately or cover and chill for up to 4 hours.

Broiling Directions: Preheat broiler. Coat unheated rack of a broiler pan with cooking spray. Broil fish on unheated rack of broiler pan about 4 inches from heat for 8 to 12 minutes or until fish flakes easily when tested with a fork, turning fish once halfway through broiling.

Chicken-Tofu Stir-Fry

Mix and match the vegetable options to create a new dish every time you make this stir-fry.

PER SERVING: 285 cal., 9 g total fat (1 g sat. fat), 32 mg chol., 331 mg sodium, 30 g carb., 4 g fiber, 20 g pro. Exchanges: 1 vegetable, 1.5 starch, 2 lean meat, 0.5 fat. Carb choices: 2.

- 2 **tablespoons olive oil**
- 2 **tablespoons orange juice**
- 1 **tablespoon reduced-sodium soy sauce**
- 1 **tablespoon Worcestershire sauce**
- 1 **tablespoon grated fresh ginger**
- 1 **teaspoon dry mustard**
- 1 **teaspoon ground turmeric**
- 8 **ounces cooked chicken breast, cubed**
- 8 **ounces tub-style extra-firm tofu (fresh bean curd), drained and cubed**
- 2 **medium carrots or 2 stalks celery, bias-sliced**
- 1 **cup pea pods and/or sliced fresh mushrooms**
- 3 **green onions, cut into ½-inch-long pieces**
- 1 **medium red and/or green sweet pepper, cut into thin bite-size strips**
- 2 **cups chopped baby bok choy and/or fresh bean sprouts**
- 3 **cups hot cooked brown or white rice**

1. In a large bowl, stir together 1 tablespoon of the oil, the orange juice, soy sauce, Worcestershire sauce, ginger, mustard, and turmeric. Add chicken and tofu; stir to coat. Cover and chill for up to 4 hours.

2. In a very large nonstick skillet, heat remaining 1 tablespoon oil over medium-high heat. Add carrot or celery; cook and stir for 2 minutes. Add pea pods and/or mushrooms; cook and stir for 2 minutes. Add green

Grilled Vegetable-Lamb Skewers

You can make your own garam masala, but you can buy the spice blend as well. Pictured on page 355.

PER SERVING: 232 cal., 4 g total fat (1 g sat. fat), 71 mg chol., 226 mg sodium, 22 g carb., 5 g fiber, 27 g pro. Exchanges: 1 starch, 1 vegetable, 3 very lean meat, 0.5 fat. Carb choices: 1.5.

1 pound lean boneless lamb
¼ cup snipped fresh cilantro
2 tablespoons chopped onion
2 tablespoons lime juice or lemon juice
4 cloves garlic, minced
2 teaspoons grated fresh ginger
1 medium jalapeño pepper, seeded and finely chopped (optional) (see tip, page 205)
1 teaspoon Homemade Garam Masala (see recipe, below) or purchased garam masala
¼ teaspoon salt
2 cups assorted vegetables (such as 1½-inch chunks of yellow summer squash or eggplant, red onion wedges, or baby patty pan squash)
  Nonstick cooking spray
1½ cups water
¾ cup bulgur
2 tablespoons snipped fresh cilantro

1. Trim fat from lamb; cut into 1½-inch pieces. Place lamb in a resealable plastic bag set in a shallow dish; set aside.

2. In a small bowl, combine ¼ cup cilantro, onion, lime juice, garlic, ginger, jalapeño pepper (if using), garam masala, and salt. Add to lamb; seal bag. Turn to coat. Chill for 4 to 6 hours.

3. On four 12-inch-long metal skewers, alternately thread lamb and vegetable pieces, leaving a ¼-inch space between pieces. Discard cilantro mixture.

4. Coat a cold grill rack with cooking spray. Grill skewers on rack of uncovered grill directly over medium heat for 12 to 14 minutes or until lamb is just pink in center, turning once.

5. In a saucepan, combine water and bulgur. Bring to boiling; reduce heat. Cover and simmer about 15 minutes or until tender. Drain bulgur; stir in 2 tablespoons cilantro.

6. Serve skewers with bulgur. Makes 4 (1 skewer plus ½ cup bulgur) servings.

Homemade Garam Masala: In a skillet, cook 1 tablespoon cumin seeds, 1 tablespoon cardamom seeds, 1 tablespoon whole black peppercorns, 12 whole cloves, and 3 inches stick cinnamon over medium heat about 3 minutes or until aromatic. Cool. In a sealed plastic bag, crush cinnamon with a rolling pin. In a spice grinder or blender, combine the spices. Cover and grind spice mixture to a powder. Store in a covered container for up to 6 months. Makes about ¼ cup.

Colorados (Red Bean Soup)

To save time, soak the dry beans the day before to make this high-fiber soup. Pictured on page 354.

PER SERVING: 273 cal., 4 g total fat (1 g sat. fat), 35 mg chol., 457 mg sodium, 33 g carb., 12 g fiber, 24 g pro. Exchanges: 0.5 vegetable, 1.5 starch, 0.5 other carb., 2.5 very lean meat, 0.5 fat. Carb choices: 2.

1 pound dry red kidney beans
¾ cup dry white wine or lower-sodium beef broth
1 medium green or red sweet pepper, chopped
1 medium onion, chopped
1 medium tomato, chopped
4 cloves garlic, minced
1 medium fresh yellow wax pepper or banana pepper, seeded and chopped
1 pound fresh beef brisket
1 ham hock
1 large russet potato
1 teaspoon salt
½ teaspoon ground black pepper

1. In a Dutch oven, combine beans and 6 cups *water*. Bring to boiling; reduce heat. Simmer for 2 minutes. Remove from heat. Cover; let stand for 1 hour. (Or place beans in 6 cups water. Cover; let soak in a cool place for 6 to 8 hours or overnight.) Drain and rinse beans.

2. Return beans to Dutch oven. Add 8 cups *water*, the wine, sweet pepper, onion, tomato, garlic, and wax pepper. Bring to boiling.

3. Trim brisket; cut into ¾-inch pieces. Add beef and ham hock to bean mixture. Return to boiling; reduce heat. Cover; simmer about 1½ hours or until beans and meat are tender. Remove hock; let cool. Mash beans slightly.

4. Peel and dice potato; stir into beans. Bring to boiling; reduce heat. Cover and simmer about 15 minutes or until potato is tender.

5. When ham is cool enough to handle, cut meat from bone; discard bone. Cut ham into bite-size pieces; stir into bean mixture. Stir in salt and black pepper. Makes 10 (1½-cup) servings.

Fresh Green Bean and Mushroom Casserole
recipe, page 360

Creole Turkey Meatballs
recipe, page 360

When Jo Ann Pegues (right photo, far right) teaches nutrition and cooking classes to Denver-area church members, everyone gets involved in making the recipes.

learning together

Where there's faith, there's a foundation for learning—so the Metro Denver Black Church Initiative has discovered. For more than 10 years, this association of more than 40 African-American churches has reached out to members with messages on living healthfully. Jo Ann Pegues, R.D., M.P.A., who is project manager of the initiative's Focus on Diabetes, conducts diabetes cooking classes as part of the program. "People come from all walks of life," Pegues says. "Some have had diabetes for years, some have just been diagnosed, some are at risk, and others are caregivers. Husbands and wives attend together to learn new ways to cook. We love it when ministers join us, because the congregation is likely to follow. There's nothing like preaching from the pulpit to encourage people to make changes!"

The classes are held where members can easily find them—in local Denver-area churches. Attendees learn about other aspects of diabetes care, especially the importance of exercise in relation to diabetes. "In the winter, we've noticed people really slack off," Pegues says. "To show them how easy it is, every class includes 15 to 20 minutes of exercise." Then it's time for students to roll up their sleeves and start cooking. Classes are very hands-on. Everyone steps up to the plate. It's a low-key time to gather around the counter for some chopping, mixing, learning, and laughing. "It's a social thing as well as a learning experience," Pegues says. "That's a key to our success."

"It's a social thing as well as a learning experience. That's a key to our success."

—Jo Ann Pegues, Focus on Diabetes
project manager, Denver, Colorado

Pecan-Cranberry Salad
recipe, page 360

Pecan-Cranberry Salad

Low-calorie gelatin thickens,
but doesn't set, this tangy relish. Pictured on page 359.

PER SERVING: 106 cal., 3 g total fat (0 g sat. fat), 0 mg chol., 27 mg sodium, 20 g carb., 2 g fiber, 1 g pro. Exchanges: 0.5 fruit, 1 other carb., 0.5 fat. Carb choices: 1.

- 1 12-ounce package fresh cranberries
- 1 cup water
- ½ cup sugar
- 1 4-serving-size package sugar-free cranberry- or raspberry-flavored gelatin
- 1 15.25-ounce can crushed pineapple (juice pack)
- ⅓ cup coarsely chopped pecans, toasted

1. In a large saucepan, combine cranberries and the water. Bring to boiling; reduce heat. Simmer, uncovered, about 3 minutes or until berries pop.

2. Remove from heat. Add sugar and gelatin, stirring to dissolve. Stir in undrained pineapple. Transfer cranberry mixture to a serving bowl. Cover and chill about 6 hours or until thick. Before serving, sprinkle with pecans. Makes 10 (⅓-cup) servings.

Fresh Green Bean and Mushroom Casserole

A toasty whole grain topper replaces the traditional fried onion rings to keep fat and sodium in check. Pictured on page 358.

PER SERVING: 107 cal., 3 g total fat (1 g sat. fat), 7 mg chol., 148 mg sodium, 14 g carb., 3 g fiber, 4 g pro. Exchanges: 1.5 vegetable, 0.5 other carb., 0.5 fat. Carb choices: 1.

- 1½ pounds fresh green beans, trimmed
- 2 tablespoons butter or margarine
- 3 tablespoons all-purpose flour
- 1 tablespoon dry ranch-style salad dressing mix
- ¼ teaspoon ground white pepper
- 1½ cups fat-free milk
- Nonstick cooking spray
- 1 cup chopped onion
- 2 cloves garlic, minced
- 1½ cups sliced fresh mushrooms
- 1 cup soft whole wheat or white bread crumbs

1. Preheat oven to 375°F. In a covered large saucepan, cook green beans in a small amount of boiling water for 10 to 15 minutes or until crisp-tender.

2. Meanwhile, for white sauce, in a medium saucepan, melt butter. Stir in flour, dressing mix, and white pepper until combined. Stir in milk. Cook and stir over medium heat until thickened and bubbly; remove from heat.

3. Coat an unheated medium nonstick skillet with cooking spray. Preheat over medium heat. Add the onion and garlic; cook for 2 to 3 minutes or until tender.

4. Remove half of the onion mixture from skillet; set aside. Add mushrooms to remaining onion mixture in skillet; cook about 5 minutes or until tender.

5. Drain beans. In a 1½-quart casserole, combine beans, mushroom mixture, and white sauce.

6. For topping, in a small bowl, stir together reserved onion mixture and bread crumbs; sprinkle onto bean mixture. Bake, uncovered, for 25 to 30 minutes or until heated through. Makes 10 (½-cup) servings.

Creole Turkey Meatballs

Look for ground turkey breast to keep the meatballs low in fat. Pictured on page 358.

PER SERVING: 94 cal., 4 g total fat (1 g sat. fat), 36 mg chol., 104 mg sodium, 5 g carb., 1 g fiber, 9 g pro. Exchanges: 0.5 other carb., 1 lean meat. Carb choices: 0.

- Nonstick cooking spray
- ¼ cup refrigerated or frozen egg product, thawed, or 1 egg
- 1 medium onion, chopped
- 1 medium green sweet pepper, chopped
- ½ cup quick-cooking rolled oats
- 2 tablespoons fat-free milk
- 2 cloves garlic, minced
- 1 teaspoon dried Italian seasoning, crushed
- 1 teaspoon salt-free seasoning
- 1 teaspoon Creole seasoning
- 1 pound uncooked ground turkey

1. Preheat oven to 375°F. Lightly coat a 15×10×1-inch baking pan with nonstick cooking spray; set aside.

2. In a large bowl, beat egg; stir in onion, pepper, oats, milk, and garlic. Stir in Italian, salt-free, and Creole seasonings. Add turkey; mix well.

3. Using a rounded tablespoon, shape mixture into 1¼-inch balls. Arrange in prepared pan.

4. Bake meatballs, uncovered, about 25 minutes or until brown and no longer pink in center (165°F). Makes 10 servings.

Citrus-Sweet Potato Pie

Using oil instead of lard in the crust lowers
the saturated fat in this pumpkin-like pie.

PER SERVING: 172 cal., 6 g total fat (1 g sat. fat), 1 mg chol.,
96 mg sodium, 25 g carb., 1 g fiber, 4 g pro. Exchanges: 1 starch,
0.5 other carb., 1 fat. Carb choices: 1.5.
PER SERVING WITH SUBSTITUTE: same as above, except 157 cal.,
21 g carb.

1½ cups mashed, cooked, peeled sweet potatoes (about
    2 medium)
¼ cup sugar or sugar substitute* equivalent to
    ¼ cup sugar
1 teaspoon vanilla
½ teaspoon finely shredded lemon peel
1 teaspoon lemon juice
¼ teaspoon ground nutmeg
¼ cup refrigerated or frozen egg product, thawed,
    or 1 egg
1 cup evaporated fat-free milk
1 recipe Baked Oil Pastry (see recipe, right)
  Frozen fat-free whipped dessert topping, thawed
    (optional)
  Ground nutmeg (optional)

1. Preheat oven to 350°F. For filling, in a large bowl,
stir together sweet potatoes, sugar, vanilla, lemon peel,
lemon juice, and the ¼ teaspoon nutmeg. Add egg. Beat
gently with a fork just until combined. Gradually add
evaporated milk; stir until combined.

2. Pour filling into Baked Oil Pastry. To prevent
overbrowning, cover edge with foil. Bake for 30 to
35 minutes or until a knife inserted near the center
comes out clean and edges are puffed. If necessary to
allow pastry to brown, remove foil for the last 5 to
10 minutes of baking. Cool on a wire rack. Cover and
refrigerate within 2 hours.

3. To serve, remove tart from pan or leave pie in pie
plate. Cut into wedges. If desired, top each serving with
topping and additional nutmeg. Makes 12 servings.

Baked Oil Pastry: Preheat oven to 450°F. In a medium
bowl, stir together 1⅓ cups all-purpose flour and
¼ teaspoon salt. Add ⅓ cup cooking oil and 3 tablespoons
fat-free milk all at once. Stir gently with a fork. Form
into a ball. On a well-floured surface, slightly flatten
dough. Roll from center to edge into an 11-inch circle.
To transfer, wrap pastry around the rolling pin. Unroll
into 9-inch tart pan with a removable bottom or a 9-inch
pie plate. Ease pastry into pan without stretching. Press
pastry into fluted sides of tart pan or crimp edge in pie
plate, trimming pastry as needed. Line pastry with a
double thickness of foil. Bake for 8 minutes. Remove foil.
Bake for 5 minutes more. Cool on a wire rack.

*Sugar Substitutes: Choose from Splenda Granular or
Sweet 'N Low bulk or packets. Follow package directions
to use product amount equivalent to ¼ cup sugar.

catering to diabetes

(pat le grand)

Pat LeGrand puts a lot of love into her cooking—and her Cleveland business that caters to people with diabetes. Her family and their favorite dishes are the inspiration. "We can eat our traditional foods as long as they're adjusted a little," she says.

When her mother was diagnosed with type 2 diabetes five years ago, Pat had no idea her life would take a dramatically different direction as a result. Pat was a high-powered corporate auditor in Cleveland who just wanted to help her 80-year-old mother, Iris, eat better to control her diabetes. Now she owns the first restaurant in the United States that caters mainly to people with diabetes.

"When Mother was diagnosed, I didn't know how much diabetes could be affected by diet and lifestyle," says Pat. "Food is normal and natural. It's a source of solace. When you find out you have diabetes, you're told all the things you've come to love and enjoy are not good for you."

Iris found it hard to cook differently and start exercising. She vacillated between not eating and having low blood glucose, then eating too much and having high blood glucose. And it upset Pat to see her mother, a great cook, eating food she didn't like.

Pat knew she had to help, but her work schedule limited her. Pat tackled her mother's diabetes just as she would solve a problem at work. She started by conducting research about diabetes from health organizations. Pat then began cooking for her mother. "I realized that there was nothing I couldn't cook for someone with diabetes," Pat says.

Pat had been cooking for her mother for about a year when opportunity knocked. Her company downsized and she got laid off. She realized she wanted to start her own business but she didn't know what it would be. While cooking for her mother one day, she thought, "I wish someone would open a restaurant so I wouldn't have to keep cooking the way I do." But there was no such place. Pat realized her wish was the "it" idea she'd been looking for for her business. Within two years A Touch of Sugar, Pat's restaurant in Cleveland, was born.

When someone had diabetes, my Southern family called it having 'a touch of sugar,' which inspired the name of my restaurant.

—Pat LeGrand, Cleveland, Ohio

Oven-Fried Chicken Breasts, Macaroni and Cheese
recipes, page 364

Pat LeGrand (below) took the foods her mother loved and made them more healthful for a diabetic meal plan. Pictured (far left) outside her Cleveland restaurant with her daughters and mom, from left: Rijalon, Iris, Pat, and Eden.

Sweet Potato Pie
recipe, page 368

Vegetable Chili and Buttermilk Corn Muffins
recipes, pages 368 and 364

Oven-Fried Chicken Breasts

Chicken crisps in the oven rather than in a deep-fat fryer. Pictured on page 363.

PER SERVING: 267 cal., 2 g total fat (1 g sat. fat), 88 mg chol., 336 mg sodium, 23 g carb., 1 g fiber, 37 g pro. Exchanges: 1.5 starch, 4.5 very lean meat. Carb choices: 1.5.

- 6 skinless, boneless chicken breast halves (about 2 pounds total)
- 1 cup buttermilk
- Olive oil nonstick cooking spray
- 1¼ cups crushed cornflakes
- 1 teaspoon garlic powder or dried minced garlic
- 1 teaspoon onion powder or dried minced onion
- 1 teaspoon paprika
- ½ teaspoon ground black pepper

1. In a large resealable plastic bag, combine chicken and buttermilk. Seal the bag; turn bag to coat chicken. Marinate chicken in the refrigerator for 2 to 8 hours, turning the bag occasionally.

2. Preheat oven to 400°F. Line a baking sheet with foil; coat foil with nonstick cooking spray. Drain chicken, discarding buttermilk.

3. In another large resealable plastic bag, combine crushed cornflakes, garlic powder, onion powder, paprika, and pepper; seal bag. Shake well to combine. Add chicken, one piece at a time, and shake bag to coat chicken well.

4. Place chicken on the prepared baking sheet. Coat chicken with nonstick cooking spray. Bake, uncovered, for 20 to 25 minutes or until chicken is no longer pink (170°F). Makes 6 servings.

Macaroni and Cheese

This updated version of the classic capitalizes on lower-fat ingredients. Pictured on page 363.

PER SERVING: 169 cal., 3 g total fat (2 g sat. fat), 9 mg chol., 210 mg sodium, 24 g carb., 1 g fiber, 11 g pro. Exchanges: 1.5 starch, 1 lean meat. Carb choices: 1.5.

- 8 ounces dried elbow macaroni
- Nonstick cooking spray
- 1 12-ounce can evaporated fat-free milk
- ½ cup refrigerated or frozen egg product, thawed, or 2 eggs, lightly beaten
- 2 teaspoons onion powder
- ½ teaspoon ground black pepper
- ¾ cup finely shredded Parmesan cheese (3 ounces)
- ¼ cup shredded reduced-fat cheddar cheese (1 ounce)
- ½ teaspoon paprika

1. Preheat oven to 350°F. Cook macaroni according to package directions. Drain and keep warm. Lightly coat a 2-quart baking dish with cooking spray; set aside.

2. In a medium bowl, whisk evaporated milk, eggs, onion powder, and pepper. Add drained macaroni, Parmesan cheese, and cheddar cheese; mix well.

3. Spread macaroni mixture in prepared baking dish. Sprinkle with paprika. Bake about 25 minutes or until heated through. Makes 9 (about ½-cup) servings.

Buttermilk Corn Muffins

These muffins are typical of Southern corn bread, which is less sweet than the Northern version. Pictured on page 363.

PER MUFFIN: 92 cal., 2 g total fat (0 g sat. fat), 1 mg chol., 129 mg sodium, 15 g carb., 1 g fiber, 3 g pro. Exchanges: 1 starch. Carb choices: 1.

- 1 cup all-purpose flour
- ¾ cup yellow cornmeal
- 1 tablespoon sugar or sugar substitute* equivalent to 1 tablespoon sugar (optional)
- 2 teaspoons baking powder
- 1 cup buttermilk
- ¼ cup refrigerated or frozen egg product, thawed, or 1 egg, lightly beaten
- 1 tablespoon canola oil
- 1 tablespoon lower-fat stick margarine, melted
- 1 teaspoon vanilla
- ½ teaspoon butter flavoring

1. Preheat oven to 400°F. Lightly coat twelve 2½-inch muffin cups with *nonstick cooking spray*. In a large bowl, stir together flour, cornmeal, sugar (if desired), baking powder, and ¼ teaspoon *salt*.

2. In a small bowl, whisk together buttermilk, egg, oil, margarine, vanilla, and butter flavoring. Add buttermilk mixture all at once to flour mixture; stir just until moistened. Don't overmix; batter should be slightly lumpy.

3. Spoon batter into prepared muffin cups. Bake about 15 minutes or until a toothpick inserted in centers comes out clean. Cool in muffin cups on a wire rack for 5 minutes. Remove from muffin cups. Serve warm. Makes 12.

*Sugar Substitutes: Choose from Splenda Granular or Sweet'N Low bulk or packets. Follow package directions to use product amount equivalent to 1 tablespoon sugar.

Chicken, Brown Rice, and Vegetable Skillet

If you need to limit gluten in your diet, this hearty gluten-free entrée is a tasty solution.

PER SERVING: 290 cal., 5 g total fat (1 g sat. fat), 48 mg chol., 661 mg sodium, 39 g carb., 6 g fiber, 23 g pro. Exchanges: 1 vegetable, 2 starch, 2 very lean meat, 0.5 fat. Carb choices: 2.5.

- **2 tablespoons dried porcini mushrooms**
- **2 teaspoons olive oil**
- **½ cup chopped onion**
- **½ cup sliced celery**
- **½ cup bite-size strips red or green sweet pepper**
- **1 14-ounce can reduced-sodium chicken broth**
- **1½ cups instant brown rice**
- **4 medium carrots, cut into thin bite-size strips**
- **2 cups chopped cooked skinless chicken breast (10 ounces)**
- **1 13.75- or 14-ounce can artichoke hearts, drained and halved**
- **1 teaspoon poultry seasoning**
- **½ teaspoon garlic-herb salt-free seasoning blend**
- **¼ teaspoon salt**
- **¼ teaspoon garlic powder**
- **¼ teaspoon ground black pepper**

1. Place mushrooms in a small bowl; add enough boiling water to cover. Let stand for 5 minutes; drain. Snip mushrooms and set aside.

2. In a very large skillet, heat oil over medium heat. Add onion, celery, and sweet pepper; cook about 4 minutes or until vegetables are tender, stirring occasionally.

3. Add broth and mushrooms to skillet. Bring to boiling. Stir in uncooked rice. Return to boiling; reduce heat. Cover and simmer for 5 minutes. Stir in carrots. Cover and cook for 5 minutes more. Stir in chicken, artichokes, poultry seasoning, seasoning blend, salt, garlic powder, and pepper. Heat through. Makes 5 (1⅓-cup) servings.

Stuffed Peppers

(10 menu picks)

Pat LeGrand is constantly trying new foods, but here are a few secrets to her top-selling items.

1. **Oven-Fried Chicken Breasts:** Pat dips the pieces into low-fat buttermilk, then bakes them instead of frying.
2. **Macaroni and Cheese:** Dreamfields pasta is Pat's secret—it has more fiber than regular pasta.
3. **Meat Loaf:** Pat chooses a lean ground meat for her meat loaf and uses whole wheat bread crumbs.
4. **Turkey Burgers:** Use lean ground turkey breast.
5. **Sweet Potato Fries:** Sweet potato has more vitamins than regular potatoes. They're baked rather than fried.
6. **Vegetable Lasagna:** No-salt-added tomato products, low-fat cheeses, and vegetables make this healthful.
7. **Stuffed Peppers:** Pat stuffs the peppers with lean ground turkey and high-fiber brown rice.
8. **Chicken, Brown Rice, and Vegetable Skillet:** This is a gluten-free item for people who have celiac disease.
9. **Turkey and Dressing:** Originally on the menu only for Thanksgiving and Christmas, roast turkey and the trimmings are popular with Pat's guests year-round.
10. **Sweet Potato Pie:** This is the number-one selling dessert. Low-fat dairy products keep it light.

Vegetable Lasagna

Vegetable Lasagna

No-boil noodles make this tempting lasagna easy; vegetables make it good for you.

PER SERVING: 287 cal., 9 g total fat (5 g sat. fat), 49 mg chol., 465 mg sodium, 35 g carb., 6 g fiber, 18 g pro. Exchanges: 2 vegetable, 1.5 starch, 1.5 lean meat, 0.5 fat. Carb choices: 2.

- 2 **10-ounce packages frozen mixed vegetables**
  Nonstick cooking spray
- 2 **14.5-ounce cans no-salt-added diced tomatoes, undrained**
- 1 **28-ounce can no-salt-added crushed tomatoes**
- 1 **tablespoon dried Italian seasoning, crushed**
- ½ **teaspoon salt**
- ½ **teaspoon garlic powder**
- 12 **no-boil lasagna noodles**
- 1 **15-ounce carton part-skim ricotta cheese**
- 1 **10-ounce package frozen chopped spinach, thawed and well drained**
- 2 **cups shredded part-skim mozzarella cheese**
- ¼ **cup grated Parmesan cheese**

1. Preheat oven to 375°F. Cook vegetables according to package directions; drain and set aside. Lightly coat a 3-quart rectangular baking dish with cooking spray.

2. In a large bowl, stir together diced tomatoes, undrained crushed tomatoes, Italian seasoning, salt, and garlic powder.

3. Spread 1 cup of the tomato mixture in the prepared dish. Arrange 4 lasagna noodles crosswise on top of the tomato mixture, overlapping the noodles slightly. Spoon ⅔ cup of the ricotta cheese in small spoonfuls onto the noodles; spread carefully over noodles. Top with a third of the drained spinach and a third of the vegetables. Sprinkle evenly with ½ cup of the mozzarella cheese.

4. Repeat layering with half of remaining tomato mixture, 4 noodles, ⅔ cup of remaining ricotta cheese, half of remaining spinach, half of remaining vegetables, and ½ cup of remaining mozzarella cheese.

5. Repeat layering with the remaining 4 noodles, remaining ricotta cheese, remaining spinach, remaining vegetables, and ½ cup of remaining mozzarella cheese. Spoon remaining tomato mixture on top.

6. Cover dish with foil; place on a foil-lined baking sheet. Bake for 40 minutes. Sprinkle with the remaining ½ cup mozzarella cheese and the Parmesan cheese.

7. Bake, uncovered, for 10 to 15 minutes more or until noodles are tender and lasagna is heated through. Let stand for 15 minutes before serving. Makes 10 servings.

Stuffed Peppers

Peppers serve as edible bowls for the turkey filling.
Pictured on page 366.

PER SERVING: 220 cal., 8 g total fat (2 g sat. fat), 60 mg chol., 337 mg sodium, 21 g carb., 4 g fiber, 16 g pro. Exchanges: 1.5 vegetable, 1 starch, 1.5 lean meat, 0.5 fat. Carb choices: 1.5.

- 3 **large yellow, green, and/or red sweet peppers (8 to 10 ounces each)**
- 1 **pound uncooked ground turkey or extra-lean ground beef**
- ¼ **cup chopped onion**
- 1½ **cups cooked brown rice**
- ½ **cup frozen stir-fry vegetables (yellow, green, and red peppers and onion) or other frozen mixed vegetables, thawed**
- ½ **cup purchased mild salsa**
- 1½ **teaspoons garlic-herb salt-free seasoning blend**
- 1 **teaspoon poultry seasoning**
- ¼ **teaspoon salt**
- ⅓ **cup soft whole wheat bread crumbs**
- 1 **tablespoon 40 to 50 percent vegetable oil spread, melted**
- ½ **teaspoon paprika**

1. Preheat oven to 350°F. Halve peppers lengthwise; remove seeds and membranes. In a Dutch oven, cook peppers in enough boiling water to cover for 2 minutes. Drain; place peppers, cut sides up, in a 13×9×2-inch baking pan. Set aside.

2. For filling, in a large skillet, cook turkey and onion until turkey is no longer pink, breaking up turkey during cooking. If necessary, drain off fat. Stir in cooked rice, vegetables, salsa, seasoning blend, poultry seasoning, and salt. Spoon filling into pepper halves. Pour ½ cup water around the stuffed peppers.

3. For topping, in a small bowl, combine crumbs, melted spread, and paprika. Sprinkle onto stuffed peppers. Cover; bake for 30 minutes. Bake, uncovered, for 5 minutes more. Makes 6 servings.

Vegetable Chili

Salt-free tomato products and seasoning blend keep the sodium down. Pictured on page 363.

PER SERVING: 209 cal., 2 g total fat (0 g sat. fat), 0 mg chol., 375 mg sodium, 42 g carb., 11 g fiber, 10 g pro. Exchanges: 2 vegetable, 2 starch. Carb choices: 3.

Nonstick cooking spray
1 teaspoon canola oil
1 cup chopped onion
1 cup chopped green sweet pepper
2 cloves garlic, minced, or
   1 teaspoon bottled minced garlic
1 14.5-ounce can no-salt-added diced tomatoes or stewed tomatoes, undrained
1 8-ounce can no-salt-added tomato sauce
1 cup water
4½ teaspoons chili powder
1 teaspoon garlic-herb salt-free seasoning blend
1 teaspoon ground cumin
⅛ teaspoon salt
1 15- to 16-ounce can kidney beans, rinsed and drained
1 cup frozen mixed vegetables
¼ cup light dairy sour cream (optional)
   Coarsely snipped fresh cilantro (optional)
⅛ teaspoon chili powder (optional)

1. Lightly coat an unheated large saucepan or Dutch oven with nonstick cooking spray. Preheat over medium-high heat. Add oil; swirl to coat the bottom of the pan. Add onion, sweet pepper, and garlic to hot oil; cook for 8 to 10 minutes or until pepper is tender, stirring often. If necessary, reduce heat to prevent burning.

2. Add tomatoes, tomato sauce, the water, the 4½ teaspoons chili powder, seasoning blend, cumin, and salt. Bring to boiling; reduce heat. Cover; simmer for 15 minutes.

3. Stir in kidney beans and mixed vegetables. Return to boiling; reduce heat. Simmer, uncovered, about 10 minutes more or until vegetables are tender.

4. If desired, top each serving with sour cream; sprinkle with cilantro and the ⅛ teaspoon chili powder. Makes 4 (1½-cup) servings.

Sweet Potato Pie

Lemon accents the flavor of this pumpkin-like pie. Pictured on page 363.

PER SERVING: 218 cal., 5 g total fat (1 g sat. fat), 1 mg chol., 119 mg sodium, 38 g carb., 3 g fiber, 5 g pro. Exchanges: 2.5 carb., 1 fat. Carb choices: 2.5.

1 recipe Oil Pastry (see recipe, below)
2¼ pounds sweet potatoes, peeled, cooked, and mashed*
1 cup evaporated fat-free milk
½ cup sugar**
½ cup refrigerated or frozen egg product, thawed, or 2 eggs, lightly beaten
2 teaspoons ground cinnamon
2 teaspoons vanilla
1 teaspoon butter flavoring
¼ teaspoon ground nutmeg
¼ teaspoon lemon extract
¾ cup frozen light whipped dessert topping, thawed (optional)
   Ground nutmeg (optional)

1. Preheat oven to 375°F. Prepare Oil Pastry. On a well-floured surface, use your hands to slightly flatten dough. Roll dough from center to edge into a 12-inch circle. To transfer pastry, wrap it around the rolling pin. Unroll pastry into a 9-inch pie plate. Ease pastry into pie plate, being careful not to stretch pastry. Trim pastry to ½ inch beyond edge of pie plate. Fold under extra pastry. Flute or crimp edge as desired. Do not prick crust.

2. For filling, in a large bowl, combine mashed sweet potatoes, evaporated milk, sugar, eggs, cinnamon, vanilla, butter flavoring, the ¼ teaspoon nutmeg, and the lemon extract; whisk until nearly smooth. Pour sweet potato filling into pastry-lined pie plate.

3. To prevent overbrowning, cover edge with foil. Bake for 25 minutes. Remove foil. Bake for 25 to 30 minutes more or until a knife comes out clean.

4. Cool the pie on a wire rack. Cover and chill within 2 hours. If desired, top each serving with whipped topping; sprinkle with additional nutmeg. Makes 12 servings.

Oil Pastry: In a medium bowl, stir together 1⅓ cups all-purpose flour and ¼ teaspoon salt. Add ¼ cup canola oil and ¼ cup fat-free milk all at once to flour mixture. Stir lightly with a fork until combined (dough will appear crumbly). Use your hands to gently work dough into a ball.

*Test Kitchen Tip: To cook sweet potatoes, peel sweet potatoes. Cut into 1½-inch chunks. In a covered large saucepan, cook sweet potatoes in enough boiling water

Butter-Rum Oatmeal Cookies

to cover for 20 to 25 minutes or until very tender. Drain. Beat potatoes until smooth using an electric mixer (you should have about 3¼ cups sweet potatoes). Cool slightly.

Test Kitchen Tip: We don't recommend sugar substitutes for this recipe.

Butter Rum Oatmeal Cookies

This soft, eggless cookie makes a delightful snack—especially with a hot cup of tea.

PER COOKIE: 67 cal., 1 g total fat (0 g sat. fat), 0 mg chol., 36 mg sodium, 12 g carb., 0 g fiber, 1 g pro. Exchanges: 1 carb. Carb choices: 1.

Butter-flavor nonstick cooking spray
½ cup packed brown sugar*
6 tablespoons lower-fat stick margarine
1 teaspoon ground cinnamon
¼ teaspoon baking soda
1 tablespoon light-color corn syrup

1 teaspoon vanilla
1 teaspoon butter flavoring
¼ teaspoon rum flavoring
1 cup all-purpose flour
¾ cup rolled oats
¼ cup raisins

1. Preheat oven to 375°F. Coat 2 cookie sheets with cooking spray; set aside. In a bowl, combine brown sugar, margarine, cinnamon, and baking soda. Beat with an electric mixer on medium speed until combined.

2. Stir in corn syrup, vanilla, butter flavoring, and rum flavoring. Using a wooden spoon, stir flour into margarine mixture. Stir in oats and raisins. Drop dough by rounded teaspoons 2 inches apart on prepared cookie sheets.

3. Bake for 8 to 10 minutes or until light brown around edges. Transfer to wire racks; cool. Makes 24 cookies.

*Test Kitchen Tip: We don't recommend sugar substitutes for this recipe.

**Peach-Berry
Frozen Dessert**
recipe, page 373

Jill's son, Lucas, burst into tears when they couldn't go to his favorite drive-through because it wasn't a healthful choice for Jill. "He thought we'd never eat burgers and fries again," Jill says. "We had to make changes in how we ate as a family, not just for us but for our kids."

breaking the pattern

With diabetes running in her family, Jill Waage didn't want her children to hear the same diagnosis that she and her father had. So with the help of her husband, Jerry, Jill embarked on a lifestyle improvement program to break the family chain of diabetes.

Jill's grandmother and father both had type 2 diabetes. And after the birth of daughter Eliza, Jill found out she had pre-diabetes. "Since I had gestational diabetes, I expected it," she says. "But I was shocked that it happened so soon." She already knew how diabetes can affect a whole family. "I remember when Dad found out in his early 40s. Mom changed the way she cooked," Jill recalls.

Thanks to her parents, Jill, knew the kind of adjustments she had to make. But how her would young family react? "We had to make changes in how we ate as a family, not just for us but for our kids," Jill acknowledges.

Jill and Jerry, who live in Urbandale, Iowa, discussed what they ate and how they could still enjoy food but make it more healthful. They also wanted everyone to eat the same thing—no special meals for Jill. "Overnight, I became the biggest label reader. I check carbs and look for whole grains," she says. "We eat a lot of vegetables, steaming them just until they're barely tender—the kids love them that way, especially edamame (fresh soybeans). I've learned how to flavor with spices and herbs and citrus.

"So much more is available today than when Mom started cooking for Dad 30 years ago," Jill continues. "Back then, her motto was 'Leave it out and do without.' Now, we have low-carb ingredients and easy ways to adapt our favorite foods."

The kids have learned that diabetes doesn't mean doing without treats, just having them at times and in amounts that are appropriate. Her son knows that if he's hungry after dessert, it's healthful food time. "Now, he'll even tell me he's hungry and ask for a 'healthy snack,'" Jill marvels.

"In many cases, I already had some great recipes. I just looked at how I could cut the fat and carbs."

—Jill Waage,
Urbandale, Iowa

Smoked Brisket with Zesty Barbecue Sauce and **Blue Cheese Coleslaw**
recipes, pages 372 and 373

Pear-Lime Salad

Pear-Lime Salad

Lime juice and peel lend a refreshing tang
to this creamy salad mold. Pictured on page 371.

PER SERVING: 82 cal., 1 g total fat (0 g sat. fat), 3 mg chol., 246 mg sodium, 12 g carb., 1 g fiber, 6 g pro. Exchanges: 0.5 fruit, 0.5 other carb., 0.5 very lean meat. Carb choices: 1.

- 1 **16-ounce can pear halves (juice pack)**
- 1 **4-serving-size package sugar-free low-calorie lime-flavored gelatin**
- ½ **cup boiling water**
- ½ **teaspoon finely shredded lime peel**
- 1 **tablespoon lime juice**
- 1 **8-ounce package fat-free cream cheese, softened**

1. Drain pears, reserving ⅔ cup juice. Chop pears; set aside. In a bowl, combine gelatin and boiling water; stir until gelatin is dissolved. Stir in reserved juice, the lime peel, and lime juice. Cover and chill about 45 minutes or until partially set (consistency of unbeaten egg whites).

2. In a bowl, beat cream cheese with an electric mixer on medium speed for 30 seconds; gradually beat in gelatin mixture. Fold in pears. Pour into a 3½- to 4-cup mold. Cover; chill about 4 hours or until firm. Unmold onto a platter. Makes 6 side-dish servings.

Smoked Brisket with Zesty Barbecue Sauce

The meat gets a big dose of flavor from a wine, a black pepper rub, and a barbecue sauce. Pictured on page 370.

PER SERVING: 232 cal., 10 g total fat (3 g sat. fat), 73 mg chol., 535 mg sodium, 8 g carb., 1 g fiber, 25 g pro. Exchanges: 0.5 other carb., 3.5 lean meat. Carb choices: 0.5.

- 8 **to 10 mesquite or hickory wood chunks**
- ¼ **cup dry red wine or reduced-sodium beef broth**
- 4 **teaspoons Worcestershire sauce**
- 1 **tablespoon cooking oil**
- 1 **tablespoon red wine vinegar or cider vinegar**
- 1 **clove garlic, minced**
- ½ **teaspoon coriander seeds, crushed**
- ½ **teaspoon hot-style mustard**
  Dash cayenne pepper
- 1 **teaspoon seasoned salt**
- 1 **teaspoon paprika**
- 1 **teaspoon ground black pepper**
- 1 **3- to 3½-pound fresh beef brisket**
- 1 **recipe Zesty Barbecue Sauce (see recipe, below)**

1. At least 1 hour before cooking, soak wood chunks in enough water to cover. Drain wood before using.

2. For mop sauce, in a small bowl, combine wine, Worcestershire sauce, oil, vinegar, garlic, coriander seeds, mustard, and cayenne. Set aside.

3. For rub, in a small bowl, combine seasoned salt, paprika, and black pepper.

4. Trim most of the visible fat from meat. Sprinkle rub mixture evenly onto the meat; rub in with your fingers.

5. In a smoker, arrange preheated coals, wood chunks, and water pan according to the manufacturer's directions. Pour water into pan.

6. Place meat on grill rack over water pan. Cover and smoke for 5 to 6 hours or until meat is tender, brushing once or twice with mop sauce during last 1 hour of smoking. Add additional coals, wood chunks, and water as needed to maintain temperature and smoke. Discard any remaining mop sauce.

7. To serve, thinly slice meat across the grain. Serve sliced meat with Zesty Barbecue Sauce. Makes 8 (3-ounce) servings.

Zesty Barbecue Sauce: Coat an unheated small saucepan with nonstick cooking spray. Preheat over medium heat. Add ½ cup chopped green sweet pepper, 2 tablespoons chopped onion, and 1 minced clove garlic; cook and stir about 5 minutes or until tender. Stir in ½ cup ketchup;

1 large tomato, peeled, seeded, and chopped; 1 tablespoon steak sauce; 1 tablespoon Worcestershire sauce; 1 teaspoon brown sugar; ¼ teaspoon ground cinnamon; ⅛ teaspoon ground nutmeg; ⅛ teaspoon ground cloves; ⅛ teaspoon ground ginger; and ⅛ teaspoon ground black pepper. Bring to boiling; reduce heat. Cover and simmer for 5 minutes. Serve warm or cool. Makes about 1¾ cups.

Peach-Berry Frozen Dessert

Fat-free cheese, yogurt, and light dessert topping keep this low in calories, carbs, and fat. Pictured on page 370.

PER SERVING: 89 cal., 2 g total fat (2 g sat. fat), 3 mg chol., 159 mg sodium, 12 g carb., 1 g fiber, 6 g pro. Exchanges: 1 other carb., 1 very lean meat. Carb choices: 1.

- **1 8-ounce package fat-free cream cheese, softened**
- **2 6-ounce cartons peach fat-free yogurt with sweetener**
- **½ of an 8-ounce container frozen light whipped dessert topping, thawed**
- **1 cup chopped, pitted, peeled fresh peaches; frozen unsweetened peach slices, thawed, drained, and chopped; or one 8.25-ounce can peach slices (juice pack), drained and chopped**
- **1 cup fresh or frozen unsweetened blueberries, raspberries, and/or strawberries, thawed and drained if frozen**
- **Fresh mint leaves (optional)**
- **Fresh berries (optional)**

1. In a medium bowl, combine the cream cheese and yogurt. Beat with an electric mixer on medium speed until smooth. Fold in the whipped topping, peaches, and the 1 cup berries.

2. Pour berry mixture into a 2-quart square baking dish. Cover and freeze about 8 hours or until mixture is firm.

3. To serve, let dessert stand at room temperature about 45 minutes to thaw slightly. Cut into squares. If desired, garnish with fresh mint leaves and additional berries. Makes 9 servings.

Make-Ahead Directions: Prepare the dessert as directed in Step 1; cover and freeze for up to 1 week.

Quick Tip

Choosing lower-fat dairy products makes good sense. But sometimes, a product you love, such as some cheeses, might not be available in lower fat. Cheeses such as blue cheese, sharp cheddar, or Gruyére have a big punch of flavor. So just use a small amount..

Blue Cheese Coleslaw

You can substitute broccoli slaw mix for the coleslaw mix. Pictured on page 371.

PER SERVING: 95 cal., 8 g total fat (1 g sat. fat), 3 mg chol., 115 mg sodium, 5 g carb., 1 g fiber, 1 g pro. Exchanges: 0.5 vegetable, 1.5 fat. Carb choices: 0.

- **½ cup cider vinegar or rice vinegar**
- **⅓ cup canola oil or salad oil**
- **1 tablespoon sugar**
- **1 teaspoon dry mustard**
- **½ teaspoon onion powder**
- **¼ teaspoon salt**
- **¼ teaspoon ground white or black pepper**
- **1 16-ounce package (5 cups) shredded cabbage with carrot (coleslaw mix)**
- **¼ cup crumbled blue cheese (1 ounce)**

1. For dressing, in a screw-top jar, combine vinegar, oil, sugar, mustard, onion powder, salt, and pepper. Cover and shake well to mix. Chill the dressing until ready to serve.

2. Before serving, in a large bowl, combine shredded cabbage and blue cheese. Shake dressing; pour over cabbage mixture. Gently toss cabbage mixture to coat. Makes 10 (½-cup) servings.

Make-Ahead Directions: Prepare the dressing through Step 1. Cover and chill for up to 1 week.

building on faith

Nechama Cohen was 35 when she was diagnosed with type 1 diabetes, more than 20 years ago. At the time, Nechama was a busy mother of five children, including a set of twins. "When the doctor told me I had diabetes," Nechama says, "I wondered how I was going to go home to five children and still lead a normal life." Especially when normal meant adhering to Jewish dietary laws and an observant Jewish lifestyle.

At first, no one could answer Nechama's questions. "I didn't feel good most of the time," says Nechama. "But when I asked for help, the doctors only knew the standard treatment. I couldn't believe diabetes had to be that way." Then she and her husband, Yossie, discovered the Joslin Diabetes Center in Boston, where they took classes on diabetes.

The more Nechama learned about diabetes, the more she wanted to know. She decided to go back to school and enroll in nutrition and nursing classes. In studying nutrition, Nechama hoped to learn how to eat healthfully and still follow Jewish dietary guidelines. She went to support groups, but no one was talking about the Jewish lifestyle. Eventually, she created a network of other Jewish women with diabetes and began having monthly meetings to discuss the challenges they faced. The meetings became so large, they had to move to larger locations. Nechama approached the American Diabetes Association (ADA) to gain support for the group. In 2000, the Jewish Diabetes Association was born, with Nechama serving as chief executive officer.

One area that concerned the group was how to adapt traditional kosher eating to adhere to diabetic eating guidelines. She began lightening her family's traditional recipes and shared the recipes in magazines. The ADA suggested she write a cookbook for Jewish people with diabetes, which resulted in *Enlitened Kosher Cooking*. "We can't put our heads in the sand," Nechama says. "Diabetes is a gift I was given. You must find joy in what you're given. Being Jewish has helped me. When you have faith, you have a tremendous strength to fall back on. I've built on that in my life."

> When I found out I had diabetes, I wondered how I was going to adhere to Jewish dietary laws and be observant of the Jewish traditions.

—Nechama Cohen,
Brooklyn, New York

It was important to Nechama to learn how to incorporate her Jewish beliefs and traditions into her diabetic meal plans. Learning how to cook for herself and her family (left and above) became very important.

Balsamic Chicken, Mock Noodle Kugel recipes, pages 378 and 379

Orange and Fennel Salad with Citrus Vinaigrette

Using less oil keeps the dressing light.

PER SERVING: 93 cal., 5 g total fat (1 g sat. fat), 0 mg chol., 76 mg sodium, 12 g carb., 3 g fiber, 2 g pro. Exchanges: 1. 5 vegetable, 0.5 fruit, 1 fat. Carb choices: 1.

PER SERVING WITH SUBSTITUTE: same as above, except 91 cal., 11 g carb.

- **1** medium fennel bulb
- **4** cups torn romaine lettuce
- **2** cups torn radicchio (½ of a small head)
- **1½** teaspoons finely shredded orange peel (set aside)
- **2** medium oranges, peeled and sectioned
- **1** small red onion, halved and thinly sliced
- **1** recipe Citrus Vinaigrette (see recipe, right)

1. Snip enough of the fennel leaves to make 1 teaspoon; reserve for vinaigrette. If desired, reserve additional leaves for garnish. Cut off and discard fennel stalks. Remove wilted outer layers of bulb; cut off a thin slice. Cut bulb lengthwise into quarters. Thinly slice quarters; set aside.

2. On a platter, arrange romaine, radicchio, orange, onion, and fennel slices. If desired, top with fennel leaves. Serve salad with Citrus Vinaigrette. Makes 6 (1½-cup) servings.

Citrus Vinaigrette: In a small bowl, combine reserved snipped fennel leaves, 3 tablespoons white wine vinegar, 2 tablespoons olive oil, 2 tablespoons water, 2 cloves minced garlic, 1½ teaspoons finely shredded orange peel, 1 teaspoon sugar or sugar substitute* equivalent to 1 teaspoon sugar, ⅛ teaspoon salt, and ⅛ teaspoon ground black pepper; whisk until mixed. For a creamier dressing, whisk in 1 tablespoon light mayonnaise or salad dressing.

*Sugar Substitutes: Choose from Splenda Granular, Equal Spoonful or packets, or Sweet'N Low bulk or packets. Follow the package directions to use product amount equivalent to 1 teaspoon sugar.

Orange and Fennel Salad with Citrus Vinaigrette

Perfect Water and Whole Wheat Challah

Serve this braided Jewish bread with dinner or for sandwiches or breakfast toast.

PER SLICE: 117 cal., 2 g total fat (0 g sat. fat), 13 mg chol., 151 mg sodium, 21 g carb., 2 g fiber, 4 g pro. Exchanges: 1.5 starch. Carb choices: 1.5.
PER SLICE WITH SUBSTITUTE: same as above, except 114 cal., 20 g carb. Carb choices: 1.

4½   to 5 cups all-purpose flour
2½   cups warm water
       (110°F to 115°F)
1   package active dry yeast
2   tablespoons sugar or sugar substitute* equivalent to
       2 tablespoons sugar
2   teaspoons salt
3   tablespoons canola oil
1   egg
1   egg white
2½   cups whole wheat flour
       Nonstick cooking spray
1   egg yolk
1   tablespoon water
1   to 2 tablespoons poppy seeds, black and/or white
       sesame seeds, or rolled oats

Perfect Water and Whole Wheat Challah

1. In a small bowl, combine ¼ cup of the all-purpose flour, ¼ cup of the warm water, the yeast, and half of the sugar. Let stand at room temperature for 10 to 15 minutes or until mixture begins to bubble.

2. Meanwhile, in a large mixing bowl, stir together 2 cups of the all-purpose flour, remaining sugar, and salt. Add remaining 2¼ cups warm water, yeast mixture, oil, egg, and egg white. Beat with an electric mixer on low to medium speed for 30 seconds, scraping sides. Beat on high speed for 3 minutes. Using a wooden spoon, stir in whole wheat flour and as much of the remaining all-purpose flour as you can.

3. Turn out dough onto a lightly floured surface. Knead in enough of the remaining all-purpose flour to make a moderately stiff dough that is smooth and elastic (6 to 8 minutes total). Cover; let rest for 10 minutes. Knead for 2 minutes more. Cover; let rest again for 10 minutes. Knead for 2 minutes. Coat a large bowl with cooking spray; add dough. Spray dough with spray. Cover; let rise in a warm place until doubled in size (about 1 hour).

4. Punch down dough; cover and let rise for 45 minutes. Punch down dough; divide in half. Cover and let rest for 10 minutes. Divide each portion of dough into three ropes (if making loaves) or 16 pieces (if making rolls).

5. For loaves, on a lightly floured surface, roll each dough portion into a 14-inch-long rope. Place ropes on a large baking sheet coated with spray. Using three ropes for each loaf, braid ropes into two loaves. Place 5 inches apart on the baking sheet. For rolls, coat two 13×9×2-inch baking pans with nonstick cooking spray; shape portions into rolls. Place 16 rolls in each pan.

6. Cover loaves or rolls; let rise in a warm place until nearly double in size (30 to 45 minutes). Preheat oven to 425°F.

7. In a bowl, combine egg yolk and the 1 tablespoon water; brush onto dough. Top with seeds or oats.

8. For loaves, bake for 10 minutes. Reduce oven temperature to 375°F. Bake for 15 to 20 minutes or until bread sounds hollow when tapped. (For rolls, bake at 425°F about 15 minutes or until tops sound hollow. Do not reduce oven temperature.)

9. Remove loaves or rolls from baking sheet or pans. Cool on wire racks. Makes 2 loaves (16 slices each) or 32 rolls.

*Sugar Substitutes: Choose from Splenda Granular or Sweet'N Low bulk or packets. Follow the package directions to use product amount equivalent to 2 tablespoons sugar.

Creamy Pumpkin Soup

Instead of flour, pumpkin thickens this soup.

per serving: 69 cal., 3 g total fat (0 g sat. fat), 0 mg chol., 304 mg sodium, 9 g carb., 1 g fiber, 3 g pro. Exchanges: 0.5 starch, 0.5 fat. Carb choices: 0.5.
PER SERVING WITH SUBSTITUTE: same as above, except 66 cal.

Nonstick cooking spray
- **1 tablespoon olive oil**
- **¾ cup chopped leeks**
- **2 cloves garlic, minced**
- **3 cups peeled and cubed pumpkin or acorn squash**
- **3 cups reduced-sodium chicken broth or homemade low-sodium chicken stock**
- **⅛ to ¼ teaspoon ground black pepper**
- **⅛ teaspoon ground cloves or ground nutmeg (optional)**
- **1 cup light plain soymilk**
- **½ to 1 cup water**
- **1 to 2 teaspoons sugar or sugar substitute* equivalent to 1 to 2 teaspoons sugar**
- **3 tablespoons pumpkin seeds or pine nuts, toasted (optional)**

1. Lightly coat an unheated large saucepan with nonstick cooking spray. Add oil; heat over medium-high heat. Add leeks and garlic; cook and stir until leeks start to brown. Stir in pumpkin, broth, pepper, and cloves, if desired.

2. Bring pumpkin mixture to boiling; reduce heat. Cover and simmer for 30 to 45 minutes or until pumpkin is tender. Remove from heat; cool slightly.

3. Transfer *half* of the pumpkin mixture to a blender or food processor; cover and blend or process until smooth. Set aside. Repeat with the remaining pumpkin mixture. Return all of the pureed mixture to the saucepan. (Or puree all of the pumpkin at once by holding an immersion blender directly in the saucepan.)

4. Stir in soymilk and enough water to reach desired consistency; heat through but do not boil. Stir in sugar to taste. Serve warm.

5. If desired, garnish with toasted pumpkin seeds or pine nuts. Makes 6 (about ¾-cup) servings.

*Sugar Substitutes: Choose from Splenda granular, Equal Spoonful or packets, or Sweet'N Low bulk or packets. Follow package directions to use product amount equivalent to 1 to 2 teaspoons sugar.

Creamy Pumpkin Soup

Balsamic Chicken

Remember this fast and flavorful chicken entrée for weeknights. Pictured on page 375.

PER SERVING: 181 cal., 5 g total fat (1 g sat. fat), 66 mg chol., 62 mg sodium, 3 g carb., 1 g fiber, 27 g pro. Exchanges: 4 very lean meat, 1 fat. Carb choices: 0.

- **4 small skinless, boneless chicken breast halves (1 to 1¼ pounds total)**
- **1 tablespoon olive oil**
- **1 tablespoon paprika**
- **½ teaspoon snipped fresh rosemary**
- **2 cloves garlic, minced**
- **¼ teaspoon ground black pepper**
- **Nonstick cooking spray**
- **¼ cup dry red wine or water**
- **3 tablespoons balsamic vinegar**
- **Fresh rosemary sprigs (optional)**

1. If desired, place chicken breast halves between two pieces of plastic wrap. Pound with flat side of a meat mallet to ¼- to ½-inch thickness.

2. Stir together oil, paprika, rosemary, garlic, and pepper to form a paste; rub paste onto chicken. Coat a 13×9×2-inch baking pan with cooking spray. Arrange chicken in pan; cover and chill for 2 to 6 hours.

3. Preheat oven to 450°F. Drizzle wine onto chicken. Bake for 10 to 12 minutes or until an instant-read meat thermometer inserted in the thickest portion of the chicken registers 170°F and juices run clear, turning pieces once halfway through cooking. (For pounded chicken, bake about 6 minutes or until chicken is no longer pink and juices run clear, turning the pieces once halfway through cooking.)

4. Remove chicken from oven. Immediately drizzle vinegar onto the chicken in the pan. Transfer chicken to plates. Stir the liquid in the baking pan; drizzle onto the chicken. If desired, garnish with fresh rosemary. Makes 4 servings.

Mock Noodle Kugel

Spaghetti squash makes a great low-carb alternative to pasta in this version of kugel. Pictured on page 375.

PER SERVING: 75 cal., 4 g total fat (1 g sat. fat), 53 mg chol., 122 mg sodium, 8 g carb., 0 g fiber, 3 g pro. Exchanges: 1.5 vegetable, 0.5 fat. Carb choices: 0.5

Nonstick cooking spray
1   2½- to 3-pound spaghetti squash
1   tablespoon olive oil
1   medium onion, chopped
2   cloves garlic, minced
2   eggs, lightly beaten*
2   egg whites, lightly beaten*
¼   teaspoon salt
    Dash ground black pepper

1. Preheat oven to 375°F. Lightly coat a 1½-quart casserole with cooking spray; set aside.

2. Cut the spaghetti squash in half lengthwise; remove seeds and strings. Place one half of the squash, cut side down, in a microwave-safe baking dish. Using a fork, prick the skin all over.

3. Microwave the spaghetti squash on 100 percent power (high) for 6 to 7 minutes or until tender; carefully remove squash from baking dish. Repeat with the other spaghetti squash half. (Or place both squash halves, cut sides down, in a shallow baking pan and bake at 375°F about 40 minutes or until tender.) Let the squash cool in the pan on a wire rack until it's easy to handle.

4. Meanwhile, in a medium skillet, heat oil over medium heat. Add onion and garlic; cook and stir about 5 minutes or until the onion starts to brown, stirring occasionally.

5. Use a fork to scrape flesh from spaghetti squash halves, holding the squash with hot pads if necessary. Place the shredded squash in a large bowl. Cool slightly.

6. Add onion mixture, eggs, egg whites, salt, and pepper to shredded squash. Stir with a wooden spoon. Pour squash mixture into the prepared casserole.

7. Bake kugel about 35 minutes or until set near the center. Cool for 15 minutes on a wire rack. Serve warm. (The kugel may water out slightly when cut.) Makes 8 (about ½-cup) servings.

Sweet Kugel: Prepare Mock Noodle Kugel as directed through Step 3. Omit the oil, onion, garlic, and pepper. Instead, to the shredded spaghetti squash, stir in ¼ cup sugar or sugar substitute** equivalent to ¼ cup sugar, 1 teaspoon ground cinnamon, and the salt. Continue baking as directed in Step 7.

PER SERVING: 79 cal., 2 g total fat (1 g sat. fat), 53 mg chol., 121 mg sodium, 14 g carb., 0 g fiber, 3 g pro. Exchanges: 1.5 vegetable, 0.5 carb. Carb choices: 1.

PER SERVING WITH SUBSTITUTE: same as above, except 55 cal., 8 g carb. Exchanges: 0 fat, 0 carb. Carb choices: 0.5.

*Test Kitchen Tip: If you like, substitute ¾ cup refrigerated or thawed egg product for the whole eggs and egg whites.

**Sugar Substitutes: Choose from Splenda Granular or Sweet'N Low bulk or packets. Follow the package directions to the use product amount that's equivalent to ¼ cup sugar.

Quick Tip

When you use flavor-packed ingredients, final recipes taste delicious without containing a lot of sodium, fat, or calories. Rely on ingredients such as garlic (roasted and unroasted), ground spices, fresh herbs, and vinegars (balsamic, flavored, and rice vinegars), just to name a few.

celebrating for life

Terry and Helene Adams learned early on that Terry's diabetes didn't have to change their holiday traditions. Every Christmas Eve, their family—from their young grandson, Peter, to Helene's elderly mother, Edythe Frette—gathers at their Ames, Iowa, home for a cozy Scandinavian-style dinner. Helene still prepares their favorite Norwegian treats, but she's careful to add a few healthful dishes of her own such as baked fish, spinach salad, and brown rice pudding. Everybody eats the same food, and Terry keeps an eye on his portions. If he indulges a little that day, he knows he'll get back on track the next morning.

In his early 70s, Terry has more energy and feels better than he has in a long time. "He's found the fountain of youth," Helene says. His diagnosis of diabetes more than five years ago provided the incentive to help him turn his health around.

The journey started at a routine physical in October 2001. Terry's doctor told him he had type 2 diabetes. His doctor's stern warning was followed by a gentle yet firm nudge from Helene. "If you don't take care of yourself, you could lose your eyesight," said his wife of more than 40 years. "I'll take care of you whatever happens, but I'd hate to see you not be able to enjoy things you love, such as reading and playing music." Terry decided to take care of his diabetes and signed on for diabetes counseling.

The real solution, Terry learned, wasn't choosing between diet and exercise—it had to be both. Initially, he had all the classic excuses for not exercising. "Walking at the gym was a challenge," he says. Then he discovered headphones, and soon marching music made the time slip away. He now walks around the neighborhood for an hour on most days.

Terry is very proud of himself, as he should be. "I feel better than I have in a long time," he says. The "fountain of youth"—in the form of eating right, exercising, and monitoring blood glucose—has definitely let Terry live the life he loves.

Christmas Ribbon Salad recipe, page 382

Terry (right) with his grandson, Peter, enjoy reading a storybook by the fire before Christmas dinner. Terry learned early on that his diabetes didn't have to change his holiday traditions—like eating Christmas Ribbon Salad.

"Terry's diagnosis of diabetes provided the incentive to help him turn his health around."

—Helene Adams,
Ames, Iowa

Spinach Salad with Glazed Almonds
recipe, page 382

Christmas Ribbon Salad

Layer the holiday colors of green, white, and red.
Pictured on page 380.

PER SERVING: 51 cal., 3 g total fat (2 g sat. fat), 7 mg chol., 140 mg sodium, 3 g carb., 0 g fiber, 3 g pro. Exchanges: 0.5 very lean meat, 0.5 fat. Carb choices: 0.

- **2 4-serving-size packages sugar-free lime-flavor gelatin**
- **1 4-serving-size package sugar-free lemon-flavor gelatin**
- **1 8-ounce tub light cream cheese, softened**
- **½ cup unsweetened pineapple juice**
- **1 cup frozen light whipped dessert topping, thawed**
- **1 4-serving-size package sugar-free raspberry-flavor gelatin**
- **1 4-serving-size package sugar-free cherry-flavor gelatin**

1. In a medium bowl, combine lime-flavor gelatin and 2½ cups *boiling water;* stir until gelatin is dissolved. Divide mixture among sixteen 4- to 6-ounce wineglasses or dessert dishes, spooning about 2 tablespoons into each glass. (Or pour mixture into a 3-quart rectangular baking dish.) Cover; chill for 1 to 2 hours or until firm.

2. In a large bowl, combine lemon-flavor gelatin and 1½ cups *boiling water;* stir until gelatin is dissolved. Whisk in cream cheese until melted and smooth. Stir in pineapple juice. Let stand for 30 minutes. Gently fold in dessert topping. Divide gelatin mixture among wineglasses, spooning about 3 tablespoons onto green layer in each. (Or carefully pour lemon gelatin mixture over lime layer in baking dish.) Cover and chill for 1 to 2 hours or until firm.

3. In a medium bowl, combine raspberry- and cherry-flavor gelatins and 2½ cups *boiling water;* stir until gelatin is dissolved. Let stand about 1 hour or until cool. Divide mixture among wineglasses, spooning about 2 tablespoons onto lemon gelatin layer in each. (Or carefully pour mixture over the lemon gelatin layer in baking dish.) Cover and chill for 2 to 3 hours or until firm. Makes 16 servings.

Spinach Salad with Glazed Almonds

Use granulated sugar for the caramel coating on the nuts, but switch to sugar substitute for the dressing, if you wish.
Pictured on page 381.

PER SERVING: 113 cal., 10 g fat (1 sat. fat), 0 mg chol., 110 mg sodium, 6 g carb., 2 g fiber, 2 g pro. Exchanges: 1.5 vegetable, 1.5 fat. Carb choices: 0.5.

PER SERVING WITH SUBSTITUTE: same as above, except 111 cal., 5 g carb. Carb choices: 0.

- **Nonstick cooking spray**
- **⅓ cup sliced almonds**
- **2 teaspoons sugar**
- **1 10-ounce package fresh spinach**
- **1 cup sliced fresh strawberries**
- **⅔ cup sliced celery**
- **2 green onions, sliced**
- **¼ cup olive oil**
- **¼ cup red wine vinegar**
- **1 teaspoon sugar or sugar substitute* equivalent to 1 teaspoon sugar**
- **¼ teaspoon salt**
- **2 drops bottled hot pepper sauce**

1. For glazed almonds, line a baking sheet with foil. Coat foil with nonstick cooking spray. In a small heavy skillet, combine almonds and the 2 teaspoons sugar. Cook over medium-high heat until sugar begins to melt, shaking skillet occasionally. Do not stir. Reduce heat to low. Continue cooking until sugar is golden brown, stirring occasionally. Remove skillet from heat. Pour nut mixture onto the prepared baking sheet. Cool completely. Break into clusters.

2. Meanwhile, in a large bowl, combine spinach, berries, celery, and green onions; set aside.

3. For dressing, in a bowl, whisk together oil, vinegar, the 1 teaspoon sugar, salt, and hot pepper sauce.

4. Drizzle dressing onto spinach mixture; toss gently to coat. To serve, top salad with glazed almonds. Makes 8 (1¼-cup) servings.

*Sugar Substitutes: Choose from Splenda Granular, Equal Spoonful or packets, or Sweet'N Low bulk or packets. Follow package directions to use product amount equivalent to 1 teaspoon sugar.

Seasoned Cod

A simple sprinkling of paprika and seasoned salt allows the fresh flavor of the fish to take center stage.

PER SERVING: 93 cal., 1 g total fat (0 g sat. fat), 48 mg chol., 156 mg sodium, 0 g carb., 0 g fiber, 20 g pro. Exchanges: 3 very lean meat. Carb choices: 0.

- 2 **pounds fresh or frozen skinless cod fillets, ¾ to 1 inch thick**
- 1 **teaspoon paprika**
- ½ **teaspoon seasoned salt**
  Lemon wedges and/or fresh parsley sprigs (optional)

1. Thaw fish, if frozen. Rinse fish; pat dry with paper towels. In a small bowl, combine paprika and seasoned salt; sprinkle onto both sides of fish. Measure the thickness of the fish.

2. Preheat broiler. Place fish on the greased unheated rack of a broiler pan. Broil 4 inches from the heat for 4 to 6 minutes per ½-inch thickness or until fish flakes easily when tested with a fork. If desired, garnish with lemon wedges and/or parsley sprigs. Makes 8 servings.

Microwave Directions: Prepare as directed in Step 1. In a 2-quart square microwave-safe baking dish, arrange fish in a single layer (do not overlap). Cover with vented plastic wrap. Microwave on 100 percent power (high) for 5 to 7 minutes or until fish flakes easily when tested with a fork, turning dish once halfway through cooking, if necessary. Serve as above.

Quick Tip

The key is to emphasize healthy eating as a lifestyle, not engaging in a crash diet, Terry points out. Yes, you must cut back, but you can eat everything—in moderation. Terry loves to eat pie, for example, but limits himself to having just two slices of his favorites a year.

Dilled Peas and Mushrooms

These colorful peas are the perfect companion to Seasoned Cod (see recipe, left).

PER SERVING: 78 cal., 2 g total fat (0 g sat. fat), 0 mg chol., 154 mg sodium, 11 g carb., 4 g fiber, 4 g pro. Exchanges: 0.5 vegetable, 0.5 starch, 0.5 fat. Carb choices: 1.

- 2 **10-ounce packages frozen peas with pearl onions**
- 1 **small red sweet pepper, seeded and coarsely chopped (⅔ cup)**
- 2 **cups sliced fresh mushrooms**
- 1 **tablespoon olive oil**
- 1 **tablespoon snipped fresh dill or 1 teaspoon dried dill**
- ¼ **teaspoon salt**
  Dash ground black pepper

1. In a covered large saucepan, cook peas and onions and sweet pepper in a small amount of boiling water about 5 minutes or until crisp-tender; drain well. Transfer to a medium bowl; set aside.

2. In the same saucepan, cook mushrooms in hot oil about 5 minutes or until tender, stirring occasionally. Stir in dill, salt, and pepper. Return mixture to saucepan; heat through. Makes 8 (½-cup) servings.

managing your diabetes

Understanding diabetes gives you a better chance of controlling it and preventing complications. It pays to learn all you can, then develop a plan that fits your lifestyle.

An estimated 21 million people in the United States, or 7 percent of the U.S. population, have diabetes, according to the Centers for Disease Control and Prevention. An additional 54 million Americans have pre-diabetes—indicating an increased risk of developing diabetes. If you're one of them, remember that you—not your doctor, dietitian, or other health professional—play the most important role in staying healthy.

Define Your Diabetes
Your health-care team will work with you to develop a personalized diabetes management plan, consisting of healthful foods, physical activity, and, if necessary, the medication that's right for you and your type of diabetes (type 1, type 2, or gestational).

Type 1 diabetes: In this type, the pancreas doesn't produce insulin, so people with type 1 diabetes must take insulin. A typical treatment plan begins with an individualized meal plan, guidelines for physical activity, and blood glucose testing. Insulin therapy is then planned around lifestyle and eating patterns.

Type 2 diabetes: In type 2 diabetes, either the pancreas doesn't produce enough insulin or the body doesn't properly respond to insulin, so too much glucose remains in the blood. Many people control type 2 diabetes by following a specially designed meal plan and engaging in regular physical activity. The right plan can help people reach and attain a desirable weight, plus healthy blood glucose, blood cholesterol, and blood pressure levels. As the disease progresses, treatment may expand to include oral medications, oral medications with insulin, or insulin alone.

Gestational diabetes: This type develops only during pregnancy. Women who've had gestational diabetes have a higher risk of developing type 2 diabetes.

Develop Your Meal Plan
Adhering to a healthful meal plan is one of the most important measures you can take to control your blood glucose. Work with a dietitian to design a meal plan that reflects your individual needs and preferences. Your meal plan should also:

- Include fruits, vegetables, and whole grains.
- Reduce the amount of saturated fat and cholesterol you eat.
- Minimize the amount of salt or sodium you eat.
- Incorporate a moderate amount of sugar because some sugar can be part of a healthful diabetes meal plan.
- Help you maintain or achieve an ideal weight.

Follow Your Meal Plan
As you start following your meal plan, you'll see that it gives you some flexibility regarding what, how much, and when you eat, but you have to be comfortable with the foods it suggests. It will guide you in eating appropriate amounts of three major nutrients—carbohydrates, protein, and fat—at the right times. Your meal plan will be nutritionally balanced, allowing you to get the vitamins, minerals, and fiber your body needs. And if you need to lose weight, it will indicate how many calories you should consume every day in order to lose the extra pounds at a realistic pace.

Your meal plan can be simple, especially if you use a proven technique to keep track of what you're eating. Two well-known meal-planning systems for diabetes are diabetic exchanges and carbohydrate counting. Your dietitian may suggest one or the other. To help you follow either system, every recipe in this book provides nutrition information, including the number of exchanges and carb choices in each serving. (Turn to page 387 to see how to use this information.)

Track the Exchanges
Exchange Lists for Meal Planning outlines a system designed by the American Diabetes Association and the American Dietetic Association. To use the exchange system, your dietitian will work with you to develop a pattern of food exchanges—or a meal plan— suited to your specific needs. You'll be able to keep track of the number of exchanges from various food groups that you eat each day. Tally those numbers and match the total

(monitor your blood glucose)

Whether you have type 1 or type 2 diabetes, it's important to test your blood glucose, especially if you're taking insulin shots or oral medication. Usually you test blood glucose before each meal. Your health-care providers will teach you how to measure your blood glucose with a simple finger-prick test, as well as how to adjust your food intake, physical activity, and/or medication when your blood glucose is too high or too low. Your health-care providers will help you set blood glucose goals. For example, the American Diabetes Association suggests a target for fasting or before meals is 90 to 130 milligrams/deciliter. At two hours after the start of a meal, the goal is less than 180 milligrams/deciliter. Your A1C level (the average amount of glucose in the blood over the last few months) should be less than 7. To keep your blood glucose at a healthy level, follow these five important guidelines:

- ❋ Eat about the same amount of food each day.
- ❋ Eat meals and snacks at about the same times each day.
- ❋ Do not skip meals or snacks.
- ❋ Take medicines at the same times each day.
- ❋ Do physical activity at about the same times each day.

to the daily allowance set in your meal plan. (For more information, see www.diabetes.org.)

Count Carbohydrates
Carbohydrate counting is the method many diabetes educators prefer for keeping tabs on what you eat. It makes sense because the carbohydrate content of

foods has the greatest effect on blood glucose levels. If you focus on carbohydrates, you can eat a variety of foods and still control your blood glucose.

When counting carbohydrates, you can tally the number of grams you eat each day. Or you can count the number of carbohydrate choices, which allows you to work with smaller numbers. We offer both numbers with our recipes.

(low-calorie sweeteners)

There's no need to dump low-calorie sweeteners just because sugar is safer than once thought. Sweeteners are "free foods" in your meal plan—and that's a good thing! They make foods taste sweet, they have no calories, and they won't raise your blood glucose levels. The following sweeteners are accepted by the Food and Drug Administration as safe to eat: aspartame (Equal and NutraSweet), acesulfame potassium (Sweet One), saccharin (Sweet'N Low and Sugar Twin), and sucralose (Splenda).

Basic carbohydrate counting relies on eating about the same amount of carbohydrates at the same times each day to keep blood glucose levels in your target range. It's a good meal-planning method if you have type 2 diabetes and take no daily oral diabetes medications or take one to two shots of insulin per day.

Advanced carbohydrate counting is a more complex method than the basic system of carbohydrate counting. It's designed for individuals who take multiple daily insulin injections or use an insulin pump. With advanced carbohydrate counting, you have to balance the amount of carbohydrates you consume with the insulin you take. You estimate the amount of carbohydrates you'll be eating and adjust your mealtime insulin dose based on your recommended insulin-to-carbohydrate ratio. To learn how to follow advanced carbohydrate counting, seek the assistance of a registered dietitian or certified diabetes educator.

The Carbohydrate Question

Although the calories from fat, protein, and carbohydrates all affect your blood glucose level, carbohydrates affect it the most. So why not just avoid carbohydrates altogether? While carbohydrates may be the main nutrient that raises blood glucose levels, you shouldn't cut them from your diet. Foods that contain carbohydrates are among the most healthful available—vegetables, fruits, whole grains, and low- or nonfat dairy foods. Eliminating these foods could compromise your health.

(be a sugar sleuth)

Knowing the different forms of sugar can make life sweeter when you're reading labels and recipes. Sugar content is included in the total grams we list for carbohydrates in recipes.

* Sucrose appears in table sugar, molasses, beet sugar, brown sugar, cane sugar, powdered sugar, raw sugar, turbinado, and maple syrup.
* Other "-ose" sugars include glucose (or dextrose), fructose, lactose, and maltose. Fructose and sugar alcohols affect blood glucose less than sucrose, but large amounts of fructose may increase blood fat levels.
* Sugar alcohols such as sorbitol, xylitol, maltitol, mannitol, lactitol, and erythritol should only be eaten in moderation because they can cause diarrhea, gas, and cramping.

How Sweet It Is

For many years, people with diabetes were told to shun sugar because it was thought that sugar caused blood glucose to soar out of control. So they diligently wiped sugary foods and sugar out of their diets, hoping to stabilize their blood glucose levels. Today, more than a dozen studies have shown sugars in foods don't cause blood glucose to spike any higher or faster than starches, such as those in potatoes and bread. The American Diabetes Association's recommendations on sugar now state "scientific evidence has shown that the use of sucrose (table sugar) as part of the meal plan does not impair blood glucose control in individuals with type 1 or type 2 diabetes."

It is important to note, however, that sugar is not a "free food." It still contains calories and offers no nutritional value beyond providing energy. So when you eat foods that contain sugar, they have to replace other carbohydrate-rich foods in your meal plan. Carbohydrates you eat contain a healthful amount of vitamins, minerals, and fiber. So it's a good idea to focus on whole grains and vegetables for your carbohydrates rather than sugar. Talk to your dietitian to determine a healthful way to include a moderate amount of sugar in your meal plan. Or you can also sweeten foods with sugar substitutes (see "Low-Calorie Sweeteners," page 385).

Stay Involved and Informed

Eating healthfully, exercising, and monitoring blood glucose levels help keep diabetes in check—all easier to do if you follow the plans you've developed with your health-care providers. Update them on your progress and request changes if something isn't working. And stay informed about diabetes by going to www.diabeticlivingonline.com to sign up for our e-mail newsletter. You're the one who can monitor your progress day by day.

(using our nutrition information)

At the top of every one of our recipes, you'll see the nutrition information listed for each serving. You'll find the amount of calories (cal.), total fat, saturated fat (sat. fat), cholesterol (chol.), sodium, total carbohydrates (carb.), fiber, and protein (pro.). In addition, you'll find the number of diabetic exchanges for each serving and the number of carbohydrate choices, in case you prefer those methods to keep track of what you're eating.

> PER SERVING: 134 cal., 9 g total fat (1 g sat. fat), 0 mg chol., 60 mg sodium, 14 g carb., 4 g fiber, 2 g pro. Exchanges: 0.5 fruit, 1 vegetable, 2 fat. Carb choices: 1.

Interpreting the Numbers
Use our nutrition analyses to keep track of the nutritional value of the foods you eat, following the meal plan you and your dietitian have decided is right for you. Refer to that plan to see how a recipe fits the number of diabetic exchanges or carbohydrate choices you're allotted for each day. When

you try a recipe, jot down our nutrition numbers to keep a running tally of what you're eating, remembering your daily allowances. At the end of each day, see how your numbers compare to your plan.

Diabetic Exchanges
The exchange system allows you to choose from a variety of items within several food groupings. Those groupings include starch, fruit, fat-free milk, carbohydrates, nonstarchy vegetables, meat and meat substitutes, fat, and free foods. To use the diabetic exchange system with our recipes, follow your plan's recommendations on the number of servings you should select from each exchange group in a day.

Carbohydrate Counting
Our recipes help you keep track of carbohydrates in two ways—tallying grams of carbohydrates and the number of carbohydrate choices. For counting grams, add the amounts of total carbohydrates to your running total for the day. For carbohydrate choices,

one choice equals 15 grams of carbohydrates. For example, a sandwich made with two slices of bread is 2 carbohydrate choices. The benefit of this system is that you're keeping track of small numbers.

Calculating Method
To calculate our nutrition information and offer flexibility in our recipes, we've made some decisions about what's included in our analyses and what's not. We follow these guidelines when we analyze recipes that list ingredient options or serving suggestions:

* When ingredient choices appear (such as yogurt or sour cream), we use the first one mentioned for the analysis.
* When an ingredient is listed as optional, such as a garnish or a suggested serve-along, we don't include it in our nutrition analysis.
* When we offer a range in the number of servings, we use the smaller number.
* For marinades, we assume most of it is discarded.

recipe index

S–T

metric information

The charts on this page provide a guide for converting measurements from the U.S. customary system, which is used throughout this book, to the metric system.

Product Differences

Most of the ingredients called for in the recipes in this book are available in most countries. However, some are known by different names. Here are some common American ingredients and their possible counterparts:

✳ All-purpose flour is enriched, bleached or unbleached white household flour. When self-rising flour is used in place of all-purpose flour in a recipe that calls for leavening, omit the leavening agent (baking soda or baking powder) and salt.

✳ Baking soda is bicarbonate of soda.

✳ Cornstarch is cornflour.

✳ Golden raisins are sultanas.

✳ Light-colored corn syrup is golden syrup.

✳ Powdered sugar is icing sugar.

✳ Sugar (white) is granulated, fine granulated, or castor sugar.

✳ Vanilla or vanilla extract is vanilla essence.

Volume and Weight

The United States traditionally uses cup measures for liquid and solid ingredients. The chart below shows the approximate imperial and metric equivalents. If you are accustomed to weighing solid ingredients, the following approximate equivalents will be helpful.

✳ 1 cup butter, castor sugar, or rice = 8 ounces = 1/2 pound = 250 grams

✳ 1 cup flour = 4 ounces = 1/4 pound = 125 grams

✳ 1 cup icing sugar = 5 ounces = 150 grams

Canadian and U.S. volume for a cup measure is 8 fluid ounces (237 ml), but the standard metric equivalent is 250 ml.

1 British imperial cup is 10 fluid ounces.

In Australia, 1 tablespoon equals 20 ml, and there are 4 teaspoons in the Australian tablespoon.

Spoon measures are used for smaller amounts of ingredients. Although the size of the tablespoon varies slightly in different countries, for practical purposes and for recipes in this book, a straight substitution is all that's necessary. Measurements made using cups or spoons always should be level unless stated otherwise.

Common Weight Range Replacements

Imperial / U.S.	Metric
1/2 ounce	15 g
1 ounce	25 g or 30 g
4 ounces (1/4 pound)	115 g or 125 g
8 ounces (1/2 pound)	225 g or 250 g
16 ounces (1 pound)	450 g or 500 g
1 1/4 pounds	625 g
1 1/2 pounds	750 g
2 pounds or 2 1/4 pounds	1,000 g or 1 Kg

Oven Temperature Equivalents

Fahrenheit Setting	Celsius Setting*	Gas Setting
300°F	150°C	Gas Mark 2 (very low)
325°F	160°C	Gas Mark 3 (low)
350°F	180°C	Gas Mark 4 (moderate)
375°F	190°C	Gas Mark 5 (moderate)
400°F	200°C	Gas Mark 6 (hot)
425°F	220°C	Gas Mark 7 (hot)
450°F	230°C	Gas Mark 8 (very hot)
475°F	240°C	Gas Mark 9 (very hot)
500°F	260°C	Gas Mark 10 (extremely hot)
Broil	Broil	Grill

*Electric and gas ovens may be calibrated using celsius. However, for an electric oven, increase celsius setting 10 to 20 degrees when cooking above 160°C. For convection or forced air ovens (gas or electric), lower the temperature setting 25°F/10°C when cooking at all heat levels.

Baking Pan Sizes

Imperial / U.S.	Metric
9×1 1/2-inch round cake pan	22- or 23×4-cm (1.5 L)
9×1 1/2-inch pie plate	22- or 23×4-cm (1 L)
8×8×2-inch square cake pan	20×5-cm (2 L)
9×9×2-inch square cake pan	22- or 23×4.5-cm (2.5 L)
11×7×1 1/2-inch baking pan	28×17×4-cm (2 L)
2-quart rectangular baking pan	30×19×4.5-cm (3 L)
13×9×2-inch baking pan	34×22×4.5-cm (3.5 L)
15×10×1-inch jelly roll pan	40×25×2-cm
9×5×3-inch loaf pan	23×13×8-cm (2 L)
2-quart casserole	2 L

U.S. / Standard Metric Equivalents

1/8 teaspoon = 0.5 ml	
1/4 teaspoon = 1 ml	
1/2 teaspoon = 2 ml	
1 teaspoon = 5 ml	
1 tablespoon = 15 ml	
2 tablespoons = 25 ml	
1/4 cup = 2 fluid ounces = 50 ml	
1/3 cup = 3 fluid ounces = 75 ml	
1/2 cup = 4 fluid ounces = 125 ml	
2/3 cup = 5 fluid ounces = 150 ml	
3/4 cup = 6 fluid ounces = 175 ml	
1 cup = 8 fluid ounces = 250 ml	
2 cups = 1 pint = 500 ml	
1 quart = 1 litre	

DIABETIC LIVING™ Best of Diabetic Living (ISBN 978-0-696-24198-7, LCCN 2008924115), Volume 1. The DIABETIC LIVING cookbook is published biannually by Meredith Corp., 1716 Locust St., Des Moines, IA 50309-3023. DIABETIC LIVING® magazine SUBSCRIPTION PRICES: U.S. and its possessions, 1 year $19.97. Canada and other countries, 1 year $23.97. © Copyright Meredith Corporation 2008. All rights reserved. Printed in the U.S.A.